Sympathetic Puritans

RELIGION IN AMERICA
Harry S. Stout, General Editor

Recent titles in the series:

FATHERS ON THE FRONTIER
French Missionaries and the Roman
Catholic Priesthood in the United
States, 1789–1870
Michael Pasquier

HOLY JUMPERS
Evangelicals and Radicals in
Progressive Era America
William Kostlevy

NO SILENT WITNESS
The Eliot Parsonage Women and
Their Unitarian World
Cynthia Grant Tucker

RACE AND REDMEPTION IN
PURITAN NEW ENGLAND
Richard A. Bailey

SACRED BORDERS
Continuing Revelation and Canonical
Restraint in Early America
David Holland

EXHIBITING MORMONISM
The Latter-day Saints and the 1893
Chicago World's Fair
Reid L. Neilson

OUT OF THE MOUTHS
OF BABES
Girl Evangelists in the Flapper Era
Thomas A. Robinson and Lanette
R. Ruff

THE VIPER ON THE HEARTH
Mormons, Myths, and the
Construction of Heresy
Updated Edition
Terryl L. Givens

THE LIFE AND DEATH OF
THE RADICAL HISTORICAL
JESUS
David Burns

MORMONS AND THE BIBLE
The Place of the Latter-day Saints in
American Religion
Updatcd Edition
Philip L. Barlow

MISSIONARIES OF
REPUBLICANISM
A Religious History of the
Mexican-American War
John C. Pinheiro

SYMPATHETIC PURITANS
Calvinist Fellow Feeling in Early
New England
Abram C. Van Engen

Sympathetic Puritans

Calvinist Fellow Feeling in
Early New England

ABRAM C. VAN ENGEN

OXFORD
UNIVERSITY PRESS

OXFORD
UNIVERSITY PRESS

Oxford University Press is a department of the University of
Oxford. It furthers the University's objective of excellence in research,
scholarship, and education by publishing worldwide.

Oxford   New York
Auckland   Cape Town   Dar es Salaam   Hong Kong   Karachi
Kuala Lumpur   Madrid   Melbourne   Mexico City   Nairobi
New Delhi   Shanghai   Taipei   Toronto

With offices in
Argentina   Austria   Brazil   Chile   Czech Republic   France   Greece
Guatemala   Hungary   Italy   Japan   Poland   Portugal   Singapore
South Korea   Switzerland   Thailand   Turkey   Ukraine   Vietnam

Published in the United States of America by
Oxford University Press
198 Madison Avenue, New York, NY 10016

CIP data is on file at the Library of Congress
ISBN 978–0–19–937963–7

9 8 7 6 5 4 3 2 1
Printed in the United States of America
on acid-free paper

For Kristin

Contents

Acknowledgments

THIS BOOK HAS a good deal to say about community, and it exists in good part because of community. First thanks go to that small community where the whole project began: my dissertation committee. Julia Stern led with enthusiasm and deep knowledge; Betsy Erkkila offered key questions, advice, and recommendations; and Tim Breen gave detailed comments on every section and chapter. I am enormously grateful to these early readers for their passion and advice. I am thankful, as well, to all the other faculty at Northwestern who deepened my thinking and prepared me for the profession. The English Department, the Graduate School, and the Society of Fellows all generously funded my early research and writing, and I count myself fortunate to have landed at Northwestern.

I was fortunate not just for financial assistance and professional advice, but also for all the smart and friendly fellow students I encountered. Thank you to Stef Bator, Sarah Blackwood, Katy Chiles, Joanne Diaz, Greg Downs, Anna Fenton-Hathaway, Nathan Hedman, Erik Gellman, Dan Gleason, Peter Jaros, Jenny Mann, Liz McCabe, Sarah Mesle, Guy Ortolano, Wendy Roberts, Gayle Rogers, Nat Small, Dave Smith, Josh Smith, Brenna Stuart, Sara VanderHaagen, Chris Verkaik, Lora Walsh, and many others. Sometimes these friends read my work and offered feedback; more often we simply shared meals, sports, and good times. Thank you for making graduate school not just something to be endured, but something to be enjoyed.

Other communities soon broadened this project. At the Newberry Library's Scholl Seminar for American History and Culture, I presented an early version of chapter 5. That chapter and other parts of the book were also enriched by an NEH Summer Institute at the Newberry Library led by Scott Stevens, who is not just brilliant but a joy to be around. My thinking for this book—especially its wider context—expanded greatly through a Warwick-Newberry Collaborative Program seminar on transatlantic

British history led by Trevor Burnard and Mark Knights. For all of these programs and events, for all its resources, and for all these people I am grateful to the Newberry Library and its staff.

At Trinity University, I was welcomed by a great faculty and wonderful students. Vicki Aarons cleared space for me to write, and an R. M. McFarlin Junior Faculty Fellowship gave me time to research and revise. Claudia Stokes befriended me, mentored me, and has never ceased offering her time to read my work and make it better. Thank you, Claudia.

Likewise, my fellow colleagues at Washington University in St. Louis have not only given me space and opportunity, but have also made St. Louis feel quickly like home. Thanks especially go to my former chair, Vince Sherry, and my current chair, Wolfram Schmidgen. All my colleagues—too many to list—have been hugely supportive, and once again I find myself fortunate to have come from one good place to another. Special thanks must go to Musa Gurnis, who in the goodness of her heart read every page of this book and offered rich and generous feedback. At Washington University I've also had the pleasure to become part of the John C. Danforth Center on Religion and Politics, another community from which I have learned so much, and I want to thank Marie Griffiths, the director, as well as Darren Dochuk, Mark Jordan, and Leigh Schmidt, all of whom offered key feedback that reshaped chapters in the final stages. Thank you.

In addition, my work has been furthered by the communities of scholars gathered at various journals. Parts of this book appeared previously in "Advertising the Domestic: Anne Bradstreet's Sentimental Poetics," *Legacy: A Journal of American Women Writers* 28.1 (2011): 47–68, as well as "Origins and Last Farewells: Bible Wars, Textual Form, and the Making of American History," *The New England Quarterly* 86.4 (December 2013): 543–592. Thank you to Theresa Strouth Gaul, Nicole Tonkovich, and Lynn Rhoads for your editorial advice. More substantially, an early version of chapter 4 was previously published as "Puritanism and the Power of Sympathy," *Early American Literature* 45.3 (Fall 2010): 533–564. Thank you to Sandra Gustafson, especially for her continued support, as well as to the anonymous readers at *EAL*.

Lastly, a huge list of scholars near and far all helped out in large and small ways over the course of several years. Special thanks go to those who read my entire manuscript at various stages of development, sometimes more than once: David D. Hall, George Marsden, Skip Stout, Mark Valeri, and another anonymous reader at OUP. In my work on Calvin and Erasmus I am particularly grateful to Luge Schemper, the theological librarian at Calvin College, and for translation help I want to thank Mark Jordan, Joshua Byron Smith, and John Van Engen (on rare occasions, it is handy to be the son of a medievalist). Thanks as well go to my current writing group—Angie Calcaterra, Travis Foster, Greta LaFleur, Wendy Roberts, Kacy Tillman, and Caroline Wigginton—where I have been able to share, learn, and improve. This writing group arose from the scholarly community that has most nourished my work and for which I am deeply grateful: the Society of Early Americanists. I attended my first conference at Bermuda and have been returning ever since. The sense of collegiality, the warm enthusiasm for each other's work, the building up through careful critique, the expansion of ideas and deepening of thought have all made the SEA a wonderful resource and strong community for the study of early American literature, history, and culture. A host of scholars have offered feedback on papers, have volunteered to read chapters, have engaged the ideas of this book in hallways and conference rooms, and have generally improved all my long research, writing, and revision. There are certainly too many names to include, but I'd like to thank in particular those who contributed directly to the shaping of this book—either through reading and commentary or through key conversations at important times—including: Melissa Adams-Campbell, Kris Bross, Michael Ditmore, Jonathan Beecher Field, Justine Murison, Meredith Neuman, Sarah Rivett, Ivy Schweitzer, Jordan Stein, Laura Stevens, Bryce Traister, Joanne van der Woude, Dan Walden, Kelly Wisecup, and Hilary Wyss. Finally, I want to thank those I have met from yet other communities who have given of their time to read, comment, and advise, especially Mitchell Breitwieser, Frank Bremer, Peter Coviello, Chris Grasso, Janice Knight, Mark Peterson, Jenny Hale Pulsipher, and Dan Shea. As is evident from even this incomplete list, the writing of a book is no solitary enterprise. What exists has been directly touched and shaped in some way by all those mentioned here, all of whom have aided me in my labors and made the end result much stronger than it ever could have been alone.

Beyond and before the many scholarly communities I have had the pleasure to know and join, there is what the Puritans considered the first community, my family, who has most shaped both me and my work. My father, John Van Engen, has modeled for me a professorial path that I happily travel down, showing me how fulfilling it can be to devote oneself to books, ideas, history, deliberation, and understanding. My mother, Suzanne Van Engen, has modeled for me all that can and must be lived both in the mind and beyond it—friendships, relationships, community itself. Both have always and fully supported me. Thank you. My brothers Hans, Stefan, and Lucas—all of whom live and move and have their beings outside of academia—continue to keep me grounded and remind me of the many worlds that exist beyond early America. I have always received strong support from them, including, I believe, a commitment to read this finished book. Pam and Sharon, Barb and Bruce, Mara and Alyssa—thank you to all my family for your love and encouragement. The world beyond my studies expanded greatly with the coming of my children, Simon and Grace. One day, looking at a new book about the Puritans that had just arrived in the mail, Simon proclaimed, "Daddy, that looks *weird!*" I'm sure my book will look strange to him, too, and it may never cease being something odd, but I thank both him and Grace for offering alternative perspectives every day and for drawing me away from the desk. Worlds beyond the realm of early America indeed; a whole world behind and beyond this book.

Lastly, and most importantly, there is Kristin—my colleague, my companion, my dearest and closest friend. You have lived with the making of this book from beginning to end; the printing of it should belong to you as well. There are not words for my gratitude, and you wouldn't want a public gushing. So let me just say this: Thank you, Kristin, for your love.

Sympathetic Puritans

Introduction

IN ALL THE *King's Men*, the Pulitzer Prize-winning novel of 1947, the main character must break some bad news to the governor's wife: her son, a spoiled boy too brash to ever heed his Christian mother, has impregnated a young and helpless girl. That might be trouble enough on its own, but given the politics—given that this is the governor's son and an election is nearing—the difficulties have only just begun. Sensing that she has not been told all there is to know, Lucy Talos, the governor's wife, asks Jack Burden, his right-hand man, to meet her at home. As he sets the scene for this encounter, Robert Penn Warren chooses a few select details to convey the deep unease: Jack walks through the yard as though he "were treading on dozens of eggs," feeling much like "a sneak thief in a dark house." Lucy meets him at the door, and they walk to the parlor. And then, to establish just the right amount of tension and gloom for all involved, Warren hangs some portraits on the wall: "big walnut and gilt frames ... enclosing the stern, malarial, Calvinistic faces whose eyes fixed you with little sympathy."[1]

It is a simple detail in a far more elaborate scene, a small line in a 600-page novel, but it functions in the moment to tie *All the King's Men* to a whole literary history of unsympathetic Calvinists, a long American tradition of stern and stoic Puritans. The novel seems obsessed with the hardness of history and the depravity no person escapes—one of the few beliefs the governor retains—and these portraits reinforce the theme. No one is clean. Scrub the surface, and the dirt will appear. And as each person's sins come to light, the Calvinists in that dark parlor will continue to stare in their stern, discerning way, untouched by human sympathy and offering no reprieve. As Nathaniel Hawthorne described them in *The Scarlet Letter*—the book read by countless high-schoolers who never encounter Calvinists again—the Puritans were "a people amongst whom religion and law were almost identical, and in whose character both were so thoroughly interfused, that the mildest and severest acts of public discipline were alike made venerable and awful. Meagre, indeed, and cold, was the sympathy that a transgressor might look for, from such bystanders at the scaffold." According to the American literary tradition, sympathy was a quality that the Puritans neither admired nor possessed. Sometimes with a hint of praise, often with a good deal of rebuke, all seem to know that those early settlers of New England were built of nothing less—or more—than iron.[2]

That unmoved, unsympathetic gaze is a function of art, not reality. Most Puritans would be surprised to hear that they were made of iron. John Winthrop, the first governor of Massachusetts Bay, seemed composed of something far softer as he sat with his dying wife, weeping so bitterly that she had to ask him to stop, "for you breake mine heart (said she) with your grievings." Nor was he alone in shedding abundant tears; as pilgrim separatists fled England, soldiers forced the families apart. Far from looking on with stern and stoic gazes, the pilgrim band broke down: "what weeping and crying on every side," William Bradford wrote, "some for their husbands that were carried away in the ship . . .; others not knowing what should become of them and their little ones; others again melted in tears, seeing their poor little ones hanging about them, crying for fear and quaking with cold." "Pitiful it was to see," he insisted, suggesting that the reader might want to lend a little sympathy as well. In fact, the absence of sympathy could be considered a serious problem, a sorrow unto itself. When Anne Bradstreet, the great New England Puritan poet, depicted the woes of a war-torn England she specifically listed the affliction of "mothers' tears unpitied," implying exactly what the New England minister William Hooke had recently preached: "It is the part of true friends and brethren, to sympathize and fellow-feele with their brethren and friends when the hand of God is upon them."[3]

Tears and grieving, melting and weeping, pity and sympathy—each of these moments fits a broad tradition of Puritan fellow feeling. Drawing together such scenes and pronouncements—both the literary depictions and the preacherly declarations—this book argues that a Calvinist theology of sympathy shaped the politics, religion, and literature of seventeenth-century New England. From the origins of Puritanism in sixteenth-century England, Reformed ministers and writers stressed fellow feeling and mutual affections as necessary for the common good.

Using scripture, they called on readers and listeners to sympathize with the joys and sorrows of citizens and saints—fellow countrymen and fellow converts. In the process, they turned sympathy into a sign of membership: the experience and expression of mutual affections helped determine who belonged with whom. Sympathy thus became both an obligation and a mark of identity, an emotional duty to be performed and an irregular, ever-shifting experience identifying who was in and who was out. In seventeenth-century New England, this dual meaning of sympathy—the active *command* to fellow-feel (a duty), as well as the passive *sign* that could indicate salvation (a discovery)—pervaded Puritan society and came to define the very boundaries of English culture, affecting conceptions of community, relations with Native Americans, and the development of American literature.[4]

Unearthing this Calvinist theology of fellow feeling helps us see the religious history of a concept that has largely been traced back to more secular roots in moral sense philosophy. The command to sympathize, after all, came from the Bible: it appears in Puritan writing because it surfaces in scripture. In attempting to live according to the Word of God, Puritan ministers and theologians had to make sense of the idea that their high priest, Christ, was "touched with the feeling of our infirmities" (Hebrews 4:15), along with the scriptural mandate to "rejoice with them that rejoice, and weep with them that weep" (Romans 12:15), to have "one suffer with another" (1 Peter 3:8), and to "remember them that are in bonds, as though ye were bound with them: and them that are in affliction, as if ye were also afflicted in the body" (Hebrews 13:3). Early English translations did not specifically use the word "sympathy" in these and other verses, but in two of them they struggled with the Greek cognate of that word, and in all of them Calvinist commentators employed the language of sympathy to make sense of what they read. Scripture, in short, commanded the godly to unite and cohere, and many Puritans understood that concord and harmony to require an imaginative reciprocation of affections that involved putting oneself in another's place and feeling as that person felt. If the Bible demanded such a thing, then it would have to be learned, interpreted, preached, and lived.[5]

Most New England Puritans dealt with sympathy on a personal level: it spoke directly to anxieties raised by election. The idea that God chose some to be saved and others to be damned before the world began caused many early Calvinists to wrestle in unique ways with the meaning and limits of mutual affection, for the right feelings toward the right people expressed and demonstrated in the right way *might* testify to one's salvation. In unpacking the scriptural "love of brethren"—most significantly from 1 John 3:14—many Puritans concluded that one of the best ways to soothe anxious souls was to highlight their sympathy with members of the church. Fellow feeling implied union and belonging; having mutual and reciprocal affections with those already admitted to the church could therefore indicate that one should be welcomed to membership as well. Or to put it differently, sympathizing with those who were *presumably* saved could witness one's own salvation. This was a comfort many took.

Yet this pious application of fellow feeling to one's personal search for assurance tied sympathy to communal bonds in other ways as well. In searching out one's salvation, it mattered *with whom* one sympathized. Such a notion translated more broadly into the construction of emotional communities—communities defined by the mutual experience and transmission of affection.[6] The borders of a Puritan community, it turns out, were often determined by mutual affections: all would-be citizens and saints needed not just oaths of allegiance and legal obedience, but also the experience of fellow feeling that defined the very boundaries of belonging. A tight-knit society of saints *felt* together—both by matching each other's emotions (rejoicing with those who rejoice and weeping with those who weep) and by responding in the same way to the same events (all fasting for Parliament or giving thanks for the banishment of heretics). A unified community meant a single affection spread equally to all.[7]

This concept of an emotional community provides an additional explanation for New England's many Fast and Thanksgiving Days. On the one hand, Puritans believed that such days had a direct impact on events, moving God to bring relief or continue prosperity; they held spiritual meaning in their own right and deepened the community's relationship with God. In that sense, they were not merely religious masks for political ends.[8] On the other hand, days of fasting and thanksgiving offered certain political benefits. Desiring an emotional unity requires someone in charge to pronounce what that emotion must be; these public days in New England enabled magistrates to reassert authority by proclaiming mourning or thanksgiving for all. And as the colonists responded, the process of fasting or rejoicing reunited the community in a shared experience of affection. On Fast Days, for example, the community conducted itself in such a way as to generate widespread mutual mourning—a repentance both experienced within and witnessed without.[9] By binding hearts together, fasting and thanksgiving rebuilt Puritan emotional communities. Unity depended on this sort of sympathetic exchange. And setting the terms of that exchange (whether joy or sorrow, rejoicing or repentance) reveals one way that Puritan sympathy mingled with aspects of power and authority.

Sympathy further mixed with politics when it came to negotiating transatlantic relations. The Puritans who left England had a special need to assure their nonemigrating godly peers that they had never separated from the Church. They were not, they repeatedly asserted, allying themselves with separatist extremists who cut all ties with the Church of England. Whatever social or geographical withdrawal might suggest, New England Puritans remained loyal subjects of the crown and members of the Church. In fact, they argued, it was precisely because they loved the Church so much—precisely because they had never left the Church—that they sought its purification and reform. This need to assert unity despite a few thousand miles of intervening ocean sent Puritans in search of any language that would overcome and downplay the basic fact that they had physically abandoned England. One language was sympathy. Even though they departed England, many Puritans asserted, fellow feeling united them with their countrymen and demonstrated their unbroken loyalty to the brethren left behind. Sympathy connected them to the cause.

In England, the cause of reformation united the godly against fellow English citizens who stood in the way of right religion. But in New England, the difference between citizen and saint more often blurred. The sympathy of *saints* involved a love of Christ that created and enabled a love of one another: such love matched sorrow and joy among a select group of the saved (or potentially saved), and it witnessed a renewed and sanctified self on its way to union with God. The sympathy of *citizens*, on the other hand, modeled itself on this elect community, but it could not signify salvation. Instead, it aimed at more practical matters involved in the common good of society. In other words, sometimes Puritans spoke of sympathy as good for one's soul, and sometimes they demanded it as necessary for the state. Yet the very fact that the term functioned in both domains occasionally made distinctions difficult in New England: if someone sympathized properly on a Fast Day with others, did that satisfy a civil duty or indicate a mark of grace? The double valence of fellow feeling in both politics and theology thus raised questions about when and how sympathy was possible, whether and to whom it could be extended, and what it revealed about a person when it was either experienced or expressed.

Finally, the Puritan linking of sympathy, salvation, and community—flowing in particular from the search for assurance—distinctly affected the concept of sincerity. The authenticity of an individual's heart took on a special value in Puritan churches, where authorities were asked to judge whether others had truly converted. In evaluating another's heart, several factors came into play: one had to have a basic, working knowledge of the catechism; one had to live a godly, pious life; and, frequently, one had to give a convincing testimony of grace.[10] In the last demand, the judgment of a sincere heart often turned on sympathy. Insofar as the Puritan minister could be moved to fellow feel with another through his or her narrative of conversion, the grace expressed in that confession would be considered a valid indication of election. That is, the operations of sympathy—the emotional exchange between narrator and listener—enabled an authoritative member of the church to judge a conversion true. Sympathy, in other words, came to play a prominent role in Puritan notions of persuasion. But here again, *who* had to be moved—and *by whom*—reveals a complex mixture of sympathy and power, nowhere more evident than in Puritan missionary activities among Native Americans.

In Puritan piety, politics, community, and sincerity, therefore, sympathy played a significant role in early New England. The Puritans were not the only ones, nor the first ones, to emphasize the importance of fellow feeling, but they *were* significant participants in a wider historical development that gradually emphasized the centrality of sympathy to ethics, literature, culture, and society, culminating in Adam Smith's *The Theory of Moral Sentiments* (1759). In sermons, treatises, poems, journals, histories, and captivity narratives, Puritans repeatedly turned to a Calvinist theology of fellow feeling, urging it on all and using it to judge the virtue of a citizen and the sanctity of a saint.

The Genealogy of Sympathy

Revealing this Calvinist theology of fellow feeling in the seventeenth century helps us reimagine that dominant portrait in American culture cited briefly by Robert Penn Warren: the grim, unfeeling, black-clothed, dour-faced Puritan. This portrait, to be sure, is not one that actual scholars of Puritanism tend to paint. Even Perry Miller, the founder of modern Puritan studies, began his magnum opus *The New England Mind* with an elegant description of inner drives. As Miller pointed out, the Puritans turned whole*heartedly* to God or they did not turn at all. Indeed, they had a name for those who merely memorized the catechism and did good deeds from day to day: such persons were "civil Christians" with a "historical faith," and they were destined for a dire end. After Miller's reign at Harvard, historians and literary critics paid increasing attention to the power and presence of feeling in seventeenth-century New England. Since the 1960s, impressive studies have mapped the various emotions needed to demonstrate election, the conversion experience of actual lay persons, the rejuvenating power of daily sanctification, the devotional exercises and literature of seventeenth-century Puritans, and the presence within Puritanism of various—and sometimes competing—emphases on desire, longing, and love. For many years now, as one scholar explains, "the dynamics of New England's hearts and souls have taken precedence over those of its heads."[11]

Yet in this regard, scholars of the Puritans remain a rather lonely crowd. The picture of Calvinism that still prevails is one of unfeeling austerity and tyrannical judgment. Such a view became ingrained in American culture primarily through the work of nineteenth-century anti-Calvinists. To defeat predestination and original sin, a wide variety of born-again preachers and liberal Protestants began to caricature Calvinism as rigorous, gloomy, heady, and heartless. The power of their portraits turned this extreme view into a new norm, so that American culture ever since has tended to see Puritanism as a religion of unemotional intellectualism. Predestination itself, as various anti-Calvinists argued, represented an impassive, arbitrary parceling out of mercy by a God more cruel than kind; anyone who believed in such a doctrine *necessarily* lacked a basic capacity for fellow feeling.[12]

This picture of Puritanism took shape not just through theological tracts and pulpit oratory; it also came about through the cultural work that framed and waged the battle. Nothing has locked into place the modern-day picture of Puritanism quite like the work of Nathaniel Hawthorne. But such a view would not have stuck so firmly in American minds were it not also for the work of Hawthorne's main nemesis: that "damned mob of scribbling women," as he called the female sentimental writers who outsold him on a regular basis. While these sentimental authors differed in their aims and aesthetics, they even more adamantly argued that whatever good Puritanism once served, it held no place in a sympathetic age. In a series of novels, writers from Catharine Maria Sedgwick to Harriet Beecher Stowe rejected Calvinism as *immoral* precisely because it lacked the sympathy so essential to forming ethical bonds. Just as these writers had left the Calvinism of their own upbringings—freeing themselves from tyrannical theology—so, they believed,

America also had to outgrow judgment, terror, and intolerance. The good of society and the salvation of one's soul depended on embracing sympathy and benevolence, not dogma and catechism. Thus, in the course of the nineteenth century, Calvinism became characterized as an intellectual love of law and doctrine enforced through the fear of God and a terror of hell. This is the portrait painted by the nation's earliest novels.

Taking such works more or less at their word, scholars of American sentimentalism—that expansive eighteenth- and nineteenth-century cultural movement which based ethics, politics, religion, and literature in theories of sympathy—have typically resisted the idea that sympathy ever found a home among the Puritans. When the literary scholar Ann Douglas opened sentimentalism to serious academic study in 1977, she described it as "feminine" and contrasted it with the "stern," "rigorous," "theological," "intellectual," "repressive, authoritarian, dogmatic, [and] patriarchal" culture of Puritanism.[13] Since then, the labors of countless historians and literary critics have vastly expanded our knowledge of sentimentalism, mapping a multitude of social, literary, political, and racial consequences. Yet while disagreements run rampant through the field, most scholars take for granted Douglas's backdrop of a rigid, unfeeling early American Puritanism. According to most accounts, Puritanism and the power of sympathy simply do not belong together; they represent separate eras, distinct movements, different phases of literary development.[14]

As for the roots of fellow feeling, the standard genealogy traces both sympathy and sentimentalism back to Latitudinarianism. Latitudinarians were members of the Anglican Church who gained prominence in England after 1660, when the Puritan Interregnum collapsed and Charles II took the throne. More moderate and liberal than other religious thinkers, Latitudinarians such as Isaac Barrow and John Tillotson believed that God cared far more for actions and morality than for the structures, disciplines, and doctrines of a national church (or any other particular sect). Elevating human nature and the power of reason, they preached a God at least as compassionate as human beings: if *we* can weep, they asserted, God must weep all the more; if *we* can sympathize, God's fellow feeling must abound. Human nature thus became the foundation for religious beliefs, which in turn reflected well on human nature. God has created us as essentially good, they claimed, and having filled us with sympathy, he expects it to play a role in the way we live.[15]

With such claims Latitudinarians paved the way to the Scottish Enlightenment, the second major phase in sentimentalism's evolution.

Over the course of more than half a century, several philosophers—including the third Earl of Shaftesbury, Francis Hutcheson, David Hume, and Adam Smith—began to theorize a moral sense guiding human action. Reacting against the Calvinist doctrine of original sin and the selfish state of nature proposed by Thomas Hobbes, these thinkers claimed that human beings were naturally sociable, not selfish; such a view, in turn, heightened the emphasis on both sympathy and benevolence. Fellow feeling became not just a basic tenet of human nature, but a pillar of virtue that could be exercised and trained.[16] These beliefs led to a cultural endorsement of refined sensibility—the catchword of the era—according to which people of good character possessed "a sympathetic heart, a quick responsiveness to the joys and sorrows of others, and a propensity toward the shedding of compassionate tears." The "central elements in morality" became "the feelings of sympathy and 'sensibility'—that is, a hair-trigger responsiveness to another person's distresses and joys."[17] Such traits would eventually define the heroes and heroines of sentimental novels in the eighteenth and nineteenth centuries. In short, the Latitudinarians enabled a more secular, anti-Calvinist moral sense philosophy that paved the way to a broader sentimental culture.[18]

So goes the standard history. This book challenges that narrative. For example, while Latitudinarians and moral sense philosophers rejected the Calvinist doctrine of original sin and instead conceived of human beings as basically good, they did not invent, but rather *continued*, a perception of humans as naturally sociable. The great bogeyman of both Latitudinarians and moral sense philosophers was Thomas Hobbes. But Hobbes's concept of the state of nature—where all fight all in lives he characterized as "solitary, poor, nasty, brutish and short"—was never a secular version of original sin and total depravity; in fact, merging Calvinist theology with Hobbesian philosophy does the Puritans a disservice, for even with their dire view of the unregenerate heart the Puritans still insisted on "natural affections," which involved a basic level of sociability even among pagans, heathens, and the reprobate. The Puritans preached sympathy not just to saints but to citizens, and they assumed that even those who lacked a love of Christ still had hearts that could be moved.[19]

Continuities between Puritanism and sentimentalism constantly emerge, as I hope to show. At the same time, it would be wrong to assert that the Puritans somehow *were* sentimental, or that they actually wrote sentimental literature. Rather, in their writing they had occasion to use techniques that would later be strongly identified with the sentimental tradition. And those occasions arose, in large part, from their thinking about sympathy. Bringing their ideas of fellow feeling and mutual affections to light will, I hope, revise the standard genealogies of both sympathy and sentimentalism, along with the traditional characterization of Puritanism that accompanies such stories. In other words, I do not challenge the usual genealogies by attempting to trace a whole new one; instead, I take a closer look at seventeenth-century Puritans and their largely unobserved language of sympathy, building on the work of those few scholars who have begun to note the significant presence of this idea and experience in early Puritanism.[20] The fact that a Calvinist theology of fellow feeling has gone so unnoticed—or that so many have assumed it could not exist based on traditional histories of sentimentalism—thus provides the impetus for a study focused primarily on the seventeenth century. Of that period, this book asks one seemingly simple question: how did sympathy shape the culture of Puritan New England?

The New England Puritans

That question, however, immediately raises two others that have to be answered: first, who were the Puritans? And second, what counts as sympathy? The former remains one of the great difficulties facing any scholar of Puritanism. In 1625, a wary King Charles, having just inherited the throne of England, asked his ally, the bishop of London William Laud, to produce a list of Puritan clergymen. Charles worried about such people because they seemed to threaten the ceremonies, hierarchies, and authority of the entire English Church. Such dissidents had existed at least since the 1570s, and the appellation "Puritan," a slur, had been slung at them for years; but Charles's sudden attempt to list and eliminate these people—to designate some and not others as Puritan—inaugurated a process of definitional ambiguity that continues still today.[21] What, then, is Puritanism? On the one hand, just as Supreme Court Justice Potter Stewart defined obscenity in 1964, everyone seems to know it when they see it. On the other hand, countless books and articles have attempted to distinguish the characteristics of this particular political, social, and devotional movement, often focusing less on the specifics of theology and more on the general mindset or attitude of those involved—to the point of avoiding the word "movement" altogether. A movement implies a unified force, whereas Puritanism often seemed more like a loose collection of zealous Protestants lacking agreement on aims or ends.[22] The trouble only mounts, meanwhile, for those who wish to speak of a Puritan New England. Over the past several decades, scholars have identified a vast diversity of persons and beliefs inhabiting seventeenth-century Massachusetts Bay, Plymouth, Connecticut, and New Haven, not to mention Rhode Island, Maine, and New Hampshire. The plurality of opinions cut not just between the clergy and the laity (who did not always share the same views), but also into and across the highest circles of society. Far from propounding a mono-lithic orthodoxy, New England comprised a host of different perspectives, doctrines, political objectives, and social ambitions. To call New England "Puritan," then, seems either to expand the word beyond its usefulness or to misconstrue the population.[23]

Yet while many have focused on New England's diversity, others have illuminated its remarkable coherence. When differentiating among the theological emphases and preaching styles *within* New England, the spectrum of viewpoints can seem vast; stepping back and placing the region in a broader context, however, reveals the presence of a distinct culture. Just as differences in similar objects fade when seen from a distance, so the gaps in New England's religious landscape narrow when nestled into one corner of the English Atlantic. Over the course of the seventeenth century, officials in England regularly viewed and treated New England as a distinct Puritan culture, different from other colonies and plantations. Indeed, the dissenters and critics of New England—many of whom had to *leave* the region in order to register their complaints—only increased the sense that this place contained one attitude, one way of life.[24] The many different settlers of New England certainly formed a disparate set of siblings who sometimes fought bitterly amongst themselves, and such distinctions should not be forgotten. But most still fit together as a family. Difference and dissent came embedded within a framework widely (though not exclusively or unanimously) accepted. In fact, it was precisely the reach and influence of Puritanism in New England that enabled it to contain—and in some cases, to *nourish*—so many tensions. In this book I try to do justice to difference, dissent, and transatlantic dimensions while focusing primarily on the people and tensions of Massachusetts Bay, where the godly were even more coherently unified than elsewhere in New England. I do so, in part, to show that the Puritan sympathy I identify was not some fluke or fleeting thought, but was instead to be found in the very heart of Puritan New England.[25]

So what was this Puritanism of New England? First, it implied a series of shared political concerns. During the English Civil Wars, when parliamentary forces squared off against the King, no one in England needed to guess where New England stood. Declarations of allegiance to the King disappeared, and all public days of Fasting or Thanksgiving responded to the fortunes of Parliament.[26] Such loyalty resulted from the fact that Parliament, like the Puritans, sought a greater restructuring and reform of the English church. Charles I, along with William Laud (now Archbishop of Canterbury), not only supported a system of hierarchical bishops that smacked of Catholicism; they advanced a theological system of Arminianism which flouted basic tenets of Reformed Calvinism. Instead of passively discovering saving grace (or searching for signs of its presence), Arminians proposed that a person could, by free will, accept or reject God's grace (often deemed a universal offer). In England, Puritan opposition to such views—along with their rejection of bishops in favor of the congregation's local authority—caused them to be silenced and pursued. Several ministers decided they could best serve the church and the cause of reform by leaving the country entirely, in many cases taking their congregations with them. By one definition, then, the Puritans of New England formed *an oppositional political party*—political precisely insofar as religious reforms inevitably concerned restructuring England's highest powers. Criticism of prelacy (the governing system of hierarchical bishops) and Arminianism (the religious position embraced by the most powerful bishops) translated into a bottom-up censure of the authorities in place.[27]

Beyond this political dimension, however, the Puritans comprised *a social movement* focused on tight-knit communities. In England, those who had been converted would travel together to hear the preaching of godly ministers (called sermon gadding), and they would gather together in conventicles—small groups of the godly—in order to share their experiences, converse about the cause of reform, study the Word of God, and refresh their spiritual lives. The experience of conversion and the piety of the saved, combined with the sense that they formed a persecuted minority, helped these gathered saints develop intense communal bonds. In other words, in a slight adaptation of Justice Potter Stewart, we might say that Puritans knew each other when they saw each other.[28] After emigrating, ministers and magistrates attempted to write such conventicles into the governing structures of New England. In many churches ministers required all would-be members to give a public conversion narrative, in effect forming a conventicle of godly persons within the wider congregation and tying it together through similar experiences of grace shared with one another. In the state, magistrates extended suffrage only to those who became members of a church, thus forming a kind of large-scale conventicle, an association of godly citizens united by shared goals and familiar accounts of conversion.

But it was *the experience of grace* itself—and the representation of that grace—which constituted Puritanism's primary distinguishing feature. Though they divided over emphases, Puritan ministers preached a remarkably similar version of the conversion process focused on the ramifications of predestination.[29] In his catechism, Thomas Shepard, the pastor of Newtown (now Cambridge), explicated the expected stages of grace. Conversion, he explained, began with *contrition*. Just as the sick do not seek a doctor until they realize they are ill, so sinners will not turn to God unless they recognize their misery. In addition, potential converts needed to acknowledge the absence of any internal, redeeming good—a process of *humiliation* in which the sinner gradually came to feel unworthy of Christ and his blessings. Only after being lowered could a convert rise. Such redemption began with *vocation*, which Shepard defined as "the Lord's call and invitation of the soul to come to Christ." Receiving such an invitation required faith—that is, "the coming of the whole soul out of itself unto Christ, for Christ, by virtue of the irresistible power of the Spirit in the call." Finally, then, by faith and through grace—both gifts of God—converts would be *justified*: "The gracious sentence of God the Father," Shepard explained, "absolves them from the guilt and condemnation of all sins, and accepts them as perfectly righteous to eternal life." Adopted and redeemed, justified sinners became new saints—children of God "crown[ed] ... with [the] privileges of sons."[30]

Yet at this point conversion had only just begun, for once sinners received God's justifying faith they began the process of *sanctification*— the process "whereby the sons of God are renewed in the whole man, unto the image of their heavenly Father in Christ Jesus." In sanctification, a person killed off his or her sin and breathed life into a new self generated by grace. Such a transformation entailed a never-ending battle, "a continual war and combat between the renewed part, assisted by Father, Son, and Holy Ghost, and the unrenewed part, assisted by Satan and this evil world." It called for *mortification*, a "daily dying to sin by virtue of Christ's death," and *vivification*, a "daily rising to newness of life, by Christ's resurrection." In sanctification, God's cosmic drama of redemption played out every day on the inner stage of each converted soul.[31]

The experience of grace mattered so much to the Puritans that it actually determined the political and social elements of their religious movement. For example, the Puritans hated the Church of England's *Book of Common Prayer* for two primary reasons: first, it violated norms of *sola Sciptura* and seemed to elevate manmade religious tradition to the same level as the Bible. Second, they believed that any form, as such, encouraged hypocrisy: written prayers, prescribed rituals, and recited sermons all prevented God from touching the heart, convicting sinners, and regenerating saints. According to many, the Church of England fostered a community of hollow Christians held together not by the inner experience of grace, but by the outward performance of ceremony. Opposition to the prelacy emerged from the same concerns: bishops gave church posts to priests according to personal preference and political need; they did not seek out those who had a proper experience of grace and could deliver the saving Word. Puritans expected preachers to change hearts; the Church of England employed them to maintain authority. Thus, for the sake of their devotion—to worship God in spirit and in truth—the Puritans of New England tied ordination to individual congregations. The local church, not some far-off bishop, would choose its own pastor and ordain him to deliver the Word.[32]

Such a view of church governance begins to reveal how communal bonds also flowed from Puritan devotion. Sermon gadding, conventicles, and the requirements for church membership in New England emerged from the basic belief that Christian conversation refreshed the heart and nourished the soul. The godly needed each other for grace.[33] And precisely because the Lord used the godly to deliver his grace, the community of Puritan saints embraced a spiritual unity that rejected the unregenerate. They bound themselves together and separated themselves from others.[34] Thus when certain Puritans met in England and discussed the possibility of emigration, Arthur Tyndal, John Winthrop's brother-in-law, resolved "to give up all my faculties, and powers both of soule, and bodie, instruments, weapons and ministers to serve yow in that unitie bond, and waie of pietie, and devocion, which your selves shall imbrace, and insue."[35] For Tyndal, as for other ardent converts, Puritanism was a "way of piety and devotion" that entailed ecclesiastical consequences (giving up one's ministers) and a new "unitie," a "bond" tighter and more significant than all the rest. That is the definition of Puritanism this book uses (one that is admittedly, but necessarily, circular): beginning with a piety and devotion aimed at both conversion and assurance of salvation, Puritanism was a way of life that collected together groups of the godly, identified them as distinct, and called on them to live lives of holiness in pursuit of wider reform—precisely so that a reformed church and society could nourish the piety and devotion aimed at true conversion and assurance.

Puritan Affections

Defining New England Puritanism, however, still leaves us with the second problem: what counts as sympathy? In tracing out a Calvinist theology of fellow feeling, one must decide whether to study words or ideas: that is, should one focus on the *term* "sympathy"—including the many words spun from a translation of the original Greek—or the *concept* of mutual affections reached through identification with another (regardless of what terms that idea attracts). In this book, I do both. Puritans focused on different aspects as the occasion required, but they understood sympathy as identification with another's experience, often involving an imaginative transfer of oneself into the place of another. In this regard, it was closer to the modern meaning of "empathy"—a word not coined until the twentieth century. Modern usage sometimes defines sympathy not as transference into another's place, but rather as an *understanding* of someone else's pain, acknowledging someone's hardship and providing comfort but not identifying with the suffering; so, for example, doctors and nurses today are often told to sympathize but not to empathize. Because of certain scriptural passages (such as Hebrews 13:3), Puritans included identification in their definition of sympathy. It applied as much to joy as to grief, and it was thought to be a reciprocal sharing of affection through the imaginative process of identification. While I study the history of a word most associated with this idea, then, I also expand my study to examine how the idea was affected by, or became conjoined to, a much larger family of terms, including "fellow feeling," "love of the brethren," and "mutual affections."[36]

The last phrase is perhaps the most important and the most difficult to define. "Affections," which the Puritans frequently wove into their definitions of faith, blurs the modern-day division of head and heart. At first, the word sounds like an affirmation of the heart—and in many cases it was—but what the Puritans understood by both "heart" and "affections" was something far more than feeling. Affections, for the Puritans, included not just particular loves and longings, but also one's understood *purpose*—one's entire orientation. To put it another way, affections were defined not just by the presence of love and longing, but also by their object: *who* or *what* one loved and desired in turn indicated the purpose of one's actions—the explanation that colored how, why, and to what end a person lived. Affections, in short, encompassed the whole bent of a person's being.[37]

The emphasis Puritans placed on the heart and the affections came from reformers like Martin Luther and John Calvin. For example, in Calvin's systematic theology *The Institutes of the Christian Religion*, he asserts that "Scripture seriously affects us only when it is sealed upon our hearts through the Spirit." For knowledge of God to be true, he emphasized, it had to "take root in the heart"; true conversion meant replacing a "heart of stone" with a "heart of flesh." That, for Puritans, was precisely the problem with the Church of England. Its uninspired preachers, its prescription of prayers, its opulence and formalism all prevented the possibility that God's word would ever change hearts. As Calvin argued, "wherever there is great ostentation in ceremonies, sincerity of heart is rare indeed."[38] He summarized the significance of a sincere heart with his personal motto: "My heart I offer to you, O Lord, promptly and sincerely." For participants in this Reformed tradition, the disposition of the heart defined the status of the person, and thus true religion dwelt primarily in religious affections—a point that would persist from John Calvin through Jonathan Edwards.[39] Here then, affections were not *feelings*; they could more properly be understood as *dispositions*.

The issue is somewhat muddled, though, for Puritans did occasionally use the word "affections" to identify particular passions or emotions, such as "joy, sorrow, love, [and] hatred." For example, when the influential Puritan theologian William Ames discussed the affections that arise from conscience, he listed joy, confidence, shame, sadness, fear, despair, and anguish. Another powerful Puritan, William Perkins, also aligned affections with emotional states resulting from the dictates of conscience. Instructing Christians to shape their affections appropriately, he gave the example of "choler and anger," which instead of being aimed at our neighbor ought to be redirected at ourselves. A third influential Puritan, Richard Sibbes, explained that godliness required both good judgment and "holy inclinations of our will and affections, that so a perfect government may be set up in our hearts, and that our knowledge may bee with al judgment, that is, with experience and feeling." Here, affections seem to encompass both the idea of a person's disposition—one's "experience"—and that more modern sense of "feeling."[40]

In preaching, the importance of the affections became even more apparent. Puritan ministers were instructed to stir up affections, which meant inducing an experience beyond mere understanding of the Word. Summarizing several preaching manuals in his *Marrow of Sacred Divinity*, Ames wrote, "Men are to be pricked to the quick so that they may feel individually what the Apostle said, namely, that the word of the Lord is a two-edged sword, piercing to the inward thoughts and affections and going through to the joining of bones and marrow." As a result, preaching should be "alive [or, 'lively'] and effective so that an unbeliever coming into the congregation of believers should be affected and, as it were, transfixed by the very hearing of the word so that he might give glory to God."[41] Congregants, in other words, had to be *moved*; the affections went beyond, but still included, an emotional state. The experience of grace required, in part, a feeling.

Yet the primary meaning of "affections" still identified a person's most basic disposition. As Perkins taught, in Adam's fall the affections "received a disorder, and by reason of this disorder they do eschew good; and pursue that which is evil." In other words, the heart of an unregenerate person *always* leans away from God. So, Ames wrote, "The fourth signe [of being in a state of sin], is perversnesse of the affections wherby men, turne away from God, and wholy cleave, and adhere, to worldly things, 1 *John*. 2. 15." Illustrating these unregenerate affections, Ames cited examples that had little to do with feeling: "The aversnesse of a man from God, is wont to be seene, 1. By his alienation from the Word of God, especially when it is preached to him powerfully ... 2. By a neglect of prayer, and other parts of Gods worship ... 3. By an alienation from the servants of God."[42] Failing to attend or be moved by a worship service, refusing to pray, distancing oneself from godly neighbors (either in action or in feeling)—all of these revealed a person's affections, the inclination of his or her heart.

In this deeper meaning of the word, no amount of effort or choice could produce godly affections. Only grace could alter the unregenerate heart, so that "through the renewing of the affections by the Holy Spirit, a man doth begin to will that which is good, and to refuse evil." Equating the affections with a person's ultimate desires, Sibbes proclaimed that nothing "sets a stampe upon a Christian so much as desires, All other things may bee counterfeit, words and actions may bee counterfeit, but the desires and affections cannot, because they are the immediate issues and productions of the soule." In other words, it took God's grace to set the affections straight—so that desiring God and Christ could in turn indicate election, the possibility that God had chosen one for salvation.[43]

The renowned Puritan minister and master of Emmanuel College, John Preston, explained that when God attracts a person to faith, "it is not such drawing as when a man is drawne by force, but it is a drawing which is done by changing the will and affections; when GOD alters the bent of the mind, when GOD justifies a man, hee will affect a mans heart so, that hee shall bee so affected with Christ, as that he shall have no rest till he have him."[44] In countless Puritan tracts, the affections indicated a leaning of the heart, which might or might not have anything to do with temporary emotional states.

Indeed, Puritan conversion required a transformation of *both* head and heart. Preston's claim that regeneration would alter not just one's affections but also "the bent of the mind" reveals the close link between intellect and will in Puritan conceptions of the human person. For the most part, Puritans accepted the dominant psychology of their day, which understood persons as possessing three primary faculties: the reason, the will, and the appetites. As one scholar explains, "The rational faculties are humanity's peculiar glory and its noblest powers; in a well-ordered soul, will commands the inferior appetite, and reason governs the passions."[45] In the tripartite human being, peace could be maintained only through proper order and subordination, the will and the passions following wherever reason might lead. Such a view lent itself to what one scholar has called the "intellectualist position," wherein "the understanding shows to the will what is to be embraced or rejected. As the understanding judges, so the will desires."[46] In general, faculty psychology moved down a hierarchy from the understanding through the will to the affections, and it identified disorders as, in part, a rebellion of the passions. Sibbes, for example, wrote that "thoughts breed desire; thoughts in the minde or braine, the braine strikes the heart presently. It goes from the understanding to the will, and affections; what we thinke of that wee desire, if it be good." Speaking of sanctification, he explained, "Light in the understanding breedeth heate of love in the affections." Thomas Hooker, the renowned minister of Hartford, Connecticut, put it more simply: "That which the Mind conceives not, the Heart affects not."[47]

But not all Puritans accepted wholesale the idea that a changed mind could or would lead to an altered will and right affections. Instead, many simultaneously maintained an Augustinian view of human persons in which the intellect and will remained separate entities, sometimes working together, sometimes not. "In this doctrine," Norman Fiering explains, "the will is not identifiable as a rational appetite at all … Instead, it comes to be almost synonymous with the inner essence of the whole man, the battleground of God and the devil. The personal drama of salvation is enacted in the will, and on the will's ultimate orientation depends one's entire fate with God." In this position, "the biblical term 'heart' was used almost interchangeably with will." The Puritans thus meshed a biblical view of human persons as based in the heart with a faculty-psychology that elevated reason.[48]

For Puritans, then, the ideal of godliness required a proper *ordering* of affections. Sibbes declared, "The first worke of grace is to set the soule in order, to subdue base affections, to sanctifie the judgement: and when it hath set the soule in tune, and order, then it is fitted to set a right price on things, to rancke and order them as it should." Temperance, Ames explained, "doth not utterly take away these affections, as being naturall, but doth govern them, that is, takes away their inordinatenesse, in regard of their degree, extent, and manner." Ordinate affections meant loves that had resisted too great an attachment to the earthly and ephemeral. Such passing goods, Preston preached, were certainly gifts of God, but they needed to be enjoyed "with weaned affections, that you doe not so enioy them as to commit *Idolatry* with them." Good Puritans set their affections first on God, and only secondarily on the blessings of God. Thus, John Winthrop praised his wife Thomasine because she was "never so adicted to any outward thinges (to my judgment) but that she could bringe hir affections to stoope to Gods will in them."[49]

Such "outward thinges" could include one's spouse and children. As Winthrop lovingly recounted Thomasine's "carriage" toward him, he lamented, "It had this onely inconvenience, that it made me delight too muche in hir to enjoye hir longe." He loved her so much, in other words, that God removed her from the world in order to set him straight—to prevent Winthrop from making Thomasine his idol. In the same way, when the Puritan poet Anne Bradstreet's granddaughter Elizabeth died, she wrote, "Farewell dear babe, my heart's *too much* content." The rest of the poem then wrestles with this love, trying to set it in its place and move past mourning into a contemplation of eternity: "Blest babe, why should I once bewail thy fate, / Or sigh thy days so soon were terminate, / Sith thou art settled in an everlasting state."[50] Such lines, along with Winthrop's praise of Thomasine's "patience" at the death of their child, have helped popularize the idea that for the Puritans "weaned affections" really meant a *lack* of feeling, a stoic turning away from sorrow and delight.

But the Puritans did not oppose extreme affections. When Thomas Bilson, the Puritan-leaning Bishop of Winchester, praised Christ's temperate affections he included an exception: Christ's affections "were moderate, till they were inflamed with piety or charitie, and then they burned more in him then in us, by reason of his abundant giftes and graces farre passing ours." Certain affections, in other words, were meant to burn. The love of God could know no limit, and because it set the bar so high—*infinitely* high—the love of others could often go a long way before it met with a worried look. The testimony of countless Puritans—John Winthrop not least among them—reveals the heights of expression that spouses could be carried to in their love for one another. As we have seen, while his love for Thomasine seems muted, it still bursts forth in so many tears that she must ask him to refrain. Meanwhile, in reviewing the letters of his third wife, Winthrop revels in a marital bliss that reveals the love of God. Recalling to his view "the love of my earthly mariages," he writes, "the more I thought upon [them], the more sensible I grewe of the most sweet love of my heavenly husband, Christ Jesus." Affections here are "weaned" not in the sense of being "made less," but rather in their leading from earth to heaven. The greater the love Winthrop has known with his wives, the more he understands the love of Christ. The same was true of Bradstreet. As often as she writes about ordering and tempering her worldly loves, she also extols marital bliss and contemplates Christ through the joys of earth.[51]

Indeed, far from preaching stoic dispassion, the Puritans repeatedly defended affections as inherently good. As one preacher declared, "Religion doth not *destroy* naturall affections, but onely *regulates* them, and *sanctifieth* them." The Puritan theologian William Fenner proclaimed, "*It is the blessing of God that we have affections implanted in our hearts.*" Even those which appeared bad—such as envy and malice—could be explained as no more "natural" than "lice and vermin are natural to Carrion, than filthy and noysome weeds are natural to a cursed ground." Such affections had to be eradicated, Fenner explained, because "to speak properly they are unnatural affections and sinful in themselves, but our natural affections are not sinful in themselves. Nay more," he continued, "the affections are not only not sinful, but it is an infinite blessing of God, that God hath given us affections."[52] Though they embraced original sin and total depravity, the Puritans never conceived of human beings in a Hobbesian state of nature. Rather, Puritans considered humans as *both* inherently selfish and naturally sociable.

The latter aspect could best be seen in familial relations, which comprised a host of natural affections. In fact, Puritans considered a love of one's family so natural that the absence of such affections would mark a person as monstrous—as essentially inhuman. In his treatise on the family, the Puritan minister Richard Greenham linked the care children ought to show their parents to human nature itself. Telling children "to wipe away the teares of griefe from your fathers eyes, and stay the sorrowfull spirites of your tender mothers," he moved readers to such actions by requiring them to "consider in your selves, if ye have any nature in you, and have not buried your use of common reason, what a shame is it to be a shame unto your fathers, to whome ye ought to be a glorie." The common reason possessed by all extended love and care from parents to children and vice versa. Greenham continued, "thinke ye, wanton wittes, that have not cast off all naturall affections, what a contempt it is to be a contempt unto your mothers, to whome you have offered as it were a despightfull violence, in that ye are a corrosive to hir griefe, when as ye should have bene a crowne unto hir comforts." Comforting one's parents came with Creation and remained in all despite the Fall, so that to despise or reject such love would be to despise or reject human nature itself. For Puritans, the fifth commandment, "Honor thy father and mother," did not create a *new* duty and impose it on humanity; it took what had always existed—the natural affections of the family—and made them holy.[53]

Here again, the meaning of affections both diverges from and overlaps with the idea of emotions. On the one hand, affections simply *were* feelings. Envy was an unregenerate, unnatural affection experienced by a particular person at a particular time. On the other hand—and more importantly—feelings could *reveal* affections. Experiencing envy suggested that the whole person might not yet be regenerate—that his or her heart rejected the good and pursued the bad. Indeed, when Fenner defended the inherent goodness of affections, he proclaimed, "How could they be set upon God, if it were not a blessing that we have them?"[54] Such a view of the affections marked them as more than feeling; often synonymous with the heart, the affections identified a person's will, and a change of affections required an infusion of grace. Yet within that process of transformation feelings still overlapped with affections, for each emotion—the tears of repentance, an experience of joy, the feeling of love for fellow saints—could indicate the outpouring of a regenerate heart. Feelings were evidence of affection.

This prolonged definition of Puritan affections is necessary because often when the idea of sympathy appeared, it came couched in a language of mutual affections. As can be seen, such a phrase might refer to the exchange of reciprocal feelings, but it could also go beyond any temporary emotional experience. Mutual affections meant, more largely, a matching of spirits—a sense of likeness that enabled not just shared experiences, but also a kind of concord in objectives. In other words, mutual affections sometimes meant a face-to-face direct and reciprocal exchange of emotion, but it also could indicate that two friends faced in the same direction and walked down the same path together, acknowledging in each other a similarity of longings and loves. Thus mutual affections often involved a third term—the goal (or God) whom both loved equally. Yet while in theory Puritan sympathy placed the love of Christ first, in actuality it often prioritized a love of others that only secondarily reflected or bespoke a love of Christ. That is, in experience, anxious Puritans would ask themselves not whether a love of Christ has united them to other persons, but rather whether their union with other persons revealed a love of Christ: do I love *that* person who seems to love Christ? And does that person seem to love me? Finally, do I experience that love through a sympathy that shares in both joy and grief? If Puritans could answer yes to questions such as these, then they could *argue* that they also possessed a saving love of Christ.

In Puritan New England, then, the meaning, value, and application of sympathy was never set in stone. Instead, it contained a whole series of tensions. Often, for example, New England Puritans used sympathy as a way of shoring up community, separating the saved from the unsaved or the godly from the rest. Yet even as the Puritans attempted to define and delimit the communion of saints, they also sought to extend its sphere, to *convert* others, to draw in those whom God had elected to be drawn in. Because of that drive, sympathy could also extend the domain and meaning of membership, sometimes purposefully (as in the case of John Eliot) and sometimes unwittingly (as in the case of Mary Rowlandson). In both situations, moreover, the importance of reciprocity remained tenuous. For the Puritans, sympathy theoretically had to be returned; the communion of saints relied on *mutual* affections. But at the same time, many individual Puritans took assurance from their private experience of sympathy *before* they knew whether or not the godly reciprocated that affection. In this process of evaluation, sympathy often ignored the need for reciprocity and became a unidirectional question: do *I* fellow-feel with *them*? Or, more properly: *with whom* do I fellow-feel? The answer to that question might indicate the community to which one belonged, even before the community knew it.

In tracing such tensions, this book becomes a project as much about the meaning and methods of sympathy as it is about a particular theology of Calvinist fellow feeling and its impact on American literature. Trying to determine who belonged with whom, using sympathy to test and guard the borders of community, the Puritans reveal again that they were not necessarily tolerant. In fact, their love of purity required intolerance, so much so that those who openly and actively attempted to institute what Puritans knew to be wrong had no more liberty than to leave. But being intolerant is not necessarily the same as lacking sympathy. In fact, valuing sympathy and valuing tolerance might bear little relation to one another—a point worth emphasizing since a good deal of modern pluralism seems to conflate them. Some recent defenses of literature, for example, seem to suggest that the very form of novels causes empathy in readers, which in turn lessens demonization, deepens ethical thinking, and builds up better citizens.[55] That can happen, certainly. And I instinctively support anyone who suggests that we all ought to read a few more novels in our lives. But the Puritan tension between active and passive sympathy—the question of whether fellow feeling can be commanded, required, encouraged, and taught, or whether it can only be discovered (and even then, only savingly by a few)—gives us another window into the working of this strange phenomenon, an account of sympathy that comes a full century before philosophers such as David Hume and Adam Smith set to theorizing the experience. Even when we subtract piety and predestination, that tension still remains. Surprisingly, the Puritans may have much to teach about how fellow feeling operates, what forms it can take, what it can signify, what consequences it entails, and in what ways it can create, expand, contract, or distinguish a community.

In the shifting emphases that exploited this active-passive tension, the idea of fellow feeling itself gradually changed. This book traces that arc of sympathy, a story in which defenses of sympathy often combine with a narrowing of its reach: the more it means and matters, the fewer it can include. When it signifies so much as salvation, for example, it can create a tightly bound community, but also one that is rather small and select. Yet what exactly mutual affections signified or how far they could extend was not always agreed upon in Puritan New England. Rather, the meaning and value of sympathy developed through complex and con-tested processes of theological debate, emigration, separation, heretical dissent, mission work, and war—each one of which could have turned out differently. In the crucible of these contingent events, the require-ment of fellow feeling and the necessity of demonstrating sincerity turned Puritan writers to literary techniques that would later be found at the heart of sentimental literature. This is the story of that development, a study of seventeenth-century Calvinist fellow feeling—a portrait, in short, of the sympathetic Puritan.

1

Puritan Sympathy

SYMPATHETIC PURITANS FORM the heart of Governor John Winthrop's 1630 "city upon a hill" sermon, *A Model of Christian Charity*. Like the Declaration of Independence many years later, this sermon attempts to speak a new community into existence. Conceived in the hurry of leaving England, delivered on the eve of entering a new land, this lay sermon both delineates and initiates an ideal society of the godly.[1] As a result, it has been made into a foundational text of New England Puritanism. Scholars attempting to understand what comprises this city upon a hill have often focused on aspects of godliness, good order, and discipline, emphasizing a stable hierarchy, a theocratic government, and a covenant with God.[2] Nor are such accounts necessarily wrong. For Governor John Winthrop, as for most other Puritans, no religious enterprise—no community, colony, or country—could thrive, or even long survive, without civil behavior, proper order, and a faithful love of God. Winthrop's friend and fellow emigrant, the minister Thomas Weld, praised God shortly after arriving because he found things "by authority commanded and performed according to the precise rule." That was a sentiment Winthrop shared and hoped would continue.[3] Yet these more legalistic elements could not stand alone. Discipline, order, and obedience operated like the blueprint of a great house: such architecture shaped people into a larger (holy) structure, but it did not, in itself, build the house or enable it to endure. Rather, a durable community required each person to form a firm and reciprocal bond with every other. When Winthrop envisioned his ideal society, therefore, he focused on the mortar, the glue, the *bonds* required to unite a community and make it stand. He spoke, that is, of sympathy.

Indeed, a hope of sympathy forms the heart of Winthrop's *Model of Christian Charity*—a vision for society in which reciprocal affections become fundamental to communal well-being. Describing New England as a city upon a hill, Winthrop proclaimed that in this new place, "a sensibleness and sympathy of each other's conditions will necessarily infuse into each parte a native desire and endeavour, to strengthen, defend, preserve and comfort the other."[4] Grounding this principle in the figure of Christ, whose sacrifice offered the ideal model of sympathy for both citizens and saints, Winthrop preached mutual affections as vital for the common good. To survive and flourish in the wilds of this new world, Winthrop declared, the community would need not just right doctrine, right worship, and right laws, but also—and especially—right hearts.[5]

Such a view, in its day, was entirely unexceptional. Those few scholars who *have* focused on Winthrop's language of affection and sympathy often miss this central point, detaching *A Model of Christian Charity* from its culture and reading it as a unique vision that quickly vanished.[6] In fact, what makes Winthrop's sermon so important is not its originality, its cultural impact, or its fame: in its own day, the sermon was never published and the manuscript was hardly known.[7] Instead, the significance of this document lies in its typicality, its commonplace culling together of basic Puritan and early modern beliefs, including the principle of sympathy. When Winthrop proclaimed the necessity of mutual affections, he relied on nearly sixty years of Puritan texts—themselves building on the work of Christian humanists and Continental Reformers—that transformed sympathy from a scientific concept into a social necessity, a Christian doctrine, and a godly duty.

Sympathy, Science, and Medicine

When "sympathy" first entered English, its associations lay entirely with ancient philosophy and the arts of healing.[8] The Stoics often receive the most credit for theorizing sympathy. It operated for them as a fundamental part of their cosmology, explaining both the unity and the animation of the entire living universe. Sympathy, they argued, depended on an underlying force called *pneuma*, which could be translated as either "spirit" or "breath." This *pneuma* permeated the world like the breath of a living body and "ensure[d] a 'sympathy' (*sympatheia*) of parts." In other words, a kind of "biology"—literally, a study of life based in breath and body—helped explain how the world worked. Moreover, Stoics argued, a wise person would recognize this concordance in the world, become attuned to it, learn to accept it, and so achieve contentment. Thus, in tying notions of wisdom and happiness to universal harmony, the Stoics made cosmology—and a physics of sympathy—central to their entire structure of thought.[9]

Yet in conceiving of the world as a sympathetic *body*, the Stoics drew on even older traditions of medicine and healing. Long before the Stoics, in the Hippocratic text *On Nourishment*, it was explained "that there is 'one confluence, one common vitality' and that 'all things are in sympathy' within the human body."[10] Extending deep into the past, sympathy helped ancient Greeks account for the human body and human health. The Stoic idea of "breath" or *pneuma* as the vitality of a body actually replaced a prior concept of "vital heat" as the source of any organism's life. Cleanthes (ca. 330–230 B.C.E.), a Stoic philosopher, took "the commonplace medical claim that innate heat is the principle of all forms of life," applied it to "the ubiquitous 'sustaining power' of heat throughout the whole world," and concluded "that the world itself owes its coherence to that vital power." It was Chryssipus (280–207 B.C.E.) who substituted "breath" for "heat," but the principle remained the same: an older, established account of what it meant for an organism to be alive became the new Stoic physics of nature.[11] This understanding of nature and anatomy opened sympathy to the arts of healing, especially as they appeared in the practice of "sympathetic cures." Such treatments took for granted not just the body's internal sympathies but also the wider harmonies of the world, attempting through them to tap into the mysterious forces of various plants and herbs. The pre-Socratic thinker Empedocles (ca. 495–435 B.C.E.) was central to this line of thinking, and he based his entire philosophy on a single, central idea: in all things, *like attracts like*. That tenet of the universe—this drawing together of like things—became a belief central to Greek notions of healing, though it was picked up and applied differently through the years.[12]

Most importantly, what persisted from these ancient Greek discussions was the continuing connection of sympathy to both physics and medicine. That legacy appears in the *Oxford English Dictionary*'s earliest definition of "sympathy" from 1567, where it illustrates "agreement, accord, harmony, consonance, concord; agreement in qualities, likeness, conformity, correspondence." Such a general "agreement" or "correspondence" could best be seen in iron and a loadstone. Just as Pliny (23–79 C.E.) explained in his *Natural History* why "the Magnet or loadstone draweth iron unto it" by reference to "this mutual affection, which the Greeks call sympathie, whereupon the frame of this world dependeth," so the English pamphleteer Anthony Nixon (d. 1616) commented on the power of music in relation to magnets: "Musicke," he wrote, "doth iubilate the heart with pleasure, excites and stirs up humors and invites to magnanimity." The only thing that explained it was "symphatie, correspondencie, and proportion." He continued, "Who can give any other reason why the Loadstone draweth yron, but a sympathy of Nature? why the needle touched but with such a stone, should never leave looking toward the North-pole? who can remember other reason then Simpathie of nature? So wee may say, that such is the nature of mens mindes, as musicke hath a certaine proportionate Simpathye with them." For Nixon as for many others, sympathy was its own explanation; certain things just agreed with one another. In nature, like attracts like, and there was little more to say. According to the philosopher and scientist Sir Thomas Browne (1605–1682), for example, no rational account could ever explain magnetism: you simply had to see it to believe it. And that empirical witness of otherwise inexplicable natural attractions served for many as proof of cosmic sympathy. Seventeenth-century Puritans would not necessarily have known or cared about the genealogy behind such a belief, but they nonetheless inherited this legacy from ancient Greece, an application of sympathy to the human anatomy and the natural world.[13]

For many early modern thinkers, then, sympathy became a kind of scientific matching game, which in turn helped explain the theological problem of the soul's relationship to one's body. How is it, many asked, that the immortal and immaterial soul could affect or be affected by the mortal and material body? The answer many gave was that they sympathized. "Great is the affinitie of soule and body," one clergyman wrote, "neerely coupled and wedded by God, like Husband & Wife, for better and worse till death depart them. ... They weepe and laugh, stand and fall, live and dye, and every way sympathize together."[14] Such sympathy explained how the spirit could trouble the body. While the soul languishes, the body can take no delight in the comforts of nature; sympathy would not permit it.

Others, however, asked the question in reverse: how could the body trouble the soul? Even supposing a person's passions were moved by certain humors—the four bodily fluids that affected mood and health—how could such physical humors distress the immaterial soul? According to Thomas Cooper, a Church of England clergyman most famous for his writings on witchcraft, "It were monstrous and preposterous, that the body should move any such Affections in the soule, contrary to it[s] immortall and impassible nature." Cooper therefore provided two possible answers to this dilemma: the soul suffers either from "sympathizing herein with the body, as a loving companion: or the justice of the Lord, by this outward chastisement of the body, arrests the soule, to give up it[s] account." Either the soul and the body work together in sympathy, or they coordinate through the just decree of God (he simply wills it that way). For many, Cooper's first answer—sympathy—seemed to make the most sense. Nicholas Byfield, a Puritan vicar in Middlesex and a noted preacher and writer, believed the soul and body had different origins (the soul came from God and the body from one's parents), yet they were "so one" in human nature "that by sympathy what one suffers, the other feeles." Despite being separate and independent entities, the body and soul coordinate suffering through sympathy. Richard Sibbes, the preacher of Gray's Inn in London and one of the preeminent English Puritans, agreed: "there is a marriage and a simpathy betweene the soule and the body," he wrote, "wherein the excessive affections of the one redound and reflect upon the other." Sympathy, in other words, worked like a companionship and a mirror, a marriage and a reflection.[15]

For Taylor, Cooper, Byfield, Sibbes, and others, then, the soul and the body were independent entities whose joint sensations could best be explained by sympathy. Yet precisely because sympathy described the cooperation of two *distinct* units, it also implied the possibility that things might go awry. The soul and the body do not always agree: sometimes the temper of the body would suggest a certain affection that does not, in fact, arise. Cooper wrote, "Though the Soule seeme to follow the temperature of the body, in regard, that the body being out of temper, the minde also fareth accordingly: yet neither is this generall, but onely in some persons, and upon some occasions." Humors therefore did not *determine* the soul's response. Instead, the soul sympathized with the body like "a loving companion"—meaning they often, but not always, moved together.[16]

Beyond the coordination of body and soul, many used sympathy to explain how the physical anatomy itself held together—a point continued from the Greeks. Each aspect of one's body sympathized with all others, spreading pain or pleasure from one part to the whole. Just as the body "doth not reiect the head, because it is bald, or but one eyed," one early modern minister explained, so the head "rageth not against the body, because it is deformed or diseased, but doth rather condole and sympathize." John Bate, a judge and politician, described such interconnections while analogizing the natural body to Christ's church. "The heart feeles the akeing of the head," he wrote, "and the head the oppression of the heart, the heart and head both doe resent a fellon in one of the fingers, and the gowt in one of the toes, the stomacke simpathizeth with the braine, and the braine with the stomacke." As the ancient Stoics once took a principle of the living body and applied it to the universe, so early modern thinkers took a principle of physics and applied it to the body.[17]

Moreover, that combination lent itself to some of the same sympathetic cures that dated back to ancient Greece. Perhaps the most famous account comes from Sir Kenelm Digby, a founding member of the Royal Society who attempted to explain and defend the "powder of sympathy." This powder healed wounds from a distance, either through use of the weapon that had caused the injury, or simply by sprinkling the powder on the injured person's unworn clothes. An international scientific community debated the realities and possibilities of this powder, and Digby defended it on the basis of empirical findings. Treating magic, rhetoric, and even *human* sympathy as problems of the fancy, Digby sought a rational, mechanical account for the powder of sympathy: as Seth Lobis has explained, he sought to make "its healing power ... independent of the power of the imagination."[18] Digby's *A Late Discourse ... Touching the Cure of Wounds by the Powder of Sympathy* reveals that sympathy still held a place in medicine and the arts of healing, even among the most respected scientists of the day. In fact, Sir Thomas Browne in the prior decade came briefly to doubt biblical miracles primarily because sympathy, so he thought, could better explain the incident. Reflecting on how Moses saved Israelites from snake bites by crafting a bronze serpent (Numbers 21:7-9), Browne wrote: "Thus having perus'd the Archidoxis and read the secret Sympathies of things, [the Devil] would disswade my beliefe from the miracle of the Brazen Serpent, make me conceit that image work'd by Sympathie, and was by an Egyptian tricke to cure their diseases without a miracle."[19] In this instance Browne managed to resist the devil's temptations, but his citation of sympathy demonstrates a wider acceptance of this concept as an element of nature. Consider, for example, the definition offered by the doctor Philemon Holland near the end of his translation of Plutarch. Providing "an explanation of sundry tearmes somewhat obscure," he defined the word "sympathie" as "[a] fellow feeling, as is betweene the head and stomacke in our bodies: also the agreement and naturall amitie in divers senslesse things, as between iron and the load-stone." In nature and the anatomy, sympathy defined the correspondence and reciprocity of distinct, but unified, elements.[20]

Erasmus and Calvin

In the work of Erasmus and Calvin—along with other Christian humanists and Reformers—sympathy began to transition from a medical and cosmological concept to a concern for human relations and the heart. Perhaps no single figure mattered quite so much for such a move as Desiderius Erasmus (1466–1536), the Christian humanist who cast his influence across all of early modern Europe. The marrow of Christian humanism lay in the intermingling of Christian theology and classical philosophy, and so in the preeminent member of this movement one can see how different discourses of sympathy came together and precipitated further developments among early modern Puritans. The impact of Erasmus spread not just to the Puritans, but also to the Puritans' enemies such as Richard Hooker (1554–1600). In fact, up until the mid-seventeenth century Oxford and Cambridge curriculums emphasized the works of Christian humanists, ensuring a continuous influence across almost 150 years. As Margo Todd has shown, "Puritans were imbued with the presuppositions of early modern England, and those were, in the final analysis, heavily Erasmian."[21]

For the history of sympathy, what matters most is the way Erasmus took the ancient principle "like rejoices in like" (*simile gaudet simili*) and applied it to both natural history and moral philosophy.[22] In a short dialogue called *Amicitia*, two characters named Ephorinus and John wonder how and why nature "mingled certain mysterious sympathies and antipathies in everything under the sun." These "natural feelings of friendship and hostility," they notice, affected even "things lacking soul or sense." Ephorinus asks: "What is that power, whether of sympathy or antipathy, between steel and a magnet that causes a substance heavy by nature to advance toward the magnet, 'cling' to it as if by a kiss, and withdraw without touching it?" For countless scientists the magnet exemplified nature's sympathy, but Erasmus does not stop there. Instead, the colloquy takes a sudden swerve toward human relations. John asks Ephorinus to explain "the point of all this talk," and Ephorinus answers, "I believe … that a person can find no surer road to happiness than by avoiding the kind of life from which he instinctively recoils and by following that to which he is attracted (always excluding what is dishonorable). Furthermore, he should avoid the company of those whose characters he finds incompatible with his own and associate with those to whom he is drawn by natural sympathy." With such a conclusion, Erasmus drew human willpower and decision-making into the realm of nature and instinct. Happiness depends on choosing friends in accordance with one's sympathies. In nature, like attracts like; in human beings, a willed decision must accept (or resist) the forces that push and pull.[23]

More important than friendship, however, was the life Erasmus located in charity and tied to Pauline teachings on the Body of Christ. "You see your brother treated unjustly, but your feelings are not disturbed as long as your own fortunes are not endangered," Erasmus wrote. "Why is the soul insensitive in these circumstances? Obviously because it is dead. Why is it dead? Because its life is not present, which is God. For where God is, there is love. 'God is love.'" Such love included a concept of fellow feeling: "If you are a living member," he continued, "why is it that when any part of the body is in pain, you feel no pain and are not even aware of it?" The life of the Body of Christ remained central to Erasmus, and often this concept implied sympathy in suffering that led to charity in action.[24] Moreover, Erasmus did not seem too particular about defining membership in this body. Sometimes he used the image to call for a love that extends to all. In the *Enchiridion*, for example, Erasmus proclaimed, "This is what Paul calls charity: to edify your neighbour, to consider everyone as members of the same body, to regard everyone as one in Christ, to rejoice in the Lord at your brother's prosperity as if it were your own and to heal his misfortunes as if they were your own." Such a pronouncement led Erasmus to a broad interpretation of Romans 12:15: "He should rejoice at another's prosperity as if it were his own, and be saddened at another's misfortune as if it were his own."[25] "Another" here indicates *anyone*, not specifically fellow Christians. At other times, however, Erasmus seemed to limit his claims to fellow Christians. In the *Enchiridion*, for example, the image of Christ's body serves as a *test* of membership. Calling on readers to remember "that we are all members of one body in Christ our Head, animated by the same spirit," Erasmus adds a conditional: "*if* we but live in him, so that we do not envy happier members and gladly come to the aid of weaker members."[26] Here, then, the Body of Christ exhibits signs of exclusivity; membership depends on a certain kind of faith and a particular way of life.

But that raises a problem: if fellow feeling applies only to fellow members (just as pain passes through a single body), how does it operate for someone *outside* the body? Does a lack of love for *those* people still indicate a failure to participate in the Body of Christ? Erasmus's paraphrase of 1 John 3 illustrates this tension. In the fourteenth verse, the epistle reads (as the King James Version has it), "We know that we have passed from death unto life, because we love the brethren. He that loveth not his brother abideth in death." At first, Erasmus substitutes the term "neighbor" for "brother," indicating a broader inclusion: "Where there is no brotherly love, the Spirit of Christ is not found either. There, everyone who hates a neighbor is dead and without inner life." Yet as he continues, Erasmus identifies distinct communities: "Pagan assists pagan, and do you, a Christian, not assist a fellow Christian? ... Do you call him brother and yet produce no evidence of brotherly feeling?" The tension comes to a head in the concluding pronouncement: "One who hates a member of Christ does not yet truly feel affection for Christ. One who wishes another human ill, one for whom Christ died, does not yet love Christ."[27] The key question here is the relation between loving "a member of Christ" and not wishing "another human" ill, for if these categories are different, then the sympathy that exists within the Body of Christ may not extend to everyone; conversely, if *anyone* can be "one for whom Christ died," then fellow feeling and compassion should spread equally to all. As the Puritans took up sympathy, this distinction would come to matter far more, for questions of membership and fellow feeling could bear directly on one's participation in the Body of Christ and one's personal search for assurance of salvation.

Beyond its implications for defining the Body of Christ, Erasmus's stress on charity entailed an Augustinian endorsement of human emotions that included compassion as a basic feature of human nature—even fallen, sinful, unredeemed human nature.[28] In *The Praise of Folly*, for example, Folly rebukes Seneca (4 BCE—65 CE), a Roman Stoic, for stripping the wise man of emotion, arguing that "by doing this he is left with something that cannot even be called human ... Who would not flee in horror from such a man, as he would from a monster or a ghost—a man who is completely deaf to all human sentiment, who is untouched by emotion?"[29] Erasmus believed that people are born with certain sociable emotions, which appear most vividly in family relations but extend outward to others as well. As he claimed in his paraphrase on 1 John 4: "Even the godless, most of whom not only do not love God but do not even believe in his existence, still show a neighbour some sort of affection either because he is a relative by blood or marriage, or because he is a close acquaintance, or simply because one human being sees that another is a human too in the same way that each species of animal possesses a natural instinct to love its own kind." While the absence of natural affections, then, would make someone a monster, their presence did not necessarily qualify as virtue, or as a sign of godliness. As a basic feature of all human beings, such affections were to be expected, not praised.[30]

In his endorsement of such affection, however, Erasmus also began to elevate the inner person and worry about sincerity. Christian humanism and the Reformation more generally began to emphasize sincerity in new and important ways. In fact, one historian has argued that this period "invented sincerity"—at least insofar as it denoted a matching of outward expression to one's distinct, individual interior self.[31] Erasmus's concern with sincerity can be seen in Folly's continuing critique of the wise. "Whatever a fool has in his heart, he reveals in his face and expresses in his speech," she remarks. "But wisemen have those two tongues ...: with one they speak the truth, with the other whatever they think convenient for the moment." In a letter to his friend Paul Volz, Erasmus took this issue further, arguing that a sincere heart might at times trump both action and achievement: "it is an element of goodness to have a sincere desire to be good, nor do I think that one should reject a heart that is sincerely devoted to such thoughts, although its efforts are sometimes unsuccessful." Erasmus repeatedly made a distinction between inner person and outward action—and placed the emphasis squarely on the former.[32]

Yet even though Erasmus elevated the inner person, he also insisted that knowledge of the heart was granted to God alone. As for human beings, we know another's character primarily through deeds. Paraphrasing 1 John 3, Erasmus claimed, "Men will know from our actions that our love for one another is not feigned; God sees the sincerity in the mind directly."[33] Building on Erasmus's and others' increased preoccupation with sincerity, Puritan ministers would take up a similar formulation in their own preaching and theology. But the desire for assurance of salvation would also invent additional routes of access to the heart, simultaneously accepting and seeking to circumvent the platitude that God alone can see inside. Such avenues were necessary not just for ministers, but also for those wanting to know whether their own love—their own acts and experiences of charity—were actually sincere (or something merely feigned). To resolve these epistemological problems, the Puritans engaged in self-examinations, morphologies of conversion, and narratives of grace that repeatedly tied sympathy to sincerity—using both as signs of membership in the Body of Christ.

While Erasmus remained an enormous influence in early modern England, the Puritans drew equally from reformers spread throughout the continent—most notably, of course, John Calvin.[34] Both the word and the idea of "sympathy" appear frequently in Calvin's writings, usually in his commentaries on Scripture. For example, in writing on 1 Peter 3:8, Calvin differentiates between "sympathy" (which belongs to all) and "love of brethren" (which applies only to the faithful). 1 Peter 3:8 reads: "Finally, be ye all of one mind: one suffer with another: love as brethren: *be* pitiful, *be* courteous." What the Geneva Bible translates as "one suffer with another" is "sympathize" in the original (from συμπάθεια). Of this passage, Calvin writes, "Sympathy (συμπάθεια) extends to all our faculties, when concord exists between us; so that everyone condoles with us in adversity as well as rejoices with us in prosperity, so that everyone not only cares for himself, but also regards the benefit of others."[35] In other words, while sympathy goes beyond feeling, it nonetheless involves the experience of mutual consolation and rejoicing. Yet whereas sympathy applies to all, Calvin goes on to explain, "What next follows, *Love as brethren*, belongs peculiarly to the faithful; for where God is known as a Father, there only brotherhood really exists."[36] In this instance Calvin identifies two kinds of reciprocal affections: one that applies broadly (sympathy), and another that relies on acknowledging the same highest good (God the Father).

What remains clear from 1 Peter 3:8, however, and reappears in other commentaries, is Calvin's sense that sympathy arises from human nature and extends to all. In fact, Calvin believes that even fallen, unredeemed human nature tends to melt at the suffering of others—a sentiment he often expresses with words like "misericordia" (mercy), "condolescere" (condolences), and "humanitas" (humanity).[37] But Calvin also turns to the Greek to make his point; finding no Latin term that would suffice, he writes of Isaiah 32:6, "Solus enim naturae sensus nos ad misericordiam et συμπάθειαν commovet," which translates: "mere natural feeling [or sense] moves us to mercy and (συμπάθειαν) compassion." He continues, "When men are so brutalized that they are not affected by the misery of others, and lay aside every feeling of humanity, they must be worse than the beasts themselves, who have some sort of pity for the wants of their own kind."[38] Here, sympathy means being affected by the misery of another, and Calvin thought such a response fundamental to being human. Even terrible people were susceptible to sympathy: "We are aware it not infrequently happens," Calvin observes, "that the long-continued misfortune of an enemy either excites the sympathy [sympathiam] of men of savage dispositions, or else makes them forget all their hatred and malevolence."[39] As such, sympathy ought to be all the *more* present in a love of brethren—a point Calvin makes in his commentary on Obadiah 13. The book of Obadiah recounts the Edomites' glee at the Israelites' exile, and it judges them for that joy, especially since Israelites and Edomites were supposed to be brethren, descending from Jacob and Esau respectively. Thus Calvin summarizes the prophet's message: "If other neighbors do this [ransack

Jerusalem], yet thou shouldest abstain, for thou art of the same blood; if thou can't not bring help, show at least some token of grief and of sympathy [συμπαθείας]: but as thou willingly and gladly lookest on their calamities, it is quite evident that there is not in thee a particle of right feeling [or 'equity']."[40] Here, as elsewhere, Calvin found no Latin word that would suit his purposes; for "sympathy" he simply used the Greek.

Although Calvin considered sympathy somewhat natural, even in corrupted human nature, he nonetheless believed it needed to be induced. And the best way to stir up feeling was through sight. In his text on Obadiah 13, Calvin observed that the most tender sense is in the eyes ("quia scimus sensum esse tenerrimum in oculis").[41] In fact, even hypocrites could use sight to make their appeal. Writing on Jeremiah 42:1–3, where the Israelites seem to repent before the prophet, Calvin argues that to move Jeremiah's heart, "they set before him their miserable state"; indeed, this explains why they added *"as thine eyes see us,"* for they presented "this sad spectacle [spectaculum], to create sympathy [sympathiam] in the Prophet."[42] The *sight* of suffering, Calvin believed, often moves others to respond. For this reason, God's worst punishment often involves a removal from view. Lamentations associates God's wrath with "thick darkness," which Calvin calls an apt metaphor: "For the eyes are the most tender sense, and we are easily inclined to mercy when a sad spectacle is presented to us." Again, even the depraved could be melted by these sights. Calvin continues, "Hence it is, that even the most savage enemies are sometimes softened, for they are led by their eyes to acts of humanity."[43] As vision is the most tender sense, so spectacle leads to sympathy; in the end, the worst calamity includes "thick darkness," for the absence of sight eliminates the possibility of consolation.[44]

Fortunately for saints, they could always count on the sympathy of at least one person: Christ. Just as human beings learn compassion for others through their own sufferings, Calvin argued, so Christ did as well.[45] Christ took on both flesh and feeling in order that from his affections and afflictions—which he endured without sin—he might console sinners in their own struggles and temptations. Thus, when Christ gets tired from so much walking in the Gospel of John, readers should know that the Lord's fatigue was not feigned: "for, in order that he might be better prepared for the exercise of sympathy [sympathiam] and compassion towards us, he took upon him our weakness."[46] In fact, John often depicts Christ in human weakness, reduced even to tears and groans. Before raising Lazarus from the dead, for example, Jesus weeps; of this moment, Calvin comments, "If Christ had not been excited to compassion by their tears, he would rather have kept his countenance unmoved, but when, of his own accord, he conforms to those mourners, so far as to weep along with them, he gives proof that he has sympathy [συμπάθειαν]."[47] Again here, Calvin uses a Greek term for which no Latin equivalent will suffice. Moreover, this term refers to fellow feeling. Christ, in short, "is as much affected by our distresses as if he had endured them in his own person."[48] But perhaps the paramount text for such an understanding comes from Hebrews 4:15. In the Geneva Bible, this verse reads: "For we have not an high Priest, which cannot be touched with the feeling of our infirmities, but was in all things tempted in like sort, *yet* without sin." Where early modern translators write "touched with feelings," the Greek New Testament has "to sympathize." For Calvin, this word created not a subtle speculation about the passions of Christ, but instead a source of encouragement to weary sinners: Christ took upon himself human misery, felt its effects, and gained sympathy from the experience   which in turn made him all the "more inclined to succor us."[49]

As a result, Christ's sympathy served as a model for others. Ministers, in particular, were told to exercise fellow feeling. "How many there are that allow all offenses to pass by unheeded—who either despise the infirmities of brethren, or trample them under foot!" Calvin railed. "This, however, arises from their having no concern for the Church. For concern, undoubtedly, produces συμπάθειαν (*sympathy*), which leads the Minister of Christ to participate in the feelings of all, and put himself in the place of all, that he may suit himself to all."[50] Just as Christ took on human flesh, so the minister of Christ was supposed to conform himself to the infirmities of others in order to exercise sympathy. Yet the lesson did not apply to ministers alone. According to Calvin, Paul teaches in Romans 12:15 that "whatever our lot may be, each should transfer [or translate, *transferat*] to himself the feeling [or sense, *sensum*] of another."[51] Calvin thus proclaims, "Let there be such a sympathy [*sympathia*] among us as may at the same time adapt us [or conform us, *conformet*] to all kinds of feelings [or affections, *affectus*]."[52] Sympathy involved a transfer of senses and affections, an adoption of someone else's inner sorrow or joy, a basic sense of identification and fellow feeling.

Yet early modern translations of Calvin's commentaries point us to an intriguing moment in the linguistic history of sympathy: where Calvin often utilized the Greek word "sympathy" or a Latin transliteration, early modern translators had no such English word. They did not write "sympathy," but instead came up with a variety of alternative translations. The clearest sign of such a lack comes from Calvin's commentary on 2 Corinthians 11:29, where he writes, "Nam cura certa συμπάθειαν generat" (For concern, undoubtedly, generates sympathy). In 1577, the minister Thomas Timme translated that sentence: "For care ingendereth a certaine compassion and mutual feeling of greefe."[53] He had to write "compassion and mutual feeling of greefe" because he did not have the single, simple word "sympathy." It wasn't yet an English word—at least not in a sense involving compassion, feeling, or human relations. Thus, when Calvin claims that Christ proves his sympathy (συμπάθειαν testator) by weeping with fellow mourners, Eusebius Pagit writes, "When as he conformeth himselfe unto them, even unto weeping, he declareth his agreement with them."[54] In 1584, Pagit interpreted συμπάθειαν as conformity and "agreement"—a meaning that dates back to ancient Greece. But Calvin used the word to indicate something more like fellow feeling—something in the same category as mercy, pity, and compassion. The point of emergence for this term in English can thus be deduced from its absence in sixteenth-century translations of Calvin's Latin commentaries.

Calvin himself, meanwhile, borrowed the Greek term "sympathy" from ancient sources and biblical passages such as 1 Peter 3:8 and Hebrews 4:15—both of which verses have to do with far more than mere "agreement."[55] More interestingly, he applied the word to passages where it never appeared in the original Greek, drawing special attention to it. For instance, 1 John 3:17 speaks in the Greek about feeling for another from one's bowels (σπλάγχνα)—the traditional seat of compassion. Yet in his commentary, Calvin explains this process with the phrase τῇ συμπαθείᾳ, which he sets again in the middle of his Latin prose.[56] So, too, in Romans 12:15, Calvin imports "sympathia" (a Latin transliteration of the Greek) to a verse that does not actually employ it, using the term to describe rejoicing with those who rejoice and weeping with those who weep. Again, the early modern translator, Christopher Rosdell, had no equivalent English word. When he translated Calvin, he wrote: "Let then that likelines or mutual combination of affection be amongst us, which may together conforme us unto all affections."[57] Sixteenth-century English translators, in short, did not know what to do with this strange term Calvin kept using to describe *not* natural attraction or agreement, but rather bowels of compassion and mutual affection.

That meaning of the term comes across rather strongly in Calvin's commentary on 1 John 3:14–19—a passage that would become foundational to

Puritan views of community and would form the basis of New England's Antinomian Controversy. Interpreting the thrust of John's message in the seventeenth verse, Calvin writes, "No act of kindness, except accompanied with sympathy [τῇ συμπαθείᾳ], is pleasing to God. There are many apparently liberal, who yet do not feel for [or are touched by] the miseries of their brethren. But the Apostle requires that our bowels should be opened; which is done, when we are endued with such a feeling as to sympathize with others in their evils, no otherwise than as though they were our own."[58] Acts of kindness, in other words, had to proceed from an inner sympathy, which Calvin defines as feeling the miseries of others as much as—or as though they *were*—one's own. The combination of Calvin's commentaries thus reveals a consistent definition of sympathy: exercised by a sorrowful spectacle, it involved a transfer of sense, feeling, or affection from one person to another by placing oneself in the position of the other (just as Christ had taken on human flesh and feeling). The mutual feeling or affection produced by this movement then grounded proper love and action, so that kindness was not truly kind unless it proceeded from the heart—from a sensibility touched by the miseries of others. Through Calvin, the Bible, Erasmus and others, therefore, "sympathy" stood poised to enter the vocabulary of the English not just as a medical and cosmological principle, but also as a social requirement and godly duty concerned with human relations.

The Body of Christ

Puritan and early modern theorists, relying on Erasmus, Calvin, and others, continued the merger of discourses relating to both the natural world and human relations. The most explicit link came through the metaphor of the body. "As it is in the naturall body: so in the politicke," wrote Henry Burton, an ardent Puritan who would eventually lose his ears for his opinions. Both the natural and the political anatomy, when sick, receive treatment in "the ill-affected part, or member," Burton continued: "yet, such is the mutuall sympathie of all the parts, that they all ioyntly suffer, as one." Thus, his censure of corrupt officials, he warned, might sting good members as well as bad. Sympathy, in other words, implied a unity of affections, a quick transmission of the same pleasure and pain throughout. When Thomas Adams, a clergyman in the Church of England, described his "Eirenopolis" (his "city of peace"), he saw the same principle at work, comparing his polis to a body joined together in love "where all are tied by bonds, ioynts, & ligaments to the head; there also by the same Nerves one to another." This single unit, this body, meant that individual members supported one another, "preserving an unanimitie in affection, a sympathy in affliction, a ready helpe to the most needful condition." In the ideal social body, one affection ran through every nerve, joint, ligament, and bond. Some writers thus counseled citizens and magistrates to practice sympathy. Offering advice for how to obtain "good order in Common-weales," Byfield urged leaders to "bring such a sympathie and love of the people, as they should both preserve their authoritie, and yet remember that they rule their brethren." Likewise, every citizen had a duty to fellow-feel with every other, discovering needs and responding with aid. When such sympathy went lacking, civil society went awry. Thus, Thomas Draxe, a Puritan clergyman in Warwickshire, hammered away at all the Papists, knights, gentlemen, lawyers, and merchants who cheated their fellow citizens, asking finally, "where o Man is thy mercie to thy poore brother? where is thy sympathy and compassion?"[59]

Yet for many writers and thinkers in the early modern era, the good of the polis depended upon the prior order of the family. And when it came to right relations between husbands and wives, many turned again to sympathy. As the head fellow-feels with the body and vice versa, so the husband (head) and wife (body) should sympathize. Guillaume de Salluste Du Bartas, an esteemed Huguenot poet of the late 1500s, put such mutual affections into meter and rhyme:

> Then see how love, so holily begunne,
> Between these two, so holy a race they runne
> (This chaste young-man and his most chastest wife)
> As if their bodies twain had but one life.
> What th'one did will, the other will'd no lesse;
> As by one mouth, their wils they do expresse.
> And as a stroke, given on the righter eye
> Offends the left: even so by Sympathie,
> Her husbands dolours made her hart unglad,
> And Iudiths sorrowes made her husband sad.[60]

As a physical body responds in sympathy to any stroke, so spouses reflect and adopt the affections of each other, thereby becoming "one life."[61] Such a sympathy, often defined as "mutual affection," was considered vital to marriage. The leading authority on Puritan domestic affairs, William

Gouge, advised, "A loving mutuall affection must passe betwixt husband and wife, or else no dutie will be well performed: this is the ground of all the rest." In particular, mutual affection preserved good reputations. Gouge told husbands and wives to treat reports about their spouses "as if the report were of their own selves." He continued, "thus shall they shew a true sympathie and fellow feeling of one anothers credit, according to that generall rule of the Apostle, *Reioyce with them that reioyce, and weepe with them that weepe.*" Likewise, in an explication of Ephesians, Gouge counseled spouses, "For the manifestation of this care, this must bee used, *viz.* that both reioyce and grieve mutually, for the good or ill name one of another, by which simpathy and fellow feeling our love and care of one anothers credit will plainely shew it selfe." When the poet and writer Richard Brathwait wondered how two bodies could be "inseparably united," therefore, he noticed this deeper principle at work: "I perceive the strange and indeed unsearchable effects of marriage, which consists not so much in the ioyning hands, as hearts. There is a sympathie equally working, equally moving in the parties loving." Sympathy, in other words, took two people and made them feel and move as one.[62]

The same principle that operated in physical, civil, and marital "bodies" also worked its way into Puritan conceptions of the church, the Body of Christ.[63] For the Puritans, this Pauline metaphor often referred to vocations: the hand did not serve the same needs as the foot, but each person, each vocation, worked together to serve the needs of the whole. Yet Christ's body also contained another important quality: it communicated one affection, via sympathy, to every member. According to John Coolidge, in fact, this feature of the Body of Christ differentiated it from the political body, in that so much emphasis on a common spirit moved a theory of order into a principle of animation arising from an infusion of grace.[64] For many Puritans, sympathizing with the church was thus seen as a natural result of joining it. In describing the phrase "in heaven" of the Lord's Prayer, for example, Gouge claimed that even angels join in this fellow feeling. Heavenly spirits, he wrote, have compassion for the earthly church: "For the Saints in earth and in heaven are fellow members of one and the same bodie: in which respect there cannot but be some sympathie and fellow-feeling of their fellow-members afflictions." That "cannot but be" signals how firmly many believed that sympathy resulted from membership. And because it came about so certainly, because it "could not but be," the reverse held equally true: those who were not members of the body did not share its sympathy. As Draxe explained, "none of the reprobate persons groane or *sympathise* with Gods children; and to none of these belongeth deliverance." Sympathy belonged only to the Body of Christ; it passed from one member to another, but never beyond the Body's bounds.[65]

If sympathy *resulted* from joining the Body of Christ, however, it also could be used as a *sign* of true membership. Viewed from a different angle, sympathy became just one more evaluative tool for determining a person's spiritual state. Glossing the command to have compassion on one another in 1 Peter 3:8, Byfield suggested that sympathy must be present among true Christians. He added, "Hereby wee prove our selves to be fellow members in the mysticall Body of Christ; which is to be doubted, if this sympathy be not in us in some measure." "Proof" and "doubt" make sympathy a sign. Arthur Hildersham, a high-profile Puritan clergyman, was even more explicit. He declared that the fourth and final "fruit" testing the presence of the Holy Spirit was "your Sympathizing with the fellow-members of Christs mysticall body."[66] For that very reason, the absence of sympathy could signal spiritual death. John Preston, mentor to many Puritan ministers, proclaimed, "A living member, if the body be in danger, will have a sympathizing and feeling of the danger ... so now if we hearing the case of Gods Church in what danger it is, if wee take it not to heart, or be not affected with it ... it is a certaine signe we are dead men." The supposed unity of affections created one more box to check when filling out the mental form that would assure one of salvation: those not saddened by ill accounts of the church should question their salvation.[67]

As was often the case, however, signs of election could also be prescribed as duties. Describing the process of conversion, Robert Bolton, a Puritan minister known mostly for his examinations of a saint's inner life, explained that a new Christian "now beginnes to delight himselfe in [the people of God], whom hee heartily hated before," and "in the meane time, he makes conscience of sympathizing, both with their felicities and miseries." The convert's heart, therefore, "is enlarged with lightsomenesse, or eclipsed with griefe; as hee heares of the prosperity or oppression of Gods people." This, Bolton wrote, is the "marke of the true convert."[68] While the passive voice ("is enlarged") ends this passage in mere description, a different voice urges listeners to "make conscience" their sympathy. The *making conscience* of sympathy moves fellow-feeling past the realm of mere description into the territory of a requirement. Indeed, many Puritans preached that sympathy was not just a sign of salvation (something that resulted from election), but also a duty, an integral part of sanctification (the process of growing in grace after one's conversion). Explicating 1 Peter

3:8, Byfield proclaimed, "The doctrine then is cleer, That we ought to have a sympathie one towards another." That "ought" signified an action, a requirement of grace. Byfield continued, "This should greatly move true Christians to strive after this virtue, and to expresse it lively, and shew it forth in all the fruits of it." Sympathy, in other words, was like a virtue, and like all virtues it could be *striven* after—trained up, practiced, and achieved in better or worse degrees. A God-given fellow feeling (and its *expression*) could improve through both time and effort.[69]

Yet as with any aspect of sanctification, theological technicalities stood in the way of prescribing and achieving godly duties. Grace enabled the fruits of grace; one had to be a member of Christ's Body before one could sympathize with it. Fellow feeling, therefore, could not really be stirred up unless one already had a disposition to fellow-feel. In a collection of sermons published in the same year as Winthrop's journey to New England, Preston danced nimbly through this nicety. He wrote:

And this further we must chiefly look to that *we love the brethren,* which for ought I see the holy Ghost points at above all other signs of this spiritual life; you have it 1 *Joh.* 3.14. *We know by this that we are passed from death to life, because we love the brethren.* You know a dead member hath no sympathie with the rest, but a living member hath a fellow-feeling, yea a quicke and exquisite sense within, when anie of the members are pained or hazzarded. Therefore let us labour to find this character of life in our selves by being affected to our neighbours and brethren, & the Churches abroad, by having bowels of compassion in us, to melt over their condition, & to desire their safty as our own.[70]

In this passage, sympathy first appears in the context of evaluation. How does one judge whether one has "new life" (the sermon's title)? Look to the love of the brethren, Preston says, the sympathy and fellow feeling that unites them. Is that feeling present? Is it "quicke and exquisite"? Up to this point, in other words, sympathy is a sign, a tool for self-examination. Then Preston turns. From describing the sign, he moves with a "therefore" to its use. "Therefore," he proclaims, "let us labour to find this character of life in our selves." It is a precarious and subtle move that turns sympathy into a practice while maintaining that only those already joined to the Body of Christ can exercise it. The congregation labors not necessarily to sympathize, but to *discover* sympathy, to find it in their lives. And yet, as Preston describes how one should look for it, the process reveals a kind of duty to be performed: they search "by being affected to our neighbours and brethren, & the Churches abroad." Indeed, searchers should have "bowels of compassion" and "melt over their condition"—prescriptions for feeling and behavior that would then signal one's election. Sympathy thus turned from sign into duty; self-examination became an encouragement to perform.

Like other aspects of sanctification, therefore, sympathy traveled on three separate registers: it constituted a result, a sign, and a duty of grace. Such movements can be illustrated by three statements, which proceed successively but obtain simultaneously:

1. You *will* sympathize with the Body of Christ (a result of grace).
2. *Are* you sympathizing with the Body of Christ? (a sign of grace).
3. You *ought* to sympathize with the Body of Christ (a duty of the godly).

The first line (a declaration) raises the second (a question), which then prompts the third (a command). And the third leads back to the first, making sanctification a tautological circle: as sympathy turns from a sign into a duty, the fulfillment of that duty leads to a ratification of the initial, theological assertion—that sympathy *results* from election. By making sympathy an essential element of sanctification, the Puritans repeatedly pressed a significant point: salvation required both the presence and the performance of fellow feeling.

What exactly a true Christian performed, moreover, was nothing less than an imaginative transfer into the place of another. Bolton makes this clear in his explanation of the Golden Rule (*"Doe as thou wouldest be done by"*). He writes, "In a fellow-feeling reall conceit, put thy selfe into the place, and impartially put on the person of the party with whom thou art to deale. Weigh well ... the whole businesse; and then returning to thy selfe, deale out ... that measure in every particular, which thou wouldest bee willing, upon good ground and sound reason, to receive at the hands of another, if thou wert in his case." Reason thus proceeds from "fellow-feeling," and "fellow-feeling" operates as an act of sympathy. In fact, an early English dictionary—written in 1604 to understand the "hard usuall" words of Scripture and sermons—defined sympathy as just that: "fellowelike feeling."[71] Such "fellowelike feeling" requires imagining another's scenario as if "thou wert in his case." This language resounds through Puritan literature. Byfield, too, asserted that sympathy "makes us like affected, as if we were in their case." The Puritan Rafe Cudworth called on Christians to have "a holy sympathie, and a fellow-feeling of [others' burdens] ... as if we were also afflicted in the bodie." Draxe explained that "wee in our prosperity ... must with such a sympathy and fellow feeling remember them that are in affliction, and so endeavour to releeve and resolve them, as if we were also afflicted in the body." The language becomes so repetitive because it quotes from the Bible, specifically Hebrews 13:3: "Remember them that are in bonds, as though ye were bound with them: and them that are in affliction, as if ye were also *afflicted* in the body."[72] According to multiple Puritans, the proper response to the afflictions of others was to imagine suffering that affliction oneself.

The imaginative work of sympathy, furthermore, constituted its own distinct practice. Puritan ministers instructed their parishioners to pray for others and provide physical aid, but before they acted, they had to be moved. According to Cudworth, Christians could bear others' burdens only if they first exercised "holy sympathie." *After* sympathy came acts of support. The same point emerges in Draxe's *Christian Armorie*. Asked what duties one must perform "to persons afflicted and persecuted," Draxe answers, "First, wee must have a fellowlike feeling of their misery, and sympathize with them." After sympathizing (and as a result of it), Christians should pray, offer counsel, and finally visit the afflicted and "minister unto their necessities." The work of fellow feeling was an inner act of the imagination that was distinct from, often preceded, and at times outweighed the outward acts of charity—just as Calvin had asserted that "no act of kindness, except accompanied with sympathy, is pleasing to God." According to Byfield, the compassion produced in sympathy "excells almes and outward workes of mercy: for when a man gives an almes, hee gives somewhat without himselfe; but when wee shew compassion, we relieve another by somewhat that is within our selves, and from our selves." Thomas Draxe agreed. According to him, "One Christian can yeeld no comfort to another, unlesse both suffer together, (if not in action) yet in fellow feeling." For the Puritans, action mattered, but sympathy came first.[73]

In fact, fellow feeling was such a necessary part of doing one's godly duty that many used a doctrine of sympathy to criticize the lack of it. Ames, for example, reprimanded the Stoics: "This may serve *to reprove* that Stoicall hardnesse," he wrote, "which hath taken hold of mens minds, whereby it comes to passe that they are no way sensible of the conditions of others." Draxe likewise reproved the apathetic: "This doctrine [of sympathy] meeteth with the Stoikes, and those that are Stoikally minded who deny affections." The affections were not obstacles to a godly life; rather, they were "wings whereby we flye, and are carryed unto God, chariots to bring us unto Christ, and ... the very heart and life of all our spiritual actions." The affections mattered not just between an individual and God, but also among believers—from one member of Christ's Body to another. Byfield used his doctrine of sympathy to "greatly humble all sorts of men for their Apathie, or want of care, or feeling, or sympathie in the distresses of others."[74] Repeatedly, Puritans separated themselves from the unfeeling and the apathetic. The godly, they claimed, must not just feel; they must *fellow*-feel.[75]

That sympathy would have first emerged in the preaching of these many sermons. When determining how to achieve their homiletic goals, Puritan ministers relied on a principle handed down from Quintilian, the first-century Roman rhetorician. Quintilian declared, "The prime essential for stirring the emotions of others is ... first to feel those emotions oneself."[76] Though Quintilian distrusted emotions, Augustine later reconceptualized affections as a prime source of knowledge. Augustine's notion enabled a passionate plain style to develop during the middle ages and Renaissance. Drawing on such a tradition, William Perkins, a famous and influential English Puritan divine, advised ministers to preach from godly affections. "Wood that is capable of burning is not set alight unless fire is put to it," he explained: "Similarly anyone who would encourage godly affections and desires in others must first have godly affections himself. Thus, whatever responses a particular sermon requires should first be stirred up privately in our minds, so that we can kindle the same flame in our hearers." The English minister and writer Richard Bernard, in perhaps the most widely read Puritan preaching manual of the seventeenth century, similarly argued that a good minister must possess the "inward sanctification and zeal of a gracious heart." Such a heart, he added, "is an excellent Rhetorician, if there bee the guift of utterance. It is the sweetest tuner of the voyce, and the most forcible perswader. It speakes to another what first it feeleth in itself; as it is affected it endevours to affect others." Perkins and Bernard, like Quintilian and Augustine, agreed that to produce feelings in others, a preacher first had to experience those feelings himself.[77]

This fellow feeling of Puritan ministers and Puritan lay persons based itself in a Christology of sympathy. That is, for many Puritans, sympathy helped explain why Christ came to earth, what he did on earth, and how he aided saints now that he was gone. According to some, Christ suffered and died not only to atone for sin, but also to experience suffering in order to sympathize with saints. Byfield's commentary on 1 Peter, for example, gives several reasons for Christ's passion, but it concludes with this: "so hee might have a sympathy of our sufferings, and have a feeling of our miseries." Taylor, too, explains Christ's temptations as necessary so that he might "sympathize with his members." In other words, Christ had something he needed to learn. Bolton writes, "*Iesus Christ* Himselfe drunke full deepe of the extremity and variety of sorest sufferings ... not only to deliver His ... but also lovingly to learne out of the sense of that sympathy, and self-feeling, to shew Himselfe tender hearted, kind, and compassionate unto them in all their extremities." Likewise, he argues that Christ had to endure spiritual agony so that "by his owne sense, and experience of such painefull passages, hee might learne, and know with a more fellow-feeling, and pittifull heart, to commiserate his poore afflicted Ones in their spirituall desertions." The ability to offer compassion implied an ability to sympathize, and Christ could only sympathize if he knew firsthand what it felt like to suffer.[78]

The main point, however, was that Christ *now* sympathized: that is, Puritans repeatedly offered Christ's sympathy as comfort to the afflicted. He was tempted, Ames explains in *The Marrow of Sacred Divinity*, so that he could "overcome temptations, and help us with συμπαθεία, sympathy."[79] The συμπάθεια was itself the help Christ gave. Likewise, Gouge offers as "a ground of great comfort unto us" the fact that Christians have "a wise, glorious and powerfull ... governor"—a wisdom, glory, and power that came down to fellow feeling: "For Christ," Gouge continues, "hath a feeling of all our wrongs and injuries, even as the head of all the hurts of the body." Byfield, too, suggested the same consolation to suffering Christians: "There is in Christ a sympathy and fellow-feeling. He is touched with our infirmities, and doth much compassionate our case." Christ felt the pains of his Body, his church; and just as Christians were prompted to act out of fellow feeling, so Christ, moved by sympathy, would rescue his saints.[80] Sympathy thus associated closely with atonement. Whether it helped atone or whether it came as a side benefit of atonement, Christ's sympathy was considered a vital comfort for the afflicted. Their sorrows were not their own; they were Christ's, too—and Christ would act quickly for relief.

Moreover, just as Calvin and others had suggested, so the sympathy of Christ set a pattern for all to follow. "As Christ hath a feeling of our infirmities," Byfield wrote, "so wee should bee like affected one to

another." In one sermon, Byfield offers five reasons to explain the doctrine that "we ought to have a sympathie one towards another": the second
is that "hereby wee shew our selves conformable and like to Christ our
Head, who excelled in this vertue." Richard Greenham, another Puritan
clergyman, argued that afflictions "conforme us unto Christ … that wee
may have the sympathie of his affections." Many Puritans believed that
affliction enabled spiritual growth, and one part of that growth involved
precisely an increase in sympathy—the same lesson Christ had learned.
Thus, in *Spirituall Preservatives Against the Pestilence*, Henry Holland, a
Calvinist who warred against the use of magic and other traditional rem-
edies for trouble, offered several fruitful uses of affliction; the eighth was
this: "I gather also by afflictions experience, and this both worketh in me
a Christian sympathie & compassion towardes other men in their miseries, and teacheth mee how to comfort them as I have beene comforted
of the Lorde."[81] Christ's active fellow feeling modeled the affections all
Christians should possess. In sympathy—as in all other matters—Christ
established the ideal.[82]

Puritan thought and practice thus included a detailed theology of sympathy. In nature, sympathy attracted like unto like, binding independent
entities (such as iron and a loadstone) into corresponding movements.
In society, it enabled good government and good order, each person feeling and responding to the needs of others. In the church, the ability to
fellow-feel with God's saints was considered both a result and a sign of
one's election—and that evaluative process turned sympathy from doctrine to duty. The duty to sympathize, moreover, concerned specifically
a movement of the affections. Charitable acts should proceed from sympathy, but they were not sympathy itself. Instead, the term applied to a
matching of affections, an ability to put oneself in the place of another
and feel as the other felt. Such a transference reached its apotheosis (so
to speak) in Christ's incarnation. Needing to know what it felt like to suffer for sin, he became human and suffered the punishment for sin. From
his own experience, then, Christ could sympathize with the afflicted, and
preachers tendered such sympathy to sorrowing souls as both comfort
and aid. Sympathy reached both horizontally (among believers) and vertically (between one believer and Christ). From the head to the foot, one
affection ran through every member, uniting the Body of Christ.

Yet such tight cohesion also entailed separation. This point must be
stressed: the Puritans certainly praised sympathy and they spoke highly
of mutual affections, but all such language came embedded within a

tightly bound and distinct community. The Puritan experience was one of a godly minority finding one another and banding together in brotherly love against a profane majority. The sympathy they felt was heightened by the sense that it extended only amongst their own. That is, fellow feeling was meant primarily for the fellow *godly*, and as such, it could be both rapturous and narrow. Just as in nature sympathy signaled the attraction of like unto like, so in theology it marked a sameness that put a difference between one kind and another, between the elect and the reprobate. Greenham, for example, suggested that when Christians bear with the infirmities of others, they must bear "especially with the frailties of the children of God." When grieving for the sins of Christians, therefore, the godly must do so "always ... with a fellow feeling and pitifull sympathie," but this pity and sympathy did *not* extend to non-Christians. Greenham continued: "we must make Gods friends our friends, without any respect of persons, howsoever they be otherwise farre distant from us, either by place, or familiaritie, or nature, or howsoever: and on the contrarie, whosoever is Gods enemie, must also be ours, howsoever we are ioyned together, yea, though we lie both together in one wombe."[83] From sympathy, in other words, Greenham turned to division—an *us* and a *them* which, he admitted, might cut even through the womb. Natural families gave way to the family of God, the Body of Christ. In Puritan sympathy, cohesion and separation went hand-in-hand. In fact, the experience of separating out from the broader profane multitude heightened the bonds of love, the sympathy of saints.

All these aspects of sympathy—its social necessity, its place in sanctification, its requirement that one transfer oneself into the place of another, its link to the affections and emotions, its model in the figure and work of Christ, and its implications for both cohesion and exclusion—would reappear in John Winthrop's *A Model of Christian Charity*. Indeed, his visionary-yet-commonplace sermon reveals in exemplary detail a Puritan sympathy that would dramatically affect the social and cultural landscape of seventeenth-century New England.

Winthrop's Sympathetic City

In the one and only surviving manuscript of Winthrop's sermon that scholars have found, *A Model of Christian Charity* begins by announcing a distinction between two classes: the rich and the poor. To modern ears, this separation often sounds rather cold: "God Almightie in his most holy and wise providence hath soe disposed of the Condicion of mankinde, as in all times some must be rich some poore, some highe and eminent in power and dignitie; others meane and in subieccion."[84] To defend this division, Winthrop offers three reasons for its existence. First, God ordained it that way; second, it gave God "more occasion to manifest the worke of his Spirit" in exercising both justice and mercy; finally, it unites. God instituted high and low ranks so that "every man might have need of other." One person could not survive alone. The good society would thrive only if each person, in devotion to his or her God-given task, supplied what others lacked. God made people diverse so that they would stick together. Vocation—this calling of each person to a distinct job or purpose—certainly matters in *Christian Charity*, but Winthrop's third reason for social division also suggests something more: bare necessity proves insufficient. One person may require another's goods, but that will not in itself cause anyone to share. Rather than emphasizing mere need or vocation, therefore, Winthrop turns, as Paul did, to love.[85] For Winthrop, love did not exist in order to fill needs; needs existed in order to increase love. *From need*—"from hence," Winthrop writes—all could be "knitt more nearly together in the Bond of brotherly Affeccion."[86] God made some rich and others poor because it would encourage love.

But Winthrop is not entirely naive. He knows that a loving response would occur only in a society of saints, and his audience includes a mixture of the presumably elect, the possibly regenerate, and the potentially reprobate.[87] As a result, he does not tell everyone to love one another and leave it at that. Instead, he introduces a "double Lawe by which we are regulated in our conversacion one towardes another": the law of nature and the law of grace. All people are born into the first; only some are *re*born into the second. The second group, moreover, constitutes its own, distinct family. The law of nature commands love of "neighbour" as "the same flesh and Image of god," but the law of grace "propounds one man to another ... as a brother in Christ allsoe." Kinship thus teaches saints "to put a difference betweene Christians and others." From its inception, therefore, brotherly affections implied the exclusion of all who are not brothers, binding together a smaller family carved from the larger community.[88]

Having distinguished between regenerate and unregenerate, Winthrop begins to address the latter. The coming times, he explains, will be difficult, necessitating "extraordinary liberality." Using lawyerly logic, he sets out the exact duties required of each during the initial period of settlement—precisely how, when, and how much the settlers should give, lend, and forgive. In other words, Winthrop *reasons* with his listeners. Where saintly affections could not be counted on, solid arguments would have to do. As he states later, the "force of Argument" can "enforce a rationall minde to some present Act of mercy." Reason will not work forever, but it may suffice for a time—just long enough, perhaps, to survive.[89]

After laying out the laws of mercy, Winthrop turns his attention to "the Bond of brotherly affeccion." That transition occurs as Winthrop shifts from the regulations of mercy to their basis in the heart. He writes, "Haveing already sett forth the practice of mercy according to the rule of God's lawe, it will be useful to lay open the groundes of it allsoe ... and that is the affection from which this exercise of mercy must arise."[90] In effect, Winthrop turns from extraordinary *times*—detailed in the rules of lending, giving, and forgiving—to extraordinary *people*, those actuated by a love springing from their union with Christ. According to Winthrop, acts of mercy proceed primarily from well-ordered affections. In keeping with the Puritan belief that outward actions spring from inward movements, Winthrop suggests that the good community will need not just the right kind of laws, but also the right kind of heart. When facing affliction— when thrown into difficult times—Christians will need mutual affections. In this claim, Winthrop conformed to the wider Puritan view of sympathy. *From* sympathy, from this inward movement of the affections, people would be prompted to offer aid. The survival and prosperity of society, in other words, depended on the motions of the heart.

To illustrate the importance of these affections, Winthrop turns to the analogy of a clock. This simile—with its coordinated gears springing from a single first movement and aimed at one final purpose—offered a ready analogy in Winthrop's day for a variety of lessons. The early modern English physician Timothie Bright, for example, used a clock to explain how a soul performed "so many and diverse actions." As the first movement in a watch produced coordinated motions, so the one soul functioned diversely through the various members of the body.[91] Yet the analogy could also spread across society and be applied to the vocations. For Perkins, clocks presented a "notable resemblance of God's special providence over mankind, which is the watch of the great world, allotting to every man his motion and calling and in that calling his particular office and function."[92] For still others, the mechanical nature of the clock explained good deeds done by bad people. Preston, for example, asserted, "Now you know there are motions, as the motions of clockes and watches, that proceede not from life, but from art; so it is in this matter of religion." The good works of the spiritually dead would last only so long as the machine ticked on, but "when that which sets them at worke is removed, there is an end of it."[93] Regardless of their precise message, each of these authors used the metaphor of a clock to speak of corresponding movements working together toward a common end and pointing back to a single origin, one spring that made the whole thing go.

For Winthrop, that spring was the "affeccions of love in the hearte." He writes:

> As when wee bid one make the clocke strike he doth not lay hand on the hammer which is the immediate instrument of the sound but setts on worke the first mover or maine wheele, knoweing that will certainely produce the sound which hee intends; soe the way to drawe men to the workes of mercy is not by force of Argument from the goodnes or necessity of the worke, for though this course may enforce a rationall minde to some present Act of mercy as is frequent in experience, yet it cannot worke such a habit in a Soule as shall make it prompt upon all occasions to produce the same effect[,] but by frameing these affeccions of love in the hearte which will as natively bring forthe the other, as any cause doth produce the effect.[94]

In Winthrop's sermon, as in Puritan theology more generally, proper deeds proceed from a godly heart. Some can be persuaded by pure reason to act well, but most must first be moved. Moreover, achieving *consistent* acts of mercy requires establishing proper dispositions, good affections; it is not about applying specific lines of logic to particular cases of conscience. Contrary to an exclusive focus on reason, laws, or discipline, Winthrop believed that the civic good depended on brotherly affection rooted in a love of Christ, responding to neighbors with acts of mercy produced by the motions of sympathy. The heart, he insisted, made the whole thing go.

If the proper affection of each citizen unites society and serves the common good, questions still linger: what *are* the proper affections, how do they operate, and where do they come from? When he introduces the metaphor of a body in *Christian Charity*, Winthrop answers these inquiries by offering as an example "the most perfect of all bodies, Christ and his church." Before Christ comes, the body is disunited, disproportionate, and disordered, each member tending its own way with "many contrary qualities or elements." But Christ changes that: "when Christ comes and by his spirit and love knitts all these partes to himselfe and each to other, it is become the most perfect and best proportioned body in the world." Winthrop, like other Puritans, believed that members of Christ's Body were knit not just vertically to God—"to himselfe"—but also horizontally, "each to other."[95]

In both the vertical and the horizontal relationships, Winthrop looks to love: "Love," he states, "is the bond of perfection." From this principle he draws five conclusions. The first three restate the position already advanced—that the perfect community is a body united in love—but the fourth and fifth expand it. In the fourth conclusion, Winthrop writes, "All the partes of this body being thus united are made soe contiguous in a speciall relacion as they must needes partake of each others strength and infirmity, ioy, and sorrowe, weale and woe." For support, Winthrop turns to 1 Corinthians 12:26—an oft-cited proof-text for Puritan views of sympathy. It reads: "Therefore if one member suffer, all suffer with it: if one member be had in honor, all the members rejoice with it." Experiences such as affliction and rejoicing are meant to be reciprocal: suffering and honor must be matched by fellow feeling. The actions that result from such reciprocity appear in Winthrop's fifth conclusion: "This sensibleness and Sympathy of each others Condicions will necessarily infuse into each parte a native desire and endeavour, to strengthen defend preserve and comfort the other." When people suffer and rejoice together, they "necessarily" respond as each occasion requires. In the ideal community, action follows from affection, and each moment's proper affection is determined through a process of sympathy rooted in a kind of sensibility—a "sensibleness" to someone else's pain. In this regard, Winthrop seems to have been guided by Romans 12:13, a verse that calls for "hospitality" in "distributing unto the necessities of the saints." Of this command, the Geneva Bible comments, "A true rule of charity, when we are no less touched with other men's wants, than with our own, and having that feeling, help them as much as we can." Sympathy, in other words, involved a fellow feeling produced by placing oneself in another's place: from that affection, so generated, the godly would be moved to offer aid.[96]

That process discovers its ideal in Christ. According to Winthrop, sympathy even explains his death on the cross. First, Christ became "a parte of this body," knit with it "in the bond of love"; second, that union produced "a native sensibleness of our infirmities and sorrows"; third, "He willingly yielded Himself to death to ease the infirmities of the rest of His body, and so healed their sorrows." Christ joined the body, felt the body's affliction,

and, on the basis of that sensibility sacrificed his life to relieve its burdens.[97] Following standard Puritan doctrine, Winthrop preached that in
dying on the cross, Christ set a pattern of sympathy for all to follow. He
continues, "From the like sympathy of partes did the Apostles and many
thousands of the Saintes lay downe theire lives for Christ." As Christ once
died for the body, so now the "Body," the church, gives its life for Christ.
Yet sympathy, again, is more than vertical. Winthrop writes, "the like wee
may see in the members of this body among themselves." He then demonstrates these communal affections with the example of Paul, who "could
have beene contented to have beene separated from Christ that the Jewes
might not be cutt off from the body," and who expresses an "affectionate
part[ak]eing with every member."[98] Winthrop then quotes two more passages from 2 Corinthians: "whoe is weake (saith hee) and I am not weake?
whoe is offended and I burne not [2 Cor: 11.21]; and againe. 2 Cor: 7.13.
therefore wee are comforted because yee were comforted." In each quotation, Winthrop demonstrates Paul's imitation of Christ's sympathy. Nor
does Paul stand alone. From the apostles and the saints down through
"the histories of the churche in all ages," Christ establishes a pattern of
fellow feeling—of grieving and rejoicing matched through identification
and reciprocation. The members of the church serve each other "out of
love," and in such service they demonstrate "the sweete Sympathie of
affeccions."[99]

There is, however, a caveat: when it comes to determining the inward
"exercise of this love," Winthrop turns to the maxim "*simile simili gaudet,*
or like will to like." Love must be grounded in "an apprehension of some
resemblance"—and that resemblance, it turns out, is one's regeneration
in Christ. Under the law of grace, "each discernes by the worke of the spirit
his owne Image and resemblance in another, and therefore cannot but
love him as he loves himselfe." In *Christian Charity*, in other words, sympathy is more often discovered than sought. Christ "found" a "native sensibleness" only after leaving the Father to be knit with the body. Likewise,
the soul loves when it "findes any thing like to it selfe." In a similar manner, Eve was "brought" to Adam, and Jonathan, who was "endued with the
spirit of Christ," loved David only after "hee Discover[ed] the same spirit
in David." Sympathy, for Winthrop, moves from self to the extension of
oneself, a likeness discovering—finding—likeness in another.[100]

Yet if "like will to like," the unlike must be left out. In this way, emotional cohesion and separation reappear in Winthrop's discussion of an
ideal community. His principle of sympathy—proposed for the whole

society—operates only within the bounds of Christ's Body. An overlap thus emerges between saint and citizen. Who should hold public office? As the colony would soon decide, public office should be reserved for those who could fellow-feel with Christ's Body, those who had the spiritual "first mover," the "affections of love in the heart" that would habitually produce good works. The body politic would be the Body of Christ, and the success of that community would depend on each member's fellow feeling—a sympathy enabled by conversion. As Gouge and Greenham had both used sympathy to distinguish the godly from the ungodly, so Winthrop did as well: "Do good to all," Winthrop proclaims, *"especially to the household of faith."*[101]

Understanding this principle of sympathy at the heart of *Christian Charity* enables a new perception of Winthrop's covenant. Winthrop proclaims, "Thus stands the cause betweene God and us, wee are entered into Covenant with him for this worke." This covenant pledges allegiance to God and promises obedience on behalf of the colony. As such, it surely forms a significant aspect of Winthrop's ideal community. Yet Winthrop does not define the *content* of the covenant according to a rigid set of outward actions or a specific form of polity; rather, he declares that "the onely way to avoyde this shipwracke"—that is, God's wrath—is by being "knitt together in this worke as one man."[102] That knitting depends on the affections. Winthrop declares:

Wee must entertaine each other in brotherly Affeccion, wee must be willing to abridge our selves of our superfluities, for the supply of others necessities, wee must uphold a familiar Commerce together in all meekenes, gentlenes, patience and liberallity, wee must delight in eache other, make others Condicions our owne[,] reioyce together, mourne together, labour, and suffer together, allwayes having before our eyes our Commission and Community in the worke, our community as members of the same body. Soe shall wee keepe the unitie of the spirit in the bond of peace.[103]

For Winthrop, the unity of the spirit and the bond of peace—a quotation from Ephesians 4:3—are precisely the point; the work *is* the community, and its perfection depends on being able to imagine another's affections as one's own, matching sorrow with sorrow and joy with joy. What the Puritans have to bear in mind, what they must always keep before their eyes, is their joint membership in one body. And just as bodily images dominated Puritan discussions of sympathy, so here Winthrop draws on such language to emphasize a coordinated movement of affections. The Puritans must not merely labor together; they must rejoice and mourn and suffer together. They must make others' conditions their own. They must entertain each other in brotherly affection. They must, in short, embody (quite literally) a theory of moral sentiments—a principle of sympathy that forms good communities through the reciprocity of fellow feeling.[104]

As these affections spread, the "one man" that emerged would, ideally, include everyone. Winthrop seemed to entertain a hope that all citizens could be saints—that the principle of "like will to like" would not, finally, exclude anyone. Admittedly, Winthrop begins his sermon with a "double lawe" that distinguishes the unregenerate from the regenerate, and the following section of rules and logic seems aimed at the former. But reason is soon set aside, and when Winthrop turns to love, he never looks back. Describing the ways in which Christ's body is knit together, the pattern of sympathy set by Christ, the affections embodied in Adam and Eve or Jonathan and David, Winthrop seems to imagine only fellow Christians—either those already regenerate, or those who might soon be. Such language culminates in Winthrop's application, where he describes the persons of this particular plantation as "a Company professing our selves fellow members of Christ." Here, the Massachusetts Bay Company overlaps fully with the Body of Christ. The persons are not just emigrants; they are, potentially, the elect.[105]

If each emigrant was potentially regenerate, then the new settlement could entertain high hopes indeed. They would be saints living together in a mutuality of affections made possible by the love of Christ. In fact, as the regenerate discovered their likeness in one another, they *could not but* love each other. United as one body, "they must needes" partake of each other's weal and woe. Such language—"must needes" and "cannot but"—shades toward the utopian.[106] But the utopia of *Christian Charity* is not premised on the eventual elimination of suffering or sorrow; rather, Winthrop bases his ideal on each citizen-saint's *response* to affliction. United as one body, one man, they would comfort one another in a love that looked to Christ and followed a pattern of sympathy traced out through the history of the church.

In so doing, this "one man" would undergo a process of sanctification. Discussing regeneration and sanctification in *Christian Charity*, Winthrop explains that Adam "rent himselfe from his Creator" and so infused in each person a principle "to love and seeke himselfe onely." That principle remains in control until Christ "takes possession of the soule and infuseth another principle, love to God and our brother." The swap, however, does not occur instantaneously. Instead, Christ *gradually* "gets the predomining in the soule" and "by little and little expells the former [principle]." In an individual Christian, this process of transformation was called sanctification; and during the process, saints experienced joy and sorrow in such a way that each occasion moved them closer to Christ. By making the community "one man," Winthrop presents his whole society as able to partake in the same spiritual development. Gradually, little by little, Winthrop's city would be sanctified.[107]

The idea of achieving some kind of perfection, however, must be tempered. On earth, sanctification never ceased; perfection remained forever out of reach—a destination that always receded into the distance. But each day, each month, each year, decade to decade, a saint came closer and closer to the goal, finally achieving glorification when he or she died and entered heaven. When envisioning this New World community, therefore, Winthrop makes clear that he does not believe it will be perfect. In a letter he signed and sent to several Church of England leaders, he and other Puritan founders declared, "Wee are not of those that dreame of perfection in this world."[108] Such an antiutopian claim seems fairly straightforward. The emigrants did not go to New England to establish heaven on earth.

Nonetheless, they did go with heavenly aspirations. The plainspoken announcement in "The Humble Request" must be set next to the statement of Winthrop's fellow colonist Thomas Weld. In a letter to his former parishioners in England, Weld writes, "Conceive us not as if we went about to justify ourselves or dream of perfection ... Only we desire to breathe after perfection and to know what is the rule and to walk in it."[109] Both Weld's letter and "The Humble Request" seek to quell accusations of separation and perfectionism—to dispel the claim that New England Puritans thought themselves superior to, and disconnected from, the Church of England. Yet Weld admits that New England Puritans do "breathe after perfection." They had some thought of getting nearer to God, some higher hopes of heaven. In *A Model of Christian Charity*, Winthrop, like Weld, breathes after perfection. The community would never *achieve* perfection, Winthrop knew—not on earth, not in this lifetime. But just as a saint approached heaven through a gradual process of sanctification, so Winthrop seemed to hope that the godly community of New England could be so unified by sympathy that each occasion of weal or woe would only sanctify them more, until, as Winthrop writes of individual Christians, "Christ be formed in them and they in him, all in eache other, knitt together by this bond of love." *A Model of Christian Charity* presents the future of New England as an asymptote: the community gets forever closer to the godly ideal without ever finally reaching it.[110]

To that end, Winthrop begins the hoped-for process of sanctification before he even finishes speaking. In the final paragraph of *Christian Charity*, Winthrop addresses his audience directly for the first time. Having spoken eloquently and at length about brotherly love—having detailed its dependence on sympathy—Winthrop suddenly stops, turns to his listeners, and calls them "Beloved": "Beloved," he says, "there is now set before us life and good, death and evil, in that we are commanded this day to love the Lord our God, and to love one another." Winthrop ends by quoting Deuteronomy 30:15–20, where Moses addresses the Israelites on the cusp of entering the Promised Land.[111] Yet he changes the first word of this passage: instead of proclaiming "Behold!" as Moses does, he calls his audience "beloved." This term comes not from Moses but from Paul, who repeatedly addressed Christian communities as his "dearly beloved." Thus, Winthrop's peroration deftly connects the Old and New Testaments, a sense of righteous law with its motivating love. New England would be—or at least *could* be—a typological Promised Land, a new fulfillment of an old promise. Yet *this* Promised Land would be known and experienced not just through a careful obedience of covenantal laws, but also and even more so through a charity enabled by the grace of Christ and lived out in the mutual affections of every member. In calling his audience "Beloved," Winthrop draws his sermon to a close by launching its vision: it begins now, he says. Now we will be a community of loved ones. Now, we will live in brotherly love. Now we will be sanctified as "one man" in the Body of Christ, sympathizing—like all bodies—from tip to toe, in both weal and woe. The broad Puritan tradition of sympathy comes to a point in Winthrop's sermon and directs his vision for a new community. Its success or failure, he proclaims, lies in the sanctified heart.

2

Love of the Brethren and the Antinomian Controversy

SIX YEARS AFTER he envisioned New England as a sanctified city on a hill, John Winthrop saw the Massachusetts Bay Colony erupt in conflict. Other skirmishes had cropped up before 1636, but nothing threatened the community quite like the Antinomian Controversy, which pitted Puritan against Puritan in a New World battle threatening the authority of leaders and the stability of the state. In the end, civic concerns (whether real or imagined) resulted in the banishment of several civilians, most famously Anne Hutchinson. But when letters first passed between Thomas Shepard and John Cotton (the leading ministers on either side), the primary issue was pastoral, not political: they debated assurance and salvation, not authority and stability. Moreover, the heart of that debate involved the same matter at the center of *A Model of Christian Charity*: in 1630, Winthrop proclaimed that the colony would flourish through a love that sympathized with brethren; in 1636, this mutual "love of brethren" marked the precise point of division. In fact, it would be only a slight exaggeration to consider the entire *theological* controversy a battle over 1 John 3:14, the verse that linked a "love of the brethren" to eternal life. Church elders, led by Shepard and Winthrop, linked a love of brethren to mutuality, reciprocity, and feeling—to sympathy—and they valued it as a sign of election; Cotton and the so-called antinomians discounted such love and declared that only a personal experience of Christ's love could assure one of salvation. In other words, the Antinomian Controversy was not, as many scholars have asserted, a battle between the moral and the spiritual, between disciplined obedience and religious experience. Instead, the Antinomian Controversy divided Puritans over the meaning and value of sympathy itself—over what sorts of spiritual experiences, what kinds of love could count as evidence of salvation. The winners would decide what sympathy could signify for the anxious, godly settlers of New England.[1]

The Antinomian Controversy

Feelings ran high in the years preceding the Antinomian Controversy. In 1633, the much-respected John Cotton immigrated to New England and joined John Wilson as a minister in Boston's church. His sermons sparked a revival. As one Dorchester layman later recalled, "God's holy Spirit in those Days was pleased to accompany the Word with such Efficacy upon the Hearts of many; that our Hearts were taken off from *Old-England* and set upon *Heaven*."[2] Such spiritual zeal, however, could not last long. It peaked and waned, and as the fervor died, new anxieties arose. Amidst these anxieties moved a woman named Anne Hutchinson. Having followed Cotton to Boston in 1634, this Puritan laywoman established herself in the community and began providing spiritual counsel to women in labor. In addition, Hutchinson began hosting meetings at her house, during which she explained and interpreted Cotton's sermons to a wider circle of Bostonians. Her talent as a teacher drew an audience, and as Boston crowded into her home, Hutchinson added critiques of other ministers to her praise of Cotton. Most, she claimed, taught a Covenant of Works, the heresy whereby sinners could *earn* salvation through good works; only a few, mainly Cotton, taught the true Covenant of Grace, in which sinners *received* salvation from Christ alone.

As word of this distinction spread, it split Puritans between those who supported Hutchinson and those who opposed her. Such divisions cut through every social rank.[3] Governor Henry Vane and John Wheelwright, a minister and brother-in-law of Hutchinson, along with several wealthy Boston merchants, all defended Hutchinson and promoted her ideas. Other powerful magistrates and ministers, led by the indomitable pastor of Newtown, Thomas Shepard, fought back. Puritan leaders initiated a series of conferences, letters, treatises, and sermons in order to sort out the differences, establish consensus, and prevent division. Yet disagreements increased; the furor rose.

To resolve the growing divisions, the magistrates of Massachusetts Bay called for a general fast. This Fast Day would address a multitude of ills, including "the miserable estate of the churches in Germany; the calamities upon our native country"; the spread of Roman Catholicism, famine, and wars; and, finally, "the dissension in our churches."[4] Wheelwright was chosen to deliver the day's main sermon, which was supposed to model repentance and reconcile the growing dissensions. Instead, he publicly supported Hutchinson's distinction between hypocrites and saints, and then set the two sides at war.[5] Technically, his sermon described a spiritual battle, not a physical fight, but the terms kept slipping and the General Court proved in no mood for assessing metaphors. It found Wheelwright guilty of contempt and sedition. As with every previous attempt to quiet opposition, however, the court's judgment only produced more protests. Several leading citizens wrote a petition in Wheelwright's defense. Then, in May 1637, called to an actual battle against the Pequot Indians, several Bostonians refused to serve in the militia when they learned that John Wilson, a putatively "legal preacher," had been appointed their chaplain.

With the colony thoroughly divided, it came time to elect a governor and members of the General Court. The election, like the Fast Day, proved a debacle. Governor Vane insisted on hearing the petition in defense of Wheelwright before anyone could vote. The gathered citizens defeated this motion, and in the ensuing election they chose Winthrop—Vane's opponent—as governor; moreover, they eliminated Hutchinson's sympathizers from the rest of the General Court. Power swung. Meeting in November 1637, the newly elected magistrates hauled antinomian leaders before the court to answer for their deeds. They found several guilty of sedition and contempt, disenfranchised others, banished a few, and fined most. Finally, the General Court removed all "guns, pistols, swords, powder, shot, and match" from anyone associated with their party.[6]

After dealing so handily with so many, the court finally turned its attention to Hutchinson. Two separate accounts of the proceedings remain, and both make it clear that the prosecution struggled. It had insufficient grounds to charge Hutchinson with a crime—that is, until she provided it herself. Rising to address the court, Hutchinson asserted that she had received an "immediate revelation." What that exactly meant could be open for interpretation, but for the elders that was all they needed to hear. Any claim to direct, extra-Scriptural, divine communication threatened society because it trumped civil law. Thus, on the basis of maintaining order and defending the state—and not, Winthrop emphasized, in regard to personal opinions—the Court banished Anne Hutchinson from Massachusetts Bay.

Hutchinson's theological opinions did matter to the church, however. Shortly after the court's sentence, therefore, she faced a second trial in front of her Boston congregation. In these proceedings, several heresies surfaced—from the mortal status of souls to the denial of resurrection—and during the course of the discussion, Hutchinson eventually recanted all of her positions and apologized to the church. But she qualified her confession: she had never held false opinions until *after* magistrates placed her under house arrest. Others, mainly Thomas Shepard, disagreed. Hutchinson was charged with lying in the very act of repenting, and the church excommunicated her.[7]

Cast out of both church and colony, Hutchinson left for Narragansett Bay in the colony of Rhode Island. After several removes, she and most of her family were killed in 1643 in the territory of New Netherlands by Native Americans at war with the Dutch (they mistook her family for Dutch settlers). Many considered these murders, along with two earlier miscarriages (one by Hutchinson and one by her supporter, Mary Dyer) as signs that New England had done right: God sided with Winthrop and Shepard. The Antinomian Controversy came to a close, and the elders—the "orthodox"—won.[8]

During the years of controversy, however, what counted as orthodox was never entirely clear. In order to set down the true position, Puritan ministers across Massachusetts Bay agreed to a synod in 1637—the first ever held in New England. From several towns they poured into Cambridge and for three weeks they publicly debated theology, inviting colonists to watch and listen. By the end of their meeting, the gathered ministers had identified and confuted nearly 90 errors, defining orthodoxy by specifying what good Puritans were not allowed to believe. In the process, they engaged in the kind of theological debate that had become a common part of the Puritan way. In England, the godly had always attempted to parse true from false, and such deliberations had nurtured many close relationships. Yet for all their arguing, most New England Puritan ministers assumed agreement on essential Christian truths—such as the nature of grace and one's assurance of salvation. Nor, it seems, would they have been forced to a synod if Anne Hutchinson had not pointed out divisions that seemed to drive deeper than mere stylistic difference. By declaring a fundamental, doctrinal opposition between various ministers, she forced them to examine what before they had assumed was just a matter of degree.[9]

If, indeed, there existed the kind of opposition Hutchinson proposed, it would have proven no small matter in New England. For Puritans, theology mapped out the meaning of human life, applying cosmic significance to the slightest details and subsuming the temporal within the breadth of the eternal. The things of this world came filtered through the prism of the next, and personal experiences always pointed back to the possibility of salvation. So, for example, when John Winthrop's sister, Lucy Downing, wrote to him about her decision to stay in England, she told him plainly that she feared the wilderness and its difficult conditions. Yet she insisted, "If wee see god withdrawinge his ordinances from us hear, and inlarginge his presence to you thear, I should then hope for comfort in the hazards of the sea, with our litell ones shrikinge about us ... and in such a case I should willinglie rather venter my chilldrins bodyes, and my owne for them, then there soulses." In the end, the consolations of salvation far outweighed the comforts of the body—which is precisely why the Antinomian Controversy ignited such deep passions in New England: its primary disagreement concerned one's assurance of salvation.[10]

Sanctification, Justification, and the Assurance of Salvation

The colonial division resulted, in part, from a spectrum of Reformed views on what Puritans called "the testimony of the Holy Spirit." All Puritans believed in such a testimony and claimed that its experience aided in assurance. But they understood this phrase diversely. The theologian and historian Joel Beeke explains three basic definitions: first, some believed "the inward evidence of grace and the testimony of the Spirit are essentially one." In other words, the Spirit's testimony *accompanied* a godly life. This definition opposed mysticism: the believer's spirit simply *is* the Holy Spirit at work in sanctification (the fruits of grace). A second view held that the Holy Spirit witnesses not only *with*, but also *to*, a believer: it was "something in addition," opening the door to some form of direct testimony or religious experience, but still tying it closely to fruits and evidence of a godly life. Finally, the most mystical group placed "the event of 'immediate' assurance by direct witness of the Holy Spirit on a higher level *practically*," describing full assurance as an "immediate light, joy unspeakable, transcendent, glorious, and intuitive."[11] In this case, a special religious rapture counted as the "testimony of the Holy Spirit." During the Antinomian Controversy, Shepard and the elders endorsed positions one and two; Cotton and the antinomians shied nearer to number three.

According to Cotton, the witness of the Spirit "applyeth and conveyeth the testimony ... imediately to the Soul." Cotton had to be careful with the word "immediately" since all Puritans believed that revelations could not come apart from Scripture. So he nuanced the term: "Imediately I say though not without the word of God nor without (sometimes in some cases) the work of God, yet with his own imediate power above the power which either the word hath of itself, or the work of any creature." In other words, some merely listened to the Word; others experienced the power of God *through* (and in addition to) this listening.[12] That power Cotton never fully defined, but he did offer clues to what he imagined. Describing the witness of the Spirit, he often used phrases such as "sheddeth abroad," "speaketh peace," "passeth understanding," "joy unspeakable," and "above."[13] Three times Cotton offered the example of Thomas Bilney from the *Book of Martyrs*: Bilney "witnesseth that the first peace and assurance he found was by the sweet comfort which the Holy Ghost shed abroad in his heart upon reading that precious promise (free from all conditions of works) 1 Timothy 1.15."[14] Scripture, on its own, meant little; what made Bilney's justification sure was the "sweet comfort ... shed abroad in his heart" that he received *while* reading. For Cotton, in other words, assurance came through the semimystical, superadded testimony of the Holy Spirit.

Because Cotton insisted on this experience, he downplayed—even, at times, dismissed—the witness of sanctification. Christ alone was the "door that must be first opened to me, and revealed to me, and entred in by me, before I can see any Assurance that the treasures of Gods House belong to me," he declared. Circumventing that entrance would be like trying to sneak into heaven through the back door—except that heaven had no back door. Christ alone opened heaven, and the experience of union with him was the only way to ground one's assurance of salvation. On this point, Cotton seemed almost to trip over his words: "It is a Spiritual thing doubtless, and consequently to be discerned Spiritually, only by Spiritual light and by Spiritual understanding and by comparing Spirituall things with Spirituall things." In so insisting, Cotton separated assurance of salvation from a Christian's daily life. When a saint sought comfort, Cotton turned him or her to those ruptures and raptures where revelations occurred.[15]

Others agreed and expanded Cotton's views. In his Fast Day sermon, Wheelwright preached that "the Lord dealeth with his children spiritually in regard of his spiritual presence." He distinguished between "the Lord himselfe" and his "fruits and effects," and he used that distinction to critique the Israelites in the wilderness: they could "procure unto themselves things from God and the blessing of God; but they did not get the Lord himselfe." The gospel, Wheelwright preached, "doth hold forth Jesus

Christ and nothing but Christ." Anne Hutchinson went further. She testified that the Lord "hath let me to distinguish between the voice of my beloved and the voice of Moses, the voice of John Baptist and the voice of antichrist, for all those voices are spoken of in scripture." These voices represented different aspects of the Puritan experience. Her "beloved," naturally, was Christ, and her ability to distinguish Christ from Moses meant that she could separate the experience of grace from the obligations of the law. John the Baptist prepared the way for Christ, and she could pick out his call from the preaching of the antichrists who obscured grace by insisting on its appearance in sanctification. Such indirectness did not hamper Hutchinson. The Lord spoke to her by "immediate revelation" and "by the voice of his own spirit to my soul." She testified that "having seen him which is invisible I fear not what man can do unto me." Cotton and Wheelwright had both called on Christians to "look to Christ" and "seek God's face"; Hutchinson proclaimed that she had done just that— and gotten results. What for Cotton was a nuanced distinction and for Wheelwright a blunt difference became for Hutchinson an unbridgeable chasm between the semimystical experience of God's love and the mundane things of this world.[16]

For the elders, in contrast, Christ could not be so easily separated from the manifestations of his grace. "Although Christ is to be the chief matter of our Consolation," they concurred, "yet a Christian ought to seek to see his interest in Christ, not only in beholding the face and hearing the voice, but also in feeling the gracious work of Christ." Thus, a careful analysis of sanctification (the "gracious work of Christ") could lead one to conclude that he or she had been justified (received a saving implantation of grace)—even if the *moment* of justification remained unclear. "When Justification is hid from the eye," the elders asserted, "Sanctification and faith are there in the heart and oftimes effectually working," and "when Sanctification is working it may be seen." Because only the justified are sanctified, the sanctified must be justified. Therefore, saints did not necessarily need an overwhelming experience of grace; they could also carefully weigh their daily experiences (their sanctification) and determine themselves elect.[17]

Yet according to the antinomians (in varying degrees of accusation), this defense of sanctification amounted to a Covenant of Works.[18] Determining one's spiritual status by searching for ordinary testimonies of election would encourage Christians to perform good deeds in order to *create* signs of grace. Rather than Christ freely opening the door of

salvation, Christians would begin to batter it down. But no one can successfully storm the gates of heaven; the misguided would be turned back.
That is what made the position such a dangerous heresy, the antinomians
claimed. What made grace *grace*, they insisted, was its status as a *gift*.

In the historiography of the Antinomian Controversy, most scholars
seem to agree that the elders were slipping into discipline and deed, mainly
because they equate sanctification with some sort of visible, outward moral
duty performed. Defining sanctification as "the moral behavior of the individual," or as "saintly behavior in the visible world," or even more simply as
"the doing of good," scholars have consistently argued that the elders were,
as one person puts it, substituting "labor for assurance."[19] Against this
works-righteousness stood a noble, embattled minority defending spontaneity, spirituality, and a mystic sense of communion with God. According
to the usual critical line, in other words, the antinomians stood for *feeling*—
for religious rapture and spiritual freedom—while the elders promoted
logic, subordination, and obedience. Since 1873, in fact, scholars have been
linking the antinomians forward two hundred years to the rise of transcendentalists, making the Antinomian Controversy into a fight for American
free-spiritedness. It is this free-spirited emotional expression, many claim,
that Puritan authorities beat down and banished before it reappeared in
Jonathan Edwards and finally came back to reign in the work of Emerson.
To give just one example: in *The Puritan Ordeal*, Andrew Delbanco favor-
ably links both Cotton and Hutchinson to Emerson because they supposedly championed "felt experience" and advocated "intimacy rather than
obeisance." The real problem with Hutchinson, Delbanco asserts, was "her
blunt charge that New England was slipping into spiritual death." Classic
accounts of this controversy thus repeatedly pit internal intuition against
external behavior, the spiritual life of antinomians against the moral living
of elders, emotions against reason, feeling against discipline, and affection against deed. As I aim to show, such an invented battle—a product of
nineteenth-century commentators and twentieth-century scholars—mis-
construes what each side was all about.[20]

Good works *did* matter to the Puritan elders of Massachusetts Bay.
That much is true and easy to prove. The call for righteous deeds resounds
through their literature. In *The Parable of the Ten Virgins*, for example, a
series of sermons preached during the Antinomian Controversy, Shepard
raged against sloth and exhorted Christians "to do the work of Christ, to
be daily at it, and finishing of it." In fact, he told his congregation to "make
this your last end, to live unto Christ and to do his work." Hypocrites

might "close with Christ to make them happy, not to make them holy"; true saints, on the other hand, sought contentment through service. "O, be not slothful then," he preached: "neglect no means, but use all means; get oil in your vessels, that you may get your desired end." Outward obedience and holy living counted as signs of grace.[21]

Or rather, they were a necessary component of grace, but nowhere near sufficient in themselves. While discipline mattered, good deeds never came divorced from proper affection. Works, in and of themselves, meant nothing; what *both* elders and antinomians cared about was the spirit in which they were performed. Shepard—the main antagonist of the antinomians—preached that Christians have a "double life": an outer one of forms and an inner one of "ineffable communion with God, vision of God, delight in God." It would not do to have the former without the latter. Shepard defined "dead works" as "good works done, but not from the principle of the life of faith, but life of nature." One minister for the elders, Peter Bulkelcy, dcfined sanctificatiun as "an inward work wrought in a man's bowels, of which he has (and can not but have) a sensible feeling in himself." For Puritans, the proper frame of heart made sanctification real. Such a view helps explain why in Shepard's church, narratives relating evidence of election always describe experience, not behavior. For *all* Puritans, saints were known not primarily by their acts, but by their hearts.[22]

On both sides of the Antinomian Controversy, then, *internal dispositions*—the affections out of which acts flowed—mattered far more than the deeds themselves. What the elders defended were not primarily deeds or discipline, but rather a certain kind of experience—an experience of sanctification that came below the level of rapture. In other words, they wanted to protect the value and significance of relatively ordinary affections. And the affection that mattered most—the one that best testified to a person's election—was brotherly love.

Love of the Brethren

The link between Puritan sympathy and the Antinomian Controversy emerges most clearly when one considers the premier example of sanctification: "love of the brethren." This phrase refers to 1 John 3:14–19:

14. We know that we are translated from death unto life, because we love the brethren: he that loveth not *his* brother, abideth in death.

15. Whosoever hateth his brother, is a manslayer: and ye know that no manslayer hath eternal life abiding in him.
16. Hereby have we perceived love, that he laid down his life for us: therefore we ought also to lay down *our* lives for the brethren.
17. And whosoever hath this world's good, and seeth his brother have need, and shutteth up his compassion from him, how dwelleth the love of God in him?
18. My little children, let us not love in word, neither in tongue *only*; but in deed and in truth.
19. For thereby we know that we are of the truth, and shall before him assure our hearts. (Geneva Bible, 1599)

On the one hand, this passage presented a practical mandate for the colony. As with Winthrop's *Model of Christian Charity*, it required those who had the most to share with those who had the least. It expected both "deed" and "truth," calling for "compassion" in the truly saved. Yet talk of life, death, eternity, and assurance also translated this passage into a higher register. Here, according to the elders, lay clear evidence that sanctification—in this case, brotherly love—could testify to election. "For thereby we know that we are of the truth," the Bible said: through their love of brethren, Christians could assure themselves that they were saved.

The significance of 1 John 3:14–19 appears in the sheer number of times it gets cited and discussed. When the elders first confronted Cotton, they suggested that a Christian can "seek his interest in Christ, not only in beholding the face and hearing the voice, but also in feeling the gracious work of Christ"—a point they supported with 1 John 3:14. Cotton responded by claiming that a love of brethren may help faith, but it could not ground assurance—a point he reiterated when the ministers met in Boston. Similarly, when Wheelwright delivered his Fast Day sermon, he offered love of the brethren as the only named example of sanctification; and, as for Cotton, it did not count. Wheelwright proclaimed, "If men have revealed to them some worke of righteousness in them selves, as love to the brethren and the like, and hereupon they come to be assured they are in a good estate, this is not the assurance of faith, for faith hath Christ revealed for the object." The example was not lost on Winthrop, who inserted Wheelwright's proclamation in his official account of the controversy. Like Wheelwright and Cotton, Hutchinson also questioned the evidentiary value of a love of the brethren, though she did so long before the controversy began (if her accusers can be believed). During her civil trial, the minister Zechariah Simmes recalled being on the boat with her while emigrating; he noticed even then "a secret opposition to things delivered" in his sermons. "The main thing that was then in hand," Simmes went on, "was about the evidencing of a good estate, and among the rest about that place in John concerning the love of brethren." Perhaps Simmes remembered her questioning of this central passage three years after it occurred; perhaps he built a case against Hutchinson by inventing her opposition to the biblical text most under dispute. Either way, Simmes's remark reveals just how central 1 John 3:14 was to the Antinomian Controversy. It should not be surprising, then, that when elders countered the errors of the antinomians in their final retelling of the story, they cited 1 John 3:14 four separate times.[23]

Love of the brethren came to the center of the controversy because it had already served so many as a sign of salvation. For example, the two main antagonists of the antinomians, Winthrop and Shepard, had previously invoked this love to assure themselves that their deceased wives had passed to heaven. In his memorial to Thomasine Clopton, Winthrop recorded that "she was sparinge in outward shewe of zeale, etc. but hir constant love to good christians, and the best things," along with her diligent use of ordinances, "did plainly shewe that truthe, and the love of God, did lye at the heart." Lacking a powerful outward display of zeal, Thomasine nonetheless proved her election true, in part by loving the saints. The same went for Shepard's wife Joanna Hooker. Among the list of virtues attributed to her, Shepard offered this: "She loved God's people dearly and studious to profit by their fellowship, and therefore loved their company."[24] God's love of Thomasine and Joanna, in other words, could be known through their love of the saints. If the love of saints no longer counted, it would not only undercut the assurance of living Puritans; it could even displace one's former wife from heaven.[25]

The fact that Thomasine and Joanna's love of the brethren could be witnessed at all, however, suggests that Puritans possibly had in mind some sort of moral performance—acts of love that remained outward and visible, something husbands could observe and record. Thomasine may have been "sparinge in outward shewe of zeale," but she still found some way to communicate her "constant love to good christians." If not conveyed entirely by conversation, that love would have required some performance of charity. On one reading, then, the love of brethren could again return to moral obedience and Christian duties. These husbands judged their wives' spiritual status by visible deeds, outward works.

Yet Puritan accounts suggest that this mark of sanctification also operated passively and inwardly. It was a feeling, an *experience*, not a deed. When Puritans discussed a love of brethren they often spoke of it as a sign discovered, not a duty performed. Recounting the initial stages of his conversion, for example, Shepard recalls not only that the minister John Preston convicted him of his sin, but also that his affections toward the preacher changed: "I began to love him much and to bless God I did see my frame and my hypocrisy and self and secret sins." Shepard's turn emerges both negatively (as a sight of sinfulness) and positively (as a love of the preacher). That love cannot be discounted. As briefly as it appears, it nonetheless remains central to his account, for if Shepard saw his sins but hated the man who revealed them, he would demonstrate little change of heart. The love of Preston—an affection distinct from any deed—testifies to and moves Shepard toward the love of Christ. Years later Shepard would exhort his congregation to "love [Christians] dearly," explaining that "a man will never get good from any Christian that he despiseth or slighteth."[26]

This love of the brethren—and the comfort it offered to weak Christians—appears most vividly in the memoir of a Puritan layman from Dorchester named Roger Clap. Recalling his own conversion, Clap could offer no specific moment when he first turned to Christ. He wrote, "If ever there were the Work of Grace wrought savingly in my Heart; the Time when, the Place where, the manner how, was never so apparent unto me, as some in their Relations say it hath been unto them." This absence of an identifying moment did not lead him to despair; it led him to the saints. Having "often heard alledged, *We know that we have passed from Death to Life, because we love the Brethren*," he looked to see whether he possessed such a love. To prove that he did, Clap offered a vignette: when a young man came among them, Clap had no particular affection for him, but when he heard that this "hard favoured" person feared God, "upon the very Report thereof my Heart was knit unto him, altho' I never spake with him that I know of." In other words, quite apart from any moral duty or act of charity, Clap experienced the love of saints and knew that he was saved.[27] This "knitting" had nothing to do with deeds or behavior, though it also seems to go beyond a simple feeling: it reminds us instead of the difficulty in assessing Puritan affections, which could be anything from ordinary passions to reorientations of the entire, redeemed self. In Clap's case, love of the brethren is a testifying experience that combines thoughts and feelings for another human being to reveal the affections of his heart.

In fact, such a movement of affections occurred whenever Clap heard about fellow saints. "To this very Day," he wrote, "if I perceive or do but hear of a Man or Woman that *feareth God*, let him be Rich or Poor, English or Indian, Portugal or Negro, my very Heart closeth with him."[28] This language of "closing" matches the terminology Puritans used to describe their union with Christ: in conversion, they "closed" with Christ. For Clap, therefore, the religious affections that bent toward Christ could also arc toward fellow Christians. And the more of Christ Clap saw in saints, the more his affections leapt. He continued, "My heart doth most close with, and most highly prize those that are most excellent, most holy, most worthy Instruments of *God's Glory* and *his People's Good*."[29] For Clap, the love of brethren was not so much an active deed as a passive reception: he did not *make* his heart leap; it jumped of its own accord. And this sensation of love, this inner experience, provided comfort in times of trial; he *must* love God and God *must* love him because, quite simply, he loved God's people. His inner response toward the community marked him as a fellow member.

Clap's accumulated assurance, however, also included a heightened religious experience. Meditating in bed one night, he asked himself whether he would commit an unspecified sin if God would still grant him salvation. No, he said. Sin was sin and he refused to commit it solely because God forbade it. In taking such a stance, Clap wrote, "my Conscience did witness to me that my State was good: And God's holy Spirit did witness (I do believe) together with my Spirit, that I was a Child of God; and did fill my Heart and Soul with such a full Assurance that Christ was mine, that it did so transport me as to make me cry out upon my Bed with a loud Voice, *He is come, He is come*."[30] In the end, it might seem, Clap's assurance depended on a moment of almost erotic rapture, not a lifetime of relationships.

Yet Clap never discounted his love of brethren or displaced it with religious rapture. Recalling the experience decades later, Clap considered it the "*most* Assurance of God's love."[31] That "most" reveals a series of degrees; Clap did not lack assurance before this event nor gain it unwaveringly afterward. Indeed, even in his recounting of the tale, Clap inserted a parenthetical doubt: "(I do believe)." More importantly, this rapture simply culminated—without replacing—Clap's earlier moments of comfort. Those experiences may have offered less assurance, but they gave comfort all the same. In fact, for Clap the love of brethren possessed a distinct *advantage* over his heightened religious experience: such a love enabled a more constant, if lesser, consolation. The problem with a spiritual high was that it too quickly passed away, as Clap himself admitted: "That Glimpse of God's eternal Love which I had at that Time was better to me than all the World; yea far better than Life itself. But Oh wretched Man that I am, I have a *Body of Death* that presseth me down, and hinders me from living always in such a heavenly Frame." When he spoke of comfort in the present tense, therefore, he did not turn to rapture, but to the brethren: "To this very Day," he explained, he still "closed" with God's people. That was Clap's continuing sign and comfort. When faced with doubt, he looked to the assurance of 1 John 3:14, the love of brethren.[32]

In emphasizing such comfort, Clap joined a chorus of Puritans who located comfort and assurance in a love of brethren. When Mistress Hibbins's husband called a fellow member of his church "sir" instead of "brother," for example, he actually found himself apologizing to the church: "How it fell from me, I know not. But it was an expression unsuitable to the covenant I am in, and the more unsuitable because the title of brother is such a phrase that I have found my heart many times enlarged with the use of it."[33] In Thomas Shepard's Newtown congregation, meanwhile, the conversion narratives of those entering church membership often highlighted 1 John 3:14. Mr. Sanders, for example, told the congregation, "And so by this we know we are translated, etc. And I thought I loved them only for the image of God in them, and the Lord hath let me find in the course of my life some power of mortification and sanctification." Sanders's Scriptural citation—"by this we know we are translated"—refers to 1 John 3:14: "We know that we are translated from death unto life, because we love the brethren."[34] In Sanders's list of evidence, love of brethren stands as its own sign of grace. The same went for Jane Holmes. She declared that upon "hearing in ministry those that were in love with brethren and trying it if they loved poor saints as well as a rich saint, some support." For the congregant William Manning, "one of [his] best evidences" of election was his "love [for] those who love Christ." Another parishioner, William Hamlet, testified, "One thing the Lord supported my heart by was love to the brethren and the ministry showing the difference between love of hypocrites and saints." Using language almost identical to Puritan accounts of sympathy, Hamlet proclaimed that he found himself sorrowing "when [he] heard God's name blasphemed in old England." The discovery of sympathetic grief, a mark of brotherly love, offered Hamlet assurance of salvation. He was elect, he knew, because his affections matched the emotional community of the elect.[35]

Beyond this sympathy of affections, love of the brethren manifested itself in Christian company. In his *Autobiography*, for example, Shepard diligently recorded the various communities he inhabited and how he responded to each. After initial signs of grace, he "fell from God to loose and lewd company, to lust and pride and gambling and bowling and drinking." The mere fact of going around with such people revealed his fall. Yet the same evidence proved his return: "The Lord left me not," Shepard wrote, "but a godly scholar, walking with me, fell to discourse about the misery of every man out of Christ, viz., that whatever they did was sin, and this did much affect me." Similar awakenings occurred whenever he "did light in godly company," but his return did not last long. "By loose company," Shepard continued, "I came to dispute in the schools and there to join to loose scholars of other colleges and was fearfully left of God and fell to drink with them." Shepard reveals the presence or absence of grace in his spiritual autobiography by detailing his movements back and forth between godly fellowship and lewd company—so that when he finally turned to God, he "began to forsake [his] loose company wholly." For many Puritans, the company they kept in life could predict where they would go in death.[36]

After Shepard finally converted, he proved his election by testifying to the Christian fellowship he *desired*. Bound to serve in Sir Richard Darly's ungodly house, Shepard wrote, "I never was so low sunk in my spirit," and that for five reasons: "(1) I was now far from all friends; (2) I was, I saw, in a profane house, not any sincerely good; (3) I was in a vile wicked town and country; (4) I was unknown and exposed to all wrongs; (5) I was unsufficient to do any work, and my sins were upon me, etc." Four out of these five causes refer specifically to Shepard's company: he was absent from friends in a profane house and wicked town with ungodly persons exposing him to wrongs. He portrays continued godliness, in other words, by displaying his emotional distance from those most physically near. Only in the last reason—and only, as it were, while trailing off—does Shepard mention sins. Company was what mattered, and by considering profane company an "afflict[ion]," Shepard evidenced his grace.[37]

Indeed, Shepard's "sunken spirit" revived only in the presence of fellow Christians. "I found in the house three servants … very careful of me, which somewhat refreshed me," he remarked. As he gradually converted the house, his spirits picked up. In the end, he concluded, "the Lord was with me and gave me favor and friends and respect of all in the family, and the Lord taught me much of his goodness and sweetness." For Shepard, as for Winthrop and many others, the goodness of the Lord was never far from the friendship of saints. Perhaps learning from this experience, Shepard preached in *The Parable of the Ten Virgins*, "I profess one day's fellowship here with a number of broken-hearted Christians, either mourning together or rejoicing in their God and King together, it outbids the many years' glory of the whole world, howsoever it is hidden from the world."[38] What this Puritan principle thus reveals is a constant assessment of company (are they wicked or good, unregenerate or godly, chosen by me or forced upon me by necessity?) and a concomitant need to examine how one *feels* about each individual at all times. Emotionally aligning oneself with saints—whether they are present or not—signifies one's union with Christ.

In like manner, many congregants of Newtown tracked their spiritual condition through the company they kept and the feelings it produced. When Francis Moore relapsed, he "fell from [God] to loose company and so to drunkenness." Nathaniel Eaton discovered "the hidden corruption of [his] own heart ... in open sins in Sabbath breaking and company keeping." Mary Angiers rested quietly in "a place of more ignorance" before she turned to God, while John Stansby, far from merely falling into wicked company, "sought a match for [his] lust ... enticing and hailing others to sin, rejoicing when I could make others drink and sin." Repeatedly, congregants recounted how they "delight[ed] in vain company and vain books" before their hearts finally turned to God. That turn, like Shepard's, appeared in the *desire* for godly company. Although William Manning first delighted in vain company, he eventually looked "on them that lived more restrainedly and civilly," deciding finally to "leave off my bad company and join myself to such as they were." John Stedman, another parishioner, "followed the Lord and found communion with God and His people so sweet that [he] resolved against ill company and hence [was] hated." Being an enemy of the enemies of God, Stedman found himself a friend of saints (and so a saint himself).[39] Sometimes, this desire for a change of company manifested itself in a longing for New England. Stansby, for example, reported that "in old England, seeing ordinances polluted, my soul desired to be there where Christ is feeding of His flock." Hamlet likewise compared the "sins and sorrows of the land" with "the sweet people that came hither" and "desired to come." More than that, he found "that when I was farthest from God then my heart was scared from coming. But when it was nearest to God then I did desire to come and content to be a servant."[40] The desire to be among saints testified to one's election—and emotional communion with the saints (loving the brethren, mourning for their sins, rejoicing for their good) witnessed divine favor.

From these accounts of the love of brethren, four points emerge. First, love of the brethren was an affection, not a deed; however much it might manifest itself in outward displays, it began as an inner movement of the heart. Second, while this affection testified to the presence of the Holy Spirit, it was nonetheless relatively ordinary.[41] It did not elevate Christians into a mystical rapture replete with tears and unspeakable joy; instead, it took delight in fellow saints, bonded (or closed) with those who feared God (including strangers), desired the company of the elect, and sympathized with the welfare of the church. These were affections that could occur on a regular basis, in daily interactions. Third, the love of brethren required daily interactions. While raptures might happen on one's bed, in one's prayer closet, or alone in one's field, the love of brethren could not occur outside of communal relations. It was a horizontal, not a vertical, sign of grace. Fourth, the love of brethren was a *legitimate* sign of grace. The comfort offered by this relatively ordinary love sometimes stood alone and sometimes received further confirmation by other religious experiences, but in either case the comfort could be trusted. The love of saints made one a saint.

Or so the elders asserted. When they broached this topic with Cotton, however, he found it difficult to agree. He had nothing against loving saints, of course, but he rejected the idea that such love could assure one of salvation. Confronted with 1 John 3:14–19, Cotton asserted that a love of brethren offered *supplementary* evidence "to such only as are formerly assured of their good estates by the seal of the Spirit." It was "an addition, or inferiour helpe, for a prop unto faith, not for a foundation to leane on." The only sure foundation was the love of God as experienced in one's union with Christ. "Even in nature," Cotton proclaimed, "children doe not first come to know their parents, either by their love to their brethren, or by their obedience to their parents; but from their parents love descending on them." The love of brethren had its uses, he granted, but grounding assurance was not one of them.[42]

The theological debate of the Antinomian Controversy, therefore, did not set up inner spiritual emotions against outer moral behavior. It was not a contest between discipline and feeling as countless scholars have suggested; rather, it opposed one view of religious experience to another. Cotton's requirement of a semimystical witness of the Spirit stood him against the elders' validation of emotions like desire, grief, and the pleasure of Christian fellowship. By authenticating such affections, the elders heightened the significance of their community's emotional bonds. If the love of brethren and the desire for godly company confirmed one's status as elect, then the individual would be knit into the community—and the community would be knit together—through relatively ordinary affections that bore extraordinary weight. By defending sanctification, the elders attempted to preserve a sympathetic "city," an emotional community of saints.

Competing Accounts of Experience and Comfort

Beyond entailing different communal effects, the opposing views of sanctification also carried significant consequences for individuals—and in particular, weak Christians. Weak Christians were those with an anxious, unsteady assurance. Like the man in the Gospel of Mark, they cried, "Lord, I believe; help thou mine unbelief."[43] For those with such a faith, anxiety needed to be assuaged and despair held at bay; on this, both elders and antinomians agreed. They disagreed, however, on how best to help. When they battled about the value of sanctification, therefore, both sides fought to comfort their flocks.[44] This deep pastoral concern has often been sidelined by scholars who favor a political story. According to many accounts, the elders were most worried about insubordination and civil unrest—a lay rebellion against Puritan laws and leaders. Morally lax, the antinomian way lessened the significance of good works, weakening the ability of magistrates to enforce discipline and obedience.[45] Civil and political concerns *were* certainly present during the controversy. Winthrop, for example, dwelt at length on the civil threats posed by Wheelwright and Hutchinson. Yet while he ended up worried about the stability of his colony he did not necessarily begin there, nor was it his sole concern throughout. And, of course, Winthrop was not always the central figure. Letters and meetings among ministers preceded the civil trials, and in these initial interactions the consistent, primary concern was pastoral care for weak Christians. The issue spiraling out of control revolved around assurance. Matters of eternal life and death hung in the balance, and those issues, at least initially, outweighed questions of civil stability or magisterial authority. In New England homes, anxious Puritans facing their eternal destiny wanted to know what comfort they could trust.[46]

When they do address this question of comfort, scholars often miss or ignore the psychological ease offered by the elders. Instead, they pose anxiety *against* assurance, composing a narrative in which the antinomians extend comfort to those whom the elders had wracked with fear.[47] This tradition has support. Shepard, for example, called the antinomians "evan-gelical hypocrites" because they hid their heresies behind the gospel: where the gospel offers rest, they took that message to heretical extremes. He preached that a person "under the terror of the law and sense of curse for his sin, will make his last refuge hither, and hide himself under the wing of the gospel, not so much out of love to Christ or gospel, but because they serve his turn, and give him ease." The Puritan minister Thomas Weld, introducing the elders' official account of the Antinomian Controversy, similarly declared that antinomian opinions opened "a faire and easie way to heaven." Certainly there were times when the elders accused their opponents of offering too much ease. But they also, and as often, charged antinomians with making demands that *increased* anxiety. The first half of this equation has received a great deal of attention; the second half usually goes unnoticed.[48]

In fact, in defending sanctification, the elders accused antinomians of not going far enough to ease anxiety and offer assurance. Cotton's way was not necessarily *wrong,* they granted; it was simply too narrow. The elders summarized his position as one in which a saint "first seeth his good Estate in Gods thoughts of peace, (or in Election) testified to him, and therein reads himself a believer, justified, sanctified; *and this is the only way,* all others going on in or aside to a Covenant of Works." Though elders doubted "that Faith in Christ is sooner discerned than Sanctification by Christ," they were nonetheless willing to "grant that sometimes it is so, *not alwaies.*" In these passages and others, elders relate that the real sting in Cotton's theology was not what it asserted, but what it rejected. Assurance could be found in more ways than one. The elders claimed that Cotton's theology actually impinged on the sovereignty of God. They objected: "But to take our first Assurance to arise from the Spirit in an absolute promise *only,* is not only difficult to us to believe (and therefore desire your grounds) but seems dangerous to maintain, as straitning the freeness of Gods Spirit in working and destroying the comfort of many, whom Christ himself doth speak comfort unto, Mathew 5.3 etc." By refus-ing all methods except his own, Cotton was binding the grace of God and destroying the assurance of many.[49]

The question at stake, then, concerned where Christians should look for comfort during their dark night of doubts. According to the cosmology of the day, stars received their light from the sun, and the ministers turned to these sources of light to make sense of the debate. Cotton argued that to understand the stars, one must first have seen the sun. That vision, that initial semimystical religious experience, offered the *only* source of comfort; when faced with doubts, troubled souls should *remember* the sun and wait for its return. He thus defined sanctification as "the setting up of another window, though a lesser, to convay the same Sun light into the house another way." In Cotton's theology, the sun, the "naked Christ," was all that mattered—not the stars, nor any other form of lesser light: one had either seen the sun or not. In contrast, the elders argued that as stars receive their light from the sun, so the lesser twinklings of sanctification could testify to the presence of Christ. In the darkest hours, the elders insisted, look to the stars, to the small signs of grace, the minor evidences of a changed heart and a godly life; such light could comfort saints while waiting for the sun to rise.[50]

The continual return of this metaphor testifies in itself to the importance of 1 John 3:14 in understanding the Antinomian Controversy, for its repetition riffs on Calvin's original commentary concerning that passage. About the sun, Calvin seemed to side with Cotton: "when we enjoy the light, we are certain that the sun shines; if the sun shines on the place in which we are, we have a clearer view of it; but *yet* when the visible rays do not come to us, we are satisfied that the sun diffuses its brightness for our benefit. So when faith is founded on Christ, some things may happen to assist it, still it rests on Christ's grace alone."[51] Even so, the commentary left room for interpretation: after all, what does it mean for the sun to "diffuse its brightness for our benefit" when its visible rays are obscured? For the elders, that meant a night sky full of stars—the diffusion of visible rays, the secondary lights that took their glimmerings from the sun.[52]

In defending the stars against Cotton's naked sun, the elders taught that comfort could come in multiple degrees. Cotton's doctrine, they claimed, identified only the high noon of assurance in a long day of revelation. "The Lord reveals not all of himself at once," Shepard preached, "the day dawns before the sun riseth." The appearance of the sun still mattered, but so did all the other lights; the glow of daybreak and the sparkle of stars testified in smaller ways to God's presence and favor. The elders agreed with Cotton "that the Consolation of the Spirit is a further degree of witness than Regeneration is of itself alone," yet they refused to reject the *gradual* witness of regeneration. They concurred with Cotton that "Full and setled Comfort [a saint] cannot take nor rest in, untill it be witnessed to him by the Spirit," but they qualified that statement by calling it "*most* full comfort." While not every believer could "sensibly hear the Witness [of the Spirit] or take notice of it," nonetheless the belief itself—the ability to "call God Father"—could not exist, they maintained, unless the believer "had this witness *in some measure.*" For the elders, rapture was not the only route to comfort; instead, assurance was a matter of accumulation, a process of degrees, a constellation of stars.[53]

Yet a distinction must be made: precisely because the elders preached varying degrees of comfort, they could distinguish it from *security.* Comfort meant taking steps in assurance toward greater sanctification; it supported Christians on their spiritual journey because it both protected against temptations and drew saints to taste more of the sweetness of Christ. Security did the opposite; it stopped spiritual progress by ending desire. Whatever it had of Christ was enough. The elders preached a theology of comfort without complacency, an ever-increasing assurance without an absolute security. In scholarly accounts privileging the psychological ease of the antinomians, the elders' pronouncements against security tend to trump (and sometimes silence) their equally persistent call to comfort.

As they defended multiple degrees of comfort, so the elders promoted the value of multiple affections, even beyond a love of brethren. Contrary to the view of several scholars, for example, it was the elders, not Cotton, who defended the validity of desire.[54] Scripture claimed that those who hungered and thirsted for righteousness would be filled, and the elders used this promise to assert that a heartfelt desire for Christ offered good evidence of salvation. They proclaimed that a "poor believing Soul some-times dare say that which the word saith: But the word saith that the poor hungry etc. are blessed: Ergo." The "hungry" here refers to those who "hunger and thirst after righteousness," as Matthew 5:6 proclaims; the "ergo," for elders, meant such desire counted as a sign of grace, a mark of election that could ease anxious souls.[55]

In his sermon series *The Parable of the Ten Virgins,* Shepard often preached on the promises attached to desire. While he agreed with Cotton that Christ was the door to God's house, he also claimed that a "sense of want" opened the door "for the Lord Jesus in all his fullness to come in." Certainly he did not believe that *any* longing would do. Sanctified desire possessed four distinct elements: it (1) proceeded from broken hearts (2) in a "sonlike spirit" (3) seeking after "grace without measure" while (4) longing for the Lord alone and for "his grace and kingdom [to] prevail in their hearts." But if desire like this existed, then saints could take comfort in it, for the "promises to them that thirst, mourn, believe, etc. are not bare words, but eternal counsels, in which you see God's purpose." Speaking to those who refused to take comfort in these promises, Shepard exclaimed, "Lord, what abundance of sweet peace do you lose!" Apart from religious rapture, he proclaimed—and far different from moral duties or outward behavior—saints could look to their inner longings and still their troubled souls.[56]

And many did. For those who joined Shepard's church, hunger and thirst repeatedly offered comfort. The congregant Elizabeth Olbon, for example, upon remembering "that teaching—blessed are those that hunger and thirst after Christ—she saw she longed after Christ to save and sanctify." George Willows was likewise "carried to long after Christ Jesus and heard those are blessed that did hunger and thirst." Mary Angier, another congregant, found "such a suitableness between Christ and me and Chapter 7—if any thirst let him come to Me and drink." John Stedman, meanwhile, "felt [his] heart longing after grace and want that grace and that was poverty yet, and this supported." The same longing assured the would-be member Mr. Haynes, who found he had a "thirsting frame." As a result, "the Lord did witness I did thirst and so the Lord did draw my heart to Himself and then I had manifest light of my estate." Because desire *counted*—because it signified a conditional promise that would ultimately come true—it could comfort a saint on the journey to Christ.[57]

For Cotton, mere desire, like a love of brethren, failed to offer assurance. It was either false, in which case it would never be fulfilled, or true, in which case it arose from a *previous* sight of Christ. "Men are not brought to mourn after Christ or for him," he insisted, "till after a gracious sight of him wrought by the Spirit of Grace." Relief, Cotton declared, lay not in desire, but in its *fulfillment*. Saints do "not drink consolation out of their thirst, but out of Christ."[58] He scoffed, "As if a suitor should satisfie his desire in conversing with the waiting maid, when he longeth for fellowship with her mistress." The right to the promises of Christ, Cotton maintained, "dependeth on our union with him; as the right of a wife to all her husbands goods dependeth not upon her good conditions or qualifications or duties about him; but upon her marriage union with him." In Cotton's mind, the elders were substituting a stop on the way to grace for grace itself. By offering comfort to longing, they forestalled the satisfaction of desire.[59]

The elders responded by rejecting Cotton's demands precisely because they were too rigorous. If his way prevailed, they feared, then multiple signs and degrees of assurance would be utterly wiped out, leaving weak Christians with nothing more than a gaping void, an anxious-ridden blankness. Under Cotton's system, they complained, "Sanctification will become of little or no account in point of Evidencing (which the Scripture layes so much weight upon) seeing the strong have little or no need of it, if the weak who much need it, can have no use at all." Shepard warned against "making graces in a Christian the weaknesses of a Christian; for this is to make darkness light and grace wantonness indeed." There were already too many "doubting, drooping spirits" rejecting solid evidence of God's good favor. Cotton's way, they wrote, reproved and censured those "who should rather be encouraged and meekly instructed to look for more of God's Spirit, not taking up their rest in what they have."[60] In critiquing Cotton, the elders did not worry that his way stripped Puritans of the ability to *do* something to ease their anxiety; no minister believed that anxious souls could answer doubts with works.[61] On the contrary, the elders feared that Cotton's doctrine of assurance canceled what comfort weak Christians had already cobbled together and replaced it with a religious experience that many could never reach.

And, it would seem, the terrifying loss of former comforts might indeed have afflicted multiple Puritans at this time. Recalling the Antinomian Controversy in his history of New England, the layman Edward Johnson commented, "The weaker sort wavered much." He illustrated that remark by narrating the story of one "poor Soule," who, upon encountering "these Erronists at his first landing," found that "hee could not skill in that new light, which was the common theame of every mans Discourse." In Johnson's narrative, the "poor Soule"—probably Johnson himself—fell into a spiritual crisis, which resolved only when he found Shepard to "cleer Christs worke of grace in the soule from all those false Doctrines, which the erronious party had afrighted him withal." For Johnson, the antinomians preached fear where Shepard offered peace. The same went for John Stedman, one of the congregants seeking membership in Shepard's church. When he arrived in New England and heard Cotton preach, he discovered "how far a man might go under a covenant of works. And so had great fears that was my condition and not sleeping quietly that I had received Christ nor could find no sense of my need of Christ." Cotton, not the elders, increased his anxiety. Like Johnson, Stedman found relief only when he "came by providence to this place [Shepard's church] and heard 2 Cor 5:20 about justification and calling." For some, Shepard eased the anxiety that arose when Cotton denied the evidence of sanctification, the witness of the stars.[62]

Yet for as much as the elders accused Cotton of destroying assurance, he, too, cared about the weak. Cotton simply believed that the elders' way offered no true consolation. To take assurance from sanctification was to proceed in self-delusion, possibly to hell. He warned the weak that "in kindling such sparks of comfort from our selves, and walking in the light thereof this they shall find at Gods hand, they shall lye down in sorrow." Christians bowed by fear and anxiety should reject the smaller lights of sanctification and instead "expect [their] comfort in the object again to be revealed; who being revealed will acknowledge his acceptance of both [them] and [their] works: and such comfort will be sound and durable." That was the assurance Cotton offered—the "sound and durable" comfort of seeing Christ.[63]

In holding out for such powerful fare, Cotton acted as much on psychological intuitions as on theological principles. His position, in one way, just made sense: if good fruits could not save, then how could people look to them for salvation? Only, he answered, if something else, something *above* such fruits, moved through them and made them valid. "You know, and all Christians know," Cotton charged, "that unless the Spirit of God set in and clear up the truth and power and grace of God in all those reasonings [about sanctification], their souls will not be able to gather clear evidences of their estates from all they hear." The Newtown congregant Nathaniel Eaton seemed to know as much. In his conversion narrative he testified, "Hence to neglect duties I durst not, and to do out of love I could not, and hence I begged the Lord would manifest something unto me that I might love Him else all my duties would not be sweet." The duties themselves did not suffice; something more—some spiritual witness—had to seal them as valid signs. A Christian, Cotton asserted, "will never be convinced to see life in his Sanctification till he see life in his justifying faith, which is that that putteth life and truth into his Sanctification: He will ever fear that without faith his best works or Sanctification are but *splendida peccata*, goodly glistering beautifull sins." For the ordinary to shine as extraordinary, it had to be distinguished from the misleading shimmer of daily life—and only the Holy Spirit could accomplish that.[64]

Instead of trying to *comfort* weak Christians, Cotton attempted to make them strong. "The way, I say, is not so much to stand to shew [doubting saints] the working of their own Sanctification within them, as to discover [reveal] the face of God in Christ which is now hid from them." The assurance that resulted from a sight of Christ would be so durable that it could persist even through the failure of sanctification. Cotton asserted that "though a Christian assured of his good estate in Christ upon safe grounds, should fall into gross sin, yet his sin is no just ground why he should weaken the assurance of his justified estate." This was not, as the elders feared, an invitation to loose living. It was a recognition that true Christians, truly justified, would live well without looking to such living for assurance. There was a "peace of justification" and a "peace of sanctification," and they were not the same—nor could the latter produce the former. They existed on wholly separate planes (the extraordinary and the ordinary), offering wholly different comfort (sound and durable versus fleeting and doubtful). What Cotton wished to instill in his congregants was not a piecemeal comfort hammered together, but a "setled comfort" assured by "the Spirit of Christ ... witness[ing] to the Soul Gods thoughts of peace." Once *that* comfort was secured, nothing could undo it.[65]

In the Antinomian Controversy, therefore, one can witness different views of experience resulting in divergent notions of comfort. Both the elders and the antinomians tried to reduce anxiety and boost assurance, but their different ideas about how best to do so nearly split the colony in two. The elders offered multiple paths and varying degrees of comfort, validating not just good deeds, but also the relatively ordinary affections of loving brethren, longing for Christ, desiring Christian fellowship and mourning for one's sins. Even if these experiences were not distinguished by some extraordinary event, they could still signal God's favor. In that sense, spiritual assurance resembled a hurdles race. The bars were not high, but they stretched on indefinitely, ending only at the point of death. As long as the race lasted, however, a Christian could look back over all the bars already leapt and accumulate comfort in an ever-increasing sanctification, knowing more certainly day-by-day that he or she would win the crown. For the elders, the ordinary counted—and comforted.

For Cotton, on the other hand, assurance was more like the pole vault. He set the bar high, but he reduced the number of leaps. The seemingly impossible height of the bar—the religious experience that Cotton demanded—daunted many, terrorized some, and led others to despair. Yet for those who could be lifted as high as Cotton required, the assurance gained would be far greater. There was just one bar, and, with Christ's support—with Christ bending and lifting and vaulting one over—all those who passed the bar could rest secure that the crown was theirs. Cotton believed that by placing consolation in smaller, daily hurdles, the elders increased doubt and eliminated the possibility of full assurance. As Christians searched for signs of sanctification, they turned their backs on the witness of the Spirit; they competed, as it were, in the wrong event. If instead they would reject all else and focus solely on a "naked Christ," Christ *might* respond by raising them into a rapture that would eliminate all fear. Cotton thus nullified ordinary comfort to make room for extraordinary relief.

When the elders took control and moved against the antinomians, they did not reject every facet of this position. Contrary to what some scholars have argued, religious rapture remained a valid part of New England Puritanism.[66] Throughout his life, it is true, Shepard remained wary of spiritual seizures. He claimed that "strange ecstasies of joy" offered "false comforts," and when he spoke of the "satisfying sweetness in God," he contrasted it with the "God-glutted Christian." At the same time, he preached that only "the Spirit of adoption" could finally remove all fears. Refusing to "exclude the work of sanctified reason from the witness of the Spirit," he nonetheless asserted "that all the men in the world, nor all the wisdom and reason of man, can never chase away all fears, scatter all mists, till the Spirit itself saith, Peace, and be still, and puts its hand and seal to the evidence; till the Spirit, not by an audible, but powerful voice, shows and persuades." In defending sanctification, Shepard still preached the power of the Spirit. The confessions of his church testify to that continued power both during and after the Antinomian Controversy. Elizabeth Olbon, to give just one example, "saw she must come to a naked Christ," and eventually "He let her feel His love."[67]

Such a view contrasts the usual way that Shepard gets positioned as a villain in this controversy. According to Michael Winship, for example, "Shepard's frequently reiterated bottom line was that Boston's methods of assurance, inaccessible to him, were the refuge of false Christians."[68] For this reason, scholars have claimed that Shepard used conversion narratives in his church primarily to guard against alternative methods of assurance.[69] Yet in Shepard's confessions, religious experiences continued unabated; Henry Dunster's narrative, for example, which came after the Antinomian Controversy had ended, clearly served an evangelical function while also calling for the seal of the Spirit.[70] Shepard does warn churches to "be very careful in receiving in of members." Yet such a warning must be balanced with his insistence that saints should not ignore their signs of grace, but embrace them. "Own the Lord Jesus," he preached; "he is yours, but you own him not." Moreover, in a section where Shepard presents various ways of waking up one's neighbors and turning them from their sins, he suggests that conversion relations would be particularly useful: "relate thy own condition," he instructs; "this is a most lovely provocation and exhortation unto another frame; for one great cause that hardeneth men in their security is because they see no such living Christianity in the world." Finally, if such confessions were used solely or primarily for surveillance, it seems odd that not one single confessor in Shepard's church was ever denied membership. It could be that barriers were established well before persons reached the stage of delivering a conversion narrative, but if so, the narrative itself still seems to have served a different purpose than mere surveillance and regulation. This is not to deny that confessions had some regulatory element; but in writing a narrative in which Shepard opposes religious ecstasy, polices it, and eventually replaces it with discipline and obedience, a great deal of counterevidence needs explaining. Cotton was not the only pastor in New England who believed these confessions might serve an evangelical function, nor was he the only one to accept and appreciate semimystical experiences. In fact, as Michael McGiffert demonstrates, "Shepard consistently sets mystical passion above and against the claims of discursive reason." Shepard certainly has his faults, but quashing mysticism in New England for the next one hundred years does not seem one of them.[71]

The difference between Cotton and Shepard, however, was that Shepard did not *require* rapture as evidence of grace. Observing the lay confessions of Shepard's church, Charles Cohen observes, "For some, a discernible event marked their crossing over the great divide between nature and grace. ... For others, the moment passed indistinctly amidst the struggles of life's routines, its occurrence registered either by later signs of regeneration or by a mere suspicion of grace."[72] That, of course, was the point—precisely what the elders fought for and won in the Antinomian Controversy. Grace could be small as well as large: there was more than one way to assurance and more than one degree of comfort. As a result, the emotional bonds of the godly community could never be divorced from the private search for grace: one's feelings—at all times and in all places and toward all people—testified to one's standing with God.

Compromise in the Form of Conversion

One result of the Antinomian Controversy is the remarkable spiritual autobiography that John Winthrop wrote in the midst of crisis. This text has usually been read as a guide to Winthrop's personal reaction, but with a fuller understanding of the dispute the autobiography emerges as more than just a testimonial: it is an attempted intervention. Nor was this the first time Winthrop tried to intervene. As the controversy boiled, he tried to cool the separate sides with a theological treatise. Before publishing it, however, he sent the document to Shepard, who read it, critiqued it, and persuaded him to destroy it. The document, Shepard commented, bore "a colour of Arminianism, which I beleeve your soule abhors." Momentarily thwarted, Winthrop turned to a different genre: spiritual autobiography. He confessed that "the Doctrine of free justification lately taught here took me in as drowsy a condition, as I had been in (to my remembrance) these twenty yeares." In the revival of his peace, Winthrop composed a personal narrative that offered a compromise between the two embattled camps. His tale moves from one side of the dispute to the other—from the elders to the antinomians and back again toward the center—relating the good and the bad of each. Denied a treatise, Winthrop wrote a tale.[73]

According to "Christian Experience," his conversion narrative, John Winthrop first took comfort as a weak Christian in his love of brethren. At the age of eighteen he "found the ministry of the word to come home to [his] heart with power" and, after a few struggles, "bid farewell to all the world." This initial conversion, however, only began Winthrop's spiritual journey. And it was at that point—as a weak Christian in the first throes of faith—that he looked to others. "I loved a Christian, and the very ground hee went upon," Winthrop writes. "I honoured a faythfull minister in my heart and could have kissed his feet." Such evidence yielded the young Winthrop "some" peace and comfort. He does not assert full assurance, but he also does not dismiss these early signs of grace. In this way, he begins in the camp of the elders: a love of brethren offers valid comfort to the weak.[74]

At the same time, Winthrop critiques the value of that assurance. His initial burst of religious zeal led to many good works, "an unsatiable thirst after the word of God," and an evangelical proselytizing of others. And yet, Winthrop admits, "those affections were not constant, but very unsetled." Studying divinity, he began to question himself more narrowly, discovering "secrett Corruptions, and some tremblings of heart (which was greatest when I was among the most Godly persons)."[75] Here Winthrop seems to comment on both the strength and the weakness of brotherly love. On the one hand, comfort remained unsteady; he needed more. On the other hand, the company of Christians constantly revealed his spiritual state and helped him move toward greater assurance.

Even as he waited for greater assurance, however, Winthrop continued to take comfort in his love of brethren. His troubles "came not all at once but by fits, for sometimes I should find refreshing in prayer, and sometimes in the Love that I had had to the saints: which though it were but poor comfort (for I durst not say before the Lord that I did love them in truth) yet the Lord upheld mee, and many times outward occasions put these feares out of my thoughts." In other words, even as Winthrop attempted to find an assurance that could not be doubted, he looked to his smaller signs of grace: he took comfort in the stars while he waited for the sun to rise. In describing this tempered assurance, he offers a mild rebuke to the antinomians. They can insist, as he himself did, on discovering a "better assurance by the seale of the spirit"; but in the meanwhile, they must leave weak Christians their lesser consolations.[76] The love of saints is a limited comfort, Winthrop admits, but it is comfort all the same.

For a long period, the young Winthrop continued in a worsening state of worry. The more he tried to be holy, the less holy he became. The more he opened himself to closing with Christ, the more Christ seemed to withdraw. He turned to works, and the anxiety out of which he performed them only deprived him of "lawful comforts." He turned to the Covenant of Grace, but he could not say "with any confidence, it had been sealed to mee."[77] Back and forth Winthrop went, from law to grace, but his state grew only worse; his anxiety increased. Then, at the age of thirty, Winthrop experienced a kind of rapturous union with Christ. In great affliction, he became lowered in his own esteem, and this lowering suddenly raised him:

> I knew I was worthy of nothing for I knew I could doe nothing for him or for my selfe. I could onely mourn, and weep to think of free mercy to such a vile wretch as I was. Though I had no power to apply it yet I felt comfort in it. I did not long continue in this estate, but the good spirit of the Lord breathed upon my soule, and said I should live. Then every promise I thought upon held forth Christ unto mee saying I am thy salvation. Now could my soule close with Christ, and rest there with sweet contentment, so ravished with his Love, as I desired nothing nor feared any thing, but was filled with joy unspeakable and glorious and with a spirit of Adoption.[78]

In such an account Winthrop gives the antinomians exactly what they required: a moment of unspeakable joy that vaulted Winthrop into sound assurance.

In the very next line, however, Winthrop qualifies what that change entailed. He writes, "Not that I could pray with more fervency or more enlargement of heart than sometimes before, but I could now cry my father with more confidence."[79] In other words, the difference was not ontological: his religious experience did not signify *the* moment of justification. Rather, it was epistemological: he could pray with *more* confidence. Throughout his narrative, then, Winthrop operates on a system of degrees where assurance can increase or decrease and where the moment of justification can remain hidden in the past. He is not an antinomian; instead, he is attempting to compromise with antinomians.

In that compromise, Winthrop maintains that the comfort offered by a religious experience really *does* satisfy more than the cobbled-together, paltry evidence of relatively ordinary emotions. His spiritual high "lasted a good time (divers months)," Winthrop comments, and while it was not always the same, nonetheless "if my comfort, and joy slackened awhile, yet my peace continued, and it would returne with advantage. I was now growne familiar with the Lord Jesus Christ[.] Hee would oft tell mee he loved mee."[80] In the shape of this relation, Winthrop acknowledges that his opponents have a valid point: religious experiences are marvelous.

At the same time, Winthrop warns about their dangers. First, they do not last. His own gave way "by degrees." More importantly, it produced negative side effects. Winthrop writes, "Though I found much spirituall strength in it yet I could not discerne but my hunger after the word of God, and my love to the saints had been as great (if not more) in former times." Searching for how this might have happened, he continues, "One reason might bee this, I found that the many blemishes and much hollow-heartednesse which I discerned in many professors, had weakned the esteem of a Christian in my heart."[81] In other words, *the danger of spiritual ecstasy lay precisely in its effect on communal relations.* Antinomians separated the strong from the weak and offered only one way—their way—to comfort. That, Winthrop argues, was their greatest fault. For all the good they offered, the antinomians finally preached a theology that resulted in a lack of love for the saints. And Winthrop could not allow that. For him, a love of brethren remained the most significant test of salvation and the cornerstone of a godly society. He would compromise with the antinomians; he would allow the marvel of rapture; but he would never relinquish the value of sympathy.

Winthrop's days of attempted compromise did not last long. Defending the significance of sympathy, Winthrop became less and less tolerant of his antagonists. The more a love of brethren mattered as a sign of grace, the less it could make room for antinomian dissent. And so, as the community continued to split into separate factions, Winthrop's search for common ground turned into a clearing of the territory. The General Court, Winthrop records, found "upon consultation, that two so opposite parties could not contain in the same body, without apparent hazard of ruin to the whole."[82] In order to maintain the importance of mutual love while banishing several members, therefore, the elders had to conclude that those removed were not of the elect. They had to condemn the antinomians so that a love of *them* would set one at odds with the love of saints: certainty of their exclusion from grace would entail withholding any sense of sympathy from extending in their direction. After all, one had to be both a friend of the godly and an enemy of the enemies of God. In the excommunication of Anne Hutchinson, therefore, the Boston church finally declared that a love of the brethren did not include this sister. They tightened the boundary of their emotional community until she stood physically, spiritually, and emotionally without.

When modern readers encounter the Antinomian Controversy, it is not surprising that their own sympathies often align with Anne Hutchinson and the antinomians. When they learn that John Winthrop exhumed the miscarried stillborn of an antinomian supporter named Mary Dyer and examined its deformities in order to prove God's judgment against her—or when they learn that for similar reasons, he also sought details of Anne Hutchinson's "monstrous birth" (her miscarriage)—modern readers often and easily find themselves repulsed with Winthrop and all the rest of the elders as well. Moreover, when most readers today encounter trial narratives where several powerful male magistrates line up against a lone, intelligent woman—as we shall witness in the next chapter—it becomes easy to celebrate Hutchinson and denounce the oppression of her persecutors. There is plenty to support such readings. Yet what these interpretations often miss is a careful examination of the antinomians' theology, along with a critical scrutiny of Anne Hutchinson's own harsh judgments against others, and—most importantly—an understanding of the consequences of antinomian tenets for weak and ordinary Christians. Surprisingly, it was the antinomians who lessened the value of sympathy (and all other relatively ordinary experiences), while the elders attempted throughout the controversy to maintain the salvific importance of fellow feeling. Precisely because it was so important to them, in fact, they could not tolerate a group of people who rejected sympathy as a sign of grace.

3

Sympathy, Persuasion, and Seduction

THE IDEA OF brotherly love, so much debated during the Antinomian Controversy, not only shaped questions of assurance; it also determined the way Puritans later wrote about and explained New England's crisis. Puritans based persuasion in the idea of brotherly love, and such a principle affected how they viewed unity and diversity. As long as mutual affections persisted, Puritans believed, differences could be worked out and consensus could be achieved; once sympathies divided, debate ceased. No amount of good logic or solid reasoning could ever win over the disaffected. When the elders set about explaining the Antinomian Controversy, therefore, they focused as much attention on the mere appearance of distinct factions as on the actual differences that defined them. The antinomians, they argued, created a clan of like-minded believers—bound by their own claims of brotherly love—and opposed it to the larger Puritan community. Once this faction formed, nothing short of political intervention could resolve the crisis, they claimed. Thus, a theology of fellow feeling—a love of brethren bound up with Puritan sympathy and tied primarily to salvation—explains the politics of faction through the principle of persuasion. According to Winthrop and his allies, the disaffected had to be exiled in order to maintain the mutual affections of the rest.

Yet the presence of distinct factions also required a good story to explain how and why separate parties even existed in New England. Having already represented their society as a unified and sanctified single body, the elders now needed to elucidate for transatlantic critics how so many good people had suddenly gone bad, all the while defending the New England Way. To accomplish this difficult task, the elders turned to a language of seduction.

Boston's godly had embraced not here*sies*, but here*tics*; they fell because they loved certain people (like Anne Hutchinson) too much, not because they understood certain doctrines (like sanctification) too little. Such an account of the controversy demonstrates the place of affection in Puritan debates while simultaneously highlighting the power of seduction in New England literature. In short, the Puritan understanding of persuasion, which depended on a theology of sympathy, turned the Antinomian Controversy into one of America's earliest stories of seduction.

Persuasion and Affection

Whether the antinomians stood within or without a wider union of affections related to a central idea held by many Puritans: dialogue, criticism, and persuasion could prosper only if they came framed by mutual love. Before leaving England, for example, John Winthrop declared to the Massachusetts Bay Company, "We must distinguish of divisions of affections and interest, the first destroys, the other preserves, as in the spoyle of Ab[raham] and Lot." Trying to determine how best to divide the joint-stock money and proceed with emigration, Winthrop maintained that success would require a unity of affections. As if rehearsing *A Model of Christian Charity*, he proclaimed, "My speeche leads cheifly to this end, that being assured of eache others sincerity in our intentions in this worke, and duely considering in what new relations we stand, we might be knit togither in a most firm bond of love and frindshippe." Differences of interest might persist, but divisions in affection would destroy.[1]

More importantly, so long as affections remained united, differences could theoretically be worked out. Such an understanding appears throughout New England literature. During the English Civil Wars, for example, the ministers Richard Mather and William Tompson wrote to their former congregation in England, "God knows, and many amongst you, we doubt not, do remember how we could not leave your Congregations, nor depart out of your coasts, without much inward affection of heart and many tears, because you were dear unto us." A tearful departure scene marks a unity of affection that knows no physical bounds. Mather and Tompson actually promise to pour forth fountains of tears for the country left behind:

> For indeed we desire to bewail the sorrows, distractions and distresses of that dear countrey where we were born, and wish we had hearts to do it more compassionately and effectually then these dull

and dry spirits of ours can yet attain unto; though we hope it is not our distance for the space of three thousand miles from that land, nor our absence from thence for the space of nine or ten years, nor all the water that in all this time hath flown in this great Atlantick Ocean between *England* and us, that hath or ever shall wash away the thought and remembrance of *England*, and of Gods people therein out of our hearts, but that we shall preferre the comfort, peace, and prosperity of it and them, before our chief joys.[2]

With such displays of emotion, Mather and Tompson show that not even the mighty Atlantic can separate the godly. *From* this avowal, Mather and Thompson then turn to persuasion: on the basis of unbroken bonds, they give advice. *"And being thus minded,"* they write, "we hope you will give us leave out of that hearty affection and good will which we bear unto our Nation, and more abundantly to you-ward, to commend unto you our dear countreymen a few words of Christian counsell and advice."[3] Their union of affection enables the possibility of persuasion. In the same way, John Norton's *Answer to ... Mr. Appollonius* begins with an address to the heart. The treatise itself comprises a host of logical arguments, carefully crafted and precise in their intellectual rigor. But the claims, counterclaims, and evidence all come framed by an opening address to the affections. In a prefatory letter to his interlocutor, Norton writes, "Since we detect ... a love of brethren, in your compassion and ... a love of truth, in your concern, admiring ... the piety, in both, we believe it will be profitable to pick up the correspondence with you in scholarly wise."[4] Here, as so often in Puritan documents, love makes way for logic.

Such love, moreover, was often based in fellow feeling. When Winthrop sent letters asking Thomas Hooker's Hartford congregation to support and aid the elders of Massachusetts Bay, the Hartford elders responded, "We have putt our selves into your place and stead in our owne apprehensions, as being the only way to work a fellow-feeling with Bretheren in the same fayth." Upon the basis of that sympathy, they were "willing therfore not only to do what you desired, but may be more then you did expect, having resolved and purposed to send both our elders in the next fitt season, to be serviceable to you to the utmost of ther ability, in the wayty occasions which now be offered to consideration."[5] In other words, not only did fellow feeling with brethren offer individual Puritans some assurance of salvation; it also operated as a basic principle of persuasion, motivation, and movement. As they engaged in fellow feeling and acknowledged mutual affections, so the Hartford elders determined to offer aid. In this way, the intimate matters of eternal destiny (the salvific value of sympathy) came tied to political realities on the ground (the offering of aid): both depended on fellowship, on a love of brethren, on the fellow feeling of saints.

In the Antinomian Controversy, this principle of persuasion—love before logic—explains a good deal of its rhetorical framing. A simple but seemingly overlooked question arises from the sources: given the depths of anger and exasperation, and given the level of punishments and persecutions, why did so many people on both sides of the debate keep insisting that they loved one another? Almost every letter sent during the controversy repeats this basic paradigm. Before Shepard broached his theological critiques of Cotton, for example, he claimed to speak for many "whose harts are much endeared to you," and he addressed his letter "*To the reverend his deare friend Mr Cotton.*" Cotton responded by opening with lines of gratitude: "I thank you unfeignedly for this labor of your love," he wrote, and closed, "Remember my Deare affection to your selfe, Brother Hookcr and others with you whom I deeply honor in the Lord," finally signing it "Your affectionate though weake Brother, JC." Such affirmations of brotherly love and affection recur throughout the controversy, though they are often set aside by scholars as either insincere or inessential. Yet however strained or sarcastic they became, however false they might seem, these statements of mutual affection remained indispensable: critiques, doubts, dialogues, and disputes had to proceed from brotherly love. When, for example, Cotton responded on behalf of several New Englanders to criticisms leveled by the English Puritan John Dodd, he first wrote, "As they do thankfully accept your brotherly love, so they our brethren here have taken your motion into serious consideration." Brotherly love enabled debate. A union of minds could arise only on the prior foundation of united hearts.[6]

The significance attached to mutual affections reveals the danger of factions. Factions, by definition, set one side against another, one party against its opponents. And separate parties, in turn, meant divvying up what had once been a united community of affection: by turning an internal disagreement into an external dispute, factions threatened the very possibility of serious consideration. In the Antinomian Controversy, therefore, the elders focused on the formation of factions. Many scholars attach this concern to matters of power and authority—both of which were certainly at stake. But something else was also at play: the obsession with factions comes from underlying Puritan conceptions about diversity and unity based in principles of persuasion. A faction represented division based in disaffection.

Such issues can be seen emerging already in Winthrop's opposition to John Wheelwright. Wheelwright, a brother-in-law of Anne Hutchinson, had been a vicar in England before converting to nonconformist views in the early 1630s. Soon suspended, he emigrated to Boston in 1636, just as Hutchinson began stirring up debate. His connection to Hutchinson and his theological views set him squarely in her camp. Concerned ministers confronted the two of them, but the meeting only increased dissension. The trouble arose when some members of the Boston church, "being of the opinion of Mrs. Hutchinson ... laboured to have Mr. Wheelwright to be called to be a teacher there."[7] They tried to replace John Wilson with John Wheelwright, and Winthrop would not allow that. Publicly opposing the move, he prevented the ordination, forcing Wheelwright to find another church.

Beyond a basic power struggle, this confrontation reveals important interlinked dynamics of affection, persuasion, unity, and diversity. When Winthrop publicly opposed Wheelwright in the Boston Church, the Boston congregants "took offense" at his behavior for three reasons: first, "he had charged the brother in public"; second, "in his speech appeared some bitterness"; and third, "he had charged [Wheelwright] to have held things which he did not." These accusations implied a criticism not just of Winthrop's theological position, but also of his *dis*position—his manner of speech. The congregation accused Winthrop of lacking brotherly love. In his defense, therefore, Winthrop argued "that he [Winthrop] did love that brother's person [Wheelwright], and did honor the gifts and graces of God in him." He acknowledged that he should have approached Wheelwright privately, but he also claimed to have done so already, requesting Wheelwright "seriously and affectionately" to lay aside certain theological terms "for the peace of the church."[8] In other words, Winthrop defended himself by narrating the deep love that drove him to his critiques. According to his own story, Winthrop's love enabled him to entertain a wider diversity of opinions within a basic unity of affections. It was Wheelwright, he charged, who refused to get along.

When similar disputes resurfaced with Governor Henry Vane, a supporter of the antinomians, Winthrop again portrayed the situation as revolving around a union of affections. "For the peace sake of the church, which all were tender of," the differing sides did not turn their dispute into a public spectacle, but instead hashed out their disagreements in writing.[9] Under a guiding concern for wider unity, differences could be worked out without undo disturbance. And indeed (if Winthrop can be believed), this particular confrontation did work itself out: "all agreeing in the chief matter of substance," he recorded, "it was earnestly desired, that the word *person* might be forborn, being a term of human invention, and tending to doubtful disputation in this case."[10] All could agree, in other words, that a terminological dispute was not worth a disturbance of the peace. Yet despite the momentary concord, factions deepened. Shortly after this truce, Winthrop recorded a court session in which Governor Henry Vane broke down weeping. Vane, in short, wanted out. Sensing God's coming wrath for "differences and dissensions," he sought to extricate himself from both the crisis and the colony before doom descended on New England.[11] Later, Vane would apologize for proclaiming such a dire prophecy, but the divisions he pointed out could hardly be ignored.

Those dissensions surface repeatedly in Winthrop's recording of the controversy. At the next court session, elders met with magistrates "to advise them about discovering and pacifying the differences among the churches in point of opinion." Not long afterward, "Mr. Wilson made a sad speech of the condition of our churches, and the inevitable danger of separation, if these differences and alienations among brethren were not speedily remedied." Again, what was at stake was not just a difference of opinion, but an alienation of affections. At one point in the crisis, for example, Winthrop claimed that theological consensus had almost been achieved, but the colonists would not reconcile because their affections were "formerly alienated." Likewise, when followers of Cotton nearly censured Wilson for rebuking antinomian opinions, Winthrop wrote, "It was strange to see, how the common people were led, by example, to condemn him in that, which (it was very probable) diverse of them did not understand." Later Winthrop would again claim that "no man could tell (except some few, who knew the bottom of the matter) where any difference was." According to Winthrop, the people divided and fought not just for specific theological positions—indeed, they hardly understood the issues—but also for competing loyalties. Congregants turned against Wilson because Wilson had turned against Cotton: one's enemies were the enemies of one's friends. What was true in matters of salvation was thus mirrored in political concerns.[12]

Brotherly Love and a Family Feud

Each of these issues came to a head when Wheelwright preached at the colony's general fast. His sermon—the turning point of the controversy—reveals not just the theological crisis at the heart of the matter, but also how that theology affected the rhetorical frame of the dispute and produced such enormous political consequences, including fines, disarmaments, and banishment. Some have argued that the elders, not the antinomians, were far more interested in making sides; they imagined and created a faction that never really existed. Michael Winship, for example, has claimed that Wheelwight's sermon made little impression at first and only came to signify sedition through the elders' skillful maneuvering. Wanting to identify and punish an adverse party, the elders finally made one up. There may be some truth to that position, but it seems to discount the actual words of Wheelwright's sermon and the fact of its delivery on a Fast Day aimed at reconciliation. The sermon reveals a distinct and persecuted band of saints bound together by their own brotherly love and set against the authorities in place. Wheelwright, in short, divided sympathies. In the most public setting possible in Puritan New England—the Fast Day pulpit—he created two separate emotional communities.[13]

The motif Wheelwright chose for his Fast Day sermon would not initially have struck Puritans as controversial. Citing Matthew 9:15, he asked, "Can the Children of the bridechamber mourne, as long as the Bridegroome is with them?" That rhetorical question led to this doctrine: "the only cause of the fasting of true beleevers is the absence of Christ." And if Christ was absent, as this Fast Day seemed to entail, then it made sense for those gathered to seek his presence. "So the children of God are a company," Wheelwright explained, "a generation that seeke the Lord and his strength and face evermore ... they do not only seeke the gifts of his spiritt, but the Lord himselfe."[14] That basic point would be repeated in multiple Puritan jeremiads throughout the seventeenth century. Nothing about it seemed problematic.

Yet Wheelwright used this doctrine to prod the debates and divisions of the Antinomian Controversy. He declared, "It standeth us all in hand, to have a care Christ be not taken from us, if we belong to the election of grace, Christ cannot be taken wholly away from us, yet he may be taken away in some degree, therefore let us have a care to keepe the Lord Jesus Christ." The "all" of "us all" would seem to include everyone, but the qualifier—"if we belong to the election of grace"—began to divide one kind from another. Moreover, Wheelwright claimed that where some had Christ and must not lose him, others fasted because of his absence. In this way, he turned the general fast into a particular separation, a sorting of sheep from goats. Such division received further delineation when Wheelwright proclaimed, "If we do not strive [in spiritual battle], those under a covenant of works will prevail." The godly "we," in other words, stood opposed to *"those* under a covenant of works"—precisely what Hutchinson charged various ministers with preaching. But Wheelwright went further. He described "those" whom the godly oppose as Antichrists. "For what is Antichrist," Wheelwright asked, "but one being against Christ, and for Christ, his being for Christ, is being against Christ, because he would put one in the roome of Christ." Covertly, that is, some Antichrists only *seem* to be for Christ when in reality they set something *else*—like sanctification—"in the room of Christ."[15] All "Antichristian spiritts," Wheelwright insisted, "take away the Christ ... and put in false Christs," attempting "to deceave the elect, if it were possible." With such lines, Wheelwright essentially called the elders—the opponents of the antinomians—Antichrists. The godly "us" held fast to the gospel, the Covenant of Grace, which according to Wheelwright "doth hold forth Jesus Christ and nothing but Christ."[16] The ungodly "them," meanwhile, replaced the gospel with a covenant of works dressed up as sanctification. During an event aimed at reconciliation, Wheelwright declared one way right and the other way wrong.

Beyond splitting his listeners in two, Wheelwright cast himself and his fellow saints as a persecuted minority. Christ is always opposed, he declared. When Christ was born, Herod tried to kill him; when he began his ministry, legions turned against him; in his death and burial, Christ showed that the world will always hate him. By drawing this lesson, Wheelwright implied that Christ had appeared in New England and that New England now sought to "bury" him. Moreover, he stated that only a small set of Christians truly stood with Christ. "I must confesse and acknowledge the saynts of God are few," Wheelwright proclaimed, "they are but a little flocke, and those that are the enimyes to the Lord, not onely Pagonish, but Antichristian, and those that run under a covenant of works are very strong." The saved would always form an embattled minority—including in New England.[17] This assigned status of the saved showed a continuation of Puritan logic from Old England to New. In England, Puritans identified each other by their committed endurance despite oppression and persecution. From the beginning, as Theodore Dwight Bozeman observes, the anger of others "drove the saints closer together and helped them better to know and esteem themselves." As a result, they began to "interpret opposition as a mark of sainthood."[18] In New England, according to Wheelwright, the game had never changed. Where Wheelwright had been suspended by authorities in England, now Winthrop resisted his ordination in Boston. In both cases, Wheelwright responded by proclaiming that persecution proved him right.

Such a division between ungodly persecutors (in the majority and typically in positions of power) and godly saints (in the minority and typically without power) lent itself to the metaphor of battle. For the most part, Wheelwright described the fight as spiritual. The children of God, he declared, must "fight with spirituall weapons, for the weapons of our warfare are not carnall but spirituall." Yet he also noted that true saints "must be willing to suffer any thing" and described just what he had in mind: "suppose those that are Gods children should loose their houses and lands and wives and freinds, and loose the acting of the guifts of grace, and loose the ordinances, yet they can never loose the Lord Jesus Christ." He even suggested that the "saynts of God" might end up "banished and deprived of all ordinances of God," though of course they could never lose Christ. In such statements, the gap between spiritual warfare and earthly consequences all but disappears. Whether he imagined a war of souls or one of flesh, Wheelwright made no bones about the coming strife. He proclaimed to fellow saints, "Therefore if we will keepe the Lord Jesus Christ and his presence and power amongst us, we must fight." To those who objected that such a call would "cause a combustion in the Church and comon wealth," Wheelwright responded, "I must confesse and acknowledge it will do so, but what then? did not Christ come to send fire upon the earth, Luke 12.49." Far from reconciling the disaffected, Wheelwright roused them for a fight.[19]

Most significantly, Wheelwright bound his followers together by using the language of love that Puritans frequently used, including in John Winthrop's *A Model of Christian Charity*. "Let us have a care all of us, that we love one another," Wheelwright insisted. "The Lord Christ delighteth in a loving people, when the saynts of God love one another, and are willing to lay downe their lives one for another, the Lord delighteth in them." Searching for biblical examples, Wheelwright first turned to Christ—just as Winthrop had—then Moses. He observed, "Moses seeing an Egiptian striving with his brother, he came and killed him. *Acts 7.24.25.26.* So Christ putetth into his people a loving spirit." Moses's love of brethren, in other words, could be seen in his murder of an Egyptian oppressor. So the love of saints bound "brothers" together in a deadly struggle against any who threatened from without. This context colors Wheelwright's exhortation: "Let us have a care, [that] we do not alienate our harts one from another, because of divers kind of expressions, but let us keepe the unity of the spiritt in the bond of peace, let us have a care to love one another, and then the Lord Jesus Christ will be still more and more present." As

Winthrop had done, so Wheelwright quoted Ephesians 4:3—a central passage for Reformed understandings of community—and proposed almost the same principle of cohesion as found in *A Model of Christian Charity*: a family of saints united by "brotherly love." But Wheelwright's family was carved from Winthrop's and turned against it.[20]

Finally, Wheelwright identified the separate families by their differing emotions. One kind of Puritan mourned for Christ's absence, while another kind—true saints—rejoiced in his presence. "So farr as Christ is present," Wheelwright insisted, "he taketh away all cause of mourning and weeping, and in his presence is fulnes of joy." Speaking to those under a covenant of grace, he declared, "Let us all have a care so to carry our selves that we may have the presence of the Lord, that he may not depart from us; for if the Lord depart we shall have cause of mourning indeede." Those for whom the Lord had not yet departed did not weep; rather, they fought to keep their joy. For this reason, the final line of Wheelwright's sermon directly contradicted the emotional contours of the entire Fast Day, calling not for repentance but rejoicing: "Therefore let the saynts of God rejoyce, that they have the Lord Jesus Christ, and their names written in the booke of life, be glad and rejoyce, for great is your reward in heaven."[21] Not only did the two families stand opposed; they differed specifically in the affections they felt for each other and the emotions displayed on that day.

The division of New England Puritans into separate emotional communities further clarifies the bonds of affection proposed in *A Model of Christian Charity* and in a host of Puritan sermons and commentaries. As multiple Puritans reiterated, society requires sympathy. But the sympathy one displays also reveals the company one keeps and the community to which one belongs. Winthrop, Shepard, and other elders had claimed that sympathizing with fellow saints (whether in joy or sorrow) offered good evidence of election; it testified to one's membership in the Body of Christ. In his Fast Day sermon Wheelwright opposed such evidence of sanctification, but still deployed a love of brethren to distinguish two opposing camps: those who mourned and those who rejoiced. And just in case anyone missed which family was saved, Wheelwright reminded his audience that on *this* day of fasting, the actual children of God rejoiced.

Far from healing the breach, then, Wheelwright's sermon blew it open. He mobilized the opposition by publicly identifying it, labeling it, and uniting it in a mutuality of affections that excluded most others. After Wheelwright spoke the colony had for the first time a clear and public binary, an "us" and a "them" set against each other in a spiritual battle that might very well entail the loss of one's house or family and banishment from the colony. According to Thomas Weld, one of the elders, Wheelwright "divided the whole Country into two ranks, some (that were of his Opinion) under a Covenant of *Grace*, and those were friends to Christ; others under a Covenant of Workes whom they might know by this, if they evidence their good estate by their Sanctification: those were (said he) enemies to Christ ... yea, Antichrists."[22] Although language about different covenants had existed long before Wheelwright spoke, no one had yet stood up with the authority of an ordained minister, labeled which Puritans belonged to which covenant, placed them in opposing emotional communities, and pitted them against each other in war.

That action, on Wheelwright's part, moved elders to a charge of sedition. Wheelwright, the elders claimed, had divided the foundational union of affections necessary to any good society and community—even to any decent disagreement and possible future concord. They wrote, "[A] brother may fall so farre into disobedience to the Gospel, as there may bee cause to separate from him, and to put him to shame, and yet hee is not to bee accounted an enemy."[23] Such a statement reveals how hard they tried to maintain the idea of a broader unity beneath the quarrel. The family was large; it contained multitudes. Disagreements did not mean divisions; they meant intrafamily disputes that the family, *as a family*, could resolve. But Wheelwright refused that formulation. On a Fast Day, he stood before the public and violently disowned the errant.

Nor did elders overlook *how* Wheelwright divided Puritans. They asked, "Did he not make himselfe a party on the other side, by often using these and the like words, We, us?" The personal pronouns separated every saved "we" from a potentially damned "them" which included the elders. That irked them, to put it mildly. But the real problem came down to Wheelwright's use of mutual affections. The elders noted that Wheelwright "raised and pressed an use of brotherly love," but only "appl[ied] it to those of his own party, to perswade them to hold together, and help one another against those of the other party."[24] Brotherly love extended neither as far nor as broadly as the elders desired. Moreover, such bonds entailed violence against outsiders, as Wheelwright's example of Moses made clear, and the elders stood on the outside in Wheelwright's formulation. For all these reasons, the elders concluded, Wheelwright had committed sedition.

Sedition, moreover, directly resulted from the formation of factions. Quoting Tully, Winthrop explained, "Sedition is the disagreement of the people among themselves when each goes his own way"; it "doth properly signifie a going aside to make a party." Defending their charge of sedition, the elders asked, "Now in our present case, did not Mr. Wheel. *make sides* when he proclaimed all to be under a Covenant of works, who did not follow him (step by step) in his description of the Covenant of Grace?" That is what upset them so much: Wheelwright made sides. Attributing all of New England's troubles to this antinomian preacher, they wrote, "Before Mr. *Wheel.* came into this country (which is not yet two yeares since) there was no strife (at least in publick observation) about [sanctification]." Strife existed, they admitted, just not in "publick observation." Yet that was precisely the point: Wheelwright *made the division public.* It was one thing for a laywoman to go around accusing ministers of walking in a covenant of works; it was quite another for a minister of God to do so on a Fast Day.[25] The elders wrote, "It began to be as common here to distinguish between men, by being under a covenant of grace or a covenant of works, as in other countries between Protestants and papists." That was Wheelwright's great fault: once such factions existed, discussion came to an end. Divided loyalties—alienated affections—would always trump reason, no matter how modest or sensible it might be. That is to say, not only did antinomians deny sympathy as a valid sign of grace; according to the elders, they actually divided the mutual affections of the broader community and so made it impossible to have a credible theological debate.[26]

The charge of contempt, meanwhile, addressed Wheelwright's call for battle. The elders stated, "To incense and heate mens minds against their Brethren, before hee had convinced or admonished them ... is not to bee termed in any truth of the Gospel." The first step in a family squabble was to convince and admonish one's siblings, not to disown them. Furthermore, the elders argued, Wheelwright falsely applied the idea of spiritual battle. Such warfare was waged not "against the persons of brethren, but against high thoughts and imaginations"; it "resist[ed] the Devill, not flesh and bloud." For *non*brethren spiritual warfare might easily issue in violence, but that was not the way to proceed with brothers and sisters in Christ.[27] When Wheelwright pointed his finger at fellow Puritans—at real flesh and blood—he committed an act of aggression unsanctioned by holy scripture. Beyond sedition, such a position and such an attitude showed contempt for reconciliation—the very purpose of the fast.

In the charges laid at Wheelwright's feet, therefore, the explanatory framework of the Antinomian Controversy first took up a language of faction and sedition—two parties where formerly there had been one. As a result of this division, the possibility of reconciliation passed. Elders and antinomians would have to fight it out, struggling for the power and authority to determine who was in and who was out, who belonged to the family of God and who opposed it. Now that two families vied for control, it was time for the real father—whoever that might be—to stand up.

After replacing Henry Vane as governor in 1637, Winthrop did just that. He asserted his paternal authority by passing a new immigration law that made it illegal for any immigrant to stay longer than three weeks without permission. In defense of this order—designed to prevent antinomians from coming to New England—Winthrop argued that a commonwealth could not receive those who would do it harm. To illustrate that principle, Winthrop turned to the analogy of a family: "A family is a little common wealth, and a common wealth is a greate family. Now as a family is not bound to entertaine all comers, no not every good man (otherwise than by way of hospitality) no more is a common wealth." New England would be hospitable to all, in other words, but not all would be invited to stay. Moreover, the head of this household, the magistrates, would be charged with deciding who brought good and who boded evil. If Wheelwright's views disturbed the peace—if they "cause[d] divisions, and ma[d]e people looke at their magistrates, ministers and brethren as enemies and Antichrists"—then, Winthrop argued, "were it not sinne and unfaithfullness in us, to receive more of those opinions?" In rejecting antinomian immigrants, therefore, Winthrop presented himself as acting like a good father. When opponents objected that Winthrop's analogy did not hold, he responded by defending it all the more. The right of receiving or rejecting was a father's prerogative; in the same way and for the same reasons (the defense of the household), it remained a magistrate's right to receive or reject. Exercising his renewed political might, Winthrop claimed he would be welcoming, but diligent. The peace of his family, his commonwealth, required nothing less.[28]

The Breeder and Nourisher of All These Distempers

The contest in New England over who controlled the family—and how wide its affections went—framed, in particular, the contentions with Anne Hutchinson. In the trials that eventually brought the Antinomian Controversy to a close, the first charge leveled against Hutchinson was that she belonged to Wheelwright's party—an accusation that had become common by the time she took the stand. Already, many of Wheelwright's supporters had been tried and sentenced. William Aspin, who signed a petition for Wheelwright, had been banished, and seven others had been fined and disenfranchised. Hutchinson entered a court that had already confirmed the existence of a faction and punished those who belonged. All the court had to do was prove her membership. Winthrop thus opened the trial by claiming that Hutchinson was known "to be nearly joined ... in affinity and affection with some of those the court had taken notice of and passed censure upon," and he asked her "to express whether you do not hold and assent in practice to those opinions and factions that have been handled in court already, that is to say, whether you do not justify Mr. Wheelwright's sermon and the petition." Winthrop wed Hutchinson to the faction in both mind and heart, both "opinions" and "affections."[29]

Rather than answering Winthrop's question, however, Hutchinson refused his argument. "Must not I then entertain the saints because I must keep my conscience," she asked. She sheltered a party of true Christians, she argued, not a faction of false heretics. Such a defense reopened the contest that Winthrop wanted closed. He and the court had definitively asserted that they alone were the true fathers of the commonwealth— and, moreover, that the commonwealth composed the family of God. Hutchinson countered that only an embattled few lived in the covenant of grace, and only they could consider themselves God's children. As the dispute continued, Winthrop charged Hutchinson with countenancing those who violated the fifth commandment—"honor thy father and mother." The fifth commandment, Winthrop instructed her, "includes all in authority, but these seditious practises of theirs, have cast reproach and dishonour upon the Fathers of the Commonwealth." Hutchinson explained that the fifth commandment did not give *all* authority to fathers, but only that power which did not contradict the ways of God. "I am to obey you only in the Lord," she asserted. Fathers had no authority when they commanded their children to perform acts which God would not permit. Hutchinson thus offered a hypothetical question in her defense: "Put case, I do feare the Lord, and my Parent doe not, may not I entertain one that feares the Lord, because my Father will not let mee?" Winthrop had to answer yes; after all, the Puritans had long used such a line of argument in England. But now the question pointed at *him: he* was the authority standing in the way of God. According to Hutchinson, the fathers of the commonwealth did not speak for the family of God.[30]

In resisting Winthrop on this point, Hutchinson did not seem to be resisting patriarchy per se.[31] Instead, she seemed to accede to patriarchal authority while also arguing that the legitimate authorities had gone astray—a claim often made in England where the Puritans had regularly disobeyed their "fathers" without questioning patriarchal rule. Winthrop, for example, tried to link Hutchinson with *men* who also broke the fifth commandment. At the same time, of course, gender inflected the controversy in multiple ways. The court case began in a long discussion about Hutchinson's teaching; the Bible forbade a woman to teach, though Puritans permitted it for private edification, so the court debated whether or not Hutchinson taught men and whether or not her teaching could be considered public. The elders' description of Hutchinson as they opened the court case in their *Short Story* also reveals just how much gender mattered, for in establishing Hutchinson as the chief agent of the crisis, they wrote: "The Court had now to do with the head of all this faction, (*Dux foemina facti*) a woman had been the breeder and nourisher of all these distempers." Such language of breeding and nourishing linked the court case to Winthrop's notorious interest in the miscarried fetuses of Hutchinson and her supporter Mary Dyer—signs, he thought, that God sided with the elders. In these and many other ways, gender mattered to the making and resolving of the controversy.[32]

But Hutchinson did not become the "head of all this faction" until the end of her court case. She was always important, but not always the "breeder and nourisher of all these distempers." That narrative developed through the trial itself. When, for example, the charge of being in league with seditious persons began to slip, the court shifted its ground to sedition itself. Where before Wheelwright had been indicted with breaking the colony's peace, now Hutchinson faced the same allegation. Thomas Dudley, the Deputy Governor, told the court that he "would go a little higher with Mrs. Hutchinson," explaining, "About three years ago we were all in peace. Mrs. Hutchinson from that time she came hath made a disturbance." And just as the elders' anger burned against Wheelwright for separating one Puritan from another, so Dudley aimed the same fire at Hutchinson, asserting that she "*made parties* in the country." According to the developing story, Wheelwright only *confirmed* a faction Hutchinson first formed. Hugh Peter, another prosecuting elder, verified Dudley's assessment. Some ministers, he reported, considered "this gentlewoman" to be "a chief agent," from whom "the spring did arise as we did conceive." The prosecution wanted to show not just that she denigrated preachers (and thus breached their authority), but also—and primarily—that she fomented factions. Division remained the central problem. If Hutchinson had critiqued the fathers from within a broader unity, it might have been possible to reconcile. But since her arrival, the elders asserted, the colonists had begun accusing one another of belonging to separate covenants. From being charged as a member of Wheelwright's party, Hutchinson thus became—through the course of her civil trial—the *source* of this separate faction.[33]

As they prosecuted Hutchinson, Winthrop and the elders both admitted an opposing party and kept denying its possibility in New England. When Hutchinson demanded that the ministers take an oath, for example, she did so on the basis that they opposed her: "they are witnesses of their own cause," she complained. In that complaint lay the whole trial—the whole problem—as Winthrop saw it. He stormed in response, "It is not their cause but the cause of the whole country and they were unwilling that it should come forth, but that it was the glory and honour of God." The country did not have two causes or two families, but one. And if all had been contained within a union of affections, then this problem of defining different covenants would never have "come forth."[34]

After Hutchinson pressed for oaths, Cotton testified on her behalf and saved her from the charge of sedition. He explained that Hutchinson did put a difference between him and others, but not nearly so much as claimed. "I told her I was very sorry that she put comparisons between my ministry and theirs," he recounted, "for she had said more than I could myself, and rather I had that she had put us in fellowship with them and not have made that discrepancy." Cotton thus told the court exactly what it wanted to hear: that he, too, wished to perceive the ministers as one fellowship. At the same time, he testified that Hutchinson had never left the family to form her own. She suggested that some might not preach *as well* as others, but, Cotton assured the court, "I did not find her saying they were under a covenant of works, nor that she said they did preach a covenant of works." With that, the second move of the prosecution—from countenancing a faction to forming one—fell apart. After a little more back-and-forth, Increase Nowell, an official of the colony, declared, "The witnesses do not answer that which you require." Winthrop responded, "I do not see that we need their testimony any further."[35]

As the prosecution disintegrated, Anne Hutchinson rose to deliver what would become her fatal speech. One historian has suggested that had Hutchinson not spoken at this point, "her judges might have felt obliged to dismiss the case for lack of evidence, or at best would have passed some vote of censure in order to save their faces."[36] But she did speak. And during the course of her spiritual autobiography, Hutchinson made an assertion that no good Puritan could accept: the Lord spoke to her "by an immediate revelation." When Dudley shouted in protest, she qualified her statement, defining immediate revelation as "the voice of his own spirit to my soul."[37] But the damage had been done. Even Cotton could no longer save her, though he still tried.

The court thus shifted its charges a third time, away from harboring and fomenting factions toward a heresy long known and hated. "Ey," Winthrop exclaimed, "it is the most desperate enthusiasm in the world." Such "enthusiasm"—a theological term for the indwelling of the Holy Spirit and its immediate guidance—led to riots, rebellions, and mass slaughters (as it had in Munster, the elders kept reminding everyone), for such revelations "being above reason and Scripture, they are not subject to control." In her acknowledgment of immediate revelations, Winthrop explained, Hutchinson "freely and fully discovered her selfe": "her owne mouth ... deliver[ed] her into the power of the Court, as guilty of that which all suspected her for, but were not furnished with proofe sufficient to proceed against her." Hutchinson's revelations became her ultimate sin—the charge which finally stuck.[38]

Even so, in two separate accounts of the proceedings, the court returned to the matter of separate parties. The "immediate revelation" did not issue in an immediate conviction. This is a point that many seem to miss: if Hutchinson's testimony was so damning, why did the trial keep going? It kept going because Hutchinson still had not been convicted of a crime. William Coddington, a Hutchinson supporter, interrupted the proceedings to remind the court that no evidence had yet surfaced that Hutchinson ever declared any minister under a covenant of works and so made a faction against them. Following his lead, two others explained that they could not censure Hutchinson because no witnesses had been produced. Coddington, building on their support, reiterated a claim Hutchinson made earlier: "every man is partial in his own cause."[39] These objections reopened the question which had driven the trial from the beginning—the making of parties. Did Hutchinson create, harbor, or in any way further a faction? If she did not do that, then all her theological questions—all of her potentially heterodox beliefs— would have to be dealt with differently: as scruples from within, rather than assaults from without.

In response, the elders argued that Hutchinson did not advance her opinions from brotherly love. Instead of critiquing from within a broader union of mutual affections, she created two separate emotional communities. But *that* point still had to be proven. To answer all reservations, Winthrop finally required an oath. Thomas Weld, John Eliot, and Hugh Peter, three prosecuting elders, swore to tell the whole truth so help them God. Eliot testified that she put "a broad difference" between Cotton and all others, claiming "we were not able ministers of the new testament and that we were not clear in our experience because we were not sealed." Weld and Peter agreed. At that, Mr. Stoughton, one of those who had previously objected, announced his satisfaction: "I say now this testimony doth convince me in the thing, and I am fully satisfied the words were pernicious and the frame of her spirit doth hold forth the same."[40] In the end, what mattered was not just the content of Hutchinson's beliefs (her "pernicious" words), but the way they were presented ("the frame of her spirit"). Winthrop called for a vote, and Hutchinson found herself without a home.

Thus just as a theology of sympathy—a love of brethren—defined the difference between these parties, so it also affected how Puritans understood communities of belonging and the possibilities of debate. Disagreement could be understood either as a critique motivated by mutual affection, or an assault prompted by pernicious spirits. In the first case, persuasion remained possible because a broader, underlying union of hearts could be assumed. In the second case, no debate remained: the disaffected had to be forcefully resisted and removed.

Seduction as Solution

For all the language of maintaining a union of affections, the elders still had not addressed a fundamental problem: how did disaffection first arise? During the controversy, many touted a golden age that preceded the advent of the antinomians. As Thomas Weld explained in his preface to the *Short Story*, the Antinomian Controversy began at a time when "our Churches [were] sweetely settled in Peace, (God abounding to us in more happy enjoyments then we could have expected)."[41] But such a picture created a conundrum: if New England had been so perfect, how did the antinomians ever gain strength? Weld raised precisely that problem in his preface. After describing the many false opinions that arose, he wrote, "Now these, most of them, being so grosse, one would wonder how they should spread so fast and suddenly amongst a people so religious and well taught."[42] Toward the end of the controversy, therefore, the elders shifted their primary concern from the fact of division to the manner in which it developed.

Elucidating how this faction formed mattered not just for the ministers of New England, but also for those watching from abroad. New England subsisted on its reputation. The Golden Age thesis, as long as it remained strong, justified the Puritans' departure from England and kept both goods and people flowing in. As one woman wrote to John Winthrop's wife, "The strongar you grow I trust the mor powar your prairs shall hav for the rest of gods children that are left hear behind."[43] More than the power of prayers, Puritans needed to demonstrate the godliness of their society to keep receiving some badly needed financial support. News of New England's success would motivate others to offer aid, join the enterprise, and replicate its model back home.[44]

In defending their reputation, moreover, the elders focused on maintaining a strong union of affection with the Puritan godly who had never left England. Just as charitable giving and the possibility of persuasion depended on brotherly love *within* New England, so between England and the colony mutual affections enabled all else. In the early days of settlement, for example, John Humfrey, an English Puritan, wrote to Isaac Johnson, one of the most powerful promoters of the colony, explaining that many had been inclined to help New England, but upon receiving an "ill report of the state of things ... straunge it was to see how little brotherly love wrought in brethren. The designe was given of as lost, and to make it worse, few shewed anie affection to save those which were likely to perish." Later, an anonymous person in England wrote to Winthrop warning him of letters from New England that contained "many weake and some dangerous passages." These documents, he cautioned, "hath caused a wonderfull disaffection in very many towards you, and which is most grievous, in many such as are they deare children of god, insomuch that there is like to be, if it be not maturely healed, a greate rent in affection betweene you and them, that though we are like to see sadd times, yet there are, till they be otherwise informed, who are resolved to undergoe much misery heere rather then ever to remove hence."[45] The disaffection had risen to such a pitch that the godly in England would risk God's destruction in a doomed land rather than sail across the sea. For these reasons, any talk of controversy—especially any rumor of heresy—posed a serious threat to New England. The Puritan colonists faced so much scrutiny from abroad that they continually had to present themselves as a community living in the unity of the spirit and the bond of peace—a communion of the faithful that had its discussions, maybe even its disagreements, but never its dissensions or divisions.

Yet despite the elders' best efforts, the Antinomian Controversy could not be contained. News of New England's problems circulated through England. As one scholar notes, "Presbyterian polemicists like Robert Baillie and Thomas Edwards leaped at the chance to use the example of Anne Hutchinson's 'abominable errours' as evidence of 'the fruits of their [Congregational] Church-way.'" A pawn in the battle between Presbyterians and Independents, a thorn in the side of magistrates, a glaring example of ungodliness on New England's sacred soil, Anne Hutchinson had to be not just banished, but explained.[46] That explanation, moreover, needed to achieve a variety of goals. Not only did it have to defend the emergent Congregational system of church and state, it also had to castigate the fallen and redeem all those who stayed within or returned to the embrace of the church. To solve all these problems, the elders turned to seduction.

That language of seduction emerges most clearly in Hutchinson's later church trial—when she ended up not just banished, but excommunicated. While the metaphor of a family dominated her civil prosecution, a new emphasis on Hutchinson's figurative and literal sexual activities pervaded the proceedings against her before her Boston congregation.[47] Gradually settling on Hutchinson as the source of all error, the elders argued that so many good people had sided with her because she had seduced them. "For she is a most dayngerous Spirit," Thomas Shepard proclaimed, "and likely with her fluent Tounge and forwardnes in Expressions to seduce and draw away many, Espetially simple Weomen of her owne sex." John Cotton, who turned against Hutchinson during the church trial, adopted the same language. He worried that many Boston women had "bine too much seduced and led aside by her." John Wilson exclaimed, "Consider how we cane or whether we may longer suffer her to goe on still in seducinge to seduce and in deacevinge to deceave and in lyinge to lye and in condeminge Authoritie and Magistracie still to contemne." When the trial ended, Cotton relied once more on this language to pronounce her excommunication: she was cast out, he told her, so that she might "learne no more to blaspheme[,] to seduce and to lye."[48] It still mattered *what* Hutchinson believed, but by this point in the controversy New England ministers and magistrates were concerned far more with how she *spread* those beliefs.

Such concerns dominate Weld's preface to the *Short Story*, which relies on a language of seduction to explain almost all that occurred in the Antinomian Controversy.[49] After listing several of Hutchinson's errors (or "brats") and asking how they could have spread, he offered two solutions: first, "the nature of the Opinions themselves" and second, the "sleights they used in fomenting their Opinions." In explaining the former, Weld suggested that Hutchinson's way would "open such a faire and easie way to Heaven, that men may passe without difficulty." In other words, antinomian theology appealed to the slothful. Those who found assurance in a "witness of the spirit" could leave behind discipline and obedience, fall "into the grossest sinnes," and yet remain perfectly secure. Weld concluded, "Then their way to life was made easie, if so, no marvell so many like of it."[50]

But theology did not remain the fullest or most adequate explanation for how these opinions spread. First, antinomian doctrines proved difficult to accept.[51] Indeed, Weld's account of "sleights" suggested that fellow Christians did not quickly embrace a supposedly easy assurance. When the antinomians told fellow Christians of "such a setled peace that they might never doubt more, though they should see no grace at all in themselves," Weld compared their speech to that of "Harlots" and concluded, "With much faire speech they caused them to yeeld, with the flattering of their lips they forced them." The need for force and flattery suggests that it took more to turn the godly than simply offering them relief. Yet the clearest indication that the *form* of seduction trumped the *substance* of antinomian doctrine can be seen in the sheer scope given to each account: two paragraphs explain how "the nature of the Opinions themselves" enabled antinomians to rise, while several pages describe their "sleights." According to the elders, the dangerous attraction lay not in the doctrines, but in the people teaching them.[52]

When he turned to "sleights," Weld described several steps by which the antinomians seduced the saints. First, they "laboured much to acquaint themselves with as many, as possibly they could, that so they might have the better opportunity to communicate their new light unto them." In other words, they waged a getting-to-know-you campaign, led in part by Hutchinson's spiritual work with pregnant women. "Once acquainted with them," Weld continued, "they would strangely labour to insinuate themselves into their affections."[53] Without any word of doctrine, they built up affection. And they did so carefully, with toil and effort. The word "labor"—which recurs frequently in Weld's account—offered three distinct advantages to him: first, it provided a subtle critique of the party that so vehemently opposed a covenant of works; second, it tied Hutchinson to her gender and her work among laboring women; and third, the *need* for labor proved the goodness of the godly. Only a great deal of premeditation, planning, and precise maneuvering enabled the seducers to sway the saints.

As Weld continued to describe antinomian "sleights," he revealed the main attraction of the Hutchinsonians: they seduced not with comely features and suave manners, but with good-looking piety and smooth-sounding prayers. Antinomians insinuated themselves into the affections of the godly "by loving salutes, humble carriage, kind invitements, [and] friendly visits." When newcomers arrived they "would be sure to welcome them, shew them all courtesie, and offer them roome in their owne houses." Meanwhile, "they would appeare very humble, holy, and spirituall Christians, and full of Christ; they would deny themselves farre, speake excellent, pray with such soule ravishing expressions and affections, that a stranger that loved goodnesse, could not but love and admire them, and so be the more easily drawne after them." The Hutchinsonians, in other words, turned virtues into vices. They appeared as saints, but they did so only to spin their own "web" to trap and "poyson [others] by degrees." Indeed, "It was rare for any man thus hooked in, to escape their Leaven."[54] According to the developing story, good Puritans fell neither for ill-gotten gains nor for easy leaps to heaven, but rather for the appearance of godliness itself.

Such seductions worked especially well on the weak. While the eminent and well-established remained the primary target, antinomians worked their way up to such Christians by preying upon the lowly. Those who "had newly tasted the sweetenesse of *Free Grace*" fell for any who claimed to defend "free grace" by "holding forth a naked Christ." The seducers, in other words, sought spiritual virgins. Yet they also turned to the troubled—any who "were full of doubts and feares about their conditions"— working themselves into their affections through flattery and "faire speech." Women, too, proved susceptible. Weld states, "They commonly laboured"—again that word—"to worke first upon women, being (as they conceived) the weaker to resist; the more flexible, tender, and ready to yield." Such language reveals how sexual the metaphor could become. And such connotations carried over into the larger plan: by seducing women, antinomians reasoned, they could then, "as by an *Eve*, ... catch their husbands also."[55] The antinomians thus focused on the inexperienced, those virginal to conversion, the young, the weak, the women—and through them, they "labored" their way into the affections of the strong.

Once they held the love of enough people, the seducers divided. Having "by all these wayes of subtilty" wrought themselves "into the hearts of the people," Weld wrote, "nextly they strongly endeavoured with all the craft they could, to undermine the good Opinion of their Ministers, and their doctrine, and to worke them cleane out of their affections." The seducers could achieve nothing so long as the seduced remained within their family; the authority of fathers had to give way. So the antinomians waged a come-away-with-us campaign, which worked so effectively, Weld recorded, "that many declined the hearing of ['legal' preachers], though they were members of their Churches." Even those who had "beene begotten to Christ" by the work of these ministers turned against "their spirituall fathers" upon "falling acquainted with those Seducers."[56] Torn from paternal protection, the seduced were left to the mercy of their new loves.

Meanwhile, the antinomians only gradually revealed the true nature of their schemes. They won hearts *before* they divulged their ideas. Weld explained, "They would not, till they knew men well, open the whole mystery of their new Religion to them." Instead, they would let out their beliefs little by little, giving "stronger and stronger potions, as they found the patient able to beare."[57] Cloaked in respectability and wearing the appearance of godliness, the seducers would wean away their virgin prey, revealing their real motives and opinions so slowly that the seduced would continue to be deceived.

With such an account, Thomas Weld turned the Antinomian Controversy into one of New England's earliest and most prominent seduction plots. But the important point is that Weld's story itself relies on Puritan principles of persuasion. Doctrine and logic cannot and do not persuade on their own; nor will they ever be heard or received if someone does not already love the person speaking. In fact, Weld's narrative enabled the story of New England's trouble to be told without any nitty gritty details of sanctification and justification, the lesser lights and the naked Christ. Instead, affections were sealed long before doctrines were revealed; and by the time doctrines *were* revealed, it was already too late. As Weld explained, the antinomians "[won] upon men, and st[o]le into their bosomes before they were aware." Nor was he alone in this assessment. When critics charged that "almost in every family some were ready to defend [the antinomians] as the Apple of their own eye," John Cotton defended the godliness of New England Puritans precisely in terms of these affections. "It is one thing to speak in the defence of erroneous persons, another to speak in defence of errours," he argued. "Multitudes there were, that thought well of the persons, who knew nothing of their errours, but heard onely of their unbottoming sandy foundations of a spirituall estate." The godly were not perpetrators of heresy; they were seduced by heretics who looked godly to all—and the seduced defended their own no matter what. As a result, the family tore apart. Fathers watched their daughters turn their backs, stop their ears, and steal away.

A Family Reunion

This framing language enabled New England elders to draw the picture of a Golden Age that antinomian seduction had ruined. Mutual affection bound the family of God, and together, the people constituted a unified body. In *A Model of Christian Charity,* Winthrop defined the ideal commu nity as knit together by "ligaments of love"—a body that operated on the principle of sympathy, so that "if one member suffer, all suffer with it: if one member be had in honor, all the members rejoice with it." That model had been achieved, these accounts argued. Before Wheelwright "broached his opinions, there was a peaceable and comely order in all affaires in the Churches, and civill state." Before Hutchinson "made parties, we were all in peace."[58] A model of Christian charity had become a reality, these elders claimed, and the Antinomian Controversy pitted those who would defend it against those who would divide it.

Such a frame for the Antinomian Controversy fit with a larger historical context concerned about unity and division—a broader transatlantic Puritan world that was beginning to split apart in the successes of the 1640s. Under Charles I and Archbishop Laud, as Tom Webster has shown, "Persecution operated as a unifying influence; an element of freedom and power provided by the 1640s led to the potential divisions becoming actual divisions." Webster explains that "it had become a common theme in godly writings to decry the contrasting divisions of the 1640s, which had replaced a perceived pre-war unity."[59] Explanations of the New England Antinomian Controversy made the same rhetorical move. With other Puritans across the Atlantic, New England authorities lamented the loss of unity—a loss not of doctrinal consensus, but rather of united hearts willing to live with disagreement. In banishing Anne Hutchinson—in refusing to tolerate her brand of intolerance—the elders of Massachusetts Bay made the claim that they were rebuilding community and returning to the unity of the spirit they had known once before.

For the story to end happily, then, it required not just a proclamation of right doctrine, but also a renewal of affections. Scholars have largely overlooked this emphasis on reunion, focusing instead on matters of intellectual disagreement resolved through the creation of a new orthodoxy defined by a long list of heresies—by what good Puritans were not allowed to believe. Philip Round, for example, claims that Weld emphasized "plaine Syllogistical despute" in his account of the synod, and that such "logical formalism" operated as "a gendered educational barrier."[60] Though Round's larger point—that the "social effect" of the synod helped gender the New England Way "in such a fashion that henceforth only men could hope to speak it"—may remain valid, this smaller point does not hold up. Weld admits that syllogisms helped some, but they did not solve New England's problem; while they settled the "indifferent" and the "wavering," they did not "effect the cure."[61] Something more than logic was needed—something aimed not at the head, but at the heart. Scriptural interpretation and doctrinal agreement remained important throughout the controversy, but such matters diminished when elders came to tell the *story* of the crisis; for them, the controversy revealed a rupture not of interpretative consensus but of *emotional* concord; a happy resolution, therefore, required a family reunion.[62]

And that renewal of affections is precisely what the elders emphasized at the conclusion of the controversy. An anonymous letter from 1637 describing the synod of that year focused on its unity of affections. Winthrop governed the event so well, the writer explained, that "the assembly is dissolved, and jarring and dissonant opinions, if not reconciled, yet are covered." More importantly, "they who came together with minds exasperated by this means depart in peace, and promise, by a mutual covenant, that no difference in opinion shall alienate their affections any more but that they will refer doubts to be resolved by the great God, at that great day when we shall appear at His tribunal."[63] Though differences might persist, affections had been healed.

In his preface to the *Short Story*, Weld made the same point. After Hutchinson's excommunication, he explained, many "came unto us, who before flew from us"; they confessed—"some of them with many teares"— the offence they had given to God and his people not just in the embrace of errors, but in the "alienation from their brethren in their affections." At that point, their eyes opened and they saw "the sleights the Adversaries had used to undermine them by, and steale away their eyes from the truth and their brethren, which before ... they could not see." The "fruit" of it all, Weld concluded, was praise, gladness, and "expressions of our renued affections by receiving them againe into our bosomes." Mutual affections had returned.[64]

More than that, such language continued the idea of communal sanctification. Puritans expected an individual Christian to experience a period of high emotions after first conversion: after Winthrop's, for example, his "peace continued" for several months, and he grew familiar with Christ, so that Christ "would oft tell mee he loved mee." According to accounts of the Antinomian Controversy, that same experience accompanied the first years of settlement in New England. Weld portrayed the churches "sweetely settled in Peace"; only then did God release an affliction, "lest we should, now, grow secure." In other words, New England had to move past its first conversion. God intended to mature the colony, and he did so through affliction. In his wisdom, said Weld, God "seldome suffers his owne, in this their wearysome Pilgrimage to be long without trouble." New England counted as God's "owne," and Hutchinson's arrival could be considered its "sorest tryall." *As a trial*, however, she did not bring judgment against the saints; instead, she proved that they *were* saints.[65]

Such logic can be clarified by a comparison of plagues in the 1630s.[66] At the same time that Hutchinson arrived in New England and "that Plague first began amongst us," as Weld wrote, a literal plague coursed through the streets of London. In three months, 57,000 people fled the city and its suburbs. New England and Old each struggled with their own "sorest tryall." Yet the interpretations of these sufferings differed dramatically. England, in short, did not face a trial; it faced a punishment—the due reward for its sins. The doom that had long been forewarned had begun to descend. Winthrop's sister, Lucy Downing, wrote to his wife Margaret that the plague showed "the arguments of the all-mighties controversie with us: and provocations incresainge to such heyghts: what can wee expect: if the sonne of god must suffer, rather then his Justis be unsatisfied." Sins could continue only so long before God's wrath would finally break forth.[67]

New England's suffering, meanwhile, came not as a punishment of the godless, but as an affliction of the godly. The antinomian plague rose and spread like the terrors in the Book of Job—calamities that had no relation to any specific sin. Certainly Puritans believed that all people deserved whatever the Lord doled out; as the Puritan poet Anne Bradstreet would write when her house burned down: "Yea so it was, and so 'twas just."[68] Yet in the same poem she puts herself in Job's position, implying that she had done nothing for which the burned house could be read as God's direct return; it was, rather, a trial, a test of faith. The elders adopted the same view when framing the Antinomian Controversy. Hutchinson arrived not in response to sins, but as God's way of preventing sins—a warning lest New England "grow secure." She was a trial, not a punishment, and all trials could be understood as the devil's attempt to disrupt the godly. According to the elders, Hutchinson came as "an instrument of Satan so fitted and trained to [the Lord's] service for interrupting the passage [of his] Kingdome in this part of the world."[69] As with Job, so with New England: the worse Hutchinson became, the better they looked. Nothing motivated Satan more than the manifestation of God's Kingdom.

Surviving Satan's malice, therefore, sanctified and matured New England beyond its first conversion. As with any Christian, so the life of the colony continually ousted the "old man" in order that the "new man" could flourish. The vivification of the colony required the mortification of its enemies. More than that, this view of the sanctified colony responded to the theological contest of the Antinomian Controversy: the golden age of a settled peace—the heightened religious experience of first conversion— could go only so far; what really assured one of salvation was not this extraordinary and momentary sense of peace, but rather the *loss* of peace and its *return*. Thus, the elders' version of the Antinomian Controversy both defended the value of sanctification and rewrote the entire episode *as* New England's sanctification.

The description of that sanctification, moreover, consistently highlights the power of united affections. Magistrates and ministers envisioned New England as a family bound by brotherly affections. As long as such affections remained strong—as long as everyone continued to imagine themselves as *one* community in the "unity of the spirit and the bond of peace"—theological debates could wander a long ways without threatening the stability or viability of either the church or state. The "boundaries of acceptable dissent" lay not so much in a definition of doctrine as in the *frame* of doctrinal dispute, the breadth of New England's emotional community: unity required responding with the same feelings to the same events—mourning together on fast days, rejoicing together on days of thanksgiving, sorrowing at dissension, praising God for unity. Any who advocated against these emotions proved themselves beyond the pale.[70] Once the frame broke—once distinct disaffected factions formed—no discussion could heal the divide. Before theology could be righted, mutual affections would have to return. The resolution of the crisis, therefore, lay not in doctrinal consensus, but rather in a family reunion—a sanctification of sympathy in Winthrop's city on a hill.

4

Transatlantic Relations and the Rhetoric of Sympathy

BEFORE LEAVING FOR America, the godly in England had joined together in bonded communities of sympathizing saints: they experienced the love of brethren in practice as they traveled to nearby sermons, met in conventicles, refreshed each other in godly conversations, and generally bound themselves together against the larger profane multitude. In New England the larger multitude was godly, and as the Antinomian Controversy revealed, the basic dynamic of sympathy needed revision. As Winthrop and others tried to transform the love of brethren from a persecuted minority into a socialized, godly society, the logic from England could not hold. Those who bound themselves together more narrowly in New England became a righteous problem, not a righteous people. Sympathy had to be extended more broadly if New England were to be perceived as—and presented as—a godly whole.

But in the wider transatlantic world of the 1630s and 1640s, Puritans still conceived of themselves as a persecuted minority bound together by a special love of brethren and fighting together for a wider reformation. At least, that is how New England Puritans thought of themselves. Not all the godly agreed. When nearly a thousand compatriots left England in 1630, many charged them with abandoning the righteous cause. Robert Ryece, a friend of John Winthrop's, argued that England had greater need of his "best abyllytie"—that Winthrop's departure would harm the homeland more than it would help the colony.[1] That charge only deepened through the 1630s and 1640s. Attempting to defend fellow colonists in 1648, John Cotton declared, "It is a serious misrepresentation unworthy of the spirit of Christian truth, to say that our brethren, either those returned from the

Netherlands or those exiled in New England, fled from England like mice from a crumbling house, anticipating its ruin, prudently looking to their own safety, and treacherously giving up the defence of the common cause of the Reformation."[2] Cotton's statement reveals just how pervasive and prolonged this accusation had become. And it was a serious charge. Real separatists existed in New England—people who denounced the Church of England and explicitly left it. For many, these separatists, such as Bradford and his pilgrims down in Plymouth, represented the limit they must not reach, partly for the reasons of persuasion that came to the fore in the Antinomian Controversy: if the Puritans left the Church of England altogether, how could they reform it? Separation would take them out of brotherly love, out of the possibility of debate and persuasion. Without a continued union, the godly of New England could be quietly ignored. As Anne Hutchinson's seduction story traveled across the sea, therefore, it joined a growing body of literature concerned with maintaining healthy transatlantic relations.

To illustrate their continued union with the godly and the godly cause, New England Puritans spoke, at times, of sympathy. As Richard Mather and William Tompson wept for England and claimed that the mighty Atlantic could never "wash away the thought and remembrance of *England*, and of Gods people therein out of our hearts," so others also claimed that whatever physical distance might suggest, a love of the brethren kept them close.[3] Faced with charges of cowardice and desertion, some New England Puritans found a handy rhetorical tool in sympathy. Yet every time sympathy was used to mediate transatlantic relations, it both resolved and revealed the problem of separation: portraying and attempting to create a union of feeling between New England and Old, the rhetoric of sympathy often showed just how far the two had drifted apart. Moreover, when Puritan writers employed sympathy to solve the problem of separation, their rhetorical needs often translated into sensational designs. In the attempt to negotiate transatlantic relations with a language of fellow feeling, one can witness sentimental techniques beginning to appear in seventeenth-century Puritanism.

Leaving Without Leaving

Transatlantic sympathy emerged even before the Puritans left England. On the eve of departure, John White, a Puritan clergyman and promoter of the Massachusetts Bay colony, penned a defense against accusations of separation. Seven leading Puritans signed the resulting document, titled *The Humble Request of his Majesties loyall Subjects, the Governour and the Company late gone for New England.*[4] The signers then sent this "humble request" to "their Brethren in and of the *Church of* England," invoking a sense of persistent family ties. In fact, the word "brethren" appears on almost every page of the original document as the emigrating Puritans reiterated the idea that brotherhood knows no bounds. Proclaiming themselves siblings, they begged that such a status be recognized and reciprocated. "We beseech you therefore," they declared, "by the mercies of the Lord Jesus to consider us as your Brethren, standing in very great need of your helpe, and earnestly imploring it." They wanted material support, certainly, but they also knew that the continuation of such aid depended on brotherly love. Thus, the document maintains that siblings did not leave their family when they left their country. The Church of England, these signers insisted, would always remain "oure deare Mother"; they received salvation "in her bosome, and suckt it from her breasts," and they could not, having thus become "members of the same body," now separate.[5]

Such imagery was fairly common in its day.[6] Only a few days before the Puritans departed, the pastor John Cotton, who would not leave England for another three years, instructed them, "Forget not the womb that bare you, and the breast that gave you suck." "As God continueth his presence with us," Cotton insisted, "so be ye present in spirit with us, though absent in body." He then defined that spiritual unity as a sibling relationship: "In the *amity* and *unity* of Brethren, the Lord hath not only *promised*, but *commanded* a Blessing, even Life for ever more."[7] The godly of England and the godly of New England would remain brothers; and siblings knew each other first and foremost not through the proximity of their homes, but through the quality of their spirits. In *The Humble Request*, emigrating Puritans defined their nonseparation in the same terms. They remained united not just because they were nourished by the same mother, but also because they *shared the same affections.* "As members of the same body," they declared, "[we] shall alwayes rejoyce in her good, and unfainedly grieve for any sorrow that shall ever betide her."[8] They would remain united, in other words, because they would constitute a single emotional community. They knew each other by how each other felt.

To make such union obvious, the writers of *The Humble Request* decided to present it physically: unity could be witnessed through weeping. The Puritans claim that they depart with "much sadnes of heart, and many teares in our eyes." Histories of New England would often portray the moment of their leaving with melting souls and breast-breaking sobs. In each case, Puritans acknowledge separation while simultaneously overcoming it through heartfelt expressions, substituting sentiment for presence. Likewise, in *The Humble Request* the godly emigrants demonstrate their continuing communal links with those in England by vowing to give God "no rest on your behalfes, wishing our heads and hearts may be as fountaines of teares for your everlasting welfare." The unity of the spirit appeared in, and relied on, a bond of tears.[9]

Years later, one of these departure scenes would find itself replayed in a sentimental novel. Near the beginning of *Hope Leslie* (1827), Catharine Maria Sedgwick depicts John Winthrop's exodus from Southampton in 1630: "truly doleful was the sight of that sad and mournful parting, to hear what sighs, and sobs, and prayers, did sound amongst them; what tears did gush from every eye, and pithy speeches pierced each other's hearts."[10] The scene concerns Winthrop, but the words are William Bradford's; they come from *Of Plymouth Plantation* and they describe the pilgrim departure from the Netherlands ten years before. For Sedgwick, Puritans and pilgrims were all one; historically, however, the depicted pain of departure aims at very different unions. Bradford unites the separatists and attempts to show that the Atlantic cannot divide the affections of the specific congregation that had gathered in Leyden; *The Humble Request*, on the other hand, pours forth fountains of tears to show New England's continued union with all those committed to reforming the Church of England.

For Sedgwick, the pain of separation in this scene gets the whole plot going, parting William Fletcher, a Puritan, from his beloved Alice, who is captured and retained by her anti-Puritan father, Sir William. Even in this more particular separation, however, Sedgwick draws again from Bradford, for what happens to William and Alice mirrors another passage from *Of Plymouth Plantation*. When the pilgrims flee England for the Netherlands, soldiers ride up and force a ship to flee, which then carries pilgrim husbands away from their wives and children on shore. "But pitiful it was to see the heavy case of these poor women in their distress," Bradford writes, "what weeping and crying on every side, some for their husbands that were carried away in the ship ...; others not knowing what should become of them and their little ones; others again melted in tears, seeing their poor little ones hanging about them, crying for fear and quaking with cold." In *Hope Leslie*, a similar event occurs. William goes on board to check arrangements for Alice, and as he is rowing back to shore, he sees "Sir William's carriage guarded by a cavalcade of armed men" driving up to Alice. Hurrying to save her, William approaches "near enough to the shore to hear Alice's last impotent cries to him—to see her beautiful face convulsed with agony, and her arms outstretched towards him—when she was forced to the carriage by her father, and driven from his sight."[11] Without citing him, Sedgwick takes another passage from *Of Plymouth Plantation* and particularizes it. This is not to say that Bradford's book or other Puritan scenes of tearful departures were secretly sentimental; it is rather to show that in their writing, Puritan writers had occasion to sensationalize tears in ways that would later be termed sentimental—so much so, sometimes, that their very words could make it into nineteenth-century fiction.

In *The Humble Request*, Puritan emigrants use such rhetorical techniques to evoke a familial, emotional community that attempts to mask actual separation. The tears caused by departure reveal that, in spirit at least, no one is really leaving.[12] According to this letter, godly siblings know each other primarily through a reciprocity of emotions, expressing the same joy and sorrow in response to the same weal and woe. No sea could separate such a spirit—a spirit of amity and unity residing in the heart and issuing in "fountaines of teares." The emigrating Puritans never separated from their family; they simply extended its reach across the sea.

Returning Home While Remaining in Place

Ten years after emigrants vowed to pour forth tears for England, civil war loomed in their homeland. Already in December 1638, news circulated of "how it is in England and Scotland even sad enough."[13] From that time forward, the godly on both sides of the Atlantic wrote numerous letters detailing the developing situation. By the summer of 1640, colonists would have known that the Scottish had invaded England and defeated an army of King Charles, that Charles had called for a parliamentary session and then dismissed it almost immediately (the Short Parliament), and that the King was now headed back to battle the Scots. While tensions remained high between Charles and Parliament, the differences had not resulted in war. Taking sides, therefore, would have been politically unwise. Although most Puritans in New England backed the Scottish resistance and hoped Parliament would restrain and reform Charles, they did not openly proclaim such support until the king raised his standard against Parliament in 1642. Moreover, most New England Puritans had family members and friends still living in England, and any war—no matter how just—would reap suffering on all. It may have been true, as some believed, that God's judgment was now descending on England for failing to reform. But however much England deserved its punishment, good people also stood to suffer. When God's wrath broke out, it always seemed to cause collateral damage.[14]

The events unfolding in England had a direct impact on those living in the colonies. Most immediately, the prospect of godly progress in the homeland caused an immediate drop in emigration. As one friend wrote to Winthrop in early 1640, "There are like to come but a small quantyty of Passengers over, in comparison of what hath beene formerly, and the reasone I conceive to be the hopes of some reformation in England by the intended parlament."[15] In addition, such hopes fueled charges of desertion. Another friend wrote Winthrop, "Now we see and feele how much we are weakened by the loss of those that are gonn from us, who should have stood in the gapp, and have wrought and wrasled mightily in this great business."[16] The great business was in England, not New England, and as a result the godly colonists faced renewed charges of indifference and irrelevance.

On the Fast Day of July 23, 1640, William Hooke, the Puritan minister of Taunton, Massachusetts, responded to these problems by calling on his listeners to pray and mourn, inflecting both actions with a principle of sympathy.[17] The doctrine of *New Englands Teares for Old Englands Feares* states, "*It is the part of true friends and brethren, to sympathize and fellow-feele with their brethren and friends when the hand of God is upon them.*" Not only was fellow feeling required, it was, in fact, "a matter of just complaint, if when friends doe mourne, their fellowes doe not weepe." Turning to biblical authority, Hooke proclaimed, "But the Scriptures are expresse in the command of this sympathy. *Rejoyce with them that rejoyce, and weepe with them that weepe; be of the same mind one towards another.*" Like others, Hooke traced a pattern of sympathy through Scripture. He first quoted 2 Corinthians 11:29, which speaks of Paul's affections for his brethren. From Paul, Hooke moved to David, the book of Lamentations, Christ, and the Psalms. He even used the example of wicked leaders sympathizing with one another to heap coals on the heads of good Puritans. Beyond providing examples, Hooke claimed that the Bible explicitly mandates fellow feeling, citing Romans 12:15, Hebrews 13:1–3, and Proverbs 17:17. In line with many other Puritan thinkers, then, Hooke turned in his sermon to the scriptural doctrine and godly duty of sympathy.[18]

After making a biblical case for sympathy, Hooke attempted to instill it.[19] The main use of his doctrine, he told his listeners, was "of Exhortation to you all, as you desire to approve your selves the true friends and brethren of your deare Country-men in old *England*, to condole with them this day in their afflictions." Instead of picking one party and rallying his audience around it, Hooke chose "not to looke upon the occasions given on the one side or the other"; rather, he instructed congregants to "looke this day simply on the event, a sad event in all likelihood, the dividing of a King from his Subjects." The phrase "in all likelihood" suggests something of a qualifier, a subtle revelation of Hooke's belief (common to many in New England) that a division from the king *might* yield benefits.[20] Though Hooke evidently leaned one way rather than another, his explicit refusal to proclaim one side right and the other side wrong resulted, in part, from the particular makeup of the two conflicting camps. Opposing the king were both Presbyterians and a loose association of religious sects later called Independents—and both groups posed special problems for New England Congregationalists. The Presbyterians, who held sway in Parliament, advocated a centralized form of church governance that would have vitiated the local autonomy of congregations in New England; the Independents, who would later dominate the army, pragmatically defended a wider degree of religious tolerance than New England Puritans could accept. United by a common enemy, the Puritans, Presbyterians, and Independents divided internally over a host of theological, ecclesiastical, and political differences.[21] In *New Englands Teares*, Hooke tries to look past these differences in order to stir up sympathy for *all* suffering saints, wherever they might be found—maintaining, in that way, a stance of neutrality.

To stir up that sympathy, Hooke employs a three-part rhetorical strategy. First, Hooke explains, he will help his listeners "see Warre described": he will aid their imagination by showing them exactly why England needs their fellow feeling. Second, he will place war "in a countrey well known to you," enabling his hearers to picture the places they had recently left, the homeland they knew so well. Finally, Hooke will command an emotional response: he will simply tell his congregants to cry. Such an approach followed the guidelines of the English preacher William Fenner, who systematized how ministers should reach the affections of their listeners. In *A Treatise of the Affections*, he laid out five principles: first, ministers stir others "by preaching to the life"—that is, by setting things before their congregation as if they were really there; second, "by being full of affections"—a point Fenner supported with Cicero, Quintilian, Calvin, and Scripture; third, "by being godly our selves"; fourth, "by the due carriage of their voices," speaking with a "weeping voice" as needed; and fifth, "by a decent action"—that is, with appropriate gestures. Such a list could be summarized as a combination of expressivity and vividness: the preacher had to feel in order to stir up feeling, and he had to present the object of that emotion in vivid and lively terms.[22]

Those vivid and lively terms began in presentation. William Perkins and Richard Bernard, the two most influential instructors of Puritan preaching, recommended several techniques to help convey the proper emotion. According to Perkins, a minister's voice needed to vary, instructing with a moderate tone and exhorting with a more "fervent and vehement" expression. Bernard agreed. "Varietie of things," he wrote, "crave variety of words, and a differing manner of speech. ... Hee that can utter the threatnings of the law with terror, and the sweete promises of God, to moove to joy and thankfulnesse, he speaketh as he ought to speak." One's voice "must not be of one sound thorow out, but rising and falling, tuneable to the matter." "To be loud in Doctrine and low in Exhortation, or alike in both," Bernard added elsewhere, "is very inconsonant, disgracefull to the speaker, and distastfull to the hearers." The pitch of one's voice, following the affections of one's heart, helped enable the demonstration of the Spirit.[23]

Preaching manuals were just as detailed about gesture. Bernard, for example, warned against "violent motion, as casting abroad the armes, often smiting upon the pulpit, hindering the hearers with the sound thereof, sometimes rising up, then stooping down againe, and many such toilesome and troublesome actions." But he also cautioned that "feare and bashfulnesse" could cause "many toyings of the hand to the face, brest, buttons, head, beard, cloke, or gowne, ridiculous to be named, besides the nodding of the head, lifting up of the shoulders, hemmings, spettings, and such like." Such annoying ticks were just as bad as beating on the pulpit. They distracted from the Spirit, rather than demonstrated it. Perkins agreed, advising Puritan preachers to practice a due measure of "gravity." "It is appropriate," he wrote, "that the preacher keep the trunk of his body erect and still, while the other parts like the arm, the hand, the face and eyes may express and (as it were) speak the spiritual affections of his heart." Again, while spiritual affections mattered most, their communication required a proper performance, a good delivery. Perkins suggested that some techniques could be found in Scripture, but for the most part, he advised watching others and emulating what worked. According to the most widely read preaching manuals of the early seventeenth century, ministers did not enable the demonstration of the Spirit solely through

syllogistic argument; they also employed oratorical skills of voice and gesture that had little to do with logic.[24]

Focused on more than a mere list of logical reasons, and presumably
drawing on manuals such as these for the manner of his delivery, Hooke
turns first in his sermon to description. Following the maxim of a lively
presence, he sets listeners in the midst of a vivid battle: "Here ride some
dead men swagging in their deep saddles; there fall others alive upon
their dead horses." Gruesome details emerge as some soldiers die, others lose limbs, and still others lie "wallowing in their sweat and goare."
Spatially, listeners find themselves surrounded. The fight happens "here"
and "there," "in yonder file" and "not far off." Positioned on the field, congregants can forget their pews and imagine themselves in the midst of
war—a war less glorious and noble than piteous and gory.[25]

Beyond the grisly fight, Hooke's sermon tries to melt hearts by turning
to women and children—to the broken family left behind. "All this while,"
Hooke writes, "the poore wife and tender children sit weeping at home." This
poor widow, he continues, "who fed yet upon a crumb of hope, teares her
haire from her head, rends her cloths, wrings her hands, lifts up her voice
to heaven, and weeps like *Rachell* that would not be comforted." The biblical reference does more than make this woman a typological abstraction. In
Scripture, Rachel weeps for the *loss* of her children (Jer. 31:15); here she weeps
with them. The children "hang about her crying and saying, O my father is
slaine, my father is dead, I shall never see my father more."[26] Such language
indicates that Hooke is interested in more than a theological point; he is writing to the heart, wrenching tears with the image of a broken home.

Such gendered divisions inflect how Hooke hopes to produce sympathy. In war, men fight and die, women wait and weep; in the sermon,
therefore, Hooke holds up the image of a suffering widow to mirror the
weeping that ought to occur in his own congregation. He uses a mother's
tears to engender a tearful response. Where others fought for the cause,
New England Puritans would weep for it. Summing up the domestic scene,
Hooke proclaims, "And so they cry and sob and sigh out their afflicted
soules, and breake their hearts together." These are the tangible signs of
lament that Hooke hopes to reproduce by putting his congregants in the
place of bereaved mothers and weeping widows. The fact that such a position would normally be gendered female can be demonstrated by another
Fast Day sermon preached in England shortly afterward. Speaking to the
House of Commons, the minister Edmund Calamy declared, "It is no
signe of *an effeminate man,* but of *a penitent man to weep this day.* It is not

vain glory, but *Gods glory* to be heard sighing and groaning." There were times, in other words, when sympathy required tears from all—when even men had to match the model of grieving mothers.[27]

The close ties of Hooke's congregation with England lead him to a second emotional appeal based in these links between one land and the other. Laws, language, and birth provide New England with a "civill relation," while the thought of "naturall relations"—the "near kinsfolke" who sit "in griefe and sorrow"—ought, Hooke says, to "challenge our sympathize" [sic]. Beyond such natural relations, Hooke also details "a spirituall relation." As members of the same Body of Christ, these congregants of Taunton share a Christian bond with their spiritual "bone" and "flesh" back home. They overlap so closely, in fact, that the distance between them all but collapses. Hooke proclaims, "Shall they be wounded with the sword and speare, and not we pierced so much as with brotherly sorrow?" A pierced gut in England thus causes (or *should* cause) a pierced heart in New England. By listing such relations, Hooke enables his listeners to "fellow-feele" across the ocean: "oh let their sorrowes be our sorrows," he pleads, "and their miseries ours." Hooke's first strategy, then, does not seem all that different from the rhetorical use of sympathy in later American sentimental fiction. As Glenn Hendler explains, the nineteenth-century reader was called not just to feel *like* certain characters, but to feel *with* them—that is, "to partially submerge his or her identity and experience in the emotions of the fictional figure in order to transform partial sameness into identity." Hooke is preaching a sermon, not writing a novel, but his first strategy—based in sympathy—seems strikingly similar.[28]

His second strategy, meanwhile—bringing the conflict home to his hearers—highlights the use of sentiment to hide separation. For the Puritans, as we have seen, sympathy relied on *resemblance*, on "like will to like." Thus, even as Hooke distinguishes New and Old England, he nonetheless begs that such differences be set aside. He pleads, "Let us therefore, I beseech you, lay aside the thoughts of all our comforts this day, and let us fasten our eyes upon the calamities of our brethren in old *England.*" To weep for others while living in comfort required closing—or atleast masking—a gap between New England and Old. By the 1650s, as Harry S. Stout observes, the Puritans of New England were "less English than they thought. In a nostalgic sense England would always be their home, but by imperceptible degrees they had changed in their cultural orientation and their millennial hopes." In 1640, this drifting apart can already be seen in how much Hooke insists they stay together. The very *call* for sympathy suggests a distance and dissimilarity that must be overcome, a move that again links Hooke's sermon forward to some of the same paradoxes and difficulties faced by later sentimental fiction.[29]

In addition to answering charges of separation, Hooke defends New England against an accusation of irrelevance. New England can contribute to England's further reformation through both prayer and tears. At one point, for example, Hooke admits that New England's failings are partly responsible for England's catastrophe, then asks, "Shall we not help to quench the fire with our teares, that we have kindled with our sinnes?" Tears, that is, held power. Hooke proclaims, "And truly, if Gods justice might be satisfied with that Lands amendment without one drop of blood, though wee should shed store both of teares and blood to effect it, wee would greatly rejoice, and soone turne this day of Humiliation into a day of gratulation, praise, and thanksgiving."[30] Hooke turns to fellow feeling as a way of involvement. Where others will be wounded with the sword and spear, New England saints will be pierced with effective, event-altering, sympathetic sorrow.

Because so much depends upon a face glazed with tears, Hooke ends by simply praying for it: "The merciful God stirre up all our affections, and give us that godly sympathy, which that Land deserveth at our hands, and teach us to expresse it upon all occasions of ill tydings coming to our eares from thence."[31] Having done all he can to reach his listeners, Hooke finally leaves it to the Lord. In doing so, however, he reveals the wider significance of Puritan sympathy. Sympathy, as Hooke observes, is "godly." In other words, before right feeling made people refined, it marked them as religious. The proper display of sympathy could indicate election and affect events across the world—which, in turn, meant that a *display* mattered. Sympathy that was felt but not seen would not suffice. Hooke prays not just that God would stir it up, but also that he would "teach us to *expresse* it."

Hooke's persistent call for tears was not lost on the anonymous writer of the preface. In fact, the preface defends New Englanders precisely on the basis of their sympathy: "for they, not seeing, nor hearing of, onely fearing the ruines of this our Countrey, were deeply affected with it; a signe they love us." True unity, the preface declares, depends not on physical proximity, but on heartfelt affections: "for certainly *they are of us*, though *they bee gone from us, for if they were not of us*, their affections would not have so *continued to us*, as to fast and pray for us." In noting the power of affection to unite distant saints, the preface praises Hooke for targeting the heart. Hooke, it claims, sought "not [so much] to inform the judgment, as to worke upon the affections." Readers, therefore, should "expect not eare-pleasing, but heart-affecting phrases." And lest there be any doubt about how to respond, the preface prepares readers directly: "If thou bring thy heart with thee to the Reading of it thou mayst find thy heart melting by Reading of it, and then thou shalt have cause to blesse God for it." Melt, the preface demands. If your heart does not melt, the fault lies with you. Not only did Puritan writers call for fellow feeling; readers were expected to respond with tears, with a physical expression of sympathy stirred up by the text.[32]

To achieve that response, Puritan preachers and writers like Hooke occasionally employed a methodology not unlike that of later sentimentalists: they attempted to have readers see and experience the sorrows of others as if they were their own, and the success of their preaching could be determined by a bodily response, by tears in the pews. One mother's dead child connected her with any mother whose child has died; and if the reader's child has not died, one might, or could, or should be able to relate through the powerful love one had for a child still living (imagine if that child died). The emotions of the text translated through the imagination, which Hooke then aids with vivid depictions and emulations of emotion. As the sermon's characters come to life, their tears become contagious. Weeping breaks through the text; tears leap from word to eye; the physical sorrow spoken in the pulpit becomes embodied in the pew. This, at any rate, is what Hooke hopes will happen. A display of emotion would prove the loyalty of New England and give it a vital role to play in England's reformation.

When war did break out with the King, that role turned from passive weeping to active rage. Where in 1640 Hooke fastened on calamities, a few years later he turned specifically to the causes of the conflict, laying blame on the English prelacy. In *New Englands Sence of Old-England and Irelands Sorrows*, Hooke highlights the "speciall cause why the Prelats in *England* doe this day stinke in the nostrils of Gods people." That stink—that odor of "noysome" sins—required immediate action; and action, this time, meant militant prayer. Picturing New England churches as "severall Regiments, or bands of Souldiers lying in ambush here under the fearn and brushet of the Wildernes," Hooke enjoined congregants to "come upon the backs of Gods Enemies with deadly Fastings and Prayer, murtherers that will kill point blanke from one end of the world to the other."[33] Rather than offer sorrowful scenes to rouse weeping, Hooke declared, "Beloved! Let us hold, and heare no more of these sad complaints; for who can have pitie, and patience too? Have we the blood of Protestants in us? Doth the spirit of Jesus runne in our veines? It is enough: We cannot want *courage*, not but *play the men* for God and pure Religion."[34] Where they had played the women and wept in 1640, now they needed to "play the men" and fight.

Yet in the transformation from grief to rage, godly sympathy remained constant. Hooke asks, "But if it be not well with them, how can it bee well with us?" What one experienced, the other must also feel—no matter what distance came between. In fact, Hooke specifically discounted physical separation: "What though we are so farre from them in place? The needle in the Compasse is never quiet till it pointeth to the North, at a thousand times greater distance. Affections touched with grace, stand firme from one end of the World to the other." Drawing on magnetic imagery common to accounts of sympathy in the early modern era, Hooke asserted that affections united allies across the ocean. He thus exhorted listeners, "Let the cause of God affect us deeply, and the people and Cities of our God be alwaies in our eyes. And let the desolations of Christendome awaken us to frequent Prayers, and constant sympathy."[35]

Together, Hooke's Fast Day sermons of the 1640s reveal the power and significance of Puritan sympathy. In *New Englands Teares*, Hooke cites fellow feeling as a doctrine, mapping its pattern with biblical figures and tracing its command from scriptural precepts. Denying that New England Puritans had ever separated from the Church, he locates their continued unity in the heart and exhorts his congregation to display that loyalty with physical expressions of fellow feeling—with tears on the face. Moreover, he strives to produce such expressions through carefully described scenes of gory battles, broken homes, and weeping mothers. Such details enable congregants to identify imaginatively with those in grief—to put themselves in the place of bereft mothers. In *New Englands Sence*, Hooke draws on the same power of sympathy but for a very different purpose. Focusing on a careful description of sins, he attempts to demonstrate New England's support for Parliament while simultaneously turning his own congregation into saintly warriors, praying soldiers who would "play the men."

United but Unequal

When civil war broke out between Parliament and the king, the Puritan poet Anne Bradstreet imagined Old England and New as women engaged in conversation. Her poem "A Dialogue between Old England and New; Concerning Their Present Troubles, Anno, 1642" constructs the two lands as mother and daughter, with the daughter speaking first:

> *Alas, dear Mother, fairest queen and best,*
> *With honour, wealth, and peace, happy and blest;*
> *What ails thee hang thy head and cross thine arms?*
> *And sit i' th' dust, to sigh these sad alarms?*
> *What deluge of new woes thus overwhelm*
> *The glories of thy ever famous realm?*
> *What means this wailing tone, this mournful guise?*
> *Ah, tell thy daughter, she may sympathize.*[36]

By opening in this fashion, Bradstreet, like Hooke, situates emotion at the center of her text: it both prompts the dialogue and structures the conversation. As others did, so Bradstreet drew on a tradition of sympathy to write toward unity and amity, a coming together of New England and Old for the cause of greater reformation. Yet Bradstreet's use of this tradition—and, in particular, her treatment of female figures—highlights in a new way the politics and paradoxes involved in a Puritan mandate to sympathize with the godly.[37]

The daughter's opening pledge, for example, presented two reversals to the contemporary reader. First, it altered the direction of pleading. Where in 1630 emigrating Puritans begged for reciprocated affections, now, twelve years later, the homeland pleads with its colony. Yet that reversal masked a second, more substantial turnaround. The remigration of the early 1640s—as godly leaders hurried home to fight for the reformation—spelled disaster for a colonial economy that depended on a steady stream of newcomers. Cast into a deep recession, New England magistrates considered sending a commission back to England in order to beg, in essence, for a bailout. Some, however, opposed the idea—precisely because it would reveal their poverty. John Endicott, for example, argued that such a trip would "confirme my Lord Say and others of his Judgment, that new England can no longer subsist without the helpe of old England." In 1642, in other words, New England needed Old England's aid, not the other way around. Yet "A Dialogue" represents the mother as desperate for her daughter's sympathy.[38]

Such pleading, moreover, does not begin with words. Instead, Bradstreet uses New England's first speech to demonstrate that for sympathy to work, it required a sign that could be seen, an appearance that moved the viewer. The daughter's opening recognition of her mother's grief depends on the mother's physical expression of sorrow: she sits in the dust, hangs her head, crosses her arms, and sighs. As in Hooke's sermons, so here sympathy centers on a weeping mother. The poem's impetus arises not from rational disquisition—no act of speech—but solely from a female bodily display. Even so, the mother's mourning does not immediately produce sympathy. Having seen her grief, the daughter wants to know what it "means"—what has caused it, certainly, but more than that, what it *feels* like.[39] Sympathy requires that she *fellow-feel*, as if the case were her own, but the daughter cannot yet imagine her mother's pain. It is that desire—the need to experience Old England's sorrow for herself—which drives the poem. The goal, from beginning to end, is the daughter's opening plea and promise: "Ah, tell thy daughter, she may sympathize."

What the mother must "tell," moreover, are not the details of her political situation, but the particulars of her grief. The daughter presses her mother for specificity: "And thus (alas) your state you much deplore / In general terms, but will not say wherefore." The word "state" indicates both a political reality and an emotional condition, but New England emphasizes the latter. She wants to see more of the "affective body"—something else that can catch and move the listener.[40] After attempting to "guess ... out" her mother's problem, she demands again: "show your grief." And when her mother merely lists a series of sins, the daughter remains unsatisfied. It is not sins she wants, but miseries; not the cause of sores, but how they *feel*—their effect. New England lifts her own "guilty hands" and suggests, "A sharer in your punishment's my due." Yet such a discussion remains beside the point. New England says:

> But all you say amounts to this effect,
> Not what you feel, but what you do expect,
> Pray in plain terms, what is your present grief?
> Then let's join head and hearts for your relief.

Knowledge alone will not suffice. The heart must be moved, and Old England's account of sins has neither revealed her grief nor touched her daughter. That is why New England pleads: "show your grief," reveal "what you feel," tell "your present grief," so that, finally, she may "sympathize," joining knowledge with affection, uniting "head and hearts" to bring relief.[41]

Finally, then, the mother describes her war-torn land: "That thousands lay on heaps, here bleeds my woes." Feeling this pain, Old England begs:

Oh pity me in this sad perturbation,
My plundred towns, my houses' devastation,
My weeping virgins and my young men slain;
My wealthy trading fall'n, my dearth of grain,
The seedtime's come, but ploughman hath no hope
Because he knows not who shall in his crop.
The poor they want their pay, their children bread,
Their woeful mothers' tears unpitied.
If any pity in thy heart remain,
Or any childlike love thou dost retain,
For my relief, do what there lies in thee,
And recompense that good I've done to thee.

In her last speech, Old England finally presents the awful effects of war. She speaks of towns plundered, virgins weeping, youth slain, and "tears unpitied." Desperate to move her daughter, the mother provides a domestic scene of sorrow to do just that.[42]

And it works. "Your griefs I pity," the daughter proclaims, and she proceeds to provide relief. That assistance, however, may not be what the mother first expects. New England goes beyond Hooke's prayers and tears, providing her mother with a new perspective. She acts from affections, but her aid primarily involves interpretation. Saying, "wipe your eyes, / Shake off your dust, cheer up, and now arise," New England reveals her belief that from these troubles "much good fruit" might come. While the grief is real, the hope is greater: "in a while," New England concludes, "you'll tell another tale."[43] This peroration by New England seems, at first, to counter any genuine sense of fellow feeling. Far from sharing emotions, New England seems to rejoice at her mother's sorrows. Suffering appears to the daughter as the first sign of peace. Old England's troubles are, in that sense, labor pains: the Puritan Reformation is being born. As such, the effects of war are cause for joy. The poem may begin in sympathy, but it seems to end in separation. The daughter and mother do not see eye-to-eye, and the daughter's duty is to put her mother straight.[44]

Even so, New England's final speech arises from continued connection. The daughter begins by claiming her tie through the body: "You are my mother nurse, and I your flesh, / Your sunken bowels gladly would refresh."[45] From the beginning of emigration, New England Puritans had proclaimed the Church of England their mother; as both *The Humble Request* and Cotton's farewell sermon stated, they received salvation from her breasts. Here, Bradstreet tightens that bond. As New England once shared her mother's body, *so she still does,* and it is precisely the shared affections of that body which prompts her speech. Having descended into her mother's "sunken bowels" and felt her pain, the daughter can then attempt to provide relief by changing her mother's point of view. She does not chide; she consoles. And she consoles her mother precisely because she herself has finally felt the sorrow that needs relief.

Yet the mother does not willingly become a spectacle for her daughter's emotions. Instead, she has to be forced into that position through the course of the poem. Responding to the initial promise of sympathy, the mother protests, "Are [you] ignorant indeed of these my woes? / Or must my *forced* tongue these griefs disclose? / And must myself dissect my tattered state, / Which 'mazed Christendom stands wond'ring at?" Not only does she initially disdain having to display her grief; she recognizes that such a requirement arises from her daughter's *lack* of feeling. A true daughter, she complains, would not demand dissection. In fact, New England's request proves a division that never should have existed. Old England accuses her: "And thou a child, a limb, and dost not feel / My fainting weak'ned body now to reel?"[46] The lack of sympathy—the promise *yet* to sympathize—reveals a rift, in the same way that Hooke's pleading for sympathy and his efforts to stir it up demonstrated how little sympathy the congregation actually felt. The more one has to beg for fellow feeling, the less fellow feeling exists—a point relating to the whole Puritan paradox of both commanding sympathy and proclaiming that it flowed from grace. A recurring conundrum for Puritans was whether or not sympathy *could* be stirred up or commanded, and whether the sympathy that arose from a particularly moving scene or sermon could actually reveal anything about the supposed sympathizer. To put it differently: what is the relation between genuine fellow feeling and rhetorical forms?

These questions come to the fore in the mother's initial answers to her daughter, and as the daughter continues to press for scenes of grief, Old England at first refuses to comply. She says, "Before I tell th' effect, I'll show the cause," launching into a series of monologues that attempt to *interpret* what is happening.[47] The daughter, impatient with such speeches, returns again to demand a bodily display, a picture to move the heart. Only after several lines of stalling does the mother finally give in and yield up a scene of grief. Such delays suggests not only the wider Puritan paradox of sympathy, but also, in Bradstreet's poem, a subtle discomfort with the use of affective bodies—weeping women who move others not with words, arguments, and explanations, but only with their tears.

In addition, being reduced to such a position alters the mother's understanding of the emotional experience. Where the daughter has originally promised sympathy, Old England pleads for pity. While both of these emotions involve some form of fellow feeling, they do not describe the same experience. In particular, pity introduces an unequal distribution of power. The mother begs, and the daughter condescends. While fellow feeling still operates, the power of sympathy nonetheless breaks down into a language of pity. In the end, New England offers an affection based not in likeness, but in a willingness to overcome *un*likeness—a willingness, that is, to lay aside her own comfort, pity her mother, and provide relief.[48]

These dynamics in "A Dialogue between Old England and New"—the political reversals, the mother's physical display of sorrow, the transition from sympathy to pity, and the daughter's final interpretative speech—reveal it in many ways to be a poem about the power of sympathy itself. Beginning with the mother's "mournful guise," the poem progresses through historical, political, and theological layers to end, finally, with a "woeful mothers' tears unpitied." This opening and closing turn the mother's two most effective statements into *non*statements: bodily displays, rather than reasoned monologues. With such bookends Bradstreet both adopts a Puritan tradition of weeping women and subtly critiques it, allowing the mother to forestall her reduction into voiceless tears. Bradstreet furthers her criticism in the character of the daughter, who does not fall into weeping but rises into speech. Throughout, however, this daughter accrues power by pressing for scenes of grief, directing the conversation through her mother's emotional need—a need which in fact reversed the historical situation. In the absence of political and financial superiority, Bradstreet accords New England an emotional and moral upper hand.

Loyal but Distinct

In the years following 1642, the unity of saints in New and Old England faced several strains. As antiroyalist divines met in Westminster to develop an ecclesiastical system and statement of faith, they quickly split between Congregationalists (allied with New England) and Presbyterians (allied with Scotland). Already in 1642, various members of Parliament sent letters to John Cotton, Thomas Hooker, and John Davenport asking them to return and help the Congregational cause. Hooker declined, Davenport could not be spared, and Cotton did not want to go alone. In place of their physical presence, these ministers and others began writing books and pamphlets to explain, defend, and promote the New England Way. Such efforts, however, met with little initial success. As Presbyterians gained power, Congregationalists allied themselves to a variety of independent sects, which in turn enabled the Presbyterians to charge them with breeding heresy.

The situation grew desperate for the Congregationalist cause in the mid-1640s, leaving many New Englanders hesitant about their relation to the homeland. Shortly after war broke out, Massachusetts Bay proclaimed its support of Parliament by omitting an oath of allegiance to King Charles and restraining all those "malignant spirits" which began to "declare themselves for the king." Parliament returned the favor by repealing tariffs and sending prisoners to serve as indentured servants. Yet these acts of unity proceeded with caution. As the Presbyterians rose in England, an assembly of New England ministers met to rebuke elders who "went about to set up some things according to the presbytery." Forced to consider in 1646 "in what relation we stood to the state of England," magistrates both declared subjection and carved out a measure of independence. In local "agitations," they wrote, "our agents shall discern the mind of the parliament toward us, which if it be propense and favorable, there may be a fit season to procure such countenance of our proceedings ... But if the parliament should be less inclinable to us, we wait upon providence for the preservation of our just liberties." When they sent a petition to Parliament declaring both obedience and autonomy, the General Court of Massachusetts was so uncertain of the outcome that it resisted sending troops against an Indian threat because it was "very probable, that their charter would be called in, as illegal." In other words, most New Englanders remained convinced about the cause of Parliament against the King, but far less certain about Parliament per se. If England turned into a Presbyterian nation, New England would have to maintain enough separation and self-governance to practice its own form of polity.[49]

Contrary to expectations in the mid-1640s, the later years of that decade and the early years of the next saw the triumph of Independency (a name for both Congregationalism and the mix of independent allies that Congregationalists joined). At the conclusion of the first civil war in 1646, the Scots grew angry with Parliament for failing to institute Presbyterianism. As a result, they pledged to help Charles I regain his throne if he would promise to succeed where Parliament failed. Such a turn led to the short-lived second civil war of 1648, in which Oliver Cromwell crushed the Scottish army. Soon afterward, Parliament purged itself of Presbyterians. Cromwell, the head of the army, continued to gain power, and the cause of Congregationalism prospered with his rise. The general turn in New England's fortunes can be glimpsed by the relative number of Fast and Thanksgiving Days it proclaimed. From 1640–1642, in the build-up to war, New England called sixteen Fasts and three Thanksgiving Days. During the first civil war, from 1643–1645, New England held twenty-one Fasts and only one Day of Thanksgiving. As New England battled Presbyterianism after the war, the numbers shifted slightly, with eleven Fast Days and four Thanksgiving Days. But as Independency gained power from 1649–1651, Fasts decreased to ten, while Thanksgivings rose to seven. 1652 represents the only year of this span when Thanksgiving Days outnumbered Fast Days, with four of the former and two of the latter.[50] The emotional contours of the broader community as prescribed in New England related directly to events across the sea.

Even so, New England remained distinct—a Congregational way that could not be collapsed back into the mother country. God had preserved New England from the sorrows of war precisely because it maintained a better covenant—because, as the minister John Norton wrote in 1648, devout men "left our country, our kindred, and our fathers' house, for the sake of a purer worship."[51] Such purity not only heightened New England's significance; it gave the leaders of that land a platform from which to teach their "brethren" back east. Thus, the relationship with England remained both dependent and independent: New England Puritans had never separated, but they *were* distinct.

When Edward Johnson, a military man and founder of Woburn, Massachusetts, began writing a history of New England in 1650, he inherited this same double-framed transatlantic relationship. In *The Wonder-Working Providence of Sions Savior in New England*, Johnson exalts New England while denying separation. Such a view comes framed, furthermore, by the transition to a new generation of New England Puritans: Hooker died in 1647, Winthrop and Shepard in 1649, and Cotton in 1652. In these deaths, Johnson records, all of New England "began to read their approaching rod in the bend of [the Lord's] brows and frowns of his former favourable countenance toward them." New England's riches and comforts had once signaled God's pleasure; now they "brought a fulness on many, even to loath the very honey-comb, insomuch that good wholesome truths would not go down."[52] As a second generation came into leadership, Johnson sought to connect it with the zeal of their mothers and fathers. And in negotiating both New England's relationship with Old and the second generation's link to the first, Johnson employed the language and literary techniques of sympathy—rhetorical devices that in many ways resemble sentimental strategies long before the rise of sentimental literature.

Wonder-Working Providence begins, however, not with connections, but distinctions. As Hooke once called upon the military might of prayer, so Johnson invokes martial imagery to describe New England's exalted place. For him, the Puritan emigrants were neither frightened refugees nor spiritual pilgrims; they were soldiers marching in the light of God. "When England began to decline in Religion, like lukewarme Laodicea," he famously begins, "and instead of purging out Popery, a farther compliance was sought ... in this very time Christ the glorious King of his Churches, raises an Army out of our English Nation, for freeing his people from their long servitude under usurping Prelacy; and ... creates a New England to muster up the first of his Forces in." Instead of deserting worldwide reformation, the Puritan emigrants strode forward to civilize a wilderness, set up a godly society, and provide a place for Christ's return. The battle is both epic and international, and New England forms the vanguard, the foremost regiment of God. In providing such grandeur to the lives of ordinary New Englanders, Johnson thus offers them a special sense of being chosen, a feeling of election.[53] That feeling of New England's election had to be tempered by avowals of continued union. Johnson published *Wonder-Working Providence* in London, after all, at a time when Congregationalist allies held greatest power. The work thus presents both a portrait of New England's blessings and a hopeful proclamation of loyalty and love. Johnson wanted to show English critics what *service* New England had provided—an assistance motivated by mutual affections. In a sense, then, Johnson faced one of the central problems of later sentimentalists: "how to create and perpetuate community once the traditional bonds of blood and geography have been loosened."[54]

This basic position of New England—a distinct mission with continued affections—emerges most clearly in Johnson's scene of the Puritan departure (book 1, chapter 12). As with his general history, the chapter opens in exalted difference. Johnson calls the exodus a "voluntary banishment," and the first dialogue only deepens the rift. Friends try to convince the emigrants to stop their foolishness, turn around, and stay put. But the emigrants refuse: "With bold resolvednesse," Johnson writes, they reject "the Pleasure, Profits and Honours of this World." Thus, the departure seems to establish precisely the irreparable separation that Johnson must disavow: he seems to distinguish between the "People of Christ" and the citizens of England.[55] Yet as this scene continues, such differences get drowned out in a flood of tears. The Puritan emigrants—those "stout Souldiers of Christ"—suddenly burst into weeping. Powerful emotions appear in two friends (one emigrating and one not), who together discuss their mutual love and "melting" souls. Soon, the friends fall silent, finding "their farther speech strangled from the depth of their inward dolor, with breast-breaking sobs, till leaning their heads each on others shoulders, they let fall the salt-dropping dews of vehement affection." When speech returns—"having a little eased their hearts with the still streames of Teares"—the nonemigrating friend lists the dangers of sea, attempting one last time to prevent departure. But before the other can answer, he "lockes his friend fast in his armes: holding each other thus for some space of time, they weepe again." Copious tears pour in a "watery-path upon their Cheekes," dropping into "the brinish Ocean." Such weeping, furthermore, arises with touch: the friends lean on each other, hold each other fast, and lead each other "hand in hand." Verbal communication again becomes secondary to bodily display: in Johnson's departure scene, sobs overtake speech.[56]

Such sobs, in addition, cannot be contained. The emigrants, trying to put Christ first, attempt to "lock up their naturall affections for a time." Yet "naturall affection will still claime her right, and manifest her selfe to bee in the body by looking out at the Windowes in a mournefull manner." These godly voyagers, Johnson emphasizes, are bound not just through "spirituall love," but also through "all Kindred of bloud that binds the bowells of affection in a true Lovers knot." For Johnson, that knot of bowels is the point. Far from being nascent separatists in a New World, the Puritans of New England were united to their English kin through their very bodies—through bowels, affections, and tears. It is not surprising, then, that Johnson's strongest statement of union arrives at the end of this chapter. Those remaining behind proclaim: "for Englands sake they are going from England to pray without ceasing for England." Then they melt back into tears, "adding many drops of salt liquor to the ebbing Ocean." And just as the ocean touches both shores, so these tears create an almost physical bond that connects the saints of one land to the "soldiers" of another. Affection, then, seeks to overcome the fact of separation with a proclamation of unity based in the heart and appearing on the face.

United by feeling, the godly can never be separated, no matter what may come between. Long before sentimental literature, Johnson's departure scene exemplifies what Marianne Noble calls "the classic paradox of sentimentalism, which is that the pain of separation fosters a unity of feeling among sufferers." Love is linked to loyalty and tears mark a separation that the tears themselves attempt to overcome.[57]

In Johnson's particular case, however, the unbroken affections witnessed in this emotional display also mask New England's lack of risk. Puritans in New England would serve the reformation through prayers and tears; their bodies and homes, meanwhile, would remain unthreatened. In other words, to go from England in order "to pray without ceasing for England" rings a bit like overcompensation: after all, while colonists prayed, others laid down their lives. The sense of survivor's guilt—of compensating for this lack of risk—also helps explain other features of *Wonder-Working Providence*, such as Johnson's martial imagery and his litany of the miseries emigrants endured. In each of these cases, Johnson seems to insist that the godly who remained to fight were not the only ones who suffered; New England also went through hell in order to bring heaven down to earth.

Although New England's hard service for worldwide reformation grounds Johnson's history, the unity of that effort still relies primarily on a language of fellow feeling. Such an appeal to unity resurfaces later in the text when Johnson lists "two sorts of persons ... whom the Elders and Brethren here do highly honour in Christ ... namely the godly Presbyterian party, and the Congregationall sincere servants of Christ." These two parties, Johnson declares, must cease fighting and get along. He adds, "The Author could wish that (with bowells of compassion, sweet simpathising affection of Brethren knit together in that transcendent love of Christ, which couples all his distanced flockes together) they would seriously ponder this History." With the rise of Independency, Johnson had the space to be generous, holding out his hand and recommending a renewal of affections.[58] Moreover, such an appeal reveals how Johnson would prefer his text to be approached. The proper way to "ponder" *Wonder-Working Providence* is with "bowells of compassion" and "sweet simpathizing affection." Read with feeling, Johnson proclaims, and you will be rewarded with a sympathy that renews affection and rebuilds a common transatlantic godly community.

Beyond working toward this tightening of bonds with England, Johnson also tries to inspire New England Puritans to take up their parents' cause. In this attempt, he likewise employs techniques of sympathetic identification. Johnson's second audience provides a different gloss on the same scenes of hardship that, for the godly in England, proved New England's difficult service. The departure scene, for example, speaks one way to English critics and another way to New England's second genera-tion. In this scene of sorrow, the children of emigrants can imagine and experience the sacrifices their mothers and fathers once made. Sharing such an experience, they can then take up with renewed enthusiasm the cause that led their parents to endure so much misery, grief, and pain. Just as Johnson draws a picture of affectionate union between New England and Old, so he appeals to the sentiments of the second generation in order to link them with the first. Addressing his colonial audience, Johnson establishes an emotional bond that runs not spatially (across the sea), but temporally (from the present to the past).

In both cases, the emotional participation of readers remains vital. In order to encourage that participation, Johnson first, quite simply, requests it: "Beloved countrymen, and our dear brethren in Christ," he writes, "step into the closet of your own hearts with us, and see if there will not be some things in this following verse that may suit your condition as well as ours, that having sown in tears, we may reap with joy."[59] Likewise, before the Puritan departure scene, Johnson writes: "Passe on and attend with teares, if thou hast any, the following discourse." Repeatedly, Johnson exhorts his readers to cry, to show feeling, to respond with emotion. When he describes the new day about to dawn in New England, he links a commit-ment to this vision with the physicality of tears: "for the day of his high Power is come, yea, his appointed time to have mercy upon Sion is at hand, all you whose eyes of pity so see her in the dust, streame down with pear-like drops of compassion, a little mixture of the unconceivable joy for the glorious worke of Christ." True saints—those who see New England's proper place—will read Johnson's work through eyes blurred with tears.[60]

Beyond exhorting tears, Johnson helps his readers to weep by listing New England's sorrows. His litany of obstacles, ailments, diseases, and deaths proves the Lord's providence—God has preserved them through such troubles—while creating space for compassion. After reproduc-ing the experience of emigration, therefore, Johnson proclaims, "Behold him whom you have peirced, preparing to peirce your hearts with his *Wonder-working Providence.*" This is the first mention of Johnson's title, and it arrives directly connected to an affective response. *Wonder-Working Providence* is nothing less than the Lord's attempt to pierce readers' hearts. To aid the Lord in such an endeavor, Johnson, like others, employs the suffering bodies of women, offering an image of "weakly Women … with their young Babes, whom they nurture up with their Breasts, while their bodies are tossed on the tumbling Waves." He ends his description of this difficult voyage by explaining that each "Remarkable Providence" shows "the Worke of Christ, is not to bee laid aside because of difficulties." Yet more occurs than mere didacticism. Johnson wraps his characters in suffering not just because deliverance proves the providence of God, but also because suffering gains the sympathy of readers.[61]

In addition to detailed miseries, Johnson employs particularity to engage his readers' emotions. Individual stories bring the larger narrative to life. For example, Johnson tells the story of the Antinomian Controversy through the figure of a single man (probably himself, though he remains unnamed), whose body takes on the colony's troubles. Broken down, weeping, wandering aimlessly through the woods, he finally seeks out the "soule-ravishing" Reverend Shepard, who obligingly ravishes the man's soul. During Shepard's sermon, Johnson writes, the man "was metamorphosed, and was faine to hang down the head often, least his watry eyes should blab abroad the secret conjunction of his affections." At that time, this person bowed his head and hid his feelings; now, however, Johnson publishes them for all. More importantly, he makes the public weeping of this private individual stand in for the entire controversy. A strong supporter of the elders' position, Johnson writes that the Lord responded to the man's tears by clearing away "all those false Doctrines" of the antinomians—just as they were washed from New England.[62]

As Johnson's account of the Antinomian Controversy indicates, he often models an emotion so that it can be reproduced in readers. In this scene, the word "echo" indicates not just what happens in the story, but also what *should* happen in the reader. In the "narrow Indian path," where Johnson's "man" weeps, he finds that "none but sencelesse Trees and eccohing Rocks make answer to his heart-easeing mone." Such a lack of sympathy magnifies the colony's distress; New England is so disordered that fellow feeling can be found only in the rocks and trees. By displaying such incongruity, Johnson implicitly invites a more human response, an echo resounding in the reader's heart. In the departure scene, Johnson displays just what such an echo should look like. After asking readers to "attend with teares," he describes the godly breaking into sobs: "Many make choise of some solitary place to eccho out their bowel-breaking affections in bidding their Friends farwell."[63] Yet while each *place* remains solitary, no person stands alone. Dialogue immediately follows as the two friends discuss their "melting" love—their mutual affections that answer sob for sob. In fact, the only solitary person at this point is, potentially, the reader. And if the reader has truly begun to attend with tears, then proper affections will continue to "eccho out."

In *Wonder-Working Providence*, therefore, Johnson's many different goals depend on readers attending to the text with tears. To achieve such a response, Johnson employs several "sentimental" strategies: he calls for emotional reactions (apostrophe); he offers vivid lists of struggles and separations (broken families and ruptured bonds); he describes historic events through specific individuals (particularity); and he models emotions with characters in the tale (mimesis). In each case, he attempts to connect his audience to the text and, through it, to each other. Each layer of union relies on the power of sympathy, the bond of tears.

In the Puritans' accounting of themselves and their relation to England, then, sympathy could be used as a handy rhetorical tool to both emphasize unity and increase the sense of it through the power of fellow feeling. The process of stirring up sympathy, moreover, could lead Puritans to literary strategies that look in many ways like precursors of sentimentalism. Puritanism, of course, could not be called "sentimental"—a term which anyway does not exist until the eighteenth century. Most Puritan publications in the 1640s disputed church polity in systematic treatises, defending the New England Way and urging it on the godly in England through writings that relied on sound logic, careful distinctions, and well-wrought definitions. Even the titles of such texts suggest efforts that have little to do with sympathy or sentimental technique: they were "defenses," "answers," and "surveys" that "cleared" proponents from accusations.[64] Yet as the Antinomian Controversy demonstrated—and as the English Civil Wars amplified—these texts came embedded in the principle that persuasion requires a broader unity of affections. Writers thus exalted New England's distinct polity while denying separation, recognizing that any lessons taught would be learned only if transatlantic readers considered themselves united by mutual affections. Meanwhile, those texts which aimed specifically at strengthening (or renewing) mutual affections relied more explicitly on a language of sympathy. And in so doing, these seventeenth-century Puritans employed techniques that would later become central aspects of sentimental literature.

5

Sympathy, Sincerity, and Sentimental Technique

THE LANGUAGE OF sympathy—and the early forms of sentimentalism it produced in Puritan literature—appears most vividly in the writings of Puritan missionaries. When Puritan ministers began evangelizing Native Americans in the mid-seventeenth century, they paid particular attention to weeping. Not only did Indian tears seem to come in torrents; they also seemed contagious. In one Puritan tract, for example, when a son entreated his father's forgiveness for the sin of drunkenness, he "took [his father] by the hand, at which his father burst forth into great weeping." Taking his mother's hand, she, too, began to weep, and from there the tears spread. More Indians wept. The English wept. Soon, "the house was filled with weeping on every side; and then we went to prayer, in all which time Cutshamekin wept, in so much that when wee had done the board he stood upon was all dropped with his teares." From father to son, from son to parents, from one family to the others, and from the Indians to the English, the weeping proliferated, and the spread of tears confirmed the presence of God.[1]

Emotional displays such as this are more often associated with sentimental novels than with Puritan ministers. Yet the issue at stake was common to them both: how to discover, witness, judge, and reveal a heart that is sincere. The Puritan focus on sincerity stretches back at least to the Reformation, linking Calvinism to later cultures of sensibility and sentimentalism. For instance, John Preston's monumental treatise *The New Covenant*—a work Perry Miller once declared "prerequisite to any understanding of thought and theology in seventeenth-century New England"—opens by claiming that "in the performance of all the Duties of

Sanctification, *Sinceritie* is all in all."[2] For Puritans, the effects of sanctification did not matter (or signify) unless they emerged sincerely; and one witness of that sincerity was an outward, visible display of emotion. But the display itself was never enough. True emotion had to spread. A moved heart had to move hearts in order for those affected to proclaim the original emotion sincere. Later sentimentalists also hoped visible expressions of feeling, along with the emotional response they produced, could evidence authentically moved (and *moveable*) hearts. And one source for that strain of thinking—one nexus of sincerity, sympathy, and emotional display, along with the way sympathy could discipline and surveill subjects—can be found in Puritan theology.[3]

This nexus powerfully influenced the writings of Puritan missionaries. During the same years that William Hooke, Anne Bradstreet, Edward Johnson, and others used sympathy to negotiate transatlantic relations, John Eliot, the Puritan minister of Roxbury, began employing fellow feeling both to convert Native Americans and to prove those conversions true. His methods, goals, and progress have been recorded in a series of texts now most often called the Eliot tracts. Written by multiple Puritans in New England and published in London between 1643 and 1671, these letters, lists, narratives, dedications, prefaces, and epilogues reveal a careful search for authentic conversions—a hunt so cautious and meticulous that it repeatedly highlights the difficulties involved in the mediation and determination of sincerity. While requiring certain objective practices (such as a knowledge of the catechism and "civilized" behavior), Puritan ministers frequently evaluated conversions based on their own gut reactions, judging as they were *moved* to judge.

Native Americans, knowing this, drew on their own cultural heritage to heighten the emotional performances of prayers, meetings, and confessions. The Algonquians of New England included the Wampanoag, Massachusett, Nipmuc, Pocumtuck, Pequot, Mohegan, Schaghticoke, Paugussett, Niantic, and Narragansett. These nations shared many cultural practices and were often intimately interlinked through marriage, alliance, and trade. Political decisions originated in the village and were negotiated both there and more broadly through the persuasive ability of sachems; these sachems often were chosen and led through their power of speech. The cultures Eliot approached, in other words, already had strong traditions of oratory.[4] And when it became clear that Puritan ministers needed to be moved by testimonials of conversion, Native converts who wished to convince them drew on their own cultures to satisfy such demands.

But the problem went beyond face-to-face meetings between Puritan ministers and Native converts. The Eliot tracts also contend with a suspicious transatlantic audience. To convince far-flung readers that Indians really had converted, therefore, writers such as Eliot amplified emotional displays on the premise that readers would believe these reports once they, too, were sufficiently moved. When confronted with the problem of judging sincerity, in other words, Puritan writers turned again to literary techniques that would later be termed "sentimental." A long theology of sympathy linked to sincerity and persuasion prepared the way for Puritan missionary activities to issue in scenes of contagious weeping.

Native Americans and the Puritan Missions

From the beginning of Puritan settlement in New England, the conversion of Native Americans formed a central—if specious—argument for emigration. Before he left England, John Winthrop, the future governor of Massachusetts Bay, justified departure by first explaining that it would serve the church "to carry the Gospell into those parts of the world." When John Endicott led an advance group to Salem in 1628, he received a letter reminding him to pursue "the main end of our Plantation, by endeavouring to bring the Indians to the knowledge of the Gospel." The 1629 Charter of the Massachusetts Bay Colony officially endorsed this position, suggesting that the inhabitants of New England should "be soe religiously, peacablie, and civilly governed, as their good life and orderlie conversation maie wynn and incite the natives of country to the knowledg and obedience of the onlie true God and Savior of mankinde, and the Christian faith"—calling this, again, the plantation's "principall ende."[5] The colony's seal put an exclamation mark on this point: it pictured an Indian pleading, "Come over and help us."[6] The reasons for leaving, the charter, letters from the founders, the seal itself—all of these early documents seemed to suggest that the Puritans had moved to New England principally to convert Native Americans.

Despite such pronouncements, the Puritans did not begin mission work for fourteen years. Such a delay sprang primarily from an underlying affective model of conversion: as the charter put it, the Puritans would win converts through a "good life and orderlie conversation," not through active missionary service. The 1628 letter to Endicott elucidates this view: conversion would "be the speedier and better effected," it explained, if "you have a diligent and watchful eye over our own people, that they live unblamable and without reproof, and demean themselves justly and courteous towards the Indians." Behaving in such a manner would "draw them to affect our persons, and consequently our religion." By *first* winning the affections of the Natives, Puritans could *then* convert them to the Gospel. So long as the Puritans lived well, the Native Americans would naturally desire to emulate their "superior" way of life.[7]

This policy persisted until the early 1640s, when the Puritans suddenly took up missionary work in earnest. At that time, New England faced a rise in criticism from abroad about their lack of efforts, some claiming that their charter's supposed "main end" had never been pursued, let alone fulfilled. It did not help that Roger Williams, a persistent nemesis, published a book in 1643 which portrayed himself as the primary missionary to Native Americans. Critical pressure coincided, moreover, with the start of hostilities in England. As many of New England's leading citizens migrated back to the homeland in order to fight the *real* fight of the reformation, missionary enterprises offered colonial Puritans a way to advance the cause of Christ on their own ground and in their own way. In addition to such external spurs, a colonial realignment of authority encouraged the start of missions. In 1644, six sachems signed themselves into the jurisdiction of Massachusetts Bay and agreed, on behalf of their nations, to receive religious instruction. When Puritan missionaries finally did set out to evangelize the Indians, they did not go to just any they could find. They specifically targeted those who lived nearest—the groups who also happened to be most weakened by disease and most dependent on English protection, especially the Nipmucks and Massachusetts.[8] In other words, the opening of missionary enterprises had as much to do with local authority, transatlantic politics, and Puritan identity as it did with any heartfelt need to save Native souls.[9]

Native Americans who actually listened to Eliot had multiple reasons for doing so. It is impossible to say, of course, what drove any particular "Praying Indian" to convert, but many motivations have been offered. Some, for example, may have seen it as the only available option: mere survival depended on conversion. Others perceived in Eliot's "Praying Towns"—towns composed entirely of converted and converting Indians—an opportunity to continue living on familiar land. In addition, conversion brought a new and different route to food, shelter, a means of livelihood, medical services, and trade goods. Some converts may have wanted to gain English literacy and saw Christianity as the best means to do so. Still others may have seen in conversion a way to rejuvenate traditional forms of authority. For example, Cutshamekin, a sachem of the Massachusetts, had grown very powerful through his exploitation of English policies, and some Native Americans under him used Christianity to lower his status and reduce their tributes, "return[ing] the office of sachem to a more consensual form."[10] Finally, some converts may have fulfilled Puritan expectations and genuinely exchanged systems of belief, deeming Christianity a better answer to their spiritual, emotional, and intellectual needs.[11]

In this chapter I do not investigate the many motivations proposed or make pronouncements about individual Indians; instead, I ask what Praying Indians had to do in order to make conversions *appear* sincere. Even the purest converts still had to convince the Puritan ministers who sat in judgment on their case. For example, in 1654, when Puritan elders refused to grant a group of Praying Indians the right to form a church, a sullen Eliot commented, "I and some others know more of the sincerity of some of them, then others doe, and are better satisfied with them."[12] Whether or not these Indians *were* sincere, as Eliot believed, they still needed to convince others besides Eliot of authentically converted hearts.

One precondition for authentic conversion was a whole new way of life. Eliot and other Puritan ministers stressed that conversion required "civility," and they imposed new forms of agriculture, new gender roles, new hair and clothing styles, and new forms of government on converts. Despite such massive changes, many Native American converts retained ties with their former ways of life: Praying Indians dwelling in Praying Towns adapted Native cultures to Christianity and Christianity to Native cultures. For instance, archaeologists have discovered that the Indians of Natick, the largest Praying Town, still buried material goods with their dead, presumably attributing *Manitou*, or spiritual power, to these items just as they had formerly done. Puritan missionary efforts, in other words, resulted in a culture all its own—a group of converts distinct from both non-Christian Native Americans and the English Puritans.[13]

This Christian Indian culture developed out of meager beginnings. In 1646 John Eliot approached Cutshamekin with the gospel, and the Massachusett sachem summarily rebuffed and ridiculed him. Eliot nearly gave up, but just then a group of Massachusett Indians settled at Nonantum (near Cambridge) asked to hear him preach. Eliot obliged the request, and he received such a welcoming response that he began to take mission work seriously.[14] Three decades later, just before the outbreak of King Philip's War, the Puritans could boast of fourteen Praying Towns, almost 2,300 Praying Indians, and multiple translations of devotional works (including the entire Bible) into the Algonquin language.[15]

John Eliot's status in New England as "the Apostle to the Indians" rose and fell with the perception of his work. When missions first began, New England badly needed converts, and leading Puritan figures, including the ministers Thomas Shepard and John Wilson, accompanied him to Nonantum. By 1650, some Puritans, including Eliot, believed that Native Americans were not in fact native at all, but actually had descended from the Hebrews and constituted the lost tribes of Israel. The attendant eschatological implications—namely, that the end times were near and that they would begin in New England—elevated the importance of missionary work. Within a decade, however, Eliot's star had fallen and many saw him as somewhat quirky. His ideas about a godly form of government, inauspiciously published just before the restoration of Charles II, advocated a commonwealth without a monarchy—a view he was forced to recant (and a book that Boston quickly burned). By 1670, most in New England, including Eliot, did not believe the Indians were Israelites. King Philip's War, waged from 1675 to 1676, increased the violence and hostility toward Native Americans in general and further isolated Eliot, especially when he defended Praying Indians against English abuses. Suspicion and antagonism, which had always existed, increased the nearer Englishpersons dwelt to Praying Towns, in part because English settlers wanted the land devoted to Native converts. For all these reasons, Eliot and his work never represented a majority position in New England. He was usually respected and occasionally revered, but he was never fully embraced.[16]

Even so, the Eliot tracts—the eleven promotional documents produced in conjunction with these Puritan missions—received the endorsement of leading Puritans in New England, for regardless of Eliot's reputation, these publications continued to serve three crucial functions. First, they boosted New England's image, particularly in England where its reputation hung in the balance. In response to criticisms leveled by Presbyterians, ex-New Englanders and anti-Puritan authorities, these texts showed accusers that the charter had indeed been fulfilled: missionaries actively pursued the principal end of their plantation. Second, Puritan leaders used these documents to raise funds: the New England Company, a missionary society established by Parliament in 1649, published them to generate cash.[17] And finally, these publications authenticated the Puritan missions themselves; beyond representing and promoting conversions, the Eliot tracts asked readers to *believe* in them—to consider both the missionary work and its results, the Native converts, sincere.

In their intense focus on sincerity, the Eliot tracts shed insight as well on beliefs and practices that were basic to much of Puritanism. John Eliot was certainly not typical, but he was not the only writer of these tracts; many leading ministers and witnesses contributed. And though Puritanism was a multifaceted religious movement consisting of many different and occasionally competing religious beliefs, the number of authors—and the reduction of Puritan theology to its most basic elements for dissemination among the Indians—enables the Eliot tracts to instruct modern readers about what many Puritans believed, especially in regard to conversion. The signs that proved sincerity in their own churches return in the evaluation of Indian converts: ministers searched for godly laws, good behavior, free prayer, righteous inquiry, and catechistical knowledge. But as these tracts demonstrate, the signs of sincere conversion also included emotional display and emotional response—often in excess and often used to confirm all the rest.

Religious Affections and Tender Hearts

The proof of a sincere conversion amounted to a demonstration of regenerate affections. These affections, for the Puritans, were not the mere stuff of transitory feelings; affections *could* be synonymous with emotions, but theologically they also indicated the basic bent of a person's heart, a leaning toward either God or sin.[18] As the Puritan theologian Richard Baxter explained, "[A] Converted man, is illuminated to discern the Loveliness of God: and so far believeth the Glory that is to be had with God, that his heart is taken up to it, and set more upon it, then on any thing in this world." Utilizing imagery often employed to describe "sympathy," Baxter continued, "As the fire doth mount upward, and the Needle that is touched with the load-stone still turneth to the North: so the Converted soul is enclined unto God."[19]

When Puritan ministers set off to discover this disposition, they searched for knowledge of Christian doctrine. After sermons, for example, Eliot would ask Native Americans for their response, and the quality of their questions demonstrated to him the presence of religious affections. Early in his enterprises he wrote, "I have heard few Christians when they begin to looke toward God, make more searching questions that they might see things really, and not onely have a notion of them." Later, he listed several such questions, adding, "by these you may perceive in what streame their minds are carried, and that the Lord Jesus hath at last an enquiring people among these poor naked men."[20] But evidence of knowledge went beyond good questions. In another tract, Eliot recorded an encounter between two Indians and a Quaker, where the Indians stood fast for anti-Quaker orthodoxy. After narrating their conversation, Eliot wrote, "I did solemnly blesse God who had given them so much understanding in his truth, and some ability to discerne between Truth and Error, and an heart to stand for the Truth, and against Error; and I cannot but take it as a Divine Testimony of Gods blessing upon my poor labours." For Puritans, a growth in knowledge could witness a new birth in Christ.[21]

By itself, however, knowledge did not count for much; what true converts learned, they also had to live. As one Puritan writer noted in *The Clear Sun-Shine*, among the Indians "every notion, breeds motion." Such motion formed an essential element of genuine conversion. Indeed, the Puritans believed that Native Americans could not join the church until they reformed their habits and behaviors to fit with the cultural norms of English civilization. As different ministers reiterated, the "degenerate" Indians "must bee brought to some civility before religion can prosper, or the word take place." When Native converts built English-style towns and established laws recognizable to him, therefore, Shepard proclaimed, "I looke upon [these things] as fruits of the ministery of the Word." In the same way, when chastising the "great uncharitableness" of English skeptics, the Puritan missionary Thomas Mayhew offered the evidence of reformed lives: Praying Indians "walk[ed] inoffensively and diligently in their way." The towns and laws, the English style of life and the godly behavior of Praying Indians all proved that they had taken the Word to heart—that their religious affections "enclined" unto God.[22]

Before saving knowledge and sanctified behavior could proceed, however, one had to experience the proper feelings. A pattern *from* feeling *to* knowledge and practice appeared already in *New Englands First Fruits*, which explains that Wequash Cooke, a Niantic warrior, upon "feeling and beholding the mighty power of God in our English forces ... went up and down bemoaning his condition; and filling every place where he came with sighes and groanes"; in the midst of his desperation, he gradually gained knowledge of religion, later testifying to his true repentance by performing good deeds and practicing Christian patience.[23] In the same way, an "Indian Maid at Salem, would often come from the Word, crying out with abundance of tears"; fearful of hell, she searched for grace, "and after this [she] grew very carefull of her carriage, proved industrious in her place, and so continued." In Puritan conversions, the Spirit came first, "awakening and humbling ..., drawing forth those affections of sorrow, and expressions of tears in abundance, which no tortures or extremities were ever observed to force from [the Indians], with lamenting." In *The Sincere Convert*, one of his sermon series, Thomas Shepard explained that spiritual truths were "either such as tend to enlarge the understanding, or such as may work chiefly upon the affections." He then passed by the former, arguing that "the understanding, although it may literally, yet it never savingly, entertains any truth, until the affections be herewith smitten and wrought upon." As Richard Baxter put it, "Few men are apt to believe that which they would not have to be true." Ministers first had to stir up desire and affection before their lessons would stick. Once tears began to flow, *then* the Indians could learn of grace and leave their sin. Affection preceded and enabled understanding.[24]

Feeling, knowledge, practice. These three supported one another and together demonstrated a sincere heart, an authentic repentance and conversion. When Eliot insisted that the Spirit of God worked among the Indians, therefore, he supported that claim by pointing to their questions, their casting off of powwows, and their "sweet and affectionate melting under the word of grace." As feelings began the process of conversion, so they remained vital to every other step. Hence, Mayhew wrote that one Christian "said (and I hope feelingly) that if all the world, the riches, plenty, and pleasures of it were presented without God, or God without all these, I would take God." The parenthetical reveals the necessity of feeling behind every statement of fact. In the same way, Eliot preached that saints believe in Christ "and know him feelingly." Saying the right words and knowing the right doctrines both mattered, but each had to be backed by a movement of the heart.[25] As Shepard warned, an unsaved person *knows* plenty about his own miserable estate, but "he never feels it, nor mourns under it, and so comes not out of it." In fact, the distinction between a saint's act and a hypocrite's deed often amounted to inner affections. God is all Spirit, Shepard pronounced, and he "abhors all worship, and all duties performed without the influence of the Spirit; as to confess thy sins without shame or sorrow, and to say the Lord's prayer without understanding—to hear the word that thou mayest only know more, and not that thou mayest be affected more." Such acts constituted "carcasses of holy duties," "most odious sacrifices before God." The Puritan search for sincerity constantly directed one's gaze through knowledge and behavior to the heart and affections within.[26]

The focus on preceding affections helps explain Eliot's opening among the Indians. On his first successful day of missionary work, he and the other elders began by praying in English. They did so, the tract explains, because they were "not so farre acquainted with the Indian language as to expresse [their] hearts herein before God or them." The "or them" suggests the performative nature of the prayer, the need to *show* Native Americans heartfelt affections, even if such feelings came embedded in a language the Indians could not understand. The Puritans prayed in English "partly to let them know that this dutie in hand was serious and sacred … partly also in regard of our selves, that wee might agree together in the same request and heart sorrowes for them." Presenting a unified emotional front, they opened themselves to the scrutiny of their hosts. Just as the sincerity of Indian converts would later be attested by a display of feeling, so here the Indians could judge the Puritan visitors purely by their affectionate demeanor—by their visible expression of feeling rather than the content of their prayer. Such a beginning reveals Eliot's investment in allure: the Indians had to be won by the missionaries before the missionaries could win them to Christ.[27]

The Puritan emphasis on inner affections did not go unnoticed by Praying Indians. Their confessions repeatedly express concern for word-only faith—belief pronounced with the lips but not felt in the heart. Waban, for example, testified, "No matter for good words, all is the true heart; and this day I do not so much desire good words, as throughly [sic] to open my heart." John Speene testified that God pardons all who repent, believe, and "pray not outwardly but inwardly." Ponampam repented for having "prayed only with my mouth"; Antony confessed, "I pray but outwardly with my mouth, not with my heart"; Nishohkou, Nookau, Ephraim—all of the Praying Indians, according to Eliot, voiced the same concern. Hypocrisy, as the Puritans taught, constituted a disconnect between outer words and inner feeling, between mere understanding and heartfelt affection.[28]

Not only did Native Americans know to look within; they also knew to search for a melted heart. Saved hearts were soft and sensitive, broken by sin and ready to weep for it. Eliot, for example, taught Praying Indians "the parable of the Nut" to instruct them "that outward acts are as the shell, which is necessary, but a broken and believing heart is the kernel." Shepard instructed readers, "Labor for a melting, tender heart for the least sin. Gold is then only fit to receive the impression when it is tender and is melted; when thine heart is heated, therefore, at a sermon, cry out, Lord, now strike, now imprint thine image upon me!" The unconverted, in contrast, hardened their hearts and refused Christ's pleadings. After explaining God's readiness to rejoice at the conversion of each sinner, Baxter proclaimed, "Doth not this turn thy heart within thee? O sinner, if thou have an heart of flesh, and not of stone in thee, methinks this should melt it." In the end, however, Baxter admitted that only God could give his readers "new and tender hearts." Either directly from Eliot or in translations of Shepard, Baxter, and others, the Indians learned that conversion required a heart able easily to melt and mourn for sins: the truly saved had "tender hearts."[29]

Moreover, this tender heart had to be seen: Puritan ministers prescribed not just the necessity of emotion, but also its display. In *The Sincere Convert*, Shepard preached, "If thine heart were truly affected, the pillow would be washed with thy tears." Faith, being precious, ought to "cost thee many a prayer, many a sob, many a tear." *The Sincere Convert* would not be translated into Algonquin until late in Eliot's career, but Eliot chose the work precisely because he supported its message and taught it himself. He preached, for example, that God would forgive all his children, if only "they fall downe and weepe, and pray, repent, and desire forgiveness for Jesus Christ's sake."[30] As a result, the Eliot tracts nearly drip with tears. In the first pamphlet, the writers informed their readers that Indian children "will sometimes tremble and melt into teares at our opening and pressing the Word upon their Consciences"; when detained from sermons, they likewise "weep and cry." Wequash and the "Indian Maid" sighed, groaned, and cried out with "abundant tears." From these first scenes forward, such sighs and tears only multiply, testifying to the movement of God's grace. As the author of *The Day-Breaking* declared, "Those aboundant teares which wee saw shed from their eies, argue a mighty and blessed presence of the spirit of Heaven in their hearts." Repeatedly, "abundant tears" form the core evidence of conversion.[31]

Displays of feeling mattered so much to the Puritans that many recorded such appearances even when they could not understand the language. In *Clear Sun-shine*, Shepard recounted a story of Indians praying after the death of a child. "What the substance of their prayer was I cannot certainly learn," he declared, but Totherswamp, the leader, "did expresse such zeale ... with such variety of gracious expressions, and abundance of teares, both of himself and most of the company, that the woods rang againe with their sighes and prayers." Shepard wanted to know what was said, and he promised to seek out the content, but without knowing the words, the emotional display still counted. Likewise, the Boston pastor John Wilson described a Praying Indian who preached "with great devotion, gravitie, decency, readines and affection, and gestures very becoming," while the audience "did joyne and attend with much Reverence, as if much affected therewith." All of this he recorded without knowing a single word spoken beyond the repetition of "Jesus Christ." The Puritan minister Richard Mather, meanwhile, opened a series of Indian confessions this way:

> And though they spake in a language of which many of us understood but little, yet we that were present that day, we saw them, and we heard them perform the duties mentioned, with such grave and sober countenances, with such comely reverence in gesture, and their whol carriage, and with such plenty of tears trickling down the cheeks of some of them, as did argue to us that they spake with much good affection, and holy fear of God.

The authenticity of Indian conversions, in other words, required an outward emotional display, a performance of sincerity based in gestures and tears.[32]

Even as the Puritans recorded weeping, however, they feared the possibility that feelings could be faked. Prescribing emotional responses made each performance untrustworthy: knowing what was expected, the Indians could put on a good show, go home, and laugh it off. Moreover, even if they did not purposefully trick the English, Native Americans might be responding only on the surface, not deep in the heart. In *The Sincere Convert*, Shepard warned, "Many a man that lives under a sound minister, under the lashes and knocks of a chiding, striving conscience, he hath some heat in him, some affections, some fears, some desires, some sorrows stirred; yet take him from the minister and his chafing conscience, and he grows cold again presently." Displays of feeling helped testify to authentic conversions, but those demonstrations often needed further grounds of evidence—something else to support their sincerity.[33]

To get at the authenticity of public tears, Puritans often sought them out in private. When Shepard claimed that the truly affected wet their pillows at night, he described a scene that could be witnessed only by "the wife in thy bosom." That was the proximity the English sought: the wife

who could prove tears true. To reach that nearness, the English attempted
to observe Indians in secret. Totherswamp's emotional prayer, for example, was reported to Shepard by a man who witnessed it "standing at some
good distance alone from them under a Tree." This added detail implies
that the man saw private, genuine affections. Even more so, Eliot's brother
informed John Wilson that "he had purposefully sometimes in the darke
walked the Round, as it were alone, and found [Indians] in their severall Families as devout in prayer, etc. as if there had been any present to
observe." Such modes of surveillance supported public expressions of
affection by tracking them back to private lives.[34]

In addition to surveillance, the Puritans employed the trope of the
hidden tear. In this literary device, Indians are observed weeping while
simultaneously attempting to *hide* their tears, thereby proving them
true. In *The Day Breaking*, for example, the author tells of one man who
"powred out many teares and shewed much affliction without affectation
of being seene, desiring rather to conceale his griefe which (as was gathered from his carriage) the Lord forced from him." The "carriage" here is
everything. If the man had wept openly, it might have been mere show;
the fact that the text portrays him as trying to cover his grief was meant
to prove that it came from the Lord. Together, the attempt and failure of
concealment enabled "the mighty power of the word" to visibly "appear."
In *Clear Sun-shine*, Eliot likewise narrated the story of a Native American
who "turned his face to the wall and wept, though with modest indeavor
to hide it." Another Englishman, Mr. Brown, "observed [the Indians] to be
much affected, and one especially did weep very much, though covered
it what hee could." The trope prevailed so much in these tracts that the
English even applied it to themselves. Authenticating Eliot's credibility,
Shepard claimed that he "writes (as is his spirit) modestly and sparingly,
and speaks the least in sundry particulars." For example, where Eliot had
reported "many teares" in one man's repentance, Shepard heard from others "that there were so many, as that the dry place of the Wigwam were hee
stood was bedirtied with them, powring them out so abundantly."[35] Eliot's
attempt to diminish the amount—to *hide* the number of tears—proved the
sincerity not only of his own testimony, but also of the weeping. Emotions,
in this trope, turn out to be more than a good show: as they are *almost* hidden, so they represent a genuine expression of the heart.

At the same time, these tears remained a good show—not necessarily
in the sense of being faked, but simply because the weeping had to be
seen. And the more, the better: Shepard proclaimed, "It is easy to drop

a tear or two, and be sermon sick, but to have a heart rent for sin and from sin, this is true humiliation; and this is hard."[36] On the one hand, such a statement reveals a Puritan distrust of emotional display; on the other hand, it ups the ante. The Indians had to do more than trickle a few wet drops down their cheeks: they had to display a rent spirit, a heart so broken it could not stop weeping. Thus, Puritans repeatedly describe an enormous outpouring, an "abundance" of weeping, a "flood" of godly sorrow wetting the floors of wigwams.

Contagion, Conversion Narratives, and Native Oratory

For all the "abundant tears" that course through the Eliot tracts, the sincerity of affections ultimately turned on the response they generated in others. If the spirit of God moved *in* a display of feeling, it would also move *through* it. Thus the Puritans often described the spreading nature of Indian tears—as in the opening scene with Cutshamekin and the wigwam filled with weeping.[37] One missionary named William Leverich, detailing the "matter of successe and incouragement" he had received, turned in his "particular observations" to the lachrymose repentance of an Indian who confessed with "teares all the while trickling downe his Cheekes." In response, Leverich's interpreter fell "suddenly and publiquely into a bitter passion, crying out, and wringing his hands, out of the like apprehension of his Condition." Likewise, when an Indian in *The Day Breaking* "fell a weeping and lamenting bitterly," another young man confessed to "the like guiltinesse with his fellow" and "burst out also into a great mourning, wherein both continued for above halfe an houre."[38]

The repeated evidence of contagious emotions highlights an underlying component of true conversion: the love of brethren. Sympathy, for the Puritans, meant primarily a love of the brethren, mutual affections among the saints. In *A Model of Christian Charity*, Winthrop had preached sympathy as essential to both sainthood and society. The Antinomian Controversy tested that position, and when the theological battle ended, love of brethren remained an essential sign of election—even as, politically, it meant excluding those who theologically disagreed. During the English Civil Wars, several Puritans again turned to this sanctified fellow feeling in order to negotiate transatlantic relations. Now, in the Puritan missions, the same principle returned. Indian converts and English saints knew each other by their reciprocal affections, by their sympathetic tears. According to Eliot, in fact, Praying Indians discovered this love of brethren without ever being taught it. He described the visit of several Christian Indians from Martha's Vineyard to others in Massachusetts Bay: "when those strangers came, and they perceived them to affect Religion, and had mutual conference about the same, there was a very great gladnesse of heart among them, and they made these strangers welcome." That experience caused the Christian neophytes to ask Eliot "what is the reason, that when a strange Indian comes among us whom we never saw before, yet if he pray unto God, we do exceedingly love him: But if my own Brother, dwelling a great way off, come unto us, he not praying to God, though we love him, yet nothing so as we love that other stranger who doth pray unto God." Eliot cited this episode as proof that the Native Americans demonstrated what "the Scripture calleth *love of the Brethren*." Ascertaining how far it spread, Eliot discovered that all the gathered Indians "found it so in their hearts." He then taught the converts that this same love extended to all saints, including the godly in England, and that such a love revealed "the unity of spirit"—a message from Ephesians 4:3 that appeared in Winthrop's *Model of Christian Charity*, reappeared in Wheelwright's Fast Day sermon during the Antinomian Controversy, and remained vital to Puritan theologies of conversion and community throughout the seventeenth century. The Praying Indians, in their mutual joy for one another, verified their membership in the Body of Christ. The emotional community of true saints comprised a worldwide spiritual brotherhood—a fraternity that was supposed to extend beyond kinship and race. In the weeping wigwam with Cutshamekin, *both* Indian and English tears served as crucial evidence for God's grace.[39]

In the Eliot tracts, therefore, Puritan writers often guaranteed the sincerity of conversions by narrating their own emotional reactions. The anonymous author of *The Day Breaking* described the scene of Eliot's first successful preaching as "a glorious affecting spectacle," which "much affected us." In the like manner, when Eliot first preached at Pawtucket, he asked how many Indians desired to pray; when they answered "*wamu*, that is, *All*," they did so "with such affection as did much affect those Christian men that I had with me in company." The affectionate expression—*and* the response it generated in English hearts—mattered as much as the word itself. Richard Mather, for example, testified to the "good affection" of several Indian confessions based not only on their "sober countenances" and the "tears trickling down [their] cheeks," but also, finally, in that they "much affected our hearts." John Endecott told a distant reading audience that "had [they] been eare and eye-witnesses of what I heard and saw on a Lecture-day amongst [the Praying Indians] about three weekes since, [they] could not but be affected therewith as I was." He then detailed his emotional response: "To speake truely I could hardly refraine teares for very joy"—and this, again, came from witnessing a scene "the matter [of which] I did not so well understand." Eliot wrote his tears into the tracts on more than one occasion, each time testifying to the truth of someone's confession or conversion. When one of the "first and principall" of the Praying Indians died, for example, he did so in such a gracious manner, with such godly words of exhortation, that the Indians with him "could not heare [him] without weeping." More significantly, Eliot himself was unable "to write his Storie without weeping." As if sealing the man's salvation, Eliot's own tears dripped onto the page.[40]

Praying Indians knew that they needed not only to display a broken heart, but also to move an English audience. Such knowledge can be glimpsed by analyzing the record of their confessions. Eliot gathered, translated, and recorded conversion narratives privately, which he then sent to fellow ministers in order to convince them they should see the confessions delivered, approve them, and let the converts form a church. Three such viewings occurred over eight years before Puritan elders permitted Praying Indians to form a congregation, and in each of these meetings Eliot translated and recorded while Native converts spoke. What survives, then, are several confessions delivered either to Eliot personally or to a gathering of Puritan elders. Apart from the content of these conversion narratives, the basic need to see them delivered—in a language unknown to almost every Puritan elder watching—suggests the necessity of *visual* witness in the evaluation of authenticity. Not satisfied to pronounce judgment on Eliot's previously recorded confessions, the elders insisted on a public day of fasting, a formal ceremony, and an oral performance. In fact, when Eliot offered to read the prerecorded confessions, the elders rejected his proposal. Demanding oral confessions, these Puritan ministers revealed the vital necessity of live testimony: sincerity, in short, had to be *seen*.[41]

In the published record of confessions, the main distinction turns on rhetoric: when relating their experiences more publicly to Puritan elders, the Praying Indians employed emotional exclamations and outbursts of feeling that went almost entirely missing in Eliot's previous accounts. In other words, faced with an audience, they performed. Monequassun, for example, ended his written confession with a series of doctrinally accurate statements. Yet when he stood before a panel of Puritan ministers, those same statements became radically transformed: "Oh! that I could go to Christ!" he exclaimed. "Oh! Christ help me to come unto thee … Oh! give me faith, and pardon my sin … Oh! Jesus Christ deliver me."[42] No "Oh!"—nor any exclamation mark—ever appears in the personal testimony to Eliot. When it came time to deliver, the rhetoric rose.

The same transformation occurred in other testimonies. Ponampam's personal confession to Eliot ended in a staid, solid, orthodox manner: "I was ashamed of my sins," he confessed, "and my heart melted, and I thought I wil give my self to God and to Christ, and do what he will for ever; and because of this promise of pardon to al that repent and beleeve, my heart desireth to pray to God as long as I live."[43] Compare that ending to the finale of his oral performance:

> Then I heard that word, If ye repent and beleeve, God pardons all sins; then I thought, Oh that I had this, I desired to repent and beleeve, and I begged of God, Oh give me Repentance and Faith, freely do it for me; and I saw God was merciful to do it, but I did not attend the Lord, only sometimes; and I now confess I am ashamed of my sins, my heart is broken, and melteth in me; I am angry at my self; I desire pardon in Christ; I betrust my soul with Christ, that he may do it for me.[44]

Where the previous confession describes a state-of-being ("I was ashamed") and trails off into abstract thought ("because of this promise of pardon"), the live testimony engages listeners with a repetition of short, quick verbs: "I heard," "I begged," "I saw," "I now confess," "I desire," "I betrust." In addition, where the oral performance *does* describe a state-of-being, it uses the present tense and centers that state on an emotion that could be visually displayed: "I am angry at my self," Ponampam declared. Adding exclamatory "Oh's!" and using short bursts of phrasing rather than long complex clauses, Ponampam ends his testimony with a rising, exhortatory rhetoric. Knowing he needed to move his Puritan judges, Ponampam would also have been familiar with the Puritans' own methods for doing so: many Puritan sermons ended with a stirring exhortation. In concluding his own testimony this way, Ponampam matched the emotional contours of a Puritan sermon as he attempted to move a set of Puritan ministers.

Such rhetorical transformations and techniques appear in every confession delivered to the Puritan elders. Monotunkquanit, for example, begged before them, "Oh Lord give me Christ," moving from this plea to a description of his broken, melted heart. Wutásakómpauin began his testimony, "Oh Christ help mee!" and incorporated throughout his confession several repetitions of this basic, emotional plea. Waban exclaimed, "Oh God I am not able to save my self, I cannot save my own soul, this is only thy work Oh God, and my heart believeth it ... Oh let God put grace into my heart; and my heart saith, Oh let me not say in vain that I believe, Oh Lord help that I may truly believe, not by my works, but by thy word Oh God." As the Praying Indians well knew, converts needed to do more than weep, more than demonstrate catechistical knowledge, more than practice a godly life; they also had to move a panel of Puritan judges.[45]

The necessity of powerful speeches, however, did not come as something new to these Indian converts. Their own Algonquian culture practiced a strong oral tradition that based authority, in part, on the ability of a speaker to move and persuade.[46] Sachems were traditional "masters of oratory," and many rituals included "the constant repetition of words or short phrases" combined with powerful gestures—what Roger Williams called "emphaticall speech and great action." Narragansett speeches, he explained, were "copious and patheticall"—that is, moving and intended to move.[47] Such oratorical practices would have blended well with Puritan preaching standards that called on ministers to stir up listeners' affections through accessible speech (the plain style) and proper gestures.

In addition to the idea of "emphaticall speech and great action," the particular person speaking carried a host of meanings. In Algonquian culture, oral performances tended to be reserved for sachems, councilors, and messengers; as a result, the Puritan requirement that all converts deliver a narrative of grace would, in a sense, have meant asking each Indian—common or not—to occupy a special position. Taking on such a role might explain why several of them seemed "daunted much to speak before so great and grave an Assembly": the Puritan demand represented a confusing clash of status and rank. Through Native eyes, the status of the visiting Puritan elders may have appeared odd: they had come as the respected leaders of the English community, but they remained silent while the converts spoke, thus reducing themselves to the position of the common people while elevating the converts, whom they had come to judge.[48] Moreover, Algonquian oral tradition would have incorporated a necessary pause that Puritans could misconstrue as hesitation: in council sessions, sachems frequently spoke last, deliberating in silence before delivering their speech. Messengers likewise "remained silent for a respectful period before announcing their news."[49] What the English understood to be a fear of public speaking, then, might have indicated instead the extension of Algonquian oral practices.[50]

Beyond the method of delivery, Algonquian oral traditions further appear in the content of these confessions. Exclamations and repetitive bursts of phrasing were used not only in ritual practices, but also in formal Indian requests. Extant petitions in the Massachusett language direct these same techniques toward multiple ends. On June 11, 1752, for example, the Indians of Mashpee, a Wampanoag Praying Town located on Cape Cod, asked New England magistrates to defend their land rights, stating:

> Oh! Our honorable gentlemen and kind gentlemen in Boston in Massachusetts Bay ... the great ones who oversee the colony in Boston, gentlemen. Oh! Oh!, gentlemen, hear us now, oh! ye, us poor Indians. We do not clearly have thorough understanding and wisdom. Therefore we now beseech you, Oh!, Boston gentlemen. Oh! Hear our weeping, and hear our beseeching of you, Oh!, and answer this beseech of you by us, Oh!, gentlemen of Boston, us poor Indians in Mashpee in Barnstable County.[51]

While removed in time and context, such language sounds almost identical to conversion narratives delivered a full century earlier. This continuity may indicate that for Praying Indians, the requirements entailed by Puritan conversion narratives would not have struck them as impossibly strange or new: instead, the demands overlapped with and engaged a strong tradition of Algonquian oratory.

For Puritan witnesses, however, such oratorical performances often appeared as spontaneous expressions of emotion—fulfilling yet another requirement in the relentless search for sincerity. In the *Sincere Convert*, Shepard railed against those who take the "form and name of religion," but not its "power and practice." Such Christians were but "stage players," and one could "trap" them by "follow[ing] them in their private houses"—something the Puritans actually did. Beyond this surveillance, however, sincerity required a proof of power that turned on spontaneous expression. For example, in a letter "concerning the success of the gospel amongst the Indians in New-England," the Boston minister Increase Mather claimed that Native preachers prayed "without a form, because from the heart."[52] Annotating and expanding upon this letter, Cotton Mather, Increase's son, contrasted the "pertinence and enlargement" of Indian prayers to the hollow petitions of English clergy who " 'read their prayers out of a book,' when they should 'pour out their souls.' " When Mayhew praised "ten, or twelve" Indians, he likewise announced that they prayed "not with any set Form like Children, but like Men induced with a good measure of the knowledg of God, their own wants, and the wants of others, with much affection, and many Spiritual Petitions, favoring of a Heavenly mind." Native converts thus proved their sincerity by praying and confessing "without a form." They could not be "stage actors" because, according to the Puritans, their powerful affections burst forth spontaneously from the heart.[53]

Despite their hatred of form, however, the Puritans still insisted on certain formulas. The confessions of Praying Indians, while unique to each individual, still followed a set pattern: the discovery of sin led to broken-heartedness and a desperate desire for mercy, which then moved each convert to complete dependence on the grace of God. One may have been a teacher; another may have been a sachem; one may have first prayed because his friends did; another may have first prayed because he wanted to earn the love of the English. While *religious* experiences remained nearly identical, each confession contained enough individual distinction to prove them authentically personal. In this way, the structures of Puritanism called on converts to produce narratives both patterned and individual—both formulaic and unique.[54]

Of course, after attempting to move audiences with carefully crafted and well-performed conversion narratives, Praying Indians still needed to prove their knowledge of doctrine and their practice of godly habits. Oral confessions, on their own, would not suffice. After the first set of testimonies, Puritan elders scheduled a later examination of doctrine; and in the final, successful trial, the Indian converts still had to transition from prepared confessions to impromptu doctrinal exams. Emotional performance remained necessary, in other words, but not sufficient. The test of sincere conversion went well beyond the stuff of feeling.

At the same time, feeling remained essential in two fundamental ways. First, each potential convert had to possess a tender heart, and such tenderness could not be judged if it were not seen. Thus sincere affections often manifested themselves in a torrent of tears. Second, these tears needed to produce a reciprocal response. No Praying Indian would be considered an authentic convert if he or she did not, at some point, move an English judge. According to the "love of brethren" and the "unity of the Spirit"—essential elements of Puritan community and salvation— God spread affections both liberally and reciprocally. In the theater of sincerity, therefore, the tender hearts of converts had to melt the softened hearts of saints.[55]

Conversion and Compassion

These two elements of sincere conversion—broken hearts and moving tears—lay the groundwork for a third: compassion. All true saints, Puritans preached, not only sympathized with one another; they pitied the unconverted. As Baxter explained, "Beloved friends; if the Lord had not awakened me to believe and lay to heart these things my self, I should have remained in the *dark* and *selfish* state, and have perished for ever: but if he have truly made me sensible of them, it will constrain me to compassionate you, as well as my self." The Puritan minister Richard Sibbes compared that compassion to Christ's and asked, "Shall we see so many poor souls in darkness, and our bowels not yearn?" Throughout the Eliot tracts, Puritan writers prove their own godliness by exhibiting concern for the Indians. *New Englands First Fruits* begins, "The Lord ... hath given us some testimony of his gracious acceptance of our poore endeavours towards [the Indians], and of our groanes to himselfe for mercy upon those miserable Soules (the very Ruines of Mankind) there amongst us; our very bowels yerning within us to see them goe downe to Hell by swarmes without remedy."[56] As Puritan writers reiterated, the full cycle of conversion began with a tender heart for one's own sins and ended with a tender heart for others.

That trajectory appears most clearly in Eliot's *Indian Dialogues*. This text, published in 1671, contains a series of conversations between Praying Indians and their unconverted friends. Intended as an instructional manual for Native missionaries, *Indian Dialogues* offers a narrative that is "partly historical ... partly instructive." In the end, Eliot's text presents "what might or should have been said" along with the hoped-for response of converts. This series of imagined conversations includes the conversion of a Native American named Pencovot by the Praying Indian Waban. In keeping with Puritan theories of persuasion, the conversion begins in the affections. Walking along a path one day, Waban and Pencovot list their many similarities. The discussion establishes a natural bond, which Waban then threatens by suggesting an important difference. Pencovot wants to know what it is, but Waban refuses to tell, thereby creating and increasing suspense: the more Waban hides his "jewel," the more Pencovot becomes "inflamed" with the need to know it. When Waban finally reveals his religious convictions, Pencovot responds, "You have ravished my soul." He then makes explicit Waban's method: "You have dealt with me like as the fishers do by the fish. You laid a bait for me to make me desire it, and bite at it. But I saw not your hook, until you had catch'd my soul." In a language replete with erotic overtones, Eliot describes Waban's holy seduction of Pencovot's soul. Conversion begins not in the transfer of knowledge, but in the building of both affection and desire.[57]

Only after Pencovot has been lured to Christianity does he finally receive instruction. Yet as Waban teaches him the moral law, Pencovot responds with an emotional display that testifies to his growing religious affections. "Oh you have killed me again," he exclaims; the new light "hath pierced me through my heart." This pierced heart becomes visible immediately: Pencovot asks, "What are these tears of mine? Can they quench hell fire?" Soon, contrition moves Pencovot to practice; he wants to *do* something to save himself. Waban then tells his friend of the only remedy—repentance and belief in Christ—explaining that God alone can provide such gifts. Of Pencovot, though, Waban expresses high hopes: "Your heart is now (in some measure) already turned away from sin." Asking whether Pencovot will return to his former ways, Pencovot satisfies Puritan demands for reformed practice by answering, "Oh no, no." With that, Waban pronounces Pencovot converted.[58]

The interchange between Waban and Pencovot thus moves from feeling—witnessed in affection, desire, a broken heart, and visible tears—through knowledge to practice. Yet one more step remains. At the end of this experience, Pencovot proclaims, "My heart also longeth after others, that they may be as I am." Returning to the village, both men encounter Nishohkou, Waban's uncle, who declares himself too old and tired to deal with this new teaching. At that point, Pencovot intervenes, explaining that he is a changed man and desiring to tell his story so "that I may stir up your heart, and the hearts of the people here present."[59] In doing so, Pencovot satisfies the final step of conversion. For the Puritans, authentic converts testified to their changed hearts by exhibiting compassion for those left behind, stirring others to seek the Lord.

That compassion, however, was all too easily limited to one's own kin or kind. Theoretically, as the Puritan layman Roger Clap claimed in his memoirs, "if I perceive or do but hear of a Man or Woman that *feareth God*, let him be Rich or Poor, English or Indian, Portugal or Negro, my very Heart closeth with him."[60] But in lived reality, culture and race still mattered. Emotional communities based in a principle of worldwide sympathy among the saints all too often followed the contours of nation or custom.[61] In speaking to their London audience, for example, the Eliot tracts often used emotion to separate Native Americans from godly Englishmen. Employing terms like "the poor Indians," "miserable Soules" and "the very Ruines of Mankind," the missionary publications reduced Native Americans to desperate objects of pity that could be redeemed only through the compassionate benevolence of the English. *New Englands First Fruits*, for example, ends by beseeching readers to lend "many hands, many prayers, [and] many teares" to the missionary work, asking God to "stirre up the bowels of some godly minded, to pitty those poore Heathen … and to reach forth an hand of soule-mercy."[62] Working hard to move readers, the Eliot tracts cleaved the objects of compassion from their subjects—the pitied from those who pitied them.

Yet the Eliot tracts also separated English readers from Indian converts by elevating converts *above* their English readers as models of sincere conversion. That ideal often turned on powerful displays of feeling. The author of *The Day-Breaking*, for example, claimed, "Indians shall weepe to heare faith and repentance preached, when English men shall mourne, too late, that are weary of such truths." The preface to *Clear Sun-shine* took the signs of new life in Native converts and turned them into an "Indian sermon" directed at degenerate Englishmen. The Indians, it chided, crave "with more affection … Gods blessing upon a little parched corn, and Indian stalks, then many of us do upon our greatest plenty and abundance." It then described England's decline, pleading, "Oh that England would be quickned by their risings, and weep over her own declinings!" Later in the same tract, when Shepard described the scene of an Indian praying with his child over "a homely dinner," he wrote, "These things me thinks should move bowels, and awaken English hearts to be thankfull." The Praying Indians repeatedly became models for the English—sincere converts flush with new life and able, through the Eliot tracts, to awaken the religious affections of godly readers.[63]

Whether setting the Indians below the English (as objects to be pitied) or above them (as objects to be emulated), Puritan writers often created an emotional divide between New England Indians and Old England saints. Each "Indian sermon" invoked a sense of competition: if *even* Native Americans could weep in thanksgiving, how much more ought English saints exhibit godly gratitude. In such a spirit, Shepard wrote, "If

I should gather and summe up together the severall gracious impressions of God upon them … I thinke it might make many Christians ashamed, who may easily see how farre they are exceeded by these naked men in so short a time." Trying to gall the godly into action, Shepard and other writers stressed the necessity of an emotional response, demanding hearts *at least* as broken as those of "naked men." Through both pity and emulation, the texts made it almost impossible to perceive Praying Indians as fellow Christians, members of the same community, the one and single Body of Christ. Instead, these texts enabled English readers to display for fellow Englishpersons both their sin-conscious brokenness and their tender-hearted compassion.[64]

The emotional divide presented in these tracts reveals the natural affections which undergirded a saintly concern for others. Eliot and others worked so hard to move readers' affections on behalf of the Native Americans in part because they realized that tender-heartedness for the unconverted most often began with compassion for one's own. The English loved Englishmen before they loved Indians, and Native Americans loved Native Americans first. The Christ-like concern of saints for others' souls still relied on the all-too-earthly, natural affections of kinship and kind. Even in his story of Praying Indians discovering a love of brethren, Eliot claimed that they found it only among fellow Algonquian converts; they had to be *taught* it concerning the English. This natural basis for godly compassion motivated Eliot to insist on the need for Native missionaries. While English missionaries might begin the work of conversion, Eliot did not expect "any great good" to come of them because, he explained, "God is wont ordinarily to convert Nations and peoples by some of their owne country men who are nearest to them, and can best speake, *and most of all pity* their brethren and countrimen." In the Eliot tracts, each time Praying Indians exhibited compassion for the unconverted, they directed it toward other Native Americans, not Englishmen. Shepard wrote that one Indian question "argue[d] some motions stirring in some of their hearts to pity and teach their poor Countreymen." That movement offered the most hope "of doing good among them" because only then would the Lord "raise up some or other like themselves to go among them and preach the Word of life unto them with fatherly or brotherly bowels." Again, saintly compassion and conversion emerged from, and depended on, kinship and kind—the natural affection of "fatherly or brotherly bowels."[65]

While natural affection raised a barrier between groups, it also created an opening for Native missionaries. Not only would Praying Indians pity unconverted Native Americans; the unconverted Native Americans would welcome Praying Indians. Indeed, in the confessions of several Indians, a natural love of brethren proves fundamental to their conversion. Sometimes Native Americans held back from Christianity because, as Totherswamp testified, he had "many friends who loved me, and I loved them, and they cared not for praying to God, and therefore I did not." At other times, such love drew Indians *to* Christianity. John Speene confessed, "When I first prayed to God, I did not pray for my soul but only I did as my friends did, because I loved them." As the final stage of conversion, a natural love of brethren would never do; as an opening, however, it remained essential. Indian missionaries would pity their kin, and their kin, in kind, would open themselves to a Christian message delivered by brothers, fathers, and friends. As the Praying Indian Antony testified, his "brothers" tracked him down when he tried to flee, and they "asked me to pray, and they pitied me, and loved me, and therefore I returned, not because I loved God, but because I loved my brothers." This testimony, which began in natural love and ended in the love of Christ, convinced the Roxbury congregation to approve Antony's conversion and welcome him as a member.[66]

On the basis of natural affections, therefore, the Eliot tracts trace out two separate emotional communities: English loving English and using the Indians to write sermons for themselves, and Native Americans loving Native Americans and learning to pray because their friends did first. Yet for all the emotional distance these documents put between Indians and Englishmen, Eliot and other writers still attempted to produce that spiritual sympathy—that worldwide communion of saints and love of brethren—that would confirm their work among the Indians. Joseph Caryl, the Puritan editor of *A Further Account*, prefaced the tract by announcing, "It were a desireable mercy, that the practise and example of our native Brethren, yea, of the native Indians in New England might kindle in us the fire of a blessed emulation in this matter." On the one hand, such a statement followed the tradition of turning Indians into object lessons; on the other hand, it acknowledged these distant Christians as "Brethren," not "naked men"; it presented them as *fellow saints*. Such a sentiment introduced a tract which would go on to narrate the founding of the first Native church. By 1660, for some Puritans, these Praying Indians could no longer be treated merely as objects of pity; they had graduated to sympathy, the love of brethren, the communion of saints.[67]

The Puritan writers of the Eliot tracts thus had three solid reasons for stirring up the affections of English readers. First, their work depended on a pity that would issue in cash. As readers aided mission work, moreover, they would demonstrate their Christ-like tender-heartedness, identifying themselves as saints. Second, Puritan writers shamed godly readers with the abundant tears of Praying Indians, forcing them to re-examine their own hearts for the softness, the sadness, the sin-conscious broken-heartedness that all true saints possessed. Finally, *some* of the Puritan writers, especially John Eliot, sought to build an emotional community not just *around* Christian Indians—using them as objects for the advancement of English spirituality and community—but *with* them, including the Praying Indians in a sympathy that would confirm the missionaries' work. All three of these motivations shaped the language and style of the Eliot tracts. The mission work, the godliness of readers, and the saintly status of Native converts all depended upon generating an emotional response.

Sincerity and Sentimentalism

To produce the proper feelings in his readers, Eliot and other writers used literary forms that would later be found at the heart of sentimental novels. Any one of these techniques by itself would suggest little, but taken together they reveal how Calvinist notions of sympathy—and its rhetorical and theological consequences—could lay groundwork for sentimental techniques. In making such a claim, I add to a rising chorus of scholars who have linked sentimentalism and its forms back to Puritanism and its texts by showing how Calvinist theology wove together sympathy, sincerity, and emotional display.[68] Finding such genealogical links helps overturn the caricatured idea that sentimentalists turned to sympathy as an antidote to their intellectual, doctrinal, stern, and rigorous Puritan past. The Eliot tracts tell a different story, one where sentimental forms arise before the advent of sentimental culture, precisely because the history of sympathy is longer and deeper than scholars have usually recognized. For the Puritans, the theological principle of sympathy, used as a vital test of sincerity, directed not just the practices of Puritan missions, but the way they appeared in texts.

To demonstrate and exercise that sympathy, the Eliot tracts first demanded from readers an emotional response. The prefaces, in particular, shaped expectations. Often, the section titled "To the Reader" addressed specifically "the Godly and well affected of this Kingdome of England." The following preface then defined such good affections: "Now to see the Gospel lifted up as an Ensigne to the Nations, and they to flow unto it, should be matter of great rejoicing to the soules of those who love the Gospel in sinceritie." Similarly, *Tears of Repentance* began, "Christian Reader, I know thy Soul longeth to hear Tydings of Gods grace powred out upon these goings down of the Sun." Introducing *A Further Account*, Caryl prayed that the Indians "may not want their compassionate and chearfull assistance, who are already (through grace) gathered into his holy flocks and folds." In other words, if readers considered themselves among the elect, they would show their godliness by responding with compassion. As the preface to *The Clear Sun-shine* put it, "If ever the love of God did center in your hearts, if ever the sense of his goodness hath begot bowels of compassion in you, draw them forth towards them whom God hath singled out to be the objects of his grace and mercy; lay out your prayers, lend your assistance to carry on this day of the Lord begun among them." Repeatedly, Puritan writers constructed an audience to which readers would *want* to belong (the godly), then prescribed the affection that would identify them as members—"bowels of compassion" for the unconverted, "great rejoicing" for every change of heart. In this way, the prefaces created a moral imperative to respond emotionally to the texts.[69]

Beyond commanding such a response, the Eliot tracts attempted to create one by describing the desperate pleading of Native Americans. Puritan writers portrayed the Indians as "cry[ing] out unto us in the bowels of compassion for the Lord Jesus sake to send them some helpe"—a cry taken straight from the seal of Massachusetts Bay. That seal, borrowed from the Bible and originally designed as a justification for emigration, served Puritan writers of the Eliot tracts as an emblem of pity, a picture meant to move the viewer. Winslow, for example, published an open letter to Parliament so that "your HONOURS might perceive how these poor Creatures cry out for help; Oh come unto us, teach us the knowledge of God, tarry longer with us, come and dwell amongst us, at least depart not so soon from us." Native converts themselves caught the spirit of this campaign. In his confession before a gathering of Puritan elders, Nishohkou begged for help not just from God, but also from "you, before whom I am in this house, help mee."[70]

In addition to pitiful pleas, writers exaggerated tearful scenes: the repeated image of an Indian *almost* concealing his God-wrought feelings; a wigwam packed with weeping; dry ground doused with tears. Instead of offering statistics and vague, general reports, the writers of the Eliot tracts focused on the visual expressions of particular individuals. While such displays helped evaluate the sincerity of conversion, they also served to generate an emotional response; and given such a goal, the writers could be easily tempted to hyberbolize (or *fictionalize*) their several scenes of weeping. Converts do not cry as most people do; instead, they fill tents with tears in a kind of flash flood of weeping that sweeps along the English—both the writers and, the writers hope, their readers. In this way, the letters themselves perform sincerity just as the converts did, opening a window onto private emotion in a gesture directed at the wider public and designed to generate a reciprocal response.[71]

In keeping with these tearful tableaus, the Eliot tracts also insert several deathbed scenes. After a series of written and oral confessions in *Tears of Repentance*, for example, Eliot added "the Confession (if I may so call it) or rather the Expression, and manifestation of faith, by two little Infants ... under three years of age when they died and departed out of this world." By calling them "confessions," Eliot rationalized their inclusion in a tract concerned with formal conversion narratives. Yet by his own admission, the dying children form more of a good tale than a proper confession: "The Story is this," he began, explaining that Nishohkou's child, "in the extremities of its torments, lay crying to God in these words, *God and Jesus Christ, God and Jesus Christ help me*." Such pathetic pleas did not constitute a full confession, but they did serve a purpose: they tugged at readers' hearts. The other toddler, Robin Speen's infant, could sense death approaching and told his father several times, "*I am going to God*." The mother made for the child "a little Basket, a little Spoon, and a little Tray," but just before dying, the toddler set these things aside, explaining, "*for I am going to God*." Attempting to stir his readers, Eliot coyly concluded his tract with a "story" of dying children.[72]

Most significantly, the sentimental goals and techniques of the Eliot tracts emerged from basic structures of Puritan belief. First, sincere conversions began with tender hearts. "Stony-hearted" sinners had to melt, mourning for their evil ways and breaking into tears as they sought a remedy for sin. When rescue came, each step of the conversion process had to be accompanied by inner feeling. Religious affections could be demonstrated by *non*emotional signs, such as knowledge and practice, but such evidence would be considered hollow, hypocritical, and void if it did not proceed from the heart. Second, these inner affections had to be *displayed*; tears communicated one's tenderness to others. Third, true saints demonstrated their new hearts by exhibiting compassion for the unregenerate: the full cycle of sincere conversion moved from feeling to feeling, from a tender heart for one's own sin to a tender heart for others. Fourth, Puritanism based compassion as much in similarities of kinship as in a spiritual love of saints. Where the one ended and the other began often blurred, but *that* one could lead to the other most Puritans acknowledged. Fifth, authenticating a person's sincere conversion depended, in part, on that person generating an emotional response. Puritan elders judged as they were moved to judge. Knowing this, Native converts drew on their own Algonquian traditions and performed the sincerity of their conversions with visible tears and a rising rhetoric meant to stir the feelings of their audience. Moreover, such confessions came embedded in narrative structures both formulaic and unique; authenticity demanded individual expression, but orthodoxy required the same experience of all. Finally, Puritans presented all of these elements *to a reading public.* In doing so, they tried to melt hearts with printed words, demanding emotional responses and defining such reactions as the highest form of reading. In the end, tender hearts appeared most—and best—in tears generated by texts.

6

Bewildered Sympathy

AS THE ELIOT tracts demonstrate, Puritan sympathy functioned both to exclude and to include. Where many writers in those tracts sought to build an emotional community of Englishmen around their shared pity for an objectified Indian figure, Eliot himself often tried to expand that community by generating a fellow feeling that would encompass Native converts as joint members in the Body of Christ. We see the reverse dynamic operating in Mary Rowlandson's hugely popular and influential captivity narrative, *The Sovereignty and Goodness of God* (1682). For Eliot, sympathy too easily stopped short of a broader communion of saints and had to be stirred up; for Rowlandson, sympathy too easily leaked beyond its bounds and had to be curtailed. *The Sovereignty and Goodness of God* reveals not only how Puritans used fellow feeling to build up, define, and bind together their communities, but also how experiences of sympathy could break down the very boundaries it was meant to construct. Rowlandson, at times, finds herself sharing mutual affections with her captors, who offer her kindness in the midst of captivity. Yet the more Rowlandson sympathizes with the Indians, and the more they sympathize with her, the more she shuts down and denies such cross-racial fellow feeling—precisely because sympathy implies a joining together, a union, a community. Instead, Rowlandson seeks throughout her narrative to identify two *opposing* emotional communities, and that effort requires her to discipline and delimit sympathy. As she reconstructs an English society held together by mutual affections, therefore, she must prevent that community from feeling compassion for the Indians and demonstrate that the Indians feel no compassion in return.[1]

In her focus on emotional communities, moreover, Rowlandson situates her narrative in a domain outside of, or set next to, politics. According to Lauren Berlant, sentimentalism constructs an "intimate public sphere" that is "juxtapolitical"—one which "flourish[es] in proximity to the political because the political is deemed an elsewhere managed by elites who are interested in reproducing the conditions of their objective superiority, not in the well-being of ordinary people or life-worlds." That process can be seen already at work in Rowlandson's narrative.[2] Longing for an imagined past of mutual affections, the homesick and alienated Rowlandson tries to rebuild a lost domestic community. While sentimental literary techniques and scenes mostly go missing from *The Sovereignty and Goodness of God*, Rowlandson's popular captivity narrative nonetheless points readers toward a basic underlying feature of later sentimental novels: the better sphere beyond politics centered on the mother and her home.

That home was lost and longed-for during King Philip's War, which came about partly through the Puritan missionary endeavors represented in the Eliot tracts.[3] In Plymouth colony, for example, the sachem of the Pokanokets, Metacom, increasingly felt threatened by the growth of Praying Indians. Since he refused to convert, he effectively lost power over, and tribute from, each of his subjects who did, especially as they moved out of traditional village structures and into John Eliot's Praying Towns. Moreover, Metacom (also called Philip) knew that no matter how much he pledged allegiance to Plymouth—and no matter what protection Plymouth promised in return—if he ever came into conflict with Praying Indians, the colony would side with its converts. For these reasons, when Wamponoag representatives met with John Easton, the Deputy Governor of Rhode Island, and listed their grievances against the English, they included the fear that "any of their Indians should be called or forced to be Christian Indians."[4] The growth of missions did not constitute the sole reason for King Philip's War—the representatives also described English practices of land snatching, the dubious death of Wamsutta (their former sachem and Metacom's older brother), the lack of legal recourse, and more—but the rise of Christian Indians and the missionary push certainly increased tensions and accelerated momentum toward war.

When a Massachusett Praying Indian named John Sassamon showed up dead in an icy pond in 1674, these tensions exploded. Sassamon had attended Harvard College and helped Eliot with his mission work before turning on the English to become a chief counselor for Metacom. But Sassamon's motivations and allegiances could never be pinned down, and in 1674 he turned again, informing the Plymouth governor, Josiah Winslow, that Metacom intended war. On his trip home, this Harvard-educated

Indian go-between disappeared. When his corpse surfaced, Christian Indians, claiming Sassamon as their own, immediately charged three of Metacom's supporters with murder, testified against them in court, and saw them hanged. What Metacom feared had now come true: in a conflict between Indians, Plymouth sided with those who prayed, accepting the testimony of Christian Indians to the point where they executed Metacom's subjects. Unable to protect his people from either the English or the Christian Indians, losing land and looking weak, Metacom struck back.[5]

By the time the war reached Mary Rowlandson's door, it had spread beyond Plymouth and the Wampanoags to the United Colonies of Massachusetts Bay, Connecticut, and New Haven, along with a host of nearby Indian nations, including the powerful Narragansetts. On February 20, 1676, a combined force of Narragansetts, Nipmucs, and Wampanoags attacked the outlying English town of Lancaster, Massachusetts, burned the garrisoned house of the minister Joseph Rowlandson, and took Mary Rowlandson, her son, two daughters, and several other women and children captive. Joseph Rowlandson himself was not present; having been warned by a Christian Indian of the impending attack, he had hurried to Boston to seek military aid. When Joseph returned, he found his town razed and his family gone.

For nearly three months, Mary Rowlandson traveled west and north from one Indian encampment to another. Her youngest child, Sarah, who was shot through the stomach during the attack, died nine days later. Rowlandson saw her older daughter, Mary, just once while in captivity and then never again until both returned to English society. Her son, Joseph, was held nearby and occasionally they met in the woods; he, too, would eventually find his freedom. After almost twelve weeks spent near starvation, witnessing multiple deaths (both of captives and of Indians), engaging in Native economies and bartering for food, being traded from one master to another—after, in general, enduring, observing, and then participating in Native American culture as a captive, Rowlandson was released and restored to English society. Christian Indians delivered a ransom of £20 to Rowlandson's captives and led her out of the wilderness. She spent one night in her abandoned Lancaster, traveled through Concord, and then settled for a time in Boston.

As for the Native Americans who captured and released Rowlandson, the war did not end well. Metacom traveled west to seek aid from the Mohawks, but his trip backfired: instead of joining the Wampanoag leader, Mohawks attacked. Hemmed in from both the east and the west, lacking access to the sea, Metacom's alliance gradually lost a war of attrition. They had pushed the English back nearly to Boston and cleared them from several outlying towns; yet in 1676, Metacom and his allies began to suffer a series of devastating defeats. As the end grew eminent, Metacom took refuge in a swamp near where the conflict began. On August 12, 1676, after an English captain named Benjamin Church and a band of Native allies tracked down Metacom, John Alderman, a Praying Indian, shot and killed him. "King Philip" (Metacom) was drawn and quartered, and his head was displayed to the public for the next twenty years.[6]

In addition to a physical reminder of the war—Metacom's staked head—many leading Puritan figures composed historical accounts. In this flood of literary material, one narrative stood out: Rowlandson's account of her captivity, which she published in 1682, became an instant bestseller. Four separate editions appeared in the first year of publication, and the book sold steadily for many years to come.[7] On the one hand, such popularity clearly indicates that Rowlandson's narrative touched something deep within her culture. On the other hand, *what* drew readers to Rowlandson's text remains uncertain. It might have been her didactic lessons on providence; it might have been her seeming resistance to orthodoxy; or it might have been simply its story of adventure—a well-told tale of one woman who had gone deep into the wilderness and returned. The largest word on the earliest surviving title page (the second edition) is "GOD," but the second largest word is "NARRATIVE": either the religious lessons or the adventurous story could have drawn a crowd.[8] In other words, as much as popularity indicates Rowlandson's connection with her culture, it also suggests her distance, her atypicality. In that sense, this bestselling narrative, which spawned a series of imitators, must be explored not only for what it borrowed from tradition, but also for what it added—what it changed. Rowlandson's narrative reflected dominant values of her day, and it acted within those values to anticipate something new. Part of what it anticipated, I argue, was sentimental literature—and it did so by engaging and altering the theology of Puritan sympathy.[9]

Pathos and Purpose

When Mary Rowlandson's captivity narrative first appeared in print, a preface explained the spiritual qualities that made the text worth publishing. The writer of the preface, most likely the influential Boston minister Increase Mather, considered the work "worthy to be exhibited to, and viewed, and pondered by all" because it represented "the excellent textures of divine providence." In other words, its virtue lay in its spiritual lessons—each of which supported Mather's social reforms.[10] In *A Brief History of the Warr with the Indians in New-England*, Mather argued that the Indians had risen up because the Puritans had declined. He detailed the sins of the second generation and called on the colonists to repent and change their ways: "*Praying* without *Reforming* will not do," he preached.[11] Throughout the war, Mather exhorted Puritans to a renewed discipline, a deeper spirituality, a longer obedience in the way first blazed by the emigrant fathers. To end the conflict and return to prosperity, the colonists would have to identify and renounce their sins—much as Rowlandson does in her text. With Mather's preface, then, Rowlandson's narrative became one more piece of rhetoric about providence and discipline, spiritual lessons and social reform.[12]

Yet within that frame, Mather focused on the affections. In order to achieve social reform, Mather knew, he had to move the heart. The appeal of Rowlandson's narrative lay as much in its emotional power as in its orthodox lessons. Just as praying without reforming would not do, so Mather preached that tearing one's garments without rending one's heart would only further provoke the Lord. In his *Essay for the Recording of Illustrious Providences*, therefore, Mather called not just for *any* example of divine direction, but specifically for "*affecting* Stories concerning the gracious Providence of God."[13] That is what Mather found in Rowlandson's tale: an "affecting story," a way to reach the reader's heart. In fact, according to the preface, Rowlandson's narrative came into print precisely because those who first read it were "*much affected* with the many passages of working providence." Moreover, Mather could pinpoint *how* Rowlandson moved her readers: "And forasmuch as not the generall but the particular knowledge of things make deepest impression upon the affections, this Narrative particularizing the several passages of this providence will not a little conduce thereunto." Mather promoted Rowlandson's narrative for its intimate details of "Life-mercies"—its "*heart-affecting* mercies, of great impression and force" which "enlarge pious hearts in the praises of God."[14]

Nor was he alone. When the publisher Samuel Green Jr. advertised Rowlandson's upcoming book in the back of *Pilgrim's Progress*, he promised "the particular circumstances of the Captivity, & Restoration of Mrs. *Mary Rowlandson*; and of her Children. Being pathetically written with her own Hand." "Pathetically" meant emotionally; as one scholar observes, it described the work as having been written " 'movingly' and 'earnestly.' The emotionalism underlying the book advertisement should have helped sales."[15] Often this word was used in relation to the horrors of war, stirring readers through powerful descriptions of suffering. "*Those* languishing, and much to be pitied, Kingdoms, which now lie bathed in blood, can attest the evils and mischiefs of War, much more pathetically than words can express," wrote one Church of England clergyman in 1679. Most often "pathetically" described verbs meant to spur readers and listeners into some kind of action: ministers "pathetically" exhorted, urged, warned, adjured, begged, and inveighed against. One pastor, preaching to several convicts on their way to execution, "pathetically laid open the deplorable Condition such sinners are in by Nature" and thus "endeavoured to awaken, and put them into a serious sense and apprehension of their lost, undone, and perishing Estate." When Green tried to boost sales by calling Rowlandson's book "pathetically written," therefore, he saw what Mather and others had also noticed: the text's ability to touch and move the heart. Its power came from its pathos.[16]

The pathos of the story hits readers in the first scene. Rowlandson does not begin her story with moral lessons or catechistical profundities: instead, she opens with action: "On the tenth of February 1675,[17] Came the *Indians* with great numbers upon *Lancaster*." The death and devastation that follows focuses in two instances on the bowels: one man "begged of [the Indians] his life, promising them Money (as they told me) but they would not hearken to him but knockt him in head, and stript him naked, and split open his Bowels." Likewise, Rowlandson's youngest child is shot "through the bowels" as she and her mother flee their burning home.[18] In the seventeenth century, the bowels were both the literal digestive track and the seat of compassion. By pointing readers to these split and pierced bowels, Rowlandson seems to exercise both meanings at once. Her scene aims not just at historical accuracy, but also at affecting readers, piercing them with words. Such a goal helps explain the many details provided, some of which go even beyond Rowlandson's immediate experience. In the splitting of the first man's bowels, for example, Rowlandson does not stand close enough to know what he said as he lay dying, yet she uses what was reported to her later in order to add "pathetic" detail, to bring readers as near to the scene as those who were involved. No lesson emerges in this opening scene of heartache and pain; instead, the action aims at generating affections and moving hearts, involving readers emotionally and imaginatively in the tale.[19]

The Puritan Family and the Sentimental Home

To reach readers' affections, Rowlandson focuses attention on the breakup of her family. That calamity appears already in the book's first scene. Hearing "Mothers & Children crying out for themselves," Rowlandson takes her and her sister's children "to go forth and leave the house"— only to be greeted by a volley of bullets. Her sister Elizabeth, seeing "the Infidels haling Mothers one way, and Children another, and some wallowing in their blood," prays for death and is instantly killed. Here, Rowlandson pauses to comment on her sister's spiritual state, trying to determine whether or not she is saved. Such a sudden excursus reminds modern readers of the multiple reasons for writing and publishing this text. Rowlandson was considering alternative possible endings to her own story, all the ways she might have died, while drawing spiritual lessons from those who did and from her own continuing afflictions—seeking, in short, to make sense and meaning of her experience. None of that should be forgotten. But when Rowlandson turns back to the telling of her tale—writing, "But to return"—she immediately picks up the theme of her broken family: "the *Indians* laid hold of us, pulling me one way, and the Children another." Rowlandson could have chosen to focus the reader's attention on any number of tragedies in this opening scene, but as it progresses, she emphasizes one: the separation of a mother from her child.[20]

For Rowlandson, the heart-tugging tragedy of familial separation becomes not just an effective rhetorical strategy, but the central motif of her text. She organizes her tale through a series of "removes"—travels through the wilderness that took her further and further from English civilization and each of her children. In the first remove, Rowlandson laments her "sad bereaved condition," concluding "All was gone, my Husband gone ... my Children gone, my Relations and Friends gone, our House and home and all our comforts within door, and without, all was gone." In the third remove, she adds, "I had one Child dead, another in the Wilderness, I knew not where, the third they would not let me come near to." Later she again records her "Heart-aking thoughts ... about my poor Children." Rowlandson's separation from family, friends, and English culture—and *especially* from her children—constitutes the motor of this text, the driving problem which builds tension and moves the story from its beginning to its end. As familial disruption causes the story to commence, so the story concludes only when her family (what is left of it) reunites. This narrative arc of separation and return creates the frame within which spiritual self-examination occurs. As with the Antinomian Controversy, so here the resolution depends on a family reunion. Yet this time the reunion is literal—the natural family, not the family of God—and the result is a significant shift in values.[21]

For Puritans, the family served as a building block of society, a school-room of obedience, a figure of order, and a model of powerful affections. When settling Springfield in 1636, for example, Puritan leaders counted families, not individuals, proposing that the town "be composed of fourty familys or if wee thinke meete after to alter our purpose yet not to exceede the number of fifty familys, rich and poore." Where families went lacking, Puritans invented makeshift replacements. The New England Company instructed Salem in 1629 that the godly should be distinguished from others and "sett over the rest devyding them into families." Meanwhile, they organized emigrating servants "into severall famylies, as wee desire and intend they should live together," and informed the Salem Puritans to "take spetiall care, in setlinge these ffamilies, that the cheife in the familie (at least some of them) bee grounded in religion."[22] Whether natural or make-shift, the family unit, Puritans believed, would serve to curb idleness, teach religion, and provide discipline for the state. As the theologian William Gouge asserted, "[A] conscionable performance of domesticall and household duties, tend to the good ordering of Church and common-wealth."[23] Many years later, the Puritan minister Eleazar Mather showed that such principles still held. In 1671, he preached, "Families are the Seminaries of Church and Common-wealth. *Keep the Lord with you in Families, and keep him then in all Societies: let him go thence, and he will quickly go from the rest.* Here begins all Apostacy and degeneration; the ruine of Churches and Country springs from thence: *Ruine Families, and ruine all.*"[24] In that sense, the figure of the family served more generally to illustrate proper hierarchical relations. Magistrates ruled as "fathers," and citizens obeyed according to the Fifth Commandment: "Honor thy father and mother." When he critiqued the Indians in 1676, for example, Increase Mather represented them as lacking order and subordination, tracing this chaos back to the home. He wrote, "The breach of the *fifth Commandment* is one of the great and *National sins*, which the Indians are guilty of: their Children have no regard nor reverence towards their Fathers." The poet Benjamin Tompson also critiqued the Native Americans for inverting Puritan values. In *New Englands Crisis*, he has Philip say, "My friends, our fathers were not half so wise / As we ourselves who see with younger eyes." The lack of respect for fathers, spoken here by an Indian "magistrate," reveals a national disorder.[25]

In addition to order and hierarchy, however, the family contained and represented the strongest affections and allegiances on earth. William Hubbard, for example, claimed, "There was no small argument in the words of Abram used to Lot, *Let us not fall out, for we are Brethren.* Nature leaves a strange instinct upon those of the same kind, even amongst the bruit creatures to defend one another, and to revenge the injury done to their owne kind." Likewise, when Eleazar Mather called on parents to pray for their children, he beseeched them on the basis of natural rela-tions: "It is not onely a Generation, but *your Generation*; now I come near indeed, *a Generation that proceeds from your own loyns, and from your own bowels.* Me-thinks this should prove a very feeling Argument." "God," he explained later, "was the God of Relations," so that, in exhorting the rising generation not to lose the faith of their parents, he preached, "As men in other things they will not part with what was their Progenitors, Oh this was my fathers and I will not part with it: so here."[26]

Yet the very power of familial affections put them under Puritan scru-tiny, for spiritual love always had to *out-do* the love one had for kin. All regenerate Christians belonged to two families: their blood relations and the household of God. As the Puritan divine William Perkins explained in *A Golden Chain*, an "effectual calling" occurred when "a sinner being severed from the world [was] entertained [entered] into God's family."[27] Grace made Christians siblings, and God's family of rebirth always trumped the kinship of mere birth. When Increase Mather published his brother's sermon, therefore, he explained that Eleazar was "a Brother ... to me by Nature, as well as in the Lord, which last is indeed ... the greatest and best Fraternity." Thus, while Puritans often assumed and enjoined familial affections, Increase Mather nonetheless could critique Native Americans for exhibiting them in excess. Not only did he repre-sent Indians as lacking proper subordination; he also claimed that the capture of Philip's wife and son "must needs be bitter as death to him ... (for the Indians are marvellous fond and affectionate toward their Children)." They loved their children so much, he implied, because they had no God—and no saints—to love more.[28]

In *The Sovereignty and Goodness of God*, Rowlandson's focus on her family shifts the proper order. Put simply, she loves her children more than she loves the saints. From the first separation to the final reunion, Rowlandson centers her story on the suffering and recovery of her offspring. The first three removes narrate the death and burial of Sarah, Rowlandson's youngest child. After this terrible blow, Rowlandson meets with her daughter Mary, but they get separated. In the ninth remove, Rowlandson again reminds readers of her woeful condition in such terms: "my Son was ill, and I could not but think of his mournfull looks ... And my poor Girl, I knew not where she was, nor whither she was sick, or well, or alive, or dead."[29] Such concern for her children even mitigates the promise of freedom; Rowlandson writes, "I was swallowed up with all thoughts of things, *viz*. that ever I should go home again; and that I must go, leaving my Children behind me in the *Wilderness*." When she does come to Boston, Rowlandson experiences "frequent heaviness of heart for our poor Children"—so much so, in fact, that she refuses to participate in a public day of Thanksgiving, instead riding out "to see if we could hear anything concerning our Children." The story ends only when the children return: "*Our family being now gathered together (those of us that were living),*" Rowlandson writes, "*the* South Church *in* Boston *hired an House for us.*"[30] The return of the family to an idealized home dominates this narrative. No matter how much Rowlandson points toward spiritual lessons, the focus remains on her natural family.

Moreover, that natural family is gathered around and centered on its mother. In the political strategies of nineteenth-century sentimental literature, the figure of the mother would serve not only as a conduit of sympathy, but also as a source of supreme authority.[31] Already in *Sovereignty and Goodness*, however, authority and responsibility lie not so much with the absent father, Joseph Rowlandson, as with the captive mother. Such a shift contrasts sharply with other accounts of the tragedy. Increase Mather, for example, recorded the event through the eyes of Joseph, writing, "Mr. *Rowlandson* (the faithful Pastor of the Church [in Lancaster]) had his House, Goods, Books, all burned; his Wife, and all his Children led away Captive before the Enemy." When he came home, Joseph "saw his *Lancaster* in flames, and his own house burnt down, not having heard of it till his eyes beheld it, and knew not what was become of the Wife of his bosome, and Children of his Bowels." According to Mather, familial separation represents a problem for the father. For Rowlandson, however, the disruption of the family, along with its restoration, appears primarily as a problem for the mother. *She* offers advice; *she* protects her children; *she* lies with Sarah; *she* becomes the center of both the narrative and the family. On the one hand, Rowlandson's representation seems to arise naturally from historical events: after all, she was the captive and thus the one physically nearest to her children. On the other hand, the absence of Joseph Rowlandson—including the absence of any reunion scene with him—suggests that familial regathering must happen through and around the mother. The mother is the center of the family, and what she seeks to restore is the home that she has lost.[32]

Throughout her captivity, then, Rowlandson endures both spiritual and earthly homesickness, the latter taking precedence over the former. Such longing, often arising in passages where Rowlandson recounts all that she has lost, appears dramatically in the story of Goodwife Joslin. Joslin is a pregnant mother who pleads with the Indians "to let her go home," but they refuse. "Vexed with her importunity," captors publicly strip her, dance around her, and kill both her and "the child in her arms." Without expressing her desire to the point of death, Rowlandson clearly shares Joslin's longing; gathering and rehearsing this alternative ending to her own tale testifies to her identification with the victim. At times, her homesickness becomes so acute that it transports her beyond her circumstances: "And here I cannot but remember," she writes, "how many times sitting in their *Wigwams*, and musing on things past, I should suddenly leap up and run out, as if I had been at home, forgetting where I was, and what my condition was." Later, she again recalls "how on the night before & after the Sabbath, when my Family was about me, and Relations and Neighbours with us, we could pray and sing, and then refresh our bodies with the good creatures of God; and then have a comfortable Bed to ly down on." Removed from her home, Rowlandson lives in memories and imaginations of the past. For readers, such reminiscences repeatedly focus attention on pleasant domestic scenes. In detailing her homesickness and in telling Joslin's story, Rowlandson not only represents the Indians as especially "hellish"; she also highlights— through its absence—a domestic sphere free from the dangers of the world. In other words, the spiritual lesson of captivity—the preparation for a *heavenly* home—focuses so much longing on the lost *earthly* home that the latter comes to dominate the former. "But the thoughts of my going homeward," Rowlandson writes, "much cheared my Spirit, and made my burden seem light, and almost nothing at all." In such language, in the careful descriptions of both her losses and her longings, Rowlandson begins to draw the outlines of a sentimental home—a paradise located in a familial, domestic setting.[33]

Nor was Rowlandson alone in drawing a sentimental home from its absence. This same transition (from the spiritual to the physical) appears also in the Puritan poet Anne Bradstreet, as seen for example in her poem "Upon the Burning of Our House." Ostensibly a didactic poem meant to turn both poet and reader toward a focus on their heavenly mansion, Bradstreet's verses provide such lovingly recollected details of her lost home that the physical seems to overtake the spiritual. She writes, "Here stood that trunk, and there that chest, / There lay that store I counted best." Then she addresses the house directly:

> Under thy roof no guest shall sit,
> Nor at thy table eat a bit.
> No pleasant tale shall e'er be told,
> Nor things recounted done of old.
> No candle e'er shall shine in thee,
> Nor bridegroom's voice e'er heard shall be.

To replace such carefully wrought, homesick details, Bradstreet offers what *ought* to be the focus of her longings:

> Thou hast an house on high erect,
> Framed by that mighty Architect,
> With glory richly furnished,
> Stands permanent though this be fled.

While heavenly splendor suggests a grandeur lacking in any earthly "pelf," the "glory" of this poem appears distant and abstract, a poor substitute for specifically remembered trunks, chests, stores, tables, tales, candles, and bridegrooms. By the end of the poem, the speaker has not yet fully embraced the spiritual substitute. She prays, "This world no longer let me love, / My hope and treasure lies above." That "let" is both a plea and a confession; the speaker still loves her own lost house, and the heavenly replacement has not yet garnered the same affection. That was the danger of Puritan metaphors: significance could shift from the spiritual meaning to the physical emblem—the well-remembered, still-longed-for, disrupted, imagined domestic sphere of peace. The Puritan insistence on a final spiritual residence laid groundwork for the sentimental home: both were nostalgic places of reunion and peace, spheres set apart from the burdens, cares, and dangers of this world.[34]

Reclaiming a Model of Christian Charity

The paradise of a peaceful home longed for in Rowlandson and appearing in other Puritan texts responded, in part, to a larger cultural outcry against "contention." Before the war broke out, Increase Mather predicted the coming of affliction because he could see signs of the Lord's displeasure, including a growing disunity in New England: "breaches and divisions," he preached, "inasmuch as they are an evidence of the Lords departure from a people, are a sign of miseries at hand." "*The love of many was grown cold*," he warned, resulting in the "ominous sign" of "*Prevailing Factions.*" In his *Brief History*, Increase Mather claimed that the Lord was removing his candlesticks from New England "because of *Contentions*, and loss of first Love." Likewise, in his *Earnest Exhortation*, he described several sins responsible for the war, but began and ended the list with "contention." The people would not be at peace, and their internal strife had provoked an external war.[35] William Hubbard, Mather's chief clerical rival for influence in Massachusetts Bay, preached the same message.[36] "Let a body politick be never so well proportioned, as to its constitution, and form of government, & never so well furnished with wise and able men for its conduct and guidance," Hubbard warned, "yet if the several members be not well tuned together, by a spirit of love and unity, there will never be any good harmony in their Administrations." New Englanders needed to be "of one heart, and of one mind." Such unity meant specifically a coherence of affections. When Hubbard enquired into "the true grounds and reasons of such Unity, or the way how it may be brought about," he claimed, "The mutual interest that the members of the same Society have in the affections of each other, gives great advantage to promote this Unity, if duly considered." Like John Winthrop in *A Model of Christian Charity*, Hubbard detailed a basic sense of sympathy as essential for the preservation of society.[37]

Moreover, those who lamented disunity saw it as a *new* disease, a degeneration from the healthy society known before. Thomas Walley, the minister of Barnstable, preached, "There is *a Burning Feaver* amongst us, a *Fire of Contention* in Towns, in Churches" so dominant now that it was "as though it were *the work of our day*, as though we had nothing else to do." Contention and disunity formed the only lament in Hubbard's election sermon *The Happiness of a People*: while order and wisdom persisted from the first generation, "such a rare pattern of unity is seldome found in our times." The jeremiad of Eleazar Mather compared the "rising generation" to their forefathers, who supposedly possessed a faith and a unity that had long since vanished. Nostalgia for such a Golden Age likewise graced the opening of Benjamin Tompson's *New England Crisis*. Describing what New England had lost, he wrote, "Freeness in judgment, *union in affections,* / Dear love, sound truth, they were our grand protection." Moreover, he made love *precede* truth, the latter following where the former led: "But if New England's love die in its youth / The grave will open next for blessed truth."[38]

When Samuel Danforth, the pastor of Roxbury, reminded the second generation of their "errand into the wilderness," he also turned to the necessity of love and lamented its loss, imbuing his jeremiad with nostalgia for an imagined Golden Age. In fact, as if channeling Winthrop's unknown sermon, Danforth mourned most of all the loss of charity and sympathy: "O how your *Love and Charity* towards each other abounded!" he proclaimed. "O what comfort of Love! what bowels and mercies! what affectionate care was there one of another! what a holy Sympathy in Crosses and Comforts, weeping with those that wept, and rejoycing with those that rejoyced!" Now, he continued, "good men grow cold in their love to God and to one another." They needed to be heated up. They needed, he said, to melt.[39] When Perry Miller penned his influential account of the Puritans' so-called "Errand into the Wilderness," the two texts that mattered most were this one by Danforth and *A Model of Christian Charity* by Winthrop. Miller makes no mention of it, but both are centered in sympathy.[40] In fact, the jeremiads surrounding Rowlandson's text proclaimed—and attempted to reclaim—a Puritan tradition in which society's good lay in its love, its unity of spirit, its mutual affections. Whatever the Puritan "errand into the wilderness" might have been, its success depended on sympathy.

In *The Sovereignty and Goodness of God*, Rowlandson extends this line of thinking to King Philip's War. At one point, reviewing "a few remarkable passages of providence," she cites Scripture to suggest that New England's afflictions might have resulted from, or at least deepened through, its loss of mutual affections. Failing to pursue the enemy, the English army left outlying towns unprotected, which leads Rowlandson to cite Scripture: "*They are not grieved for the affliction of* Joseph, *therefore shal they go Captive, with the first that go Captive.*" Rowlandson's larger citation of Amos suggests that the evil which has befallen New England "*is the Lords doing, and it should be marvelous in our eyes,*" but within that spiritual lesson lies another: that the failure to fellow-feel with fellow Puritans has left the English exposed. Indeed, in the Geneva Bible, which Rowlandson may have known, the gloss on Amos 6.6 reads: "They pitied not their brethren, whereof now many were slain and carried away captive." As Rowlandson indicates, the community's lack of mutual affections had made it vulnerable.[41]

Communal affections were so important to Rowlandson that isolation from such compassion recurs throughout the story as a special brand of suffering. As if holding a dying child were not bad enough, she adds that there was "no Christian friend near me, either to comfort or help me." In the fourth remove, she is forced to *"part with that little company I had."* Later, surrounded by Indians "as thick as the trees," Rowlandson reminds the reader that she sat in their midst with "no Christian soul near me." Such a phrase appears frequently. In the ninth remove, she praises God that no Indian attempted to rape her even though there was "no Christian soul near me"; and when she mourns for her sick son, she again laments that "no Christian Friend was near him, to do any office of love for him, either for Soul or Body."[42] As a love of brethren had been central to Puritan understandings of society and salvation, so here the loss of brotherly love—the physical isolation from a love of brethren and the absence of Christian company—adds a weight of sorrow. Rowlandson's identity, in fact, depends on her community. She is who she is in relation to her husband and children, her society and her social position. While Rowlandson often appears as a unique individual, such individuality occurs almost exclusively in the context of suffering and loss. Rowlandson longs for fellowship, for friends and family who can show her compassion and with whom she can sympathize. Even as she carves out a unique place and identity for herself in captivity, she continues to define who she is in relation to the community she has lost.

The imagery of knitting draws out this distinction. During her trial in the wilderness, Rowlandson survives through her skill with a needle. She sews and she knits, bartering her abilities and her products for food and decent treatment. She becomes, in that way, a functioning member of an Indian community with which she refuses to fellow-feel—or denies, at least, that any fellow feeling exists. Economic exchange binds this isolated individual into a community of survival. But social cohesion through such "knitting" contrasts sharply with the vision of community laid out in Winthrop's *A Model of Christian Charity*. Winthrop's commonplace sermon admits a cohesion of "every man" based on economics—on mutual need—but claims that such need had been created by God so that "from hence they might be all knit more nearly together in the Bonds of brotherly affection." Throughout *Christian Charity*, Winthrop speaks of a society knit together *by love*, functioning well not because of economic exchange, but because a "sensibleness and sympathy of each other's conditions will necessarily infuse into each parte a native desire and endeavor, to strengthen, defend, preserve and comfort the other." In contrast to Winthrop's vision, Rowlandson finds the relation of knitting to society all too literal—and lonely.[43]

Insofar as Rowlandson mourns the lack of mutual affections, her narrative attempts—through that very keening—to rebuild the community she has lost. As jeremiads imagined a former society of brotherly love and held out hopes for its return, so Rowlandson designed her narrative to reconstruct an emotional community from her suffering, a readership bound together by sympathy.[44] When describing the death of Sarah, Rowlandson focuses readers' imaginations on her "poor sick Babe" and its "lamentable condition," presenting them with a vivid "picture of death." In doing so, she notes how she "sat much alone" and describes the unsympathetic reactions of the Indians. Quoting Scripture, she complains, "*This was the comfort I had from them, miserable comforters are ye all.*" Such a biblical injunction forces readers to make a choice: they can either sympathize with Rowlandson, proving themselves good Puritans, or they can become one with the unsympathetic, un-Christian Indian captors.[45] Indeed, Rowlandson's narrative often highlights the Christian comfort of sympathy. Whenever she finds a family member in the wilderness, the two bemoan each other's condition. After Sarah dies, Rowlandson finds her daughter Mary, but when Mary weeps, Indians remove her. In other words, *preventing* the mutual expression of grief appears here and elsewhere as a choice made by evil Indians, not good Puritans. In the same remove, Rowlandson finds her son, and he, contrary to the Indians, responds to her "mourning and lamenting" by asking her "how I did." With tears in his eyes, he inquires after his sisters. When she meets up with him again later, the two ask after "each others welfare, bemoaning our dolefull condition." At yet another reunion they again "bemoaned one another a while."[46]

Such scenes of fellow feeling serve as a proper model for Rowlandson's readers; as she and her son grieve together, so the readers ought to sympathize with her plight. *The Sovereignty and Goodness of God* enjoins the community it creates to mourn together, to weep with those who weep, to fellow-feel with the characters in this story. Even when Rowlandson compares herself to Job, she does so in part to call for compassion. She writes, "I hope it is not too much to say with Job, *Have pitty upon me, have pitty upon me, O ye my friends, for the Hand of the Lord has touched me.*"[47] Calling for pity, modeling proper emotions, detailing suffering, painting pictures to life in order that readers may experience them firsthand, Rowlandson attempts to construct a virtual society of mutual affection through participation in her suffering. As readers responded emotionally to her text, they would restore the Golden Age that had been lost.

Such sympathy was so essential because Rowlandson, drawing on Puritan theology, used affections to define one's identity by having them reveal the community to which one belongs. From the opening scene to the final remove, Rowlandson differentiates the Indians from the English by the emotions they display. While the English mourn their losses, the Indians roar, sing, and rant, "as if they would have torn our very hearts out." During Rowlandson's first night of captivity, the "merciless Enemies ... were joyfull enough though we were disconsolate." The "we" here and elsewhere unifies around an emotion: those who grieve are good; those who rejoice are evil—just as in the next remove, when Rowlandson and her child are thrown from their horse, the Indians "like inhumane creatures laught, and rejoyced to see it." A lack of humanity appears as a lack of sympathy—and specifically, a lack of compassion *for the English.* Rowlandson asks not what a person believes, but *whether* and *with whom* that person sympathizes. Indian hatred of the "brethren" identifies them as hellish; just so, a love of the brethren—a sympathy for the English— makes readers godly.[48]

The development of this emotional community helps explain the many passages where Rowlandson describes her love of the English. The question put to her during her first night of captivity—"what will you love *English men* still?"—becomes the central inquiry of the narrative. Rowlandson's entire story is, in a certain sense, an extended *yes.*[49] She loved them so much that when she saw a place where English cattle had been, it comforted her; and when she stumbled on an English path, she became so homesick that, as she writes, "I thought I could have freely lyin down and dyed." In fact, she loved them so much that when she thought she saw thirty Englishmen on horseback coming toward her, her "heart skipt within [her]." Before she noticed the "vast difference between the lovely faces of Christians, and the foul looks of these Heathens," she found her identity in an emotional reaction. She was English, in other words, because her heart beat for the English, just as the Puritan layman

Roger Clap knew that he was saved because his heart leapt for the saved.[50] The contours of community follow the affections, and in *The Sovereignty and Goodness of God*, Rowlandson not only tells readers that her heart never failed; she also tries to bind their hearts to hers and to the English community more generally. The scene of the thirty riders demonstrates her proper emotions while also training readers to cheer or hiss or clap or jeer as one.

Drawing on a Puritan theology of sympathy, Rowlandson's understanding of it differs, however, in one significant detail: for her, a love of brethren divided not the regenerate from the unregenerate, but the English from the Indians. Where Clap's affections supposedly leapt at the news of *any* fellow saint, including "Rich or Poor, English or Indian, Portugal or Negro," Rowlandson's heart skips at the sight of English-looking horse-riders. Contrasting a society of unsympathetic hell-hounds to the mutual affections of her home community, Rowlandson writes upon her return, "I was not before so much hem'd in with the merciless and cruel Heathen, but now as much with pitiful, tender-hearted and compassionate Christians." In Charlestown, she again describes her many friends as "tender-hearted," so that she found herself "in the midst of love." Later, after being loaned a house in Boston, Rowlandson writes that "the Lord so moved the hearts of these and those towards us, that we wanted neither food, nor raiment." These final scenes of compassionate action contrast with the lack of food, clothing, and sympathy she supposedly experienced earlier, serving again to define communities by the presence or absence of compassion. Yet the groups so demarcated no longer correspond to religious concerns; they focus instead on nationality and ethnicity. In the end, Rowlandson equates being Christian with being a tender-hearted Englishman. Her text begins, however unwittingly, to make Christianity equivalent with refined English sensibility.[51]

Such a view demonstrates once again a Puritan investment in stirring up, rather than tamping down, readers' emotions. Within Rowlandson's narrative, in fact, only three passages support a *restraint* of tears. One occurs during the story of Goodwife Joslin and refers to Joslin facing her death. Even as Joslin refrains from weeping, however, readers and viewers are not necessarily supposed to follow suit. To face one's own death stoically might be the sign of a saint, but to view the death of a saint and not respond with sympathy would mark one as a monster. After Joslin, only two other passages cite a Bible verse suggesting restraint. At one point, for example, Rowlandson finds comfort in this verse: "*Thus saith the Lord, refrain thy voice from weeping, and thine eyes from tears, for thy work shall be rewarded, and they shall come again from the land of the Enemy."* Yet the consolation lies all in the latter half (the promise of return), not the former. In fact, whenever Rowlandson reads this verse she weeps. "This was sweet Cordial to me," she writes, "when I was ready to faint, many and many a time have I sat down, and wept sweetly over this Scripture."[52] The very fact that this call for restraint comes accompanied with tears suggests that *certain kinds* of weeping were never proscribed. The sympathy of readers seems one such kind. The calls for pity and the descriptions of comfort that accompany sympathy far surpass in both number and narrative detail these three passages. Rowlandson's constant description of her weeping—her melting, her mourning, her heavy-heartedness, her watered couch—suggest that the text has, in general, no problem with tears. The problem arises when tears go missing. Readers who do not sympathize mark themselves as standing outside the compassionate, tender-hearted community of (English) Christians.

What Rowlandson finds, however, is that no matter how much the community fellow-feels, it can never fully sympathize with her woes. "When all are fast about me, and no eye open, but his who ever waketh," she writes, "my thoughts are upon things past." Rowlandson tries to restore a model of Christian charity—a society bound by mutual affections—but she discovers that such a vision is no longer viable (if, indeed, it ever was). First, the sorrow she has experienced can never be captured by words. "It is not my tongue, or pen can express the sorrows of my heart," she writes. However much she paints a scene to life, it will not be the same as having lived it. Second, the family itself will never fully return. Mather, in his *Brief History*, writes of Rowlandson, "It is not a small mercy, that the mother and children (only one childe was killed when the others were taken) should all of them be saved alive … and at last brought home in peace." The "all" immediately erases the "one." But Rowlandson's grief for that one child seems at times to subsume her joy in all the rest. She declares, "That which was dead lay heavier upon my spirit, than those which were alive and amongst the Heathen." Finally, the audience can never quite know Rowlandson's grief without having experienced it themselves. When in prosperity, she had actually desired affliction, believing it a sign of God's love (he chastens those whom he loves). But that former wish reveals how little she understood what affliction really meant. And in some sense, despite her best efforts, such a lack of understanding remains for all who have never been through the like "tryals and afflictions." In the end, Rowlandson's heaviness of heart is unique to her—personal in a way that precludes the possibility of mutual affection. "When others are sleeping," she writes, "mine [eyes] are weeping."[53]

Yet by offering her grief to readers, by detailing its causes and describing its experience, Rowlandson turns her narrative toward the *hope* of sympathy—hoping, that is, to put others in her place and have them feel, *in some measure,* what she has felt (and still experiences). If readers can *imagine* themselves into her pain and trauma, she and they can begin to close the gap, even if they can never achieve complete understanding and mutual affection. Adding details of her tragedy, she can keep readers awake with her in the middle of the night. By publishing her captivity narrative, Rowlandson suggests that the movement toward reintegration must come not only from her, but also from them. She does not write solely to "return to English society," as one historian has claimed, but to reconstitute society itself, to draw out its Christian—its *civilized*—sympathy.[54]

The ending of Rowlandson's narrative, therefore, demonstrates again the way alienation often produces a call for sympathy. As William Hooke, years earlier, revealed a growing gap between New England and Old in his very insistence on the need for sympathy, so here, Rowlandson's isolation issues in a desperate need to generate compassion. That loneliness, moreover, emerges against the backdrop of a lost and longed-for Golden Age—a time when New England supposedly knew a union of affections. *The Sovereignty and Goodness of God* thus wrestles with fellow feeling in the midst of an emerging individualism: a self that finds (or creates) its identity in isolation from others simultaneously increases the desire to reclaim an imagined past of mutual affections. In that move alone, I would suggest, Rowlandson's narrative links forward to a good deal of sentimental literature, for sentimentalism often seems to arise from a sense of loss; and *what* is lost is precisely a mythic, imagined community of mutual affections known only by its absence. Sentimental writers strive not to build, but to *re*build a sympathetic community, a cohesion of affections detailed by visions looking forward (such as Winthrop's) and jeremiads looking back (such as Danforth's).

Disciplining Sympathy

As Rowlandson attempts to reconstruct a society of mutual affections, she tightens that community by excluding sympathy for Indians. In doing so, Rowlandson again draws on a Puritan theology of sympathy based in the principle "like will to like," but she directs that formula toward national and ethnic ends, rather than a resemblance born from belief in Christ. Winthrop spoke of a "like will to like" that flowed from regeneration, and to that end he quoted Galatians 6:10: "Do good to all, but especially to the household of God." Rowlandson altered the formulation: do good to all, *perhaps*, but especially to fellow Englishmen. As she gets drawn into Native society, therefore, Rowlandson must discipline both her and her readers' sympathies so that they side only with the English. This logic helps explain some of Rowlandson's seemingly tangential diatribes against the Indians. Apart from the opening moments of capture and captivity, they often follow scenes where Rowlandson seems incorporated into the Indian community. In *The Sovereignty and Goodness of God*, each depiction of fellow feeling between Rowlandson and her captors incites a violent denial of sympathy—an explicit statement of hatred that shores up her identity and reconfirms her membership in the English community.

Such logic winds its way through the development of the narrative, for as Rowlandson unleashes the power of sympathy, it repeatedly moves beyond its proper limits. Beginning as "murtherous wretches," "merciless Heathen," "hell-hounds," and "ravenous Beasts," Indian captors gradually transform into human beings. Kindnesses appear: one Indian gives Rowlandson a Bible; others help her cross a cold river without wetting her feet; many provide her with food. Initially, Rowlandson describes these actions "as a favour of God," who, she implies, causes even the Indians to be compassionate. At other times, however, kindness appears with no accompanying spiritual lesson. By the end of the ninth remove, she calls Indians "strangers," not "hell-hounds," and she closes the tenth remove with a blunt report: "Sometimes I met with favour, and sometimes with nothing but frowns." No Scripture makes sense of this disparity. Indians have begun to emerge as humans—some good, others bad.[55]

The first moment that Indians appear human, moreover, comes in a depiction of Native American life that matches the model of mutual affections contemporary jeremiads lamented as lost. In the eighth remove Rowlandson writes, "When I came ashore, they gathered all about me, I sitting alone in the midst: I observed they asked one another questions, and laughed, and rejoyced over their Gains and Victories." Lacking the fellowship she once enjoyed, she now witnesses the same companionship in her enemy: Native American captors converse together and rejoice with those who rejoice, united by common affections. Moreover, where all former celebrations had been either called or coded as "hellish," the Indian

mirth here does not appear malevolent. Native Americans are simply living and laughing together as human beings do—as Rowlandson once
did with her own family and friends. The humanity of the Indians in this
scene weakens Rowlandson's resolve. For the first time, she weeps before
them: "Then my heart began to fail," she writes, "and I fell a weeping
which was the first time to my remembrance, that I wept before them."
Despite the tragedies she had experienced, she had never yet "shed one
tear in their sight: but rather had been all this while in a maze, and like
one astonished."[56] Traumatic shock only partially explains this absence
of tears, for earlier she had wept and bemoaned her condition with her
children. Something different happens here—something that enables
Rowlandson to weep before her captors. For the first time in the story,
the Indians resemble Rowlandson's understanding of Christians. They
are as human as her son. And as she wept with Joseph, so now she bursts
into tears.

Even as Rowlandson breaks down, however, she maintains her separation by quoting Scripture. "Now I may say as, Psal. 137.1. *By the rivers
of* Babylon, *there we sat down; yea, we wept when we remembered Zion.*"[57]
Equating the Indian encampment with Babylon and distinguishing a community of *we* who mourn against *those* who rejoice, Rowlandson rebuilds
an emotional distinction between Indians and English. Indians do not
weep; therefore, they cannot be the "we" who long for Zion. Moreover, this
Scriptural citation glosses the situation as homesickness. Yet the cause
of this sudden homesickness—the reason Rowlandson *remembers Zion* at
this moment—is that she sees a society which so much reminds her of
home. Rowlandson witnesses "brotherly affections" in the middle of the
demon-infested woods. And so, confused and longing for what she has
lost, she weeps.

As soon as she weeps, moreover, captors respond with compassion.
Just as they had gathered about to ask each other questions, so now they
extend an inquiry to her: "There one of them asked me, why I wept."
Earlier, Rowlandson's elder daughter had wept noisily and been sent away;
Goodwife Joslin's weeping got her killed; now, instead of threatening her,
Native Americans invite Rowlandson in—they ask her why she weeps.
Rowlandson, having been asked this question, "could hardly tell what to
say" and answers that she feared "they would kill me." This response represents another attempt at separation. The Indians, contrary to her expectations, have shown concern. Moreover, they continue to demonstrate
fellow feeling by bringing Rowlandson food: "No, said he, none will hurt

you. Then came one of them and gave me two spoon-fulls of Meal *to comfort me*, and another gave me half a pint of Pease; which was more worth than many Bushels at another time."[58] They offer this succor, Rowlandson understands, out of the same motivation that lay at the heart of Winthrop's model: to comfort the afflicted. This particular scene does not conclude (as others do) with a citation of Scripture reducing the Indians to providential tools. Instead, Rowlandson simply ends it—an act of sympathy quietly rupturing the distinction between Indian hell-hounds and English Christians.

That Rowlandson is taken in by the Native American community can be observed in the later capture of an Englishman named Thomas Read. When Rowlandson arrives on the scene, she finds Read "crying bitterly, supposing they would quickly kill him. Whereupon I asked one of them, whether they intended to kill him; he answered me, they would not. He being cheered with that, I asked him about the welfare of my husband." In this instance, the situation has been reversed. Thomas Read is the isolated, weeping individual, believing that the Indians might end his life. Rowlandson, on the other hand, stands with the Indians. Not only can she somehow speak with them, she shares their response to the Englishman: Read weeps, and Native Americans, with Rowlandson, do not.[59] Moreover, just as had been done for her, so now Rowlandson extends Read a question and a kindness. She becomes the "Indian" who says, "No ... none will hurt you." In this way, her ties to both English and Indian communities have enabled her to go between.

Yet Rowlandson's gradual inclusion in Indian society leads her only to a greater denunciation of Native Americans. In one scene, Rowlandson bursts into tears when her mistress, Weetamoo, calls her home. At the sight of this weeping, an Indian woman comforts her. Rowlandson writes, "Then the old *Squaw* told me, to encourage me, that if I wanted victuals, I should come to her, and that I should ly there in her *Wigwam*." When Rowlandson returns, the same woman lays a mat for her and puts a "good Rugg" over her. These actions Rowlandson calls "the first time I had any such kindness shewed me."[60] But it is *not* the first time an Indian nurtures her in the narrative, nor even in this way. The woman's kindness becomes the "first" because Rowlandson attempts to erase what she herself records: that her captors are not necessarily "merciless Heathen"— that in fact, they often resemble compassionate Christians. She cannot let the kindnesses go unrecorded, but she also cannot permit her readers to identify or sympathize with the wrong side. Rowlandson, in short, is torn. On the one hand, some Indians *have* shown her compassion and tried to comfort her; on the other hand, such sympathy implies a joining together, a unification, a process of belonging. At each appearance of kindness, therefore, Rowlandson also portrays cruelty or cites Scripture or does something else to reaffirm her separation. Her own increasing sympathy forces her to shut it down.[61]

Such imposed boundaries help explain Rowlandson's lack of sympathy for her mistress when her mistress's baby dies. Through the first three removes, Rowlandson focuses readers on the dying of her daughter Sarah, building pity and compassion through a vivid retelling of her death. In the thirteenth remove, just before describing her mistress's tragedy, Rowlandson offers another sight strong enough "to melt a heart of flint"— the suffering of an Englishman named John Gilberd and an abandoned Indian baby. In such moments, Rowlandson attempts to stir up affection in her readers so that it can be directed toward an English community of mutual affections. At the death of the mistress's infant, however, Rowlandson must discipline and redirect sympathy. Rowlandson writes, "That night they bade me go out of the *Wigwam* again: my Mistresses Papoos was sick, and it died that night, and there was one benefit in it, that there was more room." Such a harsh treatment of this tragedy suggests an utter lack of fellow feeling, an inability to identify with another mother who has lost a child. But more is going on here. When they bury the baby the next day, a company of Native Americans comes "to mourn and howl" with Rowlandson's mistress "both morning and evening," to which Rowlandson writes: "I confess, I could not much condole with them." On the one hand, Rowlandson *confesses* a lack of sympathy—and thus critiques herself and others who fail to find compassion for the suffering. On the other hand, she admits that she *did*, to some degree, feel for the mother: she did not "much" condole. Such compassion, however, must be turned away from the Indian mourners and back to the English community. It is there where she seeks her own company "to mourn and howl." In fact, Rowlandson moves from this detail to a description of her loneliness: "Many sorrowfull dayes I had in this place: often getting alone."[62] Rowlandson's response at this moment, in other words, must be read in the context of mutual affections and emotional communities: the mistress has one and Rowlandson does not. Moreover, Rowlandson attempts through this scene to remind readers of what she lacks; by modeling the mutual affections of the Indians for one mother who lost a child, Rowlandson tries to rebuild a company of readers that can now "mourn and howl" with her. Like the Indian sermons of the Eliot tracts, Rowlandson shows that *even* Indians know how to weep with those who weep, and she implicitly calls on the English to weep with her so that she will no longer be getting by alone. At the same time, even as she begins to condole with the Indians she refuses to join in her mistress's emotional community, mourning and howling with the Native Americans, because—for the sake of her identity—those with whom Rowlandson weeps and those who weep with her must be English. Thus, the scene ends with an extended recollection of her English home, a loving remembrance of Sabbaths spent with family and friends. The emotional trajectory turns away from the Indian company to end in its proper resting place, an *English* union of affections.

The attempt to reestablish borders emerges most explicitly in Rowlandson's denunciation of Praying Indians—the very symbol of blurred boundaries. In the nineteenth remove, Rowlandson bursts into tears at the sight of Tom and Peter, two Christian Indians who negotiate for her release: "Though they were *Indians*," she writes, "I gat them by the hand, and burst out into tears; my heart was so full that I could not speak to them." Recovering herself, Rowlandson asks after her family and friends, and Tom and Peter respond, "*They are all very well, but melancholy.*"[63] They then present her with biscuits and tobacco. Such kindness threatens the strict borders Rowlandson has been trying to build. She thus follows this scene with a seemingly random list of evil Praying Indians—*seemingly* random, except that it exactly compensates for her earlier tears and reestablishes a firm wall between English and Indian. Throughout Rowlandson's text, in other words, the presence of sympathy leads to its denial: the more Rowlandson fellow-feels with Indians, the more she must denounce them.

In *The Sovereignty and Goodness of God*, therefore, sympathy both creates and blurs boundaries—each part of the process leading to the other. If sympathy for a saint made one a saint, and compassion for the English allied one with the English, then what could it mean when Indian captors responded to Rowlandson's grief with a seemingly "Christian" compassion? And if Rowlandson herself began to sympathize with the plight of the Indians—with their hunger and their suffering and the death of their children—how could she maintain her identity as English? In Puritanism, sympathy remained an essential component of communal cohesion and belonging, a basic element of Winthrop's city on a hill spread more broadly through the culture. As such, however, sympathy needed not only to be stirred up, but also to be disciplined and redirected toward fellow saints and colonists. While a lack of sympathy could mark one as inhuman, fellow-feeling with the *wrong* people could threaten one's identity. Rowlandson responds by rousing feelings of pity, compassion, and sympathy in some cases and shutting them down in others. The narrative is torn throughout by this attempt to manage affections, for as *The Sovereignty and Goodness of God* so vividly demonstrates, sympathy, once invoked, was difficult to contain. It not only built distinctions; it broke them down—sometimes to the great consternation and vehement denial of those who found themselves fellow-feeling with the foe.

Conclusion

TRANSFORMATION AND CONTINUITY AT THE END OF THE CENTURY

ON THURSDAY MORNING, March 24, 1692, the Salem Village meetinghouse crowded with spectators who had come to see a respected grandmother and longtime member of the church face examination. At seventy-one, feeling sick and looking frail, Rebecca Nurse found herself accused of witchcraft. "She beat me this morning!" one of the afflicted girls shouted. Abigail Williams said the same, and then Ann Putnam Jr., "in a grievous fit, cried out that she hurt her." Nurse proclaimed her innocence and said that God would clear her name. But the accusations went on. Goodman Kenney complained of Nurse's specter, and Ann Putnam senior, the mother of the afflicted teenager, challenged her: "Did you not bring the Black man with you? Did you not bid me tempt God & die? How oft have you eat and drunk your own damnation?" At this, Nurse spread her hands in supplication: "Oh Lord, help me," she prayed. The girls fell in another fit. And then, at just this point of spectacle and misery, John Hathorne, presiding, appealed to a Puritan theology of sympathy: "It is very awful for all to see these agonies, and you, an old professor, thus charged with contracting with the Devil by the effects of it, and yet to see you stand with dry eyes when there are so many wet." With what seems in the text like calm assurance, Nurse answered plainly: "You do not know my heart."[1]

But that, of course, was the issue at hand—what all were attempting to determine. The trials concerned themselves not primarily with invisible specters, but with the unseen dispositions—the *hearts*—of those accused. For years, Puritans had found access to the inner affections through outer displays of fellow feeling, weeping with those who weep and rejoicing with those who rejoice. If Rebecca Nurse could not weep with afflicted saints, some Puritans could conclude, she must be rejoicing with the devil. That, at any rate, is what Hathorne decided. He committed Nurse to prison, and a few months later she was hanged.

Nurse's case here is significant because it takes us to a culminating point in the long Puritan process of separating the elect from the reprobate and the unregenerate through the use of fellow feeling. That search—and its eventual demise at Salem—held significant consequences for the meaning, implications, and evolution of sympathy. Salem marks the moment when Puritan judges became so sure of grace in some that they executed others. Those not with the girls were against them. Dry eyes could signify reprobation, but only if those dry eyes gazed at a weeping group of girls known to be chosen by God. When the trials eventually collapsed, this system of judgment also seemed to implode.

While Nurse, with her inner assurance, seemed to go all too gently into that bad night, those around her were not nearly so quiet or meek. At the first mention of accusation, three days before her examination, Israel and Elizabeth Porter, along with Daniel Andrew and Peter Cloyse, went to see her. They found her unwell, but, in true Puritan fashion, she blessed God for her illness. Then, "of her own accord, she began to speak of the affliction that was amongst them." In raising the issue, moreover, Nurse showed herself on the right side of sympathy: she spoke "of Mr. Parris's family, and how she was grieved for them." Due to her sickness, she could not visit, but "she pitied them with all her heart, and went to God for them." At the same time, Nurse suggested that some of the accused were most likely innocent—a stance that, if known by the girls, might have led to the charges against her. While her loyalties were divided, then, she nonetheless declared that her pity lay with the afflicted—precisely what the court three days later wanted to see displayed in a visual performance of fellow feeling. The visitants wrote up their findings and submitted them to the court, declaring that they would be willing to testify on Nurse's behalf under oath to what they first saw and heard. They defended her to the court based on a prior display of fellow feeling.[2]

Of course, whether Nurse pitied the girls or not could not ultimately matter in a conviction of witchcraft. Witchcraft meant familiarity with the devil; moreover, in the English statute that first guided the trials, capital witchcraft required actual harm. The prosecution had to prove that Nurse not only covenanted with the devil, but also that she used her diabolical alliance to hurt others. Much of the examination, therefore—and especially her later, official trial at the Court of Oyer and Terminer—focused on specific injuries. The court eventually sentenced Nurse to hang because, according to the evidence, she choked and beat and murdered the good and godly citizens of Salem.[3]

At the same time, the language of pity and tears should not be glossed over. A lack of feeling might not make one a witch, but it could signal one's absence from the covenant of God, especially if that person had supposedly been an upstanding member of the church. Because so much faith was invested in the afflicted girls as messengers of God, one either stood with them or against them. And to stand with the girls meant to *feel* with them in their duress. All good members of the church should sympathize, embracing and experiencing the same unity of spirit. Nurse's lack of tears did not make her a witch, but it did undercut her claim to being among the elect. In fact, when Judge Hathorne commented on her dry eyes, he specifically noted with incredulity that she was "an old professor," meaning a longtime member in full communion with the church. If Nurse lacked sympathy for the girls, that absence of fellow feeling indicated—at least for Hathorne—that she actually stood *outside* the sympathy, the communion, of the elect; it meant she was less than what she had always claimed to be, and possibly something far more.[4]

Such concerns soon became a matter of explicit counsel. On the same Thursday that Hathorne called attention to Nurse's dry eyes, Deodat Lawson preached a sermon requiring sympathy with the afflicted. Visiting the town to provide assistance and relief, the former Salem minister took to the pulpit and proclaimed the afflicted and accusing girls to be "*the visible Covenant people of GOD.*" As such, anyone else in covenant with God must sympathize with them: all listeners were explicitly "Exhorted and directed, to *Exercise True Spiritual sympathy with, and Compassion towards, those poor afflicted persons, that are by Divine Permission, under the Direful Influences of Satan's malice.*" Speaking to potential witches, however, Lawson declared that all true members of the church were "constrained, to Suppress that *Kindness* and Compassion, that in their *Sacred Addresses*, they once bare unto you (as those of their *own kind*, and framed out of the *same mould*)." Sympathy meant a drawing together of like unto like; as such, it entailed a separating of the covenanted people of God from those who chose to sign the devil's book. Across that line, no compassion or kindness—no fellow feeling—should pass. When he printed the sermon shortly afterward, Lawson added a prologue that reiterated this central point: considering the troubles "of your *Reverend* and *Pious* Pastor," he wrote, "whose family also, being *so much* under the influence of these troubles, *Spiritual sympathy* cannot but stir you up, to *assist* him as at *all* times so Especially at *such* a time as this." Whatever hesitancy Lawson showed toward the accused—admitting of some that "in times past, we could draw no other *Conclusions* than that they were real members of HIS *Mystical* Body"—Lawson never suggested that fellow feeling could or should include them. Sympathy lay with the afflicted, not the accused. The agonies of the girls called for compassion, and both the presence and the *display* of that fellow feeling could place one within the visible covenant people of God.[5]

When Susannah Martin laughed during her examination, therefore, it marked precisely the absence of sympathy that signified opposition to God. Martin was almost the same age as Nurse, but she had lived a very different life. Three decades earlier she had already stood trial for witchcraft, and now she made an easy victim for the court.[6] Perhaps because she knew in advance that she was doomed, Martin felt little call to restraint. "What do you laught at it?" Judge Hathorne stammered. "Well I may at such folly," she replied. Hathorne could not believe what he heard: "Is this folly, to see these so hurt?" Martin declared her innocence: "I never hurt man, woman or child." Mercy Lewis immediately cried out that Martin "hath hurt me a great many times & plucks me down." Martin laughed again. A short time later, Hathorne pressed her further: responding to an intimation by Martin that the girls, not herself, were dealing in black magic, Hathorne declared, "I do not think that you have such affections for these whom just now you insinuated had the Devil for their Master." As the afflicted broke into further agonies, screaming and cringing, evidencing both terror and pain, Hathorne put the question baldly: "Have not you compassion on these afflicted?" Martin answered simply, "No, I have none." Three months later, she was hanged.[7]

These dry eyes, this courtroom laughter, this declaration against compassion for the afflicted—all these signs were carefully noted by court supporters. In fact, ten years after the trials had ended, Deodat Lawson reprinted his Salem sermon and appended a short defense of the proceedings, so "that those who Sate Judges in those Cases, may by the serious Consideration, of the formidable Aspect and perplexed Circumstances, of that Afflictive Providence; be in some measure excused; or at least be less Censured." As he reiterated the evidence, Lawson turned to displays of emotion. Listing a series of reasons to believe the condemned were actually and truly witches, Lawson wrote, "It was observed, both in times of

Examination and Tryal, that the Accused seemed little affected with what the Sufferers underwent, or, what was Charged against them, as being the Instruments of Satan therein; so that the Spectators were grieved at their unconcernedness."[8] To be unconcerned for the afflicted—or even worse, to laugh at their agonies—was to place oneself in the party of Satan.

Of course, most Puritans readily professed that mistakes could be made: a church contained both hypocrites and saints. As much as they could, however, New England Puritans tried to be sure. They tested knowledge of the catechism, they kept track of godly lives, and they required convincing narratives of grace in an effort to get it right—to have the invisible communion of the elect match the visible membership of the church. They attempted at every turn to know another's heart. And the more certain a group of Puritans became about who actually constituted the Covenant People of God, the more limitations they built into sympathy, using it to sort the saved from the rest and demanding that fellow feeling go one way, not another.

The sheer certainty undergirding Salem becomes evident in the preaching of Samuel Parris. On the Sunday following Rebecca Nurse's examination, Parris preached that Christ "knows us perfectly; & he knows those of us that are in the Church, that we are either Saints or Devils." For him, there existed no in between, no sense of degrees—and as a result, no hesitations, self-doubts, or room for uncertainty about others. "We are either Saints, or Devils," he repeated, "the scripture gives us no medium."[9] With that stark division, Parris proceeded to claim extraordinary knowledge about who belonged to God and who did not. The afflicted girls, certainly, were God's own children. As was Parris himself. His preaching and demeanor throughout this period exhibit none of the anxiety that filled the journals of other, earlier and more prominent Puritans such as Thomas Shepard and John Winthrop. Instead, Parris considered himself a persecuted instrument of Christ: any opposition to him could be interpreted as the work of Antichristian spirits. Shortly before eight more condemned witches hung, Parris preached again, "The Devil & his Instruments will be making war with the Lamb & his Followers as long as they can"—a war that entailed "two parties": the "Antichrist (the spiritual whore) & all her Assistants" against "the Lamb & his followers." Between these sides lay a no man's land where literally no person could stand. As if the point were not clear enough, Parris concluded, "Here are no Newters. Every one is on one side or the other."[10] A covenant of grace against a covenant of works; Antichristian spirits against the Lamb and his followers; followers and defenders of the gospel against all who would oppose it and tear it down—in New England, from the Antinomian Controversy through the Salem witch trials, a strain of Puritanism repeatedly proclaimed an ultimate conflict that eliminated all spectrums and degrees, placing everyone on one side or another, either with or against. Moreover, this strain of Puritanism often displayed a surprising lack of qualm or query about who stood with whom. Parris, like Wheelwright, knew who was saved and who was not.

By claiming such knowledge, sympathy changed; but in these separate cases the consequences varied. In the Antinomian Controversy, the meaning, purpose, and significance of sympathy were the very issues at stake: one party claimed that a love of brethren counted as a sign of salvation; the other side disagreed. Even so, Antinomians like John Wheelwright tried to reconstruct a godly community through the language of brotherly love: claiming to know who belonged to the true Covenant of Grace, they used that knowledge to create a smaller, tighter family of mutual affections drawn out of John Winthrop's more broadly conceived sympathetic city. In the Salem witch trials, Deodat Lawson, John Hathorne, Samuel Parris, and others not only attempted to build such a community; they also used sympathy—or its lack—to sort the saved from the damned, the wholesome from the hypocrites. Just as Mary Rowlandson had to reassert her English identity by disciplining her sympathy away from the Indians, so in Salem, church members had to direct their sympathy to Parris and the afflicted in order to reclaim their status in the church. Any fellow feeling that went the wrong way would raise suspicion. Sympathy meant belonging, and where there were only two possible parties, this affection had to be closely watched. Thus, an overassurance about the status of the afflicted made fellow feeling all the more significant, even as it disciplined and constrained the expression of that sympathy for anyone else. In other words, as sympathy signified more, it could extend to fewer people. Down a different path, Puritans were advancing on a lesson they had learned long before: when it comes to judging the hearts of others, certainty limits sympathy.

Years later, the great-great grandson of Judge Hathorne would depict an adulterous woman standing beneath a noose and facing a crowd of Puritans, her chest bearing a beautiful scarlet A. "Meagre, indeed, and cold," he wrote, "was the sympathy that a transgressor might look for, from such bystanders at the scaffold."[11] In such a formulation, Nathaniel Hawthorne was in fact more perceptive than he might have known. The Puritans did not lack sympathy—what he wants to suggest here—but they did direct that sympathy toward specific people at specific times. In the case of the Salem witches, a show of sympathy for the condemned might quickly land one in court, precisely because sympathy meant *so much* to the Puritans. It signaled identity and community, and as such it needed to flow toward the "visible covenant people of God"—the afflicted girls, not those condemned to die.

Even so, doubts arose. And they arose, in part, because the affections could not be limited, constrained, or disciplined away from the scaffold. That much became clear in the execution of George Burroughs, a former minister hanged as a principal leader of the witches. After being carted through the streets of Salem and forced up a ladder to his noose, Burroughs began to speak. According to Robert Calef, a critic of the proceedings, Burroughs filled his speech "with such Solemn and Serious Expressions, as were to the Admiration of all present; his Prayer (which he concluded by repeating the Lord's Prayer) was so well worded and uttered with such composedness, and such (at least seeming) fervency of Spirit, as was very affecting, and drew Tears from many (so that it seemed to some, that the Spectators would hinder the Execution)." Here sympathy threatened to bend in the wrong direction. The condemned was winning the crowd. As Mary Rowlandson had found her sympathy beginning to extend improperly, so the witnesses of Burroughs's execution did as well. The ladder gave way, the noose tightened, and Burroughs died, but Cotton Mather, a leading Boston minister, could not let the episode pass without attempting to regain the affections of the crowd. Mounting a horse, he spoke to the spectators and convinced them again of Burroughs's guilt, reminding his listeners "That the Devil has often been transformed into an Angel of Light." As Calef noted, such a speech "did somewhat appease the People, and the Executions went on." Sympathy, in other words, had been disciplined; the people had been reminded that for witches there could be no fellow feeling.[12]

At the same time, one of the judges who had condemned Burroughs marked this moment as a turning point in the trials. In his diary, Judge Samuel Sewall recorded the execution and noted the "very great number of spectators" present. Of the condemned, he observed, "All of them said they were innocent, Carrier and all. Mr. Mather says they all died by a Righteous sentence." Like Calef, so Sewall reported on Mather's need to make a speech. But his diary entry does not end with Mather mounted on his horse appeasing the crowd; instead Sewall gives the last word to Burroughs: "Mr. Burroughs by his speech, prayer, protestation of his innocence, did much move unthinking persons, which occasions their speaking hardly concerning his being executed."[13] It is hard to know what Sewall meant by the word "unthinking." On the one hand, it seems to indicate that they *should* have thought better of their fellow feeling, resisting Burroughs's appeal. On the other hand, it suggests that those who had previously thought little about the trials began to see them in a new light, precisely because they had finally been moved. For the Puritans, affections undergirded persuasion; sympathy with Burroughs could change one's judgment concerning him *and* those who had condemned him. Sewall himself thought differently soon enough: after the trials ended, he became the only judge to repent his role and ask forgiveness of his church.

But Burroughs was not the only figure who garnered sympathy and thus began to change opinions. When Captain John Alden, a prominent Boston merchant, was examined and imprisoned in Salem, the jailer found himself experiencing a change of both heart and mind. As Calef writes, "The Prison-Keeper seeing such a Man Committed, of whom he had a good esteem, was after this the more Compassionate to those that were in Prison on the like account; and did refrain from such hard things to the Prisoners, as before he had used."[14] In other words, because he admired Alden and believed him innocent, the jailer began to do precisely what Lawson had formerly prohibited: he had compassion on the imprisoned; he showed kindness to the condemned. And in the dawning of that fellow feeling, the meaning of condemnation itself began to shift—from the righteous sentence of God to the misguided injustice of the all-too-assured. As the Puritans had long taught and preached, argument depends on affection; persuasion requires a prior unity of hearts, so that where the jailer found himself in a kind of fellow feeling with the jailed, he became willing to listen to their case—and, consequentially, willing to question the arguments of those who had put them there.

Thus, in many ways the Salem witch trials amounted to a great contest of sympathies waged first in court and later in print. As David Hall has noted, the crisis opened a vent to grief; it was a way to explain and make sense of so much individual and communal suffering. In presenting evidence against the accused, members of the community narrated "stories mainly rooted in the suffering of bewildered people who watched children or their spouses die or suffer agonizing fits."[15] In the trial of Rebecca Nurse, for example, John and Hannah Putnam testified that "our poor young child was taken about midnight with strange and violent fits which did most grievously affright us, acting much like to the poor bewitched

persons, when we thought they would indeed have died." The child suffered for two days and two nights, "and then departed this life by a cruel
and violent death." Hardly mentioning Rebecca Nurse in their entire testimony, the Putnams ended only with a grief meant to stir fellow feeling: the child's death, they claimed, was "enough to pierce a stony heart,
for to the best of our understanding it was near five hours a-dying."[16] Such
a spectacle of misery aimed at moving the judges and all who listened; and
this sustained and unified movement of affections could lead finally to the
condemnation of even Rebecca Nurse, a respected church member and
grandmother in the community.

But of course, the winning of sympathies also worked in reverse.
When Robert Calef published his condemnation of the proceedings,
his literary style and rhetorical maneuverings moved audiences in the
opposite direction. Calef did not focus on the deaths and sufferings of
accusers, but on the grief and hangings of the accused. Perhaps nothing illustrates his technique better than his use of Mary Easty's petition.
Easty, a sister of Rebecca Nurse, was condemned to die September 22.
Before her execution, however, she wrote an eloquent appeal to the Court
of Oyer and Terminer that declared her innocence, accepted her fate, and
proposed ways the court could avoid killing more guiltless people in the
future. The petition, which Calef reprints in full, ends with a plea: "I beg
your Honours not to deny this my humble Petition, from a poor dying
Innocent person, and I question not but the Lord will give a blessing to
your Endeavours." As the last words of a dying person, Easty's appeal
hangs on the authority of her approaching death, but in Calef's narrative it
also does more: it begs not just for change, but for compassion. In the first
edition of Calef's book, one turns the page from this all-too-human plea
and is struck—almost slapped in the face—by the following line: "After
Execution Mr. Noyes turning him to the Bodies, said, what a sad thing it is
to see Eight Firebrands of Hell hanging there."[17] Calef could have put this
line almost anywhere; he could have organized his section in any number
of ways. But the stark contrast between Easty's human plea and Noyes's
blanket condemnation makes Calef's point without him having to state
it: no "firebrand of hell" speaks with the voice of Mary Easty. Noyes's lack
of sympathy accuses the accusers and vindicates the condemned. In such
ways, Calef's details, narratives, and rhetorical constructions invert fellow
feeling and reestablish the accused as saints—as *martyrs* now—identified
as such by the sympathy of readers. As John Eliot attempted to confirm
Native American conversions by producing tears in English readers, so

Calef sought to turn condemned witches into persecuted saints by moving the affections of those who read his text.

This contest of sympathies also may explain the surprising lack of Fast Days during the colony's crisis. From beginning to end of the entire affair, only one public Fast Day was held, and it had been called for before the crisis broke. As the historian William DeLoss Love notes, the lack of publicly proclaimed mourning may have resulted from divided opinions and affections. The Fast Day held on May 26 resulted in divergent sermons; all had to mourn, but for whom and for what should they sorrow and repent: that witches had come to dwell amongst them or that innocent people were being accused and convicted of a heinous crime? The answer depended, in part, on the leanings of particular ministers. In other words, far from unifying the colony in mutual affections—weeping with those who weep—a public Fast Day served again to exacerbate the differences. Like the 1637 Fast Day during the Antinomian Controversy, the ritual of repentance could divide colonists into *two* emotional communities.[18]

The same problem plagued the first Fast Day held after the Salem witch trials came to a close. The colony waited almost five years to make a day for public mourning, and even then the General Court split over the appropriate response: some still defended the executions while others called for repentance. In the process, the power of proclaiming public fasts passed from the clergy to the magistrates: the leading minister, Cotton Mather, drew up a proposal to be published in churches throughout the land, but the General Court rejected his draft and instead asked Samuel Sewall to write a proclamation. As the colony gathered to mourn, it still remained unclear what exactly required a fast: whether the colony should repent the execution of the condemned or the sins that had led to Satan's rise. Unable to say who stood in the Covenant of Grace—whether the afflicted or the accused—New England could not finally say for whom, with whom, or how one ought to grieve.

Such uncertainty became even more embedded through the very logic that often defended the trials. If "the Devil has often been transformed into an Angel of Light," as more than just Cotton Mather kept preaching, then eventually certainty itself loses its assurance. When is the light really light? When are the seemingly elect truly the saints of God? And how can one ever know?[19] After the Salem witch trials, more people became willing to admit that they did not and could not know. Judge Sewell asked forgiveness for his role. Members of the jury worried aloud that they had no sufficient basis for conviction and conveyed "to all in general (and to the surviving Sufferers in especial) our deep sense of, and sorrow for our Errors, in acting on such Evidence to the condemning of any person." John Hale, a nearby minister who had helped initiate the search for witches, also admitted ignorance and the possibility of error: in *A Modest Enquiry into the Nature of Witchcraft*, published a decade after the trials ended, he wrote, "Such was the darkness of that day, the tortures and lamentations of the afflicted, and the power of former presidents [precedents], that we walked in the clouds, and could not see our way."[20] What is most noticeable about these confessions and expressions of sorrow is their utter *lack* of certainty. In asking forgiveness, they did not claim that the condemned ought never to have been condemned; they claimed it was impossible to know. They repented of *assurance* and admitted ignorance about the spiritual status of other people. Of course, Puritans had *always* hedged their bets, admitting that on earth it was impossible to fully purge the church of hypocrites. In that sense, Salem represented a height of certainty unusual in Puritan New England; but at the same time, these witch trials represented the natural endpoint of the long endeavor to confirm as members only those that one could reasonably be sure were saved. When the Salem witch trials collapsed, this whole effort became, to many, suspect. People were now willing to admit what Rebecca Nurse had told them from the beginning: "You do not know my heart."

But the Salem witch trials were not alone in making this turn. The general rejection of the trials joined a series of other events in New England all of which claimed that the attempt to make visible church members match the invisible elect was inherently misguided. Turning against that attempt changed sympathy itself. Down in Connecticut, for example, a prominent minister named Solomon Stoddard had recently published a treatise that proceeded precisely along these lines. Opening communion to anyone in good standing, Stoddard denied the possibility that the elect could be determined, that saints could finally be sussed out. Meanwhile, Boston's Brattle Street Church, founded seven years after the trials ended, explicitly rejected the public examination of candidates for membership: in this prominent church, no one would use conversion narratives to detect and separate the elect, while communion would be opened to anyone with "visible sanctity." The pastor could still inquire into the spiritual state of any member, but the community as a whole would leave the inner heart to God. While Cotton Mather initially objected to Brattle Street, he was gradually mollified by Samuel Willard, the minister of Third Church, who not surprisingly also harbored suspicions about the Salem witch trials from the beginning and helped bring them to a close. Thus, Salem both joined and catalyzed a movement toward greater ecumenical uncertainty: outward obedience would be good enough; the inner heart could be left to God.[21]

It is here where we can best see both the change and the continuity in Puritan sympathy. From the beginning, Puritan sympathy had operated as both a sign and a practice. Since a love of brethren resulted from grace, it could testify to salvation; yet as part of sanctification, it could also be commanded. Ministers such as William Hooke declared it a doctrine gleaned from scripture and attempted to stir it up in both listeners and readers. As it moved forward from Puritan New England, sympathy retained this dual aspect of duty and discovery: eighteenth-century ministers, philosophers, novelists, and others would call for sympathy and attempt to induce it, but they would also use its presence—known through experience, display, and performance—as a mark, a *sign*, of gentility and refinement. In this sense, the meaning of sympathy for the godly became the function of sympathy for the gentleman.

Take, for example, the case of the first American novel, William Hill Brown's *The Power of Sympathy* (1789). At one point, the main character describes his sympathy for a slave mother in South Carolina, and he uses that discovered experience to declare, "I FEEL *that I have a soul*—and every man of sensibility feels it within himself." As the possession of sensibility replaced the possession of saving grace, those who wished to join this special club testified to their belonging by likewise experiencing and expressing soft and tender hearts. Sympathy continued as a sign of membership in a certain select society. As the main character's friend explains near the end of *The Power of Sympathy*, "[A] man without sensibility exhibits no sign of a soul." From Puritanism forward, sympathy maintained a signifying function, testifying to one's status as either godly or refined by identifying one's membership in the right sort of group.[22]

The fact that this experience in Brown's novel comes in the presence of a slave further reveals both continuity and transformation. On the one hand, the main character follows his moment of soul-discerning sensibility by telling the slave mother, "May thy soul be ever disposed to SYMPATHIZE with thy children, and with thy brethren and sisters in calamity."[23] He distinguishes one community from another—identifies two separate kinship groups—through sympathy; moreover, even as his own sensibility is touched by the sufferings of this slave mother, she mostly serves as testimony of his own goodness. There is a basic separation of emotional communities here that resembles what happened in the Puritan writings of the Eliot tracts with all their sentimental descriptions of "poor Indians" breaking into "abundant tears." Yet detached from God's sovereign election and the saint's search for assurance of salvation, the signifying of sympathy has shifted to an emphasis on its presence and practice, not its building of community or its evidence of grace. As Arminians gradually replaced Calvinists, virtuous living increasingly marked the proper path to heaven. In this process, fellow feeling moved from a concern about *with whom* one sympathized (and who sympathized with you in return) to a measure of *how much* one fellow-felt with anyone, anywhere, in any pain, suffering, or distress. Simply having sympathy came to matter more than the direction and reciprocity of that affection—in part because there was no set apart group of probable saints with whom a would-be saint ought to fellow-feel. If the true "brethren," or saints, cannot be determined, then a "love of the brethren" does not help much in the assurance of salvation. The comfort many Puritans had drawn from 1 John 3:14 required some certainty about the hearts of others. Absent that, the mere presence of sympathy came to bear more significance than either its object or its return.

Nonetheless, many of the ideas that supported the rhetorical tropes aimed at sympathy remained the same. Seventeenth-century texts invested in fellow feeling tried to produce tearful responses in readers by using deathbed scenes, modeling affections, commanding one to melt, elevating touch and gesture and tears—by, in general, employing techniques and devices that would later be replicated and amplified in sentimental fiction. When Maria Fawcet dies in *The Power of Sympathy*, she does so in a fashion that would have found many admirers in Puritan New England. Reverend Holmes, who takes her in, is certainly no Puritan; but in his letter about Maria's death he espouses a view of the affair that draws from Puritan rhetoric. Claiming that "Providence ... directed [Maria's] footsteps to my dwelling," he promises to treat her well "in this wilderness world." He then focuses on Maria's tearful repentance, arguing that it prepares the ground for reconciliation: "shall she not," he writes, "if she return with tears of repentance and contrition, be entitled to our love and charity?" As in Puritan scenes of repentance, so here, Maria's tears do a great deal of work: "however guilty she might have been," Holmes adds, "the tears of penitence do certainly make atonement therefor." But weeping signals authenticity only if it produces a sympathetic response, and the opening of Holmes's letter suggests that Maria's emotion has done just that: "We have a scene of distress at our house peculiarly pathetick and affecting," he writes.[24] As with the Puritans, so here: affecting tears seal a contrite heart as sincere.

Moreover, Maria's penitence moves her closer to salvation. Holmes writes, "I may say with assurance that I have felt an emanation of this heavenly joy animate my heart, in beholding this woman delighting to steer her course heavenward." In keeping with Puritan conversion narratives, membership in the communion of saints depends on the emotional response of those, like Holmes, who are already regarded as good. Having touched *his* heart, Maria's sorrow then becomes the very stuff of her salvation, so that in her death she resembles a Puritan saint. "Serene and composed," she presented "a spirit broken, and borne down by severe distress, yet striving to surmount all, and aspire to heaven." Striving and surmounting do not necessarily accord with Calvinist grace, but the elevation of Maria's soul through patience closely parallels the deathbed scenes of the elect. "Weep not for me," Maria proclaims, then she dies "in firm assurance of the soul's blessed immortality." Maria's tears, rather than Christ's sacrifice, open the gates of heaven; but the need for sincere repentance—known in the display of a broken heart able to move the right sort of people and leading ultimately to salvation—ties Maria's history far more to Calvinist theology than to other sources of sentimentalism. Compare Maria's passing, for example, to the deathbed scene of Thomasine Clopton, John Winthrop's second wife. As she lay dying, Thomasine asked her husband John "to be contented, for you breake mine heart (said she) with your grievings." Thomasine, meanwhile, remained serene, "comfortably resolved whither to live or die." As death drew near, she lifted up her hands, prayed, and exhorted those around her to be wary of their sins. "We might perceive that God had given her victorye," Winthrop writes, "by the comfort which she had in the meditation of hir happinesse, in the favour of God in Christ Jesus."[25] Like Maria, she resigned her mortal breath in the firm assurance of the soul's blessed immortality.

Such continuity and transformation was not wholly self-contained in the contested politics and theologies of New England. The broader shift in sympathy at the end of the seventeenth century came about both through domestic affairs—such as Salem, Stoddard, and Brattle Street—and through an influx of anti-Calvinism from Cambridge Platonists and Latitudinarians abroad.[26] The Cambridge Platonists, including Benjamin Whichcote, Henry More, and Ralph Cudworth, practiced philosophy out of backgrounds in theology, and that combination led to their central tenet: that faith and reason went hand-in-hand. From this foundation they worked up treatises defending certain religious positions as not just reasonable, but in fact far more rational than any alternative. In making these arguments, moreover, the Cambridge Platonists drew lines of continuity from natural religion to revealed religion—that is, from the principles that all humans could know and understand to the doctrines given specially in Scripture. As a result, Christian virtue became a kind of universal ethics: certain practices were good and necessary not because God commanded them; rather, God commanded them because they were universally, eternally, and immutably good. Humans anywhere could use their free will to discover and practice virtue, thus attaining the happiness that God attached to holiness.[27]

Parts of this trajectory can be witnessed already in a sermon Ralph Cudworth preached to the House of Commons on March 31, 1647. On this occasion, Cudworth wished to vanquish Antinomian stirrings unleashed by the English Civil Wars; in other words, he faced the same opponent as church elders had ten years earlier in New England's Antinomian Controversy. Yet Cudworth's approach reveals the differing direction that mainstream English religious thought would take. Cudworth opposed Antinomianism by questioning predestination itself and proposing obedience as the best sign of salvation. In other words, far more than the New England elders ever did (or ever intended to do), Cudworth transformed religion into rational morality. That shift appears first in his choice of Scripture. Where the New England Antinomian Controversy debated the meaning of 1 John 3:14—"We know that we have passed from death unto life, because we love the brethren"—Cudworth focused on a separate verse, 1 John 2:3–4: "And hereby we do know that we know him, if we keep his commandments. He that saith, I know him, and keepeth not his commandments, is a liar, and the truth is not in him." This move from 1 John 3:14 to 1 John 2:3–4 suggests, in itself, the path that sympathy would take, retaining aspects of both sign and practice but shifting the emphasis from the former to the latter—changing what sympathy signified by focusing more on how, and *how much*, it was exercised. What mattered most to the Cambridge Platonists and the Latitudinarians who came after them was not an inner experience offering bits of assurance to anxious sinners, but rather a moral life and a solid conscience.

Cudworth makes this difference clear by utilizing the same metaphor of sun and stars that guided debates during the Antinomian Controversy. Where Cotton had called on weak Christians to wait for the sun in their dark night of doubt, elders advised them to take comfort in the witness of the stars. The emphasis in both cases was on a passive perceiving, a search for signs: both sides focused on discovery and experience, not action and ethics. In contrast, Cudworth told Christians to stop gazing at the stars or blinding themselves with the sun. "We have no warrant in Scripture, to peep into these hidden Rolls and Volumes of Eternity," Cudworth preached, "and to make it our first thing that we do when we come to Christ, to spell out our name in the starres, and to perswade our selves that we are certainly elected to everlasting happinesse: before we see *the image of God*, in righteousness and true holinesse, shaped in our hearts." That righteousness and holiness meant obedience and morality, a "hearty compliance with his heavenly will." True Christians, therefore, should live a godly life of good behavior that reflected divinity like the rays of the sun.[28] In such a formulation, human beings have a free choice, an ability to act. For Cudworth, what moves us from darkness to day-light is *ourselves*. "I am sure, there be too many of us," he declared, "that have long pretended to Christ, which make little or no progress in *true Christianity*, that is, Holinesse of life: that ever hang hovering in a *Twilight of Grace*, and never seriously put our selves forwards into clear *Day-light*, but esteem that glimmering *Crepusculum*, which we are in, and like that faint *Twilight*, better then broad open day: whereas, *The Path of the just* (as the *Wiseman* speaketh) *is as the shining light, that shineth more and more unto the perfect day*."[29] Coming into the sunlight was a matter of human effort and will—of *putting ourselves forward* into clear daylight—not a matter of divine good pleasure.

Such a position directly affected Cudworth's use and understanding of sympathy. In his description of true Christians, Cudworth drew on both the ancient definition—that like attracts like—and more modern formulations. True Christians, he explained, are those who possess sparks of divinity which, in turn, create a magnetic pull of likeness between God and believer. A holy life, kindled and quickened in the heart, constituted "in a sober and qualified sence, *Divinity incarnate*; and all particular Christians, that are really possessed of it, so many *Mysticall* Christs." By being mini, mystical Christs, Christians could be assured of God's compassion: "Never was any tender Infant, so dear to those Bowels that begat it, as an *Infant new-born Christ, formed in the heart* of any true believer, to God, the *father* of it." The pitiful cry of any such "tender *Babe*" would "by strong sympathy, draw his compassionate arm to help and relieve it." We can deduce that God has compassion because we know that humans do: "If those expressions of goodnesse and tender affection here amongst the creatures, be but drops of that full Ocean that is in God; how can we then imagine, that this *Father* of our *spirits* should have so little regard to his own dear Ofspring?" Such a line moves Cudworth away from depravity and the presuppositions of predestination. Instead, the great sorter on Judgment Day—rather than being God's sovereign election—becomes sympathy itself. Relying on a view of physics infused with sympathy, Cudworth preached: "Divine wisdome hath so ordered the frame of the whole Universe, as that every thing should have a certain proper Place, that should be a Receptacle for it." In fact, a "strong *Magick* of Nature, pulls and draws every thing continually, to that place which is suitable to it, and to which it doth belong." As a result, hell will "by strong *Sympathy* pull in all sinne, and *Magnetically* draw it to it self: as true Holinesse, is alwayes breathing upwards, and fluttering towards Heaven." Set off as its own inset line in Greek is the principle that Cudworth asserts will sort all people when they come to die: "God always joins Like to Like."[30]

On the one hand, there is nothing to this statement that Puritans would find disconcerting. They believed in the same principle, embraced the same sort of physics, and understood such principles to guide both human relations and theological decrees. Sympathy was a mechanism for sorting one kind from another, for figuring out just where one belonged. But Cudworth's subtle difference lies in a point of emphasis that would have enormous ramifications: rather than being primarily an operation of discovery, sympathy had become predominately a call to action—an opening by which Christians could *place themselves* in one orb or the other, heaven or hell. In this life, Cudworth preached, "we do actually ... instate our selves in the possession of one or other of them." Far from searching out where one belonged through an examination of fellow feeling, one could instate oneself into the proper magnetic pull. "If you aime onely at your selves in your lives," Cudworth continued, "and make your *Self* the Compasse by which you sail, and the Starre, by which you steer your Course, looking at nothing higher and more noble than *your selves*; deceive not your selves, *you have neither seen Christ, nor known him*; you are deeply incorporated ... with the *Spirit of this World*, and have no true *Sympathy* with God and Christ, no *fellowship* at all with them." For Puritans, one uses a discovery of sympathy to deduce salvation; for Cudworth, one uses obedience to deduce a sympathy with Christ.[31]

In his emphasis on obedience and virtue, Cudworth tried to extend the boundaries of his imagined Christian community beyond doctrinal divides. Citing Ephesians 4:3—just as Winthrop and Wheelwright and countless others had done—Cudworth claimed, "I will therefore shut up this, with that of the *Apostle: Let us keep the unity of the Spirit in the bond of peace.* Let this soft and silken Knot of *Love,* tie our Hearts together; though our Heads and Apprehensions cannot meet, as indeed they never will, but always stand at some distance off from one another." Agreement, in other words, mattered far less than affection.[32] To some extent, Winthrop would have heartily concurred. After all, he preached a similar message in *A Model of Christian Charity,* and during the Antinomian Controversy, elders commented that disagreement ended successfully not with consensus, but with a call to brotherly love that smoothed over doctrinal differences. For Winthrop, as for Cudworth, affection outweighed agreement. And yet the trend of Cambridge Platonists like Cudworth went in a way that Winthrop could never follow. For while Winthrop and other Puritans emphasized a unity of hearts, they still tried to identity *which* hearts counted and which did not—which experience of fellow feeling put one in the communion of saints and which experiences made one an enemy of the gospel. That is, Puritans primarily used sympathy and a love of brethren as a mark of identification and separation.

Anglicans, increasingly, did not. Instead, they embraced a universalizing of both sympathy and charity that moved away from signs of election to practices of the godly. After the Restoration of Charles II to the English throne, a new generation of divines reacted to the anarchy, confusion, and bloodshed of the preceding years by calling for a universal love stripped of doctrinal separations. The proponents of this new creed were called Latitudinarians, and by the end of the seventeenth century they had become the most dominant and influential voices in England.[33] Like the Cambridge Platonists who had come before, Latitudinarians such as John Tillotson, Isaac Barrow, Simon Patrick, and Edward Stillingfleet preached a rational basis to religion that rejected predestination and focused on freely chosen ethical behavior available to all. Human nature began as essentially *good* (a creation of the infinitely good God), and anyone could freely and rationally cooperate with divine grace in achieving their best life now. In preaching such a position the Latitudinarians deliberately set themselves up against Puritans, dissenters, and anyone influenced by such traditions: the Calvinist God, they taught, was irrational, arbitrary, and false.[34]

Such a position resulted in a shifted view of sympathy, and in particular the *source* of it. For the Puritans, sympathy came both embedded in fallen nature and infused by divine grace. In the first case, it operated mostly among one's immediate kin, drawing like to like even among the heathens: sympathizing with parents or children did not constitute a sign of salvation but simply a mark of being human. Yet in addition to this natural sympathy, the Puritans also preached a divine love of brethren birthed in the heart through the operations of grace. To love the saints one had to *be* a saint. Sympathizing with the true church signified fellowship in that church, and such fellowship could happen only if God had elected one to the communion of saints. Not so for the Latitudinarians. Because they preached a good nature capable of holiness by virtue of one's reason, choice, and natural disposition, they claimed that sympathy for all bubbled up from within rather than descending from without. It was bound up with being human. As Isabel Rivers explains, for the Latitudinarians "man is seen to possess good nature, candour, and ingenuity, and his temper, complexion, inclination, disposition, constitution, and frame lead him naturally towards sympathy, benevolence, beneficence, charity, and humanity to his fellows."[35] Sympathy, in other words, was universal. According to this way of thinking, what Christianity added to nature was simply a clearer enunciation of, and a greater motive to perform, the moral obligations that all could discover. In 1690 the Latitudinarian Archbishop of Canterbury, John Tillotson—who was extraordinarily influential in New England and highly admired by the Mathers—said so explicitly:

> And therefore the Christian Religion doth only declare these Duties more plainly, and press them more earnestly upon us, and enforce the obligation of them by more powerful Arguments and Considerations, grounded upon clearer discoveries of the grace and mercy of God to mankind, and of the rewards and punishments of another World: but these Duties are in their nature still the same, and the Christian Religion is so far from releasing us from the obligation of them, that it hath very much heighten'd it, and bound them the faster upon us.[36]

Consider, however, the shift in sympathy that results from such a statement. Rather than being a *new* possibility implanted by grace, sympathy instead operates as a faculty or virtue present in all human beings and capable of being exercised at any time toward anyone. In becoming simply a "more powerful motive to the practice of [moral virtues]," grace becomes radically different than the Puritan formulation of it as *the* source of holiness. Under Tillotson the mere presence of sympathy can no longer sort one person from another; rather, the more one freely chooses to exercise it, the more he or she embraces a rational and universal truth highlighted, recommended, and further motivated by the Christian religion.

In that sense, sympathy still retains a link to its function as a sign, but not in the same way. Displays of sympathy showed not that one *might* be godly, but rather just how good and godly one already was. Such claims appeared in the rest of Tillotson's Whitsunday sermon. Enlarging on the "fruits of the spirit," he began by asserting that goodness was universal, something "which Mankind is agreed in, and which is universally approv'd by the light of nature, by Heathens, as well as Christians." A principal form of goodness, he continued, is charity, which he defined simply as "*doing good.*" It is at this particular moment that the continuing use of Puritan sympathy and the movement away from it emerges in full force, for as he defined charity, Tillotson turned to a passage also found in *A Model of Christian Charity*, Galatians 6:10. That verse reads: "As we have therefore opportunity, let us do good to all men, especially unto them who are of the household of faith." This verse contains both a universal and a particular—an embrace of "all men" and a separation of "the household of faith." Winthrop quoted it in full, and the Puritans in general spent a great deal of effort trying to determine who belonged to this "household of faith," using sympathy as a key sign of membership. Tillotson made no such move. Instead he cited Galatians 6:10 and quoted only the first half of the verse: "Do good to all men." For him, the universal trumped—even eliminated—the particular; he was not interested in identifying a particular household, but instead preached an ethics applicable to all.[37]

As Tillotson further delineated what he meant by "goodness," he turned to passages that Puritans used to understand sympathy, universalizing what they considered signs of particular membership. Supporting the idea that people ought to have "compassion, and good-will towards all men," Tillotson cited, among other verses, Romans 12:9–10, Romans 12:15, and 1 Peter 3:8–9—all of which Puritans regularly quoted when explaining and calling for sympathy. Yet in making such calls, Puritans believed that only certain people could properly respond, and that in their responses congregants would, in effect, demonstrate to themselves and to others their membership in the communion of saints. For Tillotson, sympathy still functioned as a sign of godliness, but it also became subsumed under a category of universal goodness. Summarizing these verses, Tillotson preached that they represent "unquestionable instances of Goodness, and pass for current among all Mankind, are on all hands agreed to be good, and have an universal approbation among all parties and professions, how wide soever their differences may be in other matters."[38] As a result, freely embracing these various forms of "doing good"—including sympathy—moved one toward the gospel: salvation could be approached on one's own by exercising compassion and beneficence, rather than by discovering the passive presence of a special, God-given sympathy with saints.

Here then lies the fundamental continuity and transformation in the history of seventeenth-century sympathy. For later thinkers, especially the Latitudinarians, fellow feeling still operated as a sign, but the sign had also shifted: sympathy did not signal that God had chosen one, but rather that one was already becoming godly; and it manifested that movement not by the presence of fellow feeling for the right people, but rather by the simple *fact* of sympathy—its presence and exercise *in* anyone *for* everyone. Since human nature began as good, it started with sympathy; and the more people exercised this gift of nature the better they became. In that sense, while it became broader and more ecumenical (no longer used to separate the saved from the damned), it also became more *individual*. What mattered was not so much mutual and *reciprocal* affections that built up a particular community while separating it off from others; instead what mattered was one's own individual exercise of sympathy for others, the assumption being that if everyone behaved in this way, society's accumulated exercise of individual sympathies would make everyone better off. As Tillotson preached, the virtues of charity, compassion, and beneficence are not just "excellent in their nature and use," but all have "a tendency both to the Happiness of particular persons singularly consider'd, and of human Society."[39] The difference between the Latitudinarians and the Puritans lies in whether they considered sympathy primarily as a moral practice that moves one toward the good (including godliness, happiness, holiness, and heaven), or primarily as a sign of grace providing some degree of comfort to an anxious sinner searching for assurance of salvation. At the same time, sympathy continued to operate as a sign of sensibility in sentimental culture: it separated some from others, identifying a special group as particularly refined or especially civilized. What changed sympathy, then, was a shift in emphasis resulting from theological critiques of predestination and human depravity, culminating in a greater loss of certainty about the hearts of others. With such tenets dropped, sympathy mattered less for what it suggested of some other spiritual realm. Instead, sympathy began to point *at itself*; it became its own reward. Rather than providing comfort to anxiety about one's future eternal home, feelings of sympathy provided a form of immediate pleasure to human pride; instead of alleviating one's sense of worthlessness, it confirmed one's sense of worth. Puritans, for example, might have examined themselves and determined: "My sympathy with the sorrows and sufferings of probable saints suggests that I *might* be one as well." Latitudinarians, on the other hand, declared: "My sympathy with the sorrows and sufferings of anyone shows just how saintly I've always been—and makes me even more so now." This shift represents an alteration in tone that finally enables sympathy to flourish into a developing culture of sentimentalism. But by insisting on a fundamentally *good* human nature, fellow feeling also lent itself to a kind of complacency that many would later critique; for some, it became a pat on the back for being so compassionate, a self-congratulations that eventually came under fire in eighteenth-century satire.[40]

Even so, that eighteenth-century pat on the back began long before in a Puritan search for comfort. Such a search often relied on a concept of sympathy based in interpretations of Hebrews 4:15, Hebrews 13:3, Romans 12:15, 1 Peter 3:8, and, especially, 1 John 3:14. And while emphases shifted, the dual dynamic of sign and practice remained. The history of modern sympathy, in other words, extends beyond Latitudinarianism and moral sense philosophy to the Calvinist theology of fellow feeling emerging out of early modern England. From the moment Puritans first set themselves apart and called for greater reform in the Church of England, they turned to sympathy as a Christian duty and a sign of salvation. Required of all, it was reserved for some, and in coming years, the display of a tender heart melting for the misery of certain others could mark one as godly—as a member of the communion of saints. This is the discourse that Latitudinarians subtly changed as they began to preach a universal ethics shorn of election and human depravity. Yet in changing sympathy, they still used it as a mark of identity: what it identified, however, was no longer godliness, but goodness—no longer the grace of salvation but the refinement of civilization. Thus, while the eighteenth-century sympathetic, tender-hearted man of sensibility may have been familiar only with Latitudinarian preaching and the treatises of moral sense philosophers, his ancestry went back much further. This gentleman—quick to his tears and always ready with a compassionate sigh—descended from a people concerned with predestination and the communion of saints; his presence included a past of sympathetic Puritans.

The presence of sympathy in Puritanism helps us reimagine seventeenth-century New England. Sympathy enabled Puritans like John Winthrop to envision a society that would thrive through God-given mutual affections; it formed the boundaries of community and defined the limits of membership; it functioned as the basis of a pastoral dispute that nearly split the colony in two; it shaped Calvinist views of persuasion and turned explanations of the Antinomian Controversy into narratives of seduction; it helped negotiate transatlantic relations and served as a sign of unbroken union with brethren abroad; it structured the rhetorical form of missionary tracts and shaped the Puritans' ceaseless search for sincerity; it organized the aims of Mary Rowlandson's influential captivity narrative and, in the process, began to redefine Christians as compassionate Englishmen. All these aspects of sympathy—from the anxious individual searching for a sign of grace to the rhetorical force behind a good deal of Puritan literature to the larger community's sense of its boundaries, bonds, and purposes—reveal a Calvinist theology of fellow feeling at the heart of Puritan New England.

Notes

INTRODUCTION

1. Robert Penn Warren, *All the King's Men*, restored edition (New York: Harvest, 2002), 465.

2. Nathaniel Hawthorne, *The Scarlet Letter* (New York: Modern Library, 2000), 45. See especially "The May-Pole of Merry Mount," where the words "stern" and "iron" repeatedly describe the Puritans, though interestingly John Endicott seems to soften slightly in the story's end. Hawthorne, "The May-Pole of Merry Mount," in *Nathaniel Hawthorne's Tales*, ed. James McIntosh, second edition (New York: Norton, 2013), 110–120.

3. *The Winthrop Papers*, vols. 1–7 (Boston: Massachusetts Historical Society, 1929–), I.184. William Bradford, *Of Plymouth Plantation*, ed. Samuel Eliot Morison (New York: Knopf, 2006), 14. Anne Bradstreet, "A Dialogue between Old England and New; Concerning Their Present Troubles, Anno, 1642," in *The Works of Anne Bradstreet*, ed. Jeannine Hensley (Cambridge, MA: Belknap, 1967), pp. 179–188, l. 208. William Hooke, *New Englands Teares, for Old Englands Feares* (London, 1640), 2.

4. In opening this way, I move back and forth between "feelings" and "affections," "pity" and "sympathy"—words that had a complex relationship for the Puritans. The terms have different meanings and should not be conflated, but in practice they were often linked, which partly explains my use of both here. The introduction later defines "affections" and its relation to "feelings"; pity is differentiated from sympathy especially in chapter 4.

5. In pursuing "sympathy" through such sources as sermons and commentaries, my study leans toward what Peter Stearns and Carol Stearns call "emotionality"—that is, "the attitudes or standards that a society, or a definable group within a society, maintains toward basic emotions and their appropriate expression." See Peter Stearns and Carol Stearns, "Emotionology: Clarifying the

History of Emotions and Emotional Standards," *American Historical Review* 90, no. 4 (1985): 813. More recently, scholars in the history of emotion have tried to uncover lived experience and its relation to emotionality. For a good example, see Nicole Eustace, *Passion is the Gale: Emotion, Power, and the Coming of the American Revolution* (Chapel Hill: University of North Carolina Press, 2008). While much of this book focuses on the place of sympathy in the political and theological thought of ministers and magistrates, I interweave throughout the response of English lay persons and Native Americans to the Puritan tradition of sympathy, especially in chapters 2, 5, and 6.

6. I borrow this term from Barbara Rosenwein. Rosenwein defines "emotional communities" as "groups in which people adhere to the same norms of emotional expression and value—or devalue—the same or related emotions." Barbara Rosenwein, *Emotional Communities in the Early Middle Ages* (Ithaca, NY: Cornell University Press, 2006), 2.

7. This explication of emotional communities also intersects with Benedict Anderson's idea of "imagined communities." Anderson's work about the rise of nationalism begins by defining a nation as "an imagined political community." Members rely on the imagination, he explains, because they "will never know most of their fellow-members, meet them, or even hear of them, yet in the minds of each lives the image of their communion." Benedict Anderson, *Imagined Communities: Reflections on the Origin and Spread of Nationalism*, revised ed. (London: Verso, 1991), 6. He then describes several processes that enable the "nation" to take hold. The Puritan doctrine of sympathy, coming before most of these processes, still relies on the imagination to unite a communion of saints around a common affection. But sympathy also went beyond the limits of conscious imagination (the specific image in one's mind of one's community). Because the affections were conceived of as both active and passive—because they could also happen *to* people—the *discovery* of fellow feeling might contradict what people imagined to be their community (if, for example, they found themselves sympathizing with the wrong people).

8. Michael Kaufmann discusses the anxiety that some Puritan scholars have had about taking religion seriously, instead translating it into a "mask" for something of greater interest, such as politics, economics, violence, or representational practice. Michael Kaufmann, *Institutional Individualism: Conversion, Exile, and Nostalgia in Puritan New England* (Middletown, CT: Wesleyan University Press, 1998), 7–8. That is not what I propose. Instead, while acknowledging real belief and its consequences, I also trace the social and political implications of that faith and its expression. For more on taking religion seriously, see Jordan Alexander Stein and Justine Murison, eds., "Methods for the Study of Religion in Early American Literature," *Early American Literature* 45, no. 1 (2010), especially the introduction.

9. As Webster explains, "Fasts represented one way in which voluntary religion aided the mutual recognition of the godly, one way in which communities could be formed and maintained among people divided by distance." Tom Webster, *Godly Clergy in Early Stuart England: The Caroline Puritan Movement, c. 1620–1643* (Cambridge: Cambridge University Press, 1997), 68. Matthew Brown offers a good account of these public events and the experiences they generated. See Matthew Brown, *The Pilgrim and the Bee: Reading Rituals and Book Culture in Early New England* (Philadelphia: University of Pennsylvania Press, 2007), chapter 2.

10. See Edmund Morgan, *Visible Saints: The History of a Puritan Idea* (New York: New York University Press, 1963), and Baird Tipson, "Invisible Saints: The 'Judgment of Charity' in the Early New England Churches," *Church History* 44, no. 4 (1975): 460–471.

11. Charles Lloyd Cohen, "The Post-Puritan Paradigm of Early American Religious History," *William and Mary Quarterly* 54, no. 4 (1997): 702. For a review of the turn to Puritan affections in the 1960s see Michael McGiffert, "American Puritan Studies in the 1960's," *William and Mary Quarterly* 27, no. 1 (1970): 36–67. The secondary sources on these topics are voluminous and receive their due in subsequent chapters, though three particularly significant studies deserve mention up front: Charles Lloyd Cohen, *God's Caress: The Psychology of Puritan Religious Experience* (Oxford: Oxford University Press, 1986); Charles Hambrick-Stowe, *The Practice of Piety: Puritan Devotional Disciplines in Seventeenth-Century New England* (Chapel Hill: University of North Carolina Press, 1982); and Norman Pettit, *The Heart Prepared: Grace and Conversion in Puritan Spiritual Life*, second ed. (Middletown, CT: Wesleyan University Press, 1989). In 1993, Francis Bremer claimed that Cohen and Hambrick-Stowe together had "directed attention to the life of the heart." Francis J. Bremer, "Puritan Studies: The Case for an Atlantic Approach," *Puritanism: Transatlantic Perspectives on a Seventeenth-Century Anglo-American Faith*, ed. Francis J. Bremer (Boston: Massachusetts Historical Society, 1993), xiii. I would agree, though I would add Pettit to that list.

12. See David D. Hall, "Calvin and Calvinism within Congregational and Unitarian Discourse in Nineteenth-Century America," in *John Calvin's American Legacy*, ed. Thomas J. Davis (New York: Oxford University Press, 2010), 147–164. Good representations of such views can be found in the anti-Calvinist popular poems and songs included in the appendix to Nathan Hatch, *The Democratization of American Christianity* (New Haven, CT: Yale University Press, 1989), 227–243.

13. Ann Douglas, *The Feminization of American Culture* (New York: Knopf, 1977), 6–7, 13.

14. Other scholars—some of Puritanism—have also painted Calvinism as devoid of feeling, or marked a strict division in American history between head and heart. Delbanco, for example, writes, "The process that Hawthorne cast in

dramatic form as a generational decline in the New World had in fact begun with the rationalization of religious life in Elizabeth England"—a rationalization that directed the mind of the believer "to roam among verbally delivered abstractions." Andrew Delbanco, *The Puritan Ordeal* (Cambridge, MA: Harvard University Press, 1989), 221–222. Mulford introduces the first American novel, *The Power of Sympathy* (1789), with this categorical claim: "Earlier in the century it seems that anything having to do with the passions—from emotional or sensual experiences to attitudes connoting desire, even if only of wealth—was condemned as base, beneath the dignity of humane and virtuous consideration." Carla Mulford, "Introduction," in *The Power of Sympathy* (New York: Penguin Classics, 1996), xxii. Summing up his take on the Puritans, Garry Wills, a Pulitzer Prize-winning historian, asks, "How on earth did [the Puritans] hold their odd world and their odder selves together?" He answers: "By intense intellectual effort." Wills, *Head and Heart: American Christianities* (New York: Penguin, 2007), 66.

15. For an account of Latitudinarians see Martin Griffin Jr., *Latitudinarianism in the Seventeenth-Century Church of England* (Leiden: Brill, 1992). In a much-cited article, R. S. Crane locates the theological roots of sentimentalism in the Latitudinarian tradition: see Crane, "Suggestions Toward a Genealogy of the 'Man of Feeling'," *English Literary History* 1, no. 3 (1934): 205–230. Greene critiques Crane, but Sheriff partly re-establishes Crane's position and Barker-Benfield offers an additional endorsement. Donald Greene, "Latitudinarianism and Sensibility: The Genealogy of the 'Man of Feeling' Reconsidered," *Modern Philology* 75, no. 2 (1977): 159–183. John Sheriff, *The Good-Natured Man: The Evolution of a Moral Ideal, 1660–1800* (Tuscaloosa: University of Alabama Press, 1982). G. J. Barker-Benfield, *The Culture of Sensibility: Sex and Society in Eighteenth-Century Britain* (Chicago: University of Chicago Press, 1992), 65–70.

16. As Hendler observes, Adam Smith's philosophy "implies that sympathy is not simply a natural sensation; it is a sentiment that can and should be cultivated." Glenn Hendler, *Public Sentiments: Structures of Feeling in Nineteenth-Century American Literature* (Chapel Hill: University of North Carolina Press, 2001), 4.

17. Twin Hag, *Dictionary of Literary Terms* (New Delhi: Rajat, 2003), 204. M. H. Abrams, *A Glossary of Literary Terms*, eighth edition (Boston: Thomson Wadsworth, 2005), 291. Todd defines "sentimentalism" as "the movement discerned in philosophy, politics and art, based on the belief in or hope of the natural goodness of humanity and manifested in a humanitarian concern for the unfortunate and helpless." "Sensibility," meanwhile, "came to denote [by the mid-eighteenth century] the faculty of feeling, the capacity for extremely refined emotion and a quickness to display compassion for suffering." Janet Todd, *Sensibility: An Introduction* (New York: Methuen, 1986), 7. Van Sant distinguishes between "sensibility," "sentiment," and "sentimental," but concludes, "In spite of the distinctions that can be identified ... eighteenth-century

writers and speakers were neither precise nor consistent. Their usage frequently implies that *sentiment, sensibility,* and their variants are interchangeable." Ann Van Sant, *Eighteenth-Century Sensibility and the Novel: The Senses in Social Context* (Cambridge: Cambridge University Press, 1993), 7. Dobson offers four forms of sentimentalism, but finally identifies literary sentimentalism as a genre "premised on an emotional and philosophical ethos that celebrates human connection, both personal and communal, and acknowledges the shared devastation of affectional loss." Joanne Dobson, "Reclaiming Sentimental Literature," *American Literature* 69, no. 2 (1997): 266.

18. Todd traces the origins of sensibility to Shaftesbury, Hume, and Smith. Todd, *Sensibility,* 24–27. Barnes claims that "sympathetic identification emerges in the eighteenth century as the definitive way of reading literature and human relations." Elizabeth Barnes, *States of Sympathy: Seduction and Democracy in the American Novel* (New York: Columbia University Press, 1997), 2. Stern refers to Rousseau, Smith, and Burke, endorsing Douglas's "feminization" of American culture. Julia Stern, *The Plight of Feeling: Sympathy and Dissent in the Early American Novel* (Chicago: University of Chicago Press, 1997), 7, 12. Noble finds the roots of American sentimentalism "both in the Scottish Enlightenment and in the sentimental movement in eighteenth-century Europe." She adds, "Strictly speaking, sentimental Calvinism is an oxymoron." Marianne Noble, *The Masochistic Pleasures of Sentimental Literature* (Princeton, NJ: Princeton University Press, 2000), 62. Howard puts the transatlantic and philosophical antecedents of sentimentalism in the Enlightenment, citing Shaftesbury, Hutcheson, Smith, and Rousseau. June Howard, "What is Sentimentality?," *American Literary History* 11, no. 1 (1999): 63–81. Berlant, who productively extends "the unfinished business of sentimentality" into the twentieth century, nonetheless considers it a mode that "takes up the Enlightenment project of cultivating the soul of the subject toward a visceral capacity to embody, recognize, and sanction virtue." Lauren Berlant, *The Female Complaint: The Unfinished Business of Sentimentality in American Culture* (Durham, NC: Duke University Press, 2008). When studying a wider cultural movement that emphasizes sympathy, most studies begin with Enlightenment philosophy, not Calvinist theology.

19. Thomas Hobbes, *Leviathan,* ed. A. R. Waller (Cambridge: Cambridge University Press, 1904), I.13, 84. Mainly on the basis of sociability, scholars sometimes present sentimentalism as equally opposed to both Calvinist theology and Hobbesian philosophy, essentially equating the two. Todd, for example, claims that "Hobbes proposed a kind of secular Calvinism," and Noble argues that the cult of sensibility and the man of feeling arose "as a direct challenge to Hobbesian pessimism and Calvinist determinism." Todd, *Sensibility,* 21. Noble, *Masochistic Pleasures,* 62. For an account of the sometimes *close* relation between Puritan theology and moral sense philosophy that seeks, in part, to

overturn the commonly held division of the two, see Norman Fiering, *Jonathan Edwards's Moral Thought and Its British Context* (Chapel Hill: University of North Carolina Press, 1981). My study uses Fiering as a starting point for understanding how sympathy shaped Puritan culture in the seventeenth century.

20. With case studies of moral philosophy, captivity narratives, and missionary pamphlets, scholars have claimed that the Puritans "anticipated many of the ideas and gestures that would constitute the culture of sensibility." Laura Stevens, *The Poor Indians: British Missionaries, Native Americans, and Colonial Sensibilities* (Philadelphia: University of Pennsylvania Press, 2004), 6. Fiering, for example, has searched "seventeenth-century moral thought for evidence of inchoate sentimentalism." Norman Fiering, *Moral Philosophy at Seventeenth-Century Harvard: A Discipline in Transition* (Chapel Hill: University of North Carolina Press, 1981), 5; while the literary critics Armstrong, Tennenhouse, and Burnham have all linked Mary Rowlandson's 1682 captivity narrative to Samuel Richardson's sentimental novel *Pamela* (1742). See Nancy Armstrong and Leonard Tennenhouse, *The Imaginary Puritan: Literature, Intellectual Labor, and the Origins of Personal Life* (Berkeley: University of California Press, 1992), chapter 8; and Michelle Burnham, *Captivity and Sentiment: Cultural Exchange in American Literature, 1682–1861* (Lebanon, NH: University Press of New England, 1997). In her current important book project, titled *Becoming Colonial: Indians, Immigrants, and Early American Aesthetics*, Joanne van der Woude highlights the many tears and scenes of weeping in early Puritan texts, using them to elucidate a colonial aesthetics. I am grateful to her for the opportunity to read the manuscript in advance. Working from the opposite end, Branch notes a "strange critical silence about the role of religion in sentiment" and attempts to fill that gap by analyzing Puritan "rituals of spontaneity." Lori Branch, *Rituals of Spontaneity: Sentiment and Secularism from Free Prayer to Wordsworth* (Waco, TX: Baylor University Press, 2006), 15. Seth Lobis is the one other scholar I have found who systematically studies sympathy in the seventeenth century. Our emphases, source material, and concerns are largely different—Lobis stays in England, does not study Puritanism, and seems less interested in links to sincerity and community—but in one larger argument we both concur: as a moral term guiding human relations, sympathy has a much deeper history than is usually admitted or observed. See Seth Lobis, *The Virtue of Sympathy in Seventeenth-Century England*, PhD dissertation, Yale University (Ann Arbor: ProQuest/UMI, 2005).

21. For the use of "Puritan" in its own day, see Dwight Brautigam, "Prelates and Politics: Uses of 'Puritan,' 1625–40," in *Puritanism and Its Discontents*, ed. Laura Lunger Knoppers (Newark: University of Delaware Press, 2003), 49–66. See also Patrick Collinson, "Antipuritanism," in *The Cambridge Companion to Puritanism*, ed. John Coffey and Paul C. H. Lim (Cambridge: Cambridge University Press, 2008), 19–33. Bremer locates 1625 as the year when more

distinct boundaries of Puritanism emerged because of the rise in power of its opponents (primarily Charles I and William Laud). Laud's policies of persecution, in fact, tightened and radicalized the Puritan community. See Francis Bremer, *Congregational Communion: Clerical Friendship in the Anglo-American Puritan Community, 1610–1692* (Boston: Northeastern University Press, 1994). Such a reading follows the moves of revisionist historians, such as Nicholas Tyacke and Peter Lake, who argue that the church under Charles was very different than it had been under James; after 1625, the protestant consensus—however tenuous—began to break down and Arminian doctrine took over the seats of power. See Tyacke, *Anti-Calvinists: The Rise of English Arminianism, c. 1590–1640* (New York: Oxford University Press, 1990) and Lake, "Calvinism and the English Church, 1570–1635," *Past and Present* 114 (1987): 32–76. Russell endorses Tyacke and Lake and explains the new charges of "popery" leveled at both Charles and Laud: see Conrad Russell, *The Fall of the British Monarchies 1637–1642* (New York: Oxford, 1995), chapter 1. This thesis of an Arminian Revolution, however, is not accepted by all. For a different perspective (and a good summary of the debate), see Kevin Sharpe, *The Personal Rule of Charles I* (New Haven, CT: Yale University Press, 1996), part II, chapter 6. The most important revisions of the revisionists see other dynamics shaping the Church of England in this period. Davies rereads the religious beliefs and ideologies of Laud and Charles, while Milton considers the competing claims of Catholic and Reformed movements both within England and on the Continent. See Julian Davies, *The Caroline Captivity of the Church: Charles I and the Remoulding of Anglicanism 1625–1641* (Oxford: Clarendon, 1992); and Anthony Milton, *Catholic and Reformed: The Roman and Protestant Churches in English Protestant Thought, 1600–1640* (Cambridge: Cambridge University Press, 2002).

22. In my use of the term "movement" to discuss Puritanism both here and throughout this manuscript, I accept what Webster describes as a more "fluid understanding" of the word, recognizing a wide spectrum of views. See Tom Webster, "Early Stuart Puritanism," in *The Cambridge Companion to Puritanism*, 61. On the mindset of Puritans as their most distinctive feature, Haller, for example, claims, "The disagreements that rendered Puritans into presbyterians, independents, separatists and baptists were in the long run not so significant as the qualities of character, of mind and of imagination, which kept them all alike Puritan." William Haller, *The Rise of Puritanism*, 1938 (Philadelphia: University of Pennsylvania Press, 1972), 17. Knoppers admits that there is no easy way to define the Puritans, but claims "that a distinctive 'discontent'—with selves, others, community, church, and state—marked Puritans and Puritanism in seventeenth-century England and America." Laura Lunger Knoppers, "Introduction," in *Puritanism and Its Discontents*, 11. Lake summarizes three different definitions of the Puritans: as a political movement, as a style of piety, and as a combination of Reformed strands of thought. His inclination is to

unite the second and third. Peter Lake, "Defining Puritanism—Again?," in *Puritanism: Transatlantic Perspectives on a Seventeenth-Century Anglo-American Faith*, ed. Francis Bremer (Boston: Massachusetts Historical Society, 1993), 3–5. All these approaches—and many more could be added—have two things in common: first, they recognize how difficult it is to define the Puritans; and second, they mark Puritans primarily by their devotion, zeal, and way of life.

23. As Breen noted long ago, "New England was not a single, monolithic 'fragment' separating off from the mother country. It was a body of loosely joined fragments, and some of the disputes that developed in the New World grew out of differences that had existed in the Old." T. H. Breen, "Persistent Localism: English Social Change and the Shaping of New England Institutions," in *Puritans and Adventurers: Change and Persistence in Early America* (New York: Oxford University Press, 1980), 16. Already in 1970, McGiffert could comment on the rise of pluralism in Puritan studies. McGiffert, "American Puritan Studies," 40–42. In a later review of Puritan studies, Hall observed the same emphasis, calling the narrative of Puritan New England a story not "of monolithic unity, but of dialogue and ambivalence." David D. Hall, "On Common Ground: The Coherence of American Puritan Studies," *William and Mary Quarterly* 44, no. 2 (1987): 199. More recently, Cohen has identified what he calls the post-Puritan paradigm, which contributes to pluralism by setting a nonmonolithic New England among "the varieties of colonial religious experience" spanning the New World. Cohen, "Post-Puritan Paradigm," 697.

24. Field, building on other developments in Puritan studies, highlights the place of dissent in transatlantic disputes and objects to a monolithic New England often defined as Massachusetts Bay. His point is well taken, but it also illustrates my claim: dissidents were always *dissidents*, objectors to the majority who found little respite outside of Rhode Island. See Jonathan Beecher Field, *Errands into the Metropolis: New England Dissidents in Revolutionary London* (Lebanon: Dartmouth College Press, 2009).

25. Cohen aptly summarizes the approach I take here, claiming: "It is now easier to conceive of Puritanism as a predominating cultural force without having to demonstrate its absolute stranglehold on New England minds and mores, an impossibility in any event given the intrusions of Separatists, Baptists, and Quakers by the mid-seventeenth century." Cohen, "Post-Puritan Paradigm," 702. Hall's work reiterates this point. He asserts, "Conflict was intrinsic to the congregational system despite agreement on its basic principles." In the midst of debate, "the clergy helped maintain a common system. They had all been trained alike; they all thought alike." David D. Hall, *Worlds of Wonder, Days of Judgment: Popular Religious Belief in Early New England* (Cambridge, MA: Harvard University Press, 1989), 12, 6. On the differences between laity and clergy, Hall admits that lay persons were "irregular in practicing the duties of religion," but rejects an antithesis between ministers and their flocks. Hall, "Common

Ground," 225–226. See also David D. Hall, "The World of Print and Collective Mentality in Seventeenth-Century New England," in *New Directions in American Intellectual History*, ed. John and Paul K. Conkin Higham (Baltimore: Johns Hopkins University Press, 1979). In short, "the commonalities outweighed the differences." David D. Hall, "Toward a History of Popular Religion in Early New England," *William and Mary Quarterly* 41, no. 1 (1984): 51. Breen and Foster claim that "social cohesion" was the "Puritans' greatest achievement" in the seventeenth century, listing several reasons for "relative social peace." T. H. Breen and Stephen Foster, "The Puritans' Greatest Achievement: A Study of Social Cohesion in Seventeenth-Century Massachusetts," *The Journal of American History* 60, no. 1 (1973): 5. See also George Selement, *Keepers of the Vineyard: The Puritan Ministry and Collective Culture in Colonial New England* (Lanham, MD: University Press of America, 1984).

26. Carla Gardina Pestana, *The English Atlantic in an Age of Revolution, 1640–1661* (Cambridge, MA: Harvard University Press, 2004), 40. As Pestana writes later, "New England symbolized aggressive puritanism." Pestana, *English Atlantic*, 57.

27. The issue is, of course, more complicated than this quick summary. As Collinson has shown, many moderate Puritans accepted the ecclesiastical structures in place, at least through the reigns of Elizabeth and James I. See Patrick Collinson, *The Elizabethan Puritan Movement* (Berkeley: University of California Press, 1967). In fact, some of the strongest supporters of the episcopacy before the Civil War had roots in Calvinism and puritanism. For more on the defense of the episcopacy and its relation to the king's authority, see Collinson, *The Religion of Protestants: The Church in English Society, 1539–1625* (Oxford: Oxford University Press, 1982), chapter 1. Still, the experiential religion of many Puritans often lent itself to a re-envisioning of church structures. Webster has advised us that many Puritans who conformed did so unwillingly: they were "conformable" rather than conformists. See Webster, *Godly Clergy*.

28. As Spurr writes, puritanism was "that which puritans saw in each other." John Spurr, *English Puritanism, 1603–1689* (London: Macmillan, 1998), 7–8. For good accounts of these conventicles along with the social networks and ties of Puritans, see Bremer, *Congregational Communion*, and Webster, *Godly Clergy*.

29. Webster, while admitting variation, emphasizes the convergence of godly preachers on a common *ordo salutis*, even to the point of using the same metaphor for different stages of salvation. The differences, he argues, were "differences of emphasis within an agreed framework." See Webster, *Godly Clergy*, 109–112.

30. Thomas Shepard, "The First Principles of the Oracles of God," in *The Works of Thomas Shepard* (Ligonier, PA: Soli Deo Gloria, 1991), 346.

31. Ibid., 347. The morphology had different emphases depending on the preacher: some stressed the active duties of the sinner in preparing to receive God's call; others emphasized passivity and God's overwhelming grace.

The best account of differing views remains Janice Knight, *Orthodoxies in Massachusetts: Rereading American Puritanism* (Cambridge, MA: Harvard University Press, 1994).

32. Webster, for example, uses the term "puritan" to "denote an antiformalist search for 'heart religion,' for truly valid religious experience that found it difficult to endure any stumbling block to that search." Webster, *Godly Clergy*, 3. In this vein, Sargent Bush Jr. explains that the Puritan plain style necessarily contained a political dimension as well. By rejecting the ornamentation of Anglican rhetoric in favor of a style aimed solely at reaching and regenerating hearts (not pleasing the ear), the Puritans revealed that "aesthetics and politics were inseparably conjoined." Sargent Bush Jr., *The Writings of Thomas Hooker: Spiritual Adventure in Two Worlds* (Madison: University of Wisconsin Press, 1980), 15.

33. As Coolidge writes, "Indeed, the interrelation which Puritans insist on between Christian liberty and edification expresses with remarkable clarity the principle that individual identity comes about only through social relationship; but at the same time it defines a social organism which itself arises uniquely from the process of growth in spiritual freedom in its members." John Coolidge, *The Pauline Renaissance in England: Puritanism and the Bible* (Oxford: Clarendon, 1970), 148. Likewise, Webster argues, "The construction of the godly self was necessarily a communal activity." Webster, *Godly Clergy*, 135.

34. In *Congregational Communion*, Bremer focuses "on the experience of regeneration that brought men and women together in a godly communion, simultaneously binding them to each other and distancing them from contemporaries who did not share the illumination of grace." Bremer, *Congregational Communion*, xii. See also Webster, *Godly Clergy*, chapters 1–2.

35. *Winthrop Papers*, II.166.

36. Lobis describes these alternatives well. Citing Leo Spitzer, he calls the different approaches "semasiological" and "onamasiological," and writes: "The follower of the former method, as Leo Spitzer explains in *Essays on Historical Semantics*, begins with a particular word and studies its meaning or range of meanings over time in various 'cultural stylizations,' whereas the follower of the latter begins with a particular concept, or thing, and studies 'the variety of word-material' it has 'attracted.'" Lobis, *Virtue of Sympathy*, 5–6. In those places where I track the word itself, I further a methodology of "key words" that scholars have been adopting and adapting for several years. For a good recent example, see Phil Withington, *Society in Early Modern England: The Vernacular Origins of Some Powerful Ideas* (Cambridge: Polity, 2010).

37. Bouwsma, for example, delineates an Augustinian humanism—basic to later Puritanism—that considered the will to "take its direction not from reason but from the affections, which are in turn not merely the disorderly impulses of the treacherous body but expressions of the energy and quality of

the heart." William Bouwsma, "The Two Faces of Humanism: Stoicism and Augustinianism in Renaissance Thought," in *A Usable Past: Essays in European Cultural History* (Berkeley: University of California Press, 1990), 47.

38. John Calvin, *Institutes of the Christian Religion*, ed. John T. McNeill, trans. Ford Lewis Battles, 2 vols. (Louisville: Westminster John Knox, 1960), I.vii.5, 80; I.v.9, 61–62; II.iii.6, 297; I.ii.2, 43.

39. Jonathan Edwards claimed, "True religion, in great part, consists in holy affections." Jonathan Edwards, *Religious Affections*, ed. John E. Smith, vol. 2, *The Works of Jonathan Edwards* (New Haven, CT: Yale University Press, 1959), 95.

40. William Perkins, *A Discourse of Conscience* (London, 1596), 1. William Ames, *Conscience with the power and cases thereof* (London, 1639), 32–33. Perkins, *Discourse of Conscience*, 168. Richard Sibbes, *The Bruised Reede, and Smoaking Flax* (London, 1630), 236–237.

41. William Ames, *The Marrow of Theology*, trans. John Dykstra Eusden (Grand Rapids: Baker Books, 1997), 193–194.

42. William Perkins, *An abridgement of the whole body of divinity extracted from the learned works of that ever-famous and reverend divine* (London, 1654), 33. Ames, *Conscience*, 5.

43. Perkins, *Abridgement*, 150. Richard Sibbes, *A breathing after God* (London, 1639), 42. This point would eventually become a site of intense theological debate during the Antinomian Controversy in New England. For more on this topic, see chapter 2.

44. John Preston, *The Breast-Plate of Faith and Love* (London, 1630), 102–103.

45. Cohen, *God's Caress*, 28. Cohen's first chapter provides one of the best explanations of the predominant faculty humor psychology, and how Puritans adapted it to fit with more biblical views of the human person.

46. Norman Fiering, "Will and Intellect in the New England Mind," *William and Mary Quarterly* 29, no. 4 (1972): 523. Fiering's account, like Cohen's, is particularly detailed and clear.

47. Sibbes, *Breathing after God*, 37. Sibbes, *Bruised Reede*, 103. Thomas Hooker, *The Application of Redemption … The First Eight Books* (London, 1656), 208. When Miller made this intellectualist position central to seventeenth-century New England culture, he contributed to a prevailing view of the Puritans as centered on reason and understanding: ministers changed lives through logic. Fiering shows that Miller attributed the intellectualist position to Ames, but Ames was citing it as the view of his *opponents*; such a misreading, Fiering continues, led Miller to "an illogical severance of eighteenth-century evangelicism from seventeenth-century Puritan thought." Fiering, "Will and Intellect," 533.

48. Fiering, "Will and Intellect," 529. See also Cohen, *God's Caress*, 34. As Fiering concludes, "It can be established then that coexisting with theological quarrels, and relatively independent of the question of the freedom of the will in its classic forms, there existed in seventeenth-century New England a deep-running

debate concerning psychological models, which in the end may be assessed as a debate based ultimately on temperamental preferences." Fiering, "Will and Intellect," 549.

49. Sibbes, *Breathing after God*, 35–36. Ames, *Conscience*, 76. John Preston, *The New Covenant* (London, 1629), 156. *Winthrop Papers*, I.190.

50. *Winthrop Papers*, I.190. Bradstreet, *Works*, 235 (emphasis added).

51. Bilson, *Survey*, 383. *Winthrop Papers*, I.184, I.203. For an account of Puritan affections and the impact they had on poetry and Puritan literature more generally, see Robert Daly, *God's Altar: The World and the Flesh in Puritan Poetry* (Berkeley: University of California Press, 1978).

52. Edmund Calamy, *The Monster of Sinful Self-Seeking* (London, 1655), 6. Fenner, *A Treatise of the Affections, or, the Souls Pulse* (London, 1650), 56–57.

53. Richard Greenham, *A godlie exhortation, and fruitfull admonition to vertuous parents and modest matrons* (London, 1584), B3v-B3r.

54. Fenner, *Treatise of the Affections*, 54.

55. The most famous proponent of this position is Martha Nussbaum, who has advanced the links among literature, empathy, and ethics in a number of works. See especially *Poetic Justice: The Literary Imagination and Public Life* (Boston: Beacon Press, 1995) and *Not for Profit: Why Democracy Needs the Humanities* (Princeton, NJ: Princeton University Press, 2010). In addition, see Steven Pinker, *The Better Angels of our Nature* (New York: Viking, 2011), and Lynn Hunt, *Inventing Human Rights* (New York: Norton, 2007). The issues are far more complex, and these scholars are far more nuanced, than my quick summary here. For a good account of the various arguments about novels and empathy, see Suzanne Keen, *Empathy and the Novel* (New York: Oxford University Press, 2007).

CHAPTER 1

1. Just where and when Winthrop spoke this sermon remains under some dispute. For many years, scholars believed Winthrop delivered his sermon while crossing the Atlantic. Dawson threw that assumption into doubt, claiming that Winthrop gave this sermon with John Cotton's *Gods Promises to his Plantations* just prior to leaving and arguing that such a setting changes how we ought to read the text. See Hugh Dawson, " 'Christian Charitie' as Colonial Discourse: Rereading Winthrop's Sermon in Its English Context," *Early American Literature* 33, no. 2 (1998): 117–148; Hugh Dawson, "John Winthrop's Rite of Passage: The Origins of the 'Christian Charitie' Discourse," *Early American Literature* 26, no. 3 (1991): 219–231.

2. Perry Miller considered *A Model of Christian Charity* "the fundamental document for understanding the Puritan mind," and interpretations of the Puritan venture regularly run through this piece of writing. Perry Miller, ed., *The*

American Puritans: Their Prose and Poetry (New York: Columbia University Press, 1956), 78. Miller used this text to assert the Puritans' sense of a special mission; later scholars have argued that the Puritans were not establishing a model society, but *fleeing* one they thought doomed. As early as 1965, Rutman claimed that Winthrop sought "the refuge of a secular monastery." Darrett Rutman, *Winthrop's Boston: A Portrait of a Puritan Town, 1630–1649* (University of North Carolina Press, 1965; reprint ed., New York: Norton, 1972), 22. Leverenz likewise suggested that, according to Winthrop, "failure, not success, is what the world is watching for, and what literature would recount. If we prevail, he implies, no one need pay attention but God." David Leverenz, *The Language of Puritan Feeling: An Exploration in Literature, Psychology and Social History* (New Brunswick, NJ: Rutgers University Press, 1980), 265. For other important revisions, see Theodore Dwight Bozeman, "The Puritans' 'Errand into the Wilderness' Reconsidered," *New England Quarterly* 59, no. 2 (1986): 231–251; and Andrew Delbanco, "The Puritan Errand Re-Viewed," *Journal of American Studies* 18, no. 3 (1984): 343–360. For a good review of the reasons many Puritans left England and what they hoped to achieve, see Theodore Dwight Bozeman, *To Live Ancient Lives: The Primitivist Dimension in Puritanism* (Chapel Hill: University of North Carolina Press, 1988), 90–119. His account should be balanced with Francis Bremer, "To Live Exemplary Lives: Puritans and Puritan Communities as Lofty Lights," *Seventeenth Century* 7, no. 1 (1992): 27–39. Bremer argues that the Puritans intended to be *a* light (not *the* light) for others. For good recent challenges to the idea that Puritans created an oligarchic, authoritarian theocracy, see David D. Hall, *A Reforming People: Puritanism and the Transformation of Public Life in New England* (New York: Knopf, 2011) and Michael Winship, *Godly Republicanism: Puritans, Pilgrims, and a City on a Hill* (Cambridge, MA: Harvard University Press, 2012).

3. Thomas Weld, "We Dream Not of Perfection," in *Puritans in the New World: A Critical Anthology*, ed. David D. Hall (Princeton. NJ: Princeton University Press, 2004), 34.

4. John Winthrop, "A Model of Christian Charity," in *The Winthrop Papers*, vols. 1–7 (Boston: Massachusetts Historical Society, 1929–), II.294, II.289.

5. One way to decipher what parts of Winthrop's sermon scholars have deemed most important is to track the passages they choose to publish in anthologies cramped for space: most eliminate Winthrop's language of sympathy at the center of his sermon. Prominent examples include Perry Miller and Thomas Johnson, eds., *The Puritans: A Sourcebook of Their Writings* (Mineola, NY: Dover, 2001), 195–199; Alan Heimert and Andrew Delbanco, eds., *The Puritans in America: A Narrative Anthology* (Cambridge, MA: Harvard University Press, 1985), 82–92; and David D. Hall, ed., *Puritans in the New World: A Critical Anthology* (Princeton. NJ: Princeton University Press, 2004), 165–170.

6. Over the years, a handful of scholars have argued that affections are central to *Christian Charity*. For an early example see Stephen Foster, *Their Solitary Way: The Puritan Social Ethic in the First Century of Settlement in New England* (New Haven, CT: Yale University Press, 1971), chapter 2. Most who focus on sympathy and affection are literary scholars. Coviello, for example, offers a revaluation of affection in early America more generally, claiming that "the capacity to feel, properly and deeply, was an essential measure of one's civic virtue." Peter Coviello, "Agonizing Affection: Affect and Nation in Early America," *Early American Literature* 37, no. 3 (2002): 442. For other readings of the affections in *Christian Charity*, see Douglas Anderson, *A House Divided: Domesticity and Community in American Literature* (Cambridge: Cambridge University Press, 1990), 9–13; Kristin Boudreau, *Sympathy in American Literature: American Sentiments from Jefferson to the Jameses* (Gainesville: University of Florida Press, 2002), 3–5; Andrew Delbanco, *The Puritan Ordeal* (Cambridge, MA: Harvard University Press, 1989), 72–74; Ivy Schweitzer, *Perfecting Friendship: Politics and Affiliation in Early American Literature* (Chapel Hill: University of North Carolina Press, 2006), 73–102. I am indebted to these accounts, but in each case, scholars *abstract* Winthrop from his context. Coviello moves from Winthrop to Edwards to Jefferson. Boudreau uses Winthrop as background to Hawthorne. Schweitzer skips from Winthrop to *The Coquette*, a novel published in 1797. The implication is that Winthrop's sermon is not representative of his culture, an approach best summed up by Delbanco, who comments on the "fleetingness" of *A Model of Christian Charity* and ties its ideas to later thinkers, such as Edwards, Melville, and Whitman. Delbanco, *Puritan Ordeal*, 74. I place Winthrop in a broader context of seventeenth-century Puritan sympathy and instead endorse Bremer's assertion that "the ideas which have struck so many later commentators as original and influential were commonplaces of their time." Francis Bremer, *John Winthrop: America's Forgotten Founding Father* (Oxford: Oxford University Press, 2003), 175. For his correlation of commonplace ideas, see Francis Bremer, "The Heritage of John Winthrop: Religion along the Stour Valley, 1548–1630," *The New England Quarterly* 70, no. 4 (Dec., 1997): 515–547.

7. I have argued elsewhere that the text was almost entirely unknown in its own day and that what remains to posterity is an incomplete manuscript. Winthrop's sermon became central to claims about the purpose of the Puritan migration (and, in turn, the exceptionalism of America) only in the twentieth century. See Abram C. Van Engen, "Origins and Last Farewells: Bible Wars, Textual Form, and the Making of American History," *The New England Quarterly* 86, no. 4 (December 2013): 543–92.

8. As Lobis states well: "The history of sympathy did not begin with a new science of man, nor did it begin with a new religion of man; it began, rather, with the old system of the world." Seth Lobis, *The Virtue of Sympathy in Seventeenth-Century*

England, PhD dissertation, Yale University (Ann Arbor: ProQuest/UMI, 2005), 27.

9. Michael Lapidge, "Stoic Cosmology," *The Stoics*, ed. John M. Rist (Berkeley: University of California Press, 1978), 175–176. See also A. A. Long and D. N. Sedley, *The Hellenistic Philosophers*, vol. 1 (Cambridge: Cambridge University Press, 1987), 7.

10. Lapidge, "Stoic Cosmology," 176.

11. Long and Sedley, *Hellenistic Philosophers*, 287.

12. See Peter Kingsley, *Ancient Philosophy, Mystery, and Magic: Empedocles and Pythagorean Tradition* (Oxford: Clarendon, 1995), 296–298; see also 339. Edelstein writes, "The sympathetic effect to the ancients is a natural phenomenon and proved by experiments, not by any magical theory." He notes that these experiments convinced even the Skeptics by gathering "facts," though Skeptics explained sympathy "not by a divine spirit but by the spontaneity of nature." Meanwhile, he claims that "it is Theophrastus who gives sympathy its place in natural science." Ludwig Edelstein, *Ancient Medicine: Selected Papers of Ludwig Edelstein*, trans. C. Lilian Temkin, ed. Owsei Temkin and C. Lilian Temkin (Baltimore: Johns Hopkins University Press, 1967), 232, 234.

13. "Sympathy," in *Oxford English Dictionary Online* (Oxford University Press, 2010). Anthony Nixon, *A True Relation of the Travels of M. Bush* (London, 1607), Ev–E2r. Thomas Browne, *Religio Medici* (London, 1643), 107–108.

14. Thomas Taylor, *Davids Learning, or The way to true happinesse in a commentarie upon the 32. Psalme* (London, 1617), ¶2r–¶2v.

15. Thomas Cooper, *The Mysterie of the Holy Government of our Affections* (London, 1620), 8–9. Nicholas Byfield, *A Commentary: or, sermons upon the second chapter of the first epistle of Saint Peter* (London, 1623), 443. Richard Sibbes, *Bowels opened, or, A discovery of the neere and deere love, union and communion betwixt Christ and the Church, and consequently betwixt Him and every beleeving soule* (London, 1639), 320.

16. Cooper, *Mysterie*, 8. The relationship of soul to body concerned a related theological question of the day: in what manner did Christ suffer? All agreed that he suffered in both body and soul, but how did his soul suffer? Most answered that Christ's soul suffered partly through sympathy with his body, but directly and immediately from God. See, for example, William Ames, *The Marrow of Theology*, trans. John Dykstra Eusden (Grand Rapids: Baker Books, 1997), 142; Robert Bolton, *Instructions for a Right Comforting Afflicted Consciences* (London, 1631), 527; Thomas Draxe, *The Churches Securitie* (London, 1608), 47.

17. Robert Bolton, *Some Generall Directions for a Comfortable Walking with God* (London, 1626), 242. John Bate, *The psalme of mercy, or, A meditation upon the 51. psalme by a true penitent* (London, 1625), 321.

18. Lobis, *Virtue of Sympathy*, 250. In his excellent article on the subject, which this paragraph draws from, Lobis sets Digby in the context of the history of

science and suggests that he represents a turning point occurring more generally from 1630–1680, where sympathy moves from a scientific concept to a matter of human morality. See Seth Lobis, "Sir Kenelm Digby and the Power of Sympathy," *Huntington Library Quarterly* 74, no. 2 (2011): 243–260.

19. Browne, *Religio Medici*, 44.

20. Plutarch, *The philosophie, commonlie called, the morals written by the learned philosopher Plutarch of Chaeronea*, trans. Philemon Holland (London, 1603). This included an explanation of species. In fact, the sympathy of animals for their own kind was sometimes used as a lesson. Thomas Taylor, for example, declared, "Every creature by nature gather to their likes. Birds of a feather, Beasts of one kinde. For every Creature hath agreement, and sympathy with his kinde: and things thrive best among their like." For Taylor, that meant God's *new* creatures, his converts, should take themselves "to the societie of the Saints." William Gouge, meanwhile, used this sympathy to chastise Christians: "Even unreasonable creatures are ready to run at the cry of such as are of their own kind. Should reasonable men have lesse sympathy then unreasonable beasts?" If even *beasts* sympathized, Christians should do so all the more. Thomas Taylor, *A Man in Christ, or a New Creature* (London, 1629), 105–106. William Gouge, *Gods Three Arrowes: Plague, Famine, Sword* (London, 1631), 278.

21. Margo Todd, *Christian Humanism and the Puritan Social Order* (Cambridge: Cambridge University Press, 1987), 17–18; for a great deal of information on what students read in the sixteenth century, see 54–71. As Eden writes, "Proclaiming himself the rightful heir of both early Christian and classical traditions, Erasmus reinvests his Augustinian legacy in order to advance his claim, as did Augustine before him, to the ancient philosophical, especially Platonic, tradition." Kathy Eden, *Friends Hold All Things in Common: Tradition, Intellectual Property, and the Adages of Erasmus* (New Haven, CT: Yale University Press, 2001), 17. For Hooker, see R. J. Shoeck, "From Erasmus to Hooker," *Richard Hooker and the Construction of Christian Community*, ed. Arthur Stephen McGrade (Tempe: Arizona State University Press, 1997), 59–73.

22. He also applied it to piety. Furey notes, "This biblical imperative—with the holy thou shalt be holy—reflects what had for over a millennium been a key premise of Christian soteriology, that like can only be known by like. Thus one who desires to be saved, to dwell with God, must seek to become like God." Constance Furey, "Bound by Likeness: Vives and Erasmus on Marriage and Friendship," *Discourses and Representations of Friendship in Early Modern Europe, 1500–1700*, ed. Daniel T. Lochman, Maritere Lopez, and Lorna Hutson (Burlington, VT: Ashgate, 2011), 40.

23. Desiderius Erasmus, *"Sympathy / Amicitia,"* trans. Craig Thompson, in *The Collected Works of Erasmus*, vol. 40 (Toronto: University of Toronto Press, 1997), 1036, 1043, 1044, 1046. This analysis of Erasmus's *Amicitia* briefly summarizes and paraphrases an excellent article by Seth Lobis. "Activating two major

senses of its title word," Lobis argues, "the colloquy moves from one semantic field to another, from *amicitia* as natural affinity—whether between animals, plants, persons, or things—to *amicitia* as personal friendship." Analyzing the strange ending, Lobis writes, "Erasmus transfers agency from a remote and mysterious Nature to the individual Christian, who must balance the claims of his own nature with his duty to all." Lobis, "Erasmus and the Natural History of Friendship," *Erasmus of Rotterdam Society Yearbook* 30 (2010): 24–25.

24. Desiderius Erasmus, *The Handbook of the Christian Soldier (Enchiridion militis christiani)*, trans. Charles Fantazzi, in *The Collected Works of Erasmus*, vol. 66 (Toronto: University of Toronto Press, 1988), 28.

25. Erasmus, *Enchiridion*, 79, 94. Similarly, he says later, "Christian charity knows no exclusivity. Let him [the Christian soldier] love the pious in Christ and the impious for the sake of Christ." Ibid., 93. Erasmus quotes Romans 12:15 here and amplifies the argument: a good Christian, he claims, will "bear another's suffering even more grievously than his own, and be happier at another's good fortune than at his own."

26. Ibid., 95.

27. Desiderius Erasmus, *Paraphrases on The Epistles to Timothy, Titus, and Philemon, The Epistles of Peter and Jude, The Epistle of James, The Epistles of John, The Epistle to the Hebrews*, trans. John J. Bateman, in *The Collected Works of Erasmus*, vol. 44, ed. Robert Sider (Toronto: University of Toronto Press, 1993), 190–192.

28. Bouwsma notes that humanists "were also inclined to treat positively the passions, so close to the biblical heart; they saw the passions not simply as potential rebels against reason but as powerful resources for good, especially in human relationships." William Bouwsma, "Hooker in the Context of European Cultural History," in *Richard Hooker and the Construction of Christian Community*, ed. Arthur Stephen McGrade (Tempe: Arizona State University Press, 1997), 48–49.

29. Desiderius Erasmus, *The Praise of Folly*, trans. Clarence H. Miller (New Haven, CT: Yale University Press, 1979), 45–46.

30. Erasmus, *Paraphrases*, 196. As Erasmus writes, "Whatever comes from nature cannot be ascribed to merit." Erasmus, *Handbook*, 52.

31. See John Martin, "Inventing Sincerity, Refashioning Prudence: The Discovery of the Individual in the Renaissance." *American Historical Review* 102, no. 5 (1997): 1309–1342. Martin claims that "there was something significantly new about the way in which men and women in the Renaissance began to conceptualize the relation between what they saw as the interior self on the one hand and the expressions of one's thoughts, feelings, or beliefs on the other." Ibid., 1322–1323.

32. Erasmus, *Praise of Folly*, 56. Erasmus, *Enchiridion*, 8. Calling for repentance, Erasmus wrote, "I am not concerned with what you manifest externally. But if by a complete reversal you begin to hate what you once loved, to flee from it

and shudder at it, if what once tasted like gall becomes sweet to your affections, then I regard this as proof of your return to good health." *Enchiridion*, 83.

33. Erasmus, *Paraphrases*, 191. He also claimed that brotherly love should emanate in provisions of food, shelter, comfort, teaching, and admonition. "If we do this without hesitation, we shall know by this sign that we are children of truth and that our love is not feigned but sincere." Ibid., 191. The lack of hesitation—the *way* an outward act was performed—revealed the quality of one's heart.

34. Over time, the Puritans adapted and transformed Calvin's theology, but reverence for his thought persisted. Thus for example, John Cotton, the eminent Puritan minister of Boston, declared that every night he "sweeten[ed] his mouth with a bit of Calvin." Quoted in David Thomson, "The Antinomian Crisis: Prelude to Puritan Missions," *Early American Literature* 38, no. 3 (2003): 404. Some argue that the Puritans differed dramatically from John Calvin. As Beeke notes, "The post-Reformers are viewed as having injected a cold, systematic scholasticism into the doctrines of faith and assurance, thereby supplanting the warm biblicism of the Reformers." His book effectively repudiates "the sharp distinction contemporary scholarship has drafted between Calvin and Calvinism." The difference was a matter of degree, not substance. In the fundamentals they agreed, but "Calvin was concerned largely with the assurance of God's benevolence; the Puritans, with the assurance of personal faith. Calvin focused on the certainty of salvation in Christ; the Puritans dwelt on how the believer could be assured of his own salvation in Christ." Joel Beeke, *Assurance of Faith: Calvin, English Puritanism, and the Dutch Second Reformation* (New York: Peter Lang, 1991), 1–2, 157.

35. John Calvin, *Commentaries on the Catholic Epistles*, trans. John Owen (Edinburgh: Calvin Translation Society, 1855), 102. The Latin reads: "Συμπάθεια ad omnes sensus extenditur, quum ea inter nos viget concordia, ut quisque proximorum malis non secus ac suis condoleat, prosperis rebus laetetur, non seipsum modo curet, sed alios etiam complectatur." Ioannis Calvini, *Comentarii in Epistolas Canonicas*, in *Opera Exegetica*, vol. 20, ed. Kenneth Hagen (Genève: Librairie Droz, 2009), 90. As becomes clear in comparison to scripture, Calvin in a sense transforms the biblical command to "sympathize" into an abstract noun, "sympathy."

36. Calvin, *Commentaries on the Catholic Epistles*, 102.

37. See, for example, his commentaries on Psalm 109:12 and Jeremiah 15:5.

38. John Calvin, *Commentary on the Book of the Prophet Isaiah*, trans. William Pringle (Edinburgh: Calvin Translation Society, 1851), 411–412. Ioannis Calvini, *Opera Quae Supersunt Omnia*, vol. 36, in *Corpus Reformatorum*, vol. 64, ed. Guilielmus Baum, Eduardus Cunitz, and Eduardus Reuss (Brunsvigae: Appelhans, 1888), 546.

39. John Calvin, *Commentary on the Book of Psalms*, vol. 4, trans. James Anderson (Edinburgh: Calvin Translation Society, 1847), 280. This is a comment on Psalm 109:12.

40. John Calvin, *Commentaries on the Twelve Minor Prophets*, vol. 2, *Joel, Amos Obadiah*, trans. John Owen (Edinburgh: Calvin Translation Society, 1846), 443. In the context of this chapter—concerned as it is with emotion—what John Owen translates here as "right feeling" is actually misleading; the word is better translated as "justice," "fairness," "equanimity," or "equity." Here is the Latin: "Si alii vicini hoc faciunt, tamen abstineas tu, quia es consanguineous: si non possis opem ferre, saltem ostende signum aliquod doloris et συμπαθείας. Quum autem tu et alacriter, et cupide adspicias ipsorum calamitates, hinc apparet nullam esse in te guttam aequitatis." Ioannis Calvini, *Opera Quae Supersunt Omnia*, vol. 43, in *Corpus Reformatorum*, vol. 71, ed. Guilielmus Baum, Eduardus Cunitz, and Eduardus Reuss (Brunsvigae: Appelhans and Pfenningstorff, 1890), 192.

41. Calvini, *Opera*, vol. 43, p. 192.

42. John Calvin, *Commentaries on the Book of the Prophet Jeremiah and The Lamentations*, vol. 4 (Edinburgh: Calvin Translation Society, 1850; repr., Grand Rapids: W.B. Eerdmans Pub. Co., 1950), 480.

43. These passages are from Calvin's commentary on Lamentations 3:43, and the translations have been aided by Joshua Byron Smith. Owen translates the first as follows: "For an object presented to the eye produces sympathy, and we are easily inclined to mercy when a sad spectacle is presented to us." John Calvin, *Commentaries on the Book of the Prophet Jeremiah and The Lamentations*, vol. 5 (Edinburgh: Calvin Translation Society, 1850; repr., Grand Rapids: W.B. Eerdmans Pub. Co., 1950), 437. But Calvin does not use the word "sympathia" here; instead he describes the eyes as *tender*, writing, "Nam sensus occulorum est tenerior, et facile ad misericordiam flectimur ubi occurrit nobis triste spectaculum." The second quotation reads: "Hinc fit, ut etiam saevissimi hostes interdum mansuescant, quia oculis suis feruntur ad humanitatem." Ioannis Calvini, *Opera Quae Supersunt Omnia*, vol. 39, in *Corpus Reformatorum*, vol. 67, ed. Guilielmus Baum, Eduardus Cunitz, and Eduardus Reuss (Brunsvigae: Appelhans and Pfenningstorff, 1889), 594.

44. Many years later, Adam Smith would depict a similar nadir for the wicked. Detailing the various emotions felt by a "violator of the more sacred laws of justice," Smith paints a vivid picture of that person fleeing into solitude and slowly creeping back to society, begging a "little protection from the countenance of those very judges, who he knows have already all unanimously condemned him." This wicked person sympathizes with "the hatred and abhorrence which other men must entertain for him" and becomes, therefore, "in some measure the object of his own hatred and abhorrence." He is full of grief and regret, "thrown out from the affections of all mankind," and—significantly—utterly without hope "for the consolation of sympathy." Adam Smith, *The Theory of Moral Sentiment* (Mineola, NY: Dover, 2006), II.ii.2, 83–84.

45. Of human affliction and sympathy, Calvin writes (on Genesis 40:6–7): "For thus men become softened by their own afflictions, so that they not despise others who are in misery; and, in this way, common sufferings generate sympathy [sympathiam]. Wherefore it is not wonderful that God should exercise us with various sorrows; since nothing is more becoming than humanity towards our brethren, who, being weighed down with trials, lie under contempt. This humanity, however, must be learned by experience; because our innate ferocity is more and more inflated by prosperity." John Calvin, *Commentaries on the First Book of Moses Called Genesis*, vol. 2 (Edinburgh: Calvin Translation Society, 1847; repr., Grand Rapids: Wm. B. Eerdmans, 1948), 309. Thus, while Calvin argued that sympathy was natural even to "savage men," he also claimed that it had to be learned through affliction. A similar sort of tension would appear much later in moral sense philosophers, who believed both that sympathy was innate and that it needed to be educated (though the process of refinement did not necessarily involve personal affliction, nor would they have endorsed Calvin's picture of "innate ferocity").

46. John Calvin, *Commentary on the Gospel According to John*, vol. 1, trans. William Pringle (Edinburgh: Calvin Translation Society, 1847), 145. Calvin writes, "Non simulavit lassitudinem, sed revera fessus erat. Nam quo magis ad sympathiam propensus foret nobisque condolosceret, infirmitates in se nostras suscepit, quemadmodum docet Apostolus." Ioannis Calvini, *In Evangelium Secundum Johannem Commentarius Pars Altera*, in *Opera Exegetica*, vol. XI/1, ed. Helmut Feld (Genève: Librairie Droz, 1997), 118.

47. Calvin, *Commentary on … John*, vol. 1, 439. The Latin is as follows: "Nisi condoluisset Christus illorum lachrymis, stetisset potius vultu rigido. Quum autem sponte se illis conformat usque ad fletum, συμπάθειαν testatur." Ioannis Calvini, *In Evangelium Secundum Johannem Commentarius Pars Altera*, in *Opera Exegetica*, vol. XI/2, ed. Helmut Feld (Genève: Librairie Droz, 1998), 62.

48. Calvin, *Commentary on … John*, vol. 1, 439. The full sentence reads: "Ergo Lazaraum suscitaturus, antequam remedium opemque afferat, fremitus spiritus, arcto doloris sensu et lachrymis testator malis nostris perinde se affici, acsi ea in se pateretur." Calvini, *In Evangelium Secundum Johannem Commentarius Pars Altera*, XI/2, 62–63.

49. John Calvin, *Commentaries on the Epistle of Paul the Apostle to the Hebrews*, trans. John Owen (Edinburgh: Calvin Translation Society, 1853), 108.

50. John Calvin, *Commentary on the Epistles of Paul the Apostle to the Corinthians*, vol. 2, trans. John Pringle (Edinburgh: Calvin Translation Society, 1849), 362. This is from Calvin's commentary on 2 Cor. 11:29.

51. As Joshua Byron Smith has pointed out to me, linking "translation" to "sense" means a transfer of meaning, not form; one must make a foreign feeling, in a sense, native. It is not enough just to act like someone; you have to take their *sensus* on (or rather *in*) and not just their outward appearance.

52. John Calvin, *Commentaries on the Epistle of Paul the Apostle to the Romans*, trans. John Owen (Edinburgh: Calvin Translation Society, 1849), 470.

53. John Calvin, *A commentarie vpon S. Paules epistles to the Corinthians*, trans. Thomas Timme (London, 1577), 292.

54. John Calvin, *A harmonie vpon the the three Euangelists, Matthew, Mark and Luke with the commentarie of M. Iohn Caluine*, trans. Eusebius Pagit (London, 1584), 269.

55. He could have also gleaned the word from the French. Lobis notes that "the French *sympathie* goes back to the fifteenth century." Lobis, *Virtue of Sympathy*, n. 11, p. 6. Calvin was French, and so he could have been familiar with the term from his original language as well, making the Latin transliteration, "sympathia," a natural fit.

56. Here again the translator did not know quite what to do with the term. He compromised by keeping the Greek in his English translation, but interpreted it as "compassion." John Calvin, *The comentaries of M. Iohn Caluin vpon the first Epistle of Sainct Ihon, and vpon the Epistle of Iude ... Translated into Englishe by W. H.* (London, 1580), 59.

57. John Calvin, *A commentarie vpon the Epistle of Saint Paul to the Romanes*, trans. Christopher Rosdell (London, 1583), 168.

58. Calvin, *Commentaries on the Catholic Epistles*, 220. Calvin does not use the Greek word for sympathy twice. Another possible translation would read: "No good act is pleasing to God unless it is joined with sympathy. Many are generous in appearance, who nonetheless are hardly [or, not at all] touched by the miseries of their brethren. Truly the Apostle enjoins that the bowels/innards are to be opened. That happens when we put on (in the sense of "dressing") the same sensibility/feeling so that we might not [or should not] feel the pain of others' evils any less than our own." The Latin is as follows: "Quarta, nullam beneficentiam, nisi τῇ συμπαθείᾳ coniuncta, Deo placere. Multi in speciem sunt liberals, qui tamen fratrum miseriis minime tanguntur. Verum Apostolus praecipit aperienda esse viscera, quod fit dum induimus fere eundem sensum, ut aliorum malis non secus condolescamus ac nostris." Calvini, *Comentarii in Epistolas Canonicas*, 198.

59. Henry Burton, *A Censure of Simonie* (London, 1624), Sr. Thomas Adams, *Eirenopolis: = the citie of peace Surveyed and commended to all Christians* (London, 1622), 25–26. Nicholas Byfield, *An Exposition upon the epistle to the Colossians* (London, 1615), II.15. Thomas Draxe, *The Earnest of Our Inheritance* (London, 1613), 26. Staines argues, "Early modern understandings of political rhetoric began with an understanding of the passions and how they spread from body to body; thus the shared passion of *compassion*—known also as *mercy, pity,* or *sympathy*—was one model for public politics." He then critiques Habermas's version of a public sphere based solely in rational-critical debate. See John Staines, "Compassion in the Public Sphere of Milton and King Charles," in *Reading the*

Early Modern Passions: Essays in the Cultural History of Emotion, ed. Gail Kern Paster, Katherine Rowe, and Mary Floyd-Wilson (Philadelphia: University of Pennsylvania Press, 2004), 92.

60. Guillaume de Salluste Du Bartas, *Du Bartas his deuine weekes and workes translated*, trans. Joshua Sylvester (London, 1611), 51–2.

61. Du Bartas probably drew this analogy from Plutarch. As the early modern translation of Plutarch reads: "These words ['mine' and 'not mine'] ought rather to be banished out of the state of matrimonie, unlesse it be (as the Physicians holde) that the blowes or woundes which are given on the left side of the body, are felt on the right; even so a wife ought to have a fellow-feeling (by way of sympathie and compassion) of her husbands calamities, and the husband of his wives, much more." Plutarch, *Philosophie*, 318. Lobis sees Du Bartas as a potentially important figure in the linguistic rise of sympathy: "The direction of influence and the chronology itself are hard to pin down, but I would speculate that wider interest in the word was generated by the appearance of Josuah Sylvester's translations of du Bartas starting in the 1580s." Lobis, *Virtue of Sympathy*, n. 11, p. 6. As a reformed poet beloved by English Calvinists, this would further explain how "sympathy," as a term, entered the Puritan vocabulary.

62. Gouge, *Of Domesticall Duties* (London, 1622), 225, 250–251. William Gouge, "An Exposition of part of the fift and sixt chapters of S. Paules Epistle to the Ephesians," in *An Exposition on the whole fifth chapter of S. Iohns Gospell: Also Notes on other choice places of Scripture* (London, 1630), 12. Richard Brathwait, *Essaies upon the five senses with a pithie one upon detraction* (London, 1620), 125.

63. In what follows, I will be citing and quoting many Puritans to understand their interpretation of sympathy. In doing so, I do not mean to conflate these various Puritans as all speaking with one mind; instead, recognizing their divergence on multiple issues, I seek the ways they often converged on a single matter: sympathy.

64. See Coolidge, *Pauline Renaissance*, 38. More generally, Coolidge offers a good account of the Puritan insistence on an "organic" and living ecclesial order.

65. William Gouge, *A Guide to Goe to God* (London, 1626), 75. Draxe, *Earnest*, 5.

66. The other fruits were as follows: "The first is your Charity; the second is your Constancy in cleaving to the truth which you have received; the third is your Taking to heart the cause of God and religion." Each of these fruits receives a full explication in a series of lectures. Unfortunately, Hildersham died just before he could get to sympathy. See Arthur Hildersham, *CLII lectures upon Psalme LI* (London, 1635), 747. Draxe likewise made sympathy a culminating sign of grace; see Draxe, *Churches Securitie*, 34–35.

67. Nicholas Byfield, *Sermons upon the ten first verses of the third chapter of the first Epistle of S. Peter* (London, 1626), 188. John Preston, *A Liveless Life: or, Mans spirituall death in sinne* (London, 1633), 30. Such sympathy included the church's good fortunes. Any failure to give thanks, Gouge warned, "sheweth that they

have no fellow-feeling of the good of the mysticall Body of Christ, or of the severall members thereof; which might make them feare that they themselves are scarce sound members of that body: if they were, there would assuredly be some sympathy betwixt themselves and other members, some mutual compassion, and fellow-feeling: they would reioyce with them that reioice." William Gouge, *The Whole-Armor of God* (London, 1619), 417.

68. Bolton, *Instructions*, 330–331.

69. Byfield, *Sermons*, 187, 188–189. Byfield offered similar commentary on Col. 3:12: "There should be a *Sympathy* and fellow-feeling in the distresses of others." See Byfield, *Exposition*, III.78. These "ought's" and "should's" turned sympathy from a predictable result of grace into a pressing demand of godliness.

70. John Preston, *Sermons Preached before the Maiestie; and upon other speciall occasions* (London, 1630), 48–49.

71. Bolton, *Generall Directions*, 207–208. Robert Cawdry, *The First English Dictionary, 1604: Robert Cawdrey's A Table Alphabetical*, ed. John Simpson (Oxford: Oxford University Press, 2007), 145. The title of the dictionary reads: "A Table Alphabeticall, conteyning and teaching the true writing, and understanding of hard usuall English wordes ... With the interpretation thereof by *plaine English words, gathered for the benefit & helpe of Ladies, Gentle-women, or any other unskil-full persons.* Whereby they may the more easilie and better understand many hard English wordes, which they shall heare or read in Scriptures, Sermons, or elswhere, and also be made able to use the same aptly themselves."

72. Byfield, *Sermons*, 187. Rafe Cudworth, "Supplement: Galatians 6," in *A Commentarie or Exposition, upon the five first chapters of the Epistle to the Galatians* (London, 1604), 489. See also Cudworth, "Supplement: Galatians 6," 651. Thomas Draxe, *The Christian Armorie* (London, 1611), II.164. See the *1599 Geneva Bible* (White Hall, WV: Tolle Lege Press, 2006), 1274. Puritans would also have known the Geneva Bible's gloss on Hebrews 13:3, which explains that each person must "be so much touched, as if their misery were yours." Compare these Puritan descriptions of sympathy to Adam Smith's assessment in 1759. Smith writes, "As we have no immediate experience of what other men feel, we can form no idea of the manner in which they are affected, but by conceiving what we ourselves should feel in the like situation." The imagination, he adds, represents "to us what would be our own, if we were in his case." See Adam Smith, *Moral Sentiments*, 3–4. James Chandler, in his recent work on the "sentimental mode," spends time discussing the sentimental "case," which he traces back to Adam Smith and claims arises as a response to Catholic casuistry; I would trace that "case" much further back and link it to Puritan practical divinity. See James Chandler, *An Archaelogy of Sympathy: The Sentimental Mode in Literature and Cinema* (Chicago: University of Chicago Press, 2013), 172–175. Keith Thomas, studying Puritan casuistry in the seventeenth century, observes "a shift from a conception of morality as the application of divine laws to human affairs to the idea of it as the simple love of God

and pursuit of goodness. Instead of thinking of life as made up of a series of discrete problems, each to be solved separately in accordance with the rulebook, theologians were increasingly inclined to place their emphasis upon the formation of an individuals' general moral character. As John Preston had stressed long before, no one should be judged on the basis of one or two particular actions: 'the only measure to esteem ourselves or others is the continued tenor of the course and actions. This proceeds from inward principles and from the frame of the heart.'" Thomas then ties this shift into a wider historical development ending in "the triumph of the proto-Romantic belief in the authenticity of individual sentiment." Keith Thomas, "Cases of Conscience in Seventeenth-Century England," in *Public Duty and Private Conscience in Seventeenth-Century England: Essays Presented to G.E. Aylmer*, ed. John Morrill, Paul Slack, and Daniel Woolf (Oxford: Clarendon, 1993), 51, 52. That development, in part, is what this study maps, asking how it shaped—and took its shape from—Puritan New England.

73. Cudworth, "Supplement: Galatians 6," 489. Draxe, *Christian Armorie*, II.125–126. Byfield, *Sermons*, 188. Draxe, *Christian Armorie*, II.125.

74. As can be seen, Puritans critiqued Stoics both for their lack of affection *and* for their lack of feeling, revealing again that while these words were importantly distinct, they often overlapped. For more on the meaning of "affection," see the introduction.

75. William Ames, *An Analyticall Exposition of both the Epistles of the Apostle Peter* (London, 1641), 73. Draxe, *Churches Securitie*, 48. Byfield, *Sermons*, 188. It is important not to get too carried away, however, for as much as Draxe praises emotion, he still qualifies it by discussing only those affections which are "set upon their right obiect, and that in due proportion." See Draxe, *Churches Securitie*, 48. As Gail Kern Paster, Katherine Rowe, and Mary Floyd-Wilson note, "Rather than seeking to quell emotions in the Stoic sense, many Renaissance writers appealed instead to the classical tradition of controlling affections with other affections." See Gail Kern Paster, Katherine Rowe, and Mary Floyd-Wilson, "Introduction," in *Reading the Early Modern Passions: Essays in the Cultural History of Emotion* (Philadelphia: University of Pennsylvania Press), 12. On the other hand, controlling them did not necessarily mean repressing them. The "due proportion" did not automatically translate to a lesser degree. There was no limit, for example, to the love one should have (or express) for God.

76. Quintilian, *Institutio Oratoria*, trans. H.E. Butler, *Loeb Classical Library* (Cambridge, MA: Harvard University Press, 1969), II.6.2.26, 431–432. Skinner has done foundational work tracing the influence of Quintilian and Cicero on the politics and rhetorical practices of early modern England. See, for example, Quentin Skinner, "Hobbes's Changing Conception of Civil Science," in *Visions of Politics: Hobbes and Civil Science* (Cambridge: Cambridge University Press, 2002).

77. William Perkins, *The Art of Prophesying* (Edinburgh: The Banner of Truth Trust, 1996), 74. Richard Bernard, *The Faithfull Shepeard*, revised ed. (London, 1621),

75. In an excellent chapter on Puritan preaching, Gordis lists several manuals and rhetorics that ministers would have consulted, but concludes that Perkins and Bernard were the most important and most widely read. Lisa Gordis, *Opening Scripture: Bible Reading and Interpretative Authority in Puritan New England* (Chicago: University of Chicago Press, 2002), 15–16. Cockroft has compared this rhetorical principle to an "emotional laser" in which the emotions transmitted and intensified between orator and audience resemble "the energy built up between mirrors in a laser tube." Robert Cockroft, *Rhetorical Affect in Early Modern Writing: Renaissance Passions Reconsidered* (Basingstoke: Palgrave Macmillan, 2003), 74. Many have noted this principle, though I rely here mostly on Deborah Shuger's foundational *Sacred Rhetoric: The Christian Grand Style in the English Renaissance* (Princeton, NJ: Princeton University Press, 1988). In his book on nineteenth-century American literature, Hendler identifies this principle as a quintessential formulation of sentimentalism, describing "a recursive emotional exchange" and presenting "the necessarily sympathetic qualities of a great orator." Glenn Hendler, *Public Sentiments: Structures of Feeling in Nineteenth-Century American Literature* (Chapel Hill: University of North Carolina Press, 2001), 3.

78. Byfield, *Commentary*, 797. Thomas Taylor, *Christes Combate and Conquest* (London, 1618), 191. Bolton, *Instructions*, 491–492, 529. Here a significant difference from Adam Smith's concept of sympathy may emerge: where Smith activated the imagination to move one into another's place, the Puritans sometimes still relied on an older idea of the more generic (rather than individual) self, so that the best way to fellow feel with another's misery was to *remember* one's own experience of affliction. As Shuger observes of this period, "Sacred discourse expresses a selfhood created by the activity of the Spirit within the heart, a selfhood both personal and yet generic." Shuger, *Sacred Rhetoric*, 233; see also 248. In this sense, experience was not necessarily *unique* (and so opened only by the imagination), but also *generic* (and so accessible through memory).

79. Ames, *Marrow*, 140. Where sympathy appears in Ames's text, it usually occurs in Greek, just as it often did for Calvin.

80. Gouge, "Exposition," 63. Nicholas Byfield, *The Promises: or, A treatise shewing how a godly Christian may support his heart with comfort against all the distresses which by reason of any afflictions or temptations can befall him in this life* (London, 1619), 122. See also Nicholas Byfield, *The Marrow of the Oracles of God* (London, 1630), 354; and Thomas Draxe, *The Lambes Spouse, or The Heavenly Bride* (London, 1608).

81. Byfield, *Commentary*, 329–330. Byfield, *Sermons*, 188. Richard Greenham, *The workes of the reverend and faithfull servant of Iesus Christ M. Richard Greenham* (London, 1612), 640. Henry Holland, *Spirituall Preservatives against the Pestilence* (London, 1603), 81.

82. Christ's example applied to more than just the godly. Reminding princes and rulers that they were still men—"knit ... in a sympathy of affection with [other men]"—the ever-outspoken and fearless Burton told these authorities to contemplate the example of Christ: "Even Christ," he wrote, "tooke our Nature, with the infirmities of it, that he might be a mercifull High-priest, and having experience of our temptations, hee might succour them that are tempted." The descent of high to low, prompted by mercy and enabling sympathy, was a pattern for all to emulate. Henry Burton, *Israels Fast. Or, a Meditation upon the seventh chapter of Ioshuah* (London, 1628), 10.

83. Greenham, *Workes*, 545.

84. Winthrop, "Christian Charity," 282. According to Miller, Winthrop propounded this "European class structure" in order to keep people in their place. Perry Miller, *Errand into the Wilderness* (Cambridge, MA: Belknap, 1956), 5. For others, such as Foster, Winthrop was not so much planning a society as defining it: "social distinctions were part of a set of assumptions held in common by all ranks of society." Foster, *Their Solitary Way*, 7, 41. Morgan combines both readings, calling the opening lines "the central platitude of sixteenth- and seventeenth-century social and political thought, invoked whenever the occasion seemed to suggest a need for reinforcing authority." Edmund Morgan, "John Winthrop's 'Modell of Christian Charity' in a Wider Context," *Huntington Library Quarterly* 50, no. 2 (1987): 145–146. Still others claim that Winthrop established his doctrine only to move past it, driving through rank toward spiritual equality. For such interpretations, see Anderson, *House Divided*, 10; and Lee Schweninger, *John Winthrop* (Boston: Twayne, 1990), 42.

85. See Van Engen, "Origins and Last Farewells," where I map Winthrop's sermon to Galatians 5 and Romans 12, both places where Paul moves, like Winthrop, from rules about what we owe one another to love as the solution.

86. *1599 Geneva Bible*, 1157. Winthrop, "Christian Charity," 283.

87. As Bremer comments, "There was no simple bi-polar division of saints and sinners. Men and women were regenerate and elect, elect but not yet regenerate, or unregenerate—those who were not yet born again might be in the middle category and yet be chosen. New England's Puritans were willing to give the latter the benefit of the doubt even though they did not welcome them to communion." Francis J. Bremer, "Puritan Studies: The Case for an Atlantic Approach," *Puritanism: Transatlantic Perspectives on a Seventeenth-Century Anglo-American Faith*, ed. Francis J. Bremer (Boston: Massachusetts Historical Society, 1993), xiii.

88. Winthrop, "Christian Charity," 283–284.

89. Ibid., 284, 288.

90. Ibid., 288.

91. Bright writes, "We see it evident in automaticall instruments, as Clockes, Watches, and Larums, how one right and straight motion, through the aptnesse of the first wheele, not only causeth circular motion in the same, but in divers

others also: and not only so, but distinct in pace, and time of motion: some wheeles passing swifther then other some, by diverse rases." Timothy Bright, *A Treatise of Melancholie* (London, 1613), 82.

92. Before this line, Perkins writes, "The order and manner of living in this world is called a vocation, because every man is to live as he is called of God. . . . In a clock made by the art and handiwork of man there be many wheels: and every one hath his several motion—some turn this way, some that way, some go softly, some apace, and they are all ordered by the motion of the watch." The analogy proves, for Perkins, that "God himself is the author and beginning of callings." William Perkins, *The Work of William Perkins*, ed. Ian Breward (Appleford: Sutton Courtenay Press, 1970), 447.

93. Preston, *Sermons*, 34–35.

94. Winthrop, "Christian Charity," 288.

95. Ibid., 288–289.

96. Ibid., 289.

97. Ibid.

98. Ibid. The first reference is to Romans 9, where Paul has "great heaviness, and continual sorrow in [his] heart" for his "brethren that are my kinsmen according to the flesh" (9:2–3)—that is, for the unconverted Jews.

99. Ibid., 289–290.

100. Ibid., 289–291.

101. Ibid., 284 (emphasis added).

102. Ibid., 294.

103. Ibid., 294.

104. My reading thus agrees most strongly with Schweitzer's interpretation. She argues that in *Christian Charity*, "saints must 'feel' what others, in very different social circumstances but who are part of their magic circle, feel, thus exercising the wildly unstable, but potent force of imagination. Such power is necessary to overcome the effects of the Fall and produce saintly action . . . as an outcome and expression of a spiritually produced affective realignment." Ivy Schweitzer, "John Winthrop's 'Model' of American Affiliation," *Early American Literature* 40, no. 3 (2005): 449. See also Schweitzer, *Perfecting Friendship*, 73–102. Yet I differ from her larger claim that such reciprocal love is idealized in homosocial friendship. In *Christian Charity*, the biblical imagery of family (the household of God) and body (Christ's church) matter more it seems to me, and the perfect example of sympathy is Christ himself.

105. Winthrop, "Christian Charity," 292. I agree, then, with Baritz's observation that "the love which was necessary for the creation and operation of the body politic could come only when that body was made up of the converted." Loren Baritz, *City on a Hill: A History of Ideas and Myths in America* (New York: Wiley and Sons, 1964), 15. Foster makes the same point; see *Their Solitary Way*, 42–44, 64.

Likewise, Lang argues that Winthrop makes "the capacity for love an outcome
of new birth, thereby making election the condition for true community."
Amy Schrager Lang, *Prophetic Woman: Anne Hutchinson and the Problem of
Dissent in the Literature of New England* (Berkeley: University of California
Press, 1987), 28.

106. Winthrop, "Christian Charity," 289–290. As Gouge had argued that in
a true body there "cannot but be some sympathie and fellow-feeling of
their fellow-members afflictions," so now Winthrop seems to envision a
communal sympathy that was almost guaranteed: the saints, as they discover each other, "cannot but" love. Gouge, *Guide*, 75. Winthrop, "Christian
Charity," 290.

107. Winthrop, "Christian Charity," 289. Perkins defined sanctification as that
process "whereby such as believe, being delivered from the tyranny of sin,
are by little and little renewed in holiness and righteousness." Perkins,
Work, 234.

108. *The Winthrop Papers*, vols. 1–7 (Boston: Massachusetts Historical Society, 1929–
), II.232.

109. Thomas Weld, "We Dream Not of Perfection," in *Puritans in the New
World: A Critical Anthology*, ed. David D. Hall (Princeton: Princeton University
Press, 2004), 35.

110. Winthrop, "Christian Charity," 292.

111. Winthrop, "Christian Charity," 294. For a fuller analysis of this ending, see Van
Engen, "Origins and Last Farewells," 578–583.

CHAPTER 2

1. The most recent, compelling narrative of the Antinomian Controversy highlights the contingent nature of the crisis and rejects an approach that "presume[s]
the clash of structural opposites." Michael Winship, *Making Heretics: Militant
Protestantism and Free Grace in Massachusetts, 1636–1641* (Princeton,
NJ: Princeton University Press, 2002), 2. Winship properly reminds scholars
of the "underdetermined" nature of the controversy; yet examining the clash of
ideas, as debated in the sources, does not necessarily overdetermine the results.
In fact, focusing on personalities can just as easily cause problems. Winship's
narrative, for all its merits, relies too heavily on his portrait of Thomas Shepard
as a rather flat, uncomplicated villain stirring up the controversy. By emphasizing this overdrawn image, Winship actually misses some of the points Shepard
tried to make. McGiffert, for example, paints quite a different portrait of the
man. See Michael McGiffert, "Thomas Shepard: The Practice of Piety," in *God's
Plot: Puritan Spirituality in Thomas Shepard's Cambridge*, revised and expanded
ed. (Amherst: University of Massachusetts Press, 1994), 3–33. I do track structural oppositions, but they require a note about my terms: throughout this

chapter, I refer to the "elders" and the "antinomians." The term "antinomian," however, is a misnomer. At their most extreme, Antinomians abrogated moral law in favor of immediate revelations ("antinomian" means "against the law"), and at no point did New England's supposed antinomians begin to live (or propose living) morally unguided lives. For this reason (among others), Winship calls it the "free grace controversy." Winship, *Making Heretics*, 1. Yet the fullest account of Antinomianism, by David Como, offers a set of characteristics that in many ways *do* describe the positions of John Cotton, John Wheelwright, Anne Hutchinson, and their followers. I thus retain the more recognizable terms, but use a lower case "a" to emphasize the wide variety of "antinomian" positions. See David Como, *Blown by the Spirit: Puritanism and the Emergence of an Antinomian Underground in Pre-Civil-War England* (Redwood City, CA: Stanford University Press, 2004), 33–38.

2. Roger Clap, *Memoirs of Capt. Roger Clap* (Boston, 1731), 4.

3. Como has shown that in London, antinomianism also had "no obvious class bias." Como, *Blown by the Spirit*, 51.

4. John Winthrop, *Winthrop's Journal, 1630 1649*, ed. James Kendall Hosmer (New York: Scribners, 1908), 208.

5. One reason structural oppositions are still worth investigating in the Antinomian Controversy is simply because so many Puritans kept invoking them.

6. David D. Hall, ed., *The Antinomian Controversy, 1636–1638: A Documentary History*, second ed. (Durham, NC: Duke University Press, 1990), 10.

7. For more on the mortal status of souls and its place in the controversy, see James Fulton Maclear, "Anne Hutchinson and the Mortalist Heresy," *New England Quarterly* 54, no. 1 (1981): 74–105.

8. For more detailed narratives of the Antinomian Controversy, see Philip Gura, *A Glimpse of Sion's Glory: Puritan Radicalism in New England, 1620–1660* (Middletown, CT: Wesleyan University Press, 1984), 237–275; William Stoever, *"A Faire and Easie Way to Heaven": Covenant Theology and Antinomianism in Early Massachusetts* (Middletown, CT: Wesleyan University Press, 1978), 21–33; Michael Winship, *Times and Trials of Anne Hutchinson: Puritans Divided* (Lawrence: University Press of Kansas, 2005).

9. As Lisa Gordis has noted, Hutchinson "challenged ideals of communal unity and consensus, particularly ideas of ministerial consensus." Lisa Gordis, *Opening Scripture: Bible Reading and Interpretative Authority in Puritan New England* (Chicago: University of Chicago Press, 2002), 178.

10. *The Winthrop Papers*, vols. 1–7 (Boston: Massachusetts Historical Society, 1929–), III.279. Two traditions of interpretation have differed on whether the fundamental issue was preparation or assurance. Miller suggested that against a growing preparationist camp, Cotton stuck to a stricter Calvinist line. Perry Miller, "'Preparation for Salvation' in Seventeenth-Century New England," *Journal*

of the History of Ideas 4, no. 3 (1943): 253–286. Morgan adopted a similar line. Edmund Morgan, *The Puritan Dilemma: The Story of John Winthrop*, 3rd edition (Prentice Hall: Pearson, 2006), 136–138. Pettit, Delbanco and Knight also maintained preparation as the primary *theological* issue (though Pettit partly redefined preparation as a spiritual search for assurance). See Norman Pettit, *The Heart Prepared: Grace and Conversion in Puritan Spiritual Life*, second ed. (Middletown, CT: Wesleyan University Press, 1989), 14–21; Andrew Delbanco, *The Puritan Ordeal* (Cambridge, MA: Harvard University Press, 1989), n. 24, p. 279; and Janice Knight, *Orthodoxies in Massachusetts: Rereading American Puritanism* (Cambridge, MA: Harvard University Press, 1994), 20. Yet a second tradition has asserted that the controversy concerned assurance, not preparation. Hall, for example, claims that "assurance of salvation was the central issue in the controversy." Hall, *Antinomian Controversy*, xiv. The question was not how one might prepare for grace, but what counted as a sign that one had already received it. William Stoever has argued that "'preparation' in 1636–1638 was at most an issue only incidentally." Instead, "the immediate practical context of the controversy between Cotton and the other ministers, clearly, was the problem of personal assurance of election." William Stoever, "Nature, Grace and John Cotton: The Theological Dimension in the New England Antinomian Controversy," *Church History* 44, no. 1 (1975): 23–24. Winship concurs with this tradition: see Winship, *Making Heretics*, 4. Stoever offers a particularly good explanation of why preparation was not the primary concern: see Stoever, *Faire and Easie*, 192–199. For the reasons offered there and elsewhere, I agree with this latter camp.

11. Joel Beeke, *Assurance of Faith: Calvin, English Puritanism, and the Dutch Second Reformation* (New York: Peter Lang, 1991), 170–172.

12. Hall, *Antinomian Controversy*, 80. This statement comes from "Mr. Cottons Rejoynder." That text and several other central documents of the Antinomian Controversy have been collected together in David Hall's documentary history of the controversy. Hereafter, I will cite his edition, not the specific document.

13. As Abraham "rejoyced with joy unspeakable and glorious" when he received the promise, so any saint would respond in kind. Ibid., 86. The Holy Spirit, Cotton wrote, "beareth a peculiar and distinct witness of his own revealing the grace of God in greater peace and power." He explained, "In greater peace, for it is he that sheddeth abroad the love of God into our hearts … and he speaketh peace to us … even peace that passeth understanding … from whence springeth the joy unspeakable and glorious, which is therefore called the joy of the Holy Ghost because it floweth immediately from him and his testimony. … Again, He revealeth the grace of God in greater power to us in Christ … to wit, above the power they had received whilst Christ was conversant with them upon the Earth." Hall, *Antinomian Controversy*, 80–81.

14. Hall, *Antinomian Controversy*, 94; see also 184 and 334. For more on Bilney and Cotton's use of the example in the Antinomian Controversy, see Adrian

Chastain Weimer, *Martyrs' Mirror: Persecution and Holiness in Early New England* (New York: Oxford University Press, 2011), chapter 3.

15. Hall, *Antinomian Controversy*, 99, 140. According to Gura, the "radical spiritist" wing of Puritanism "maintained that at the moment of conversion God overruled the natural order and endowed the saint with an overwhelming and undeniable sense of his salvation." Gura, *Glimpse*, 51. Cotton never fully fit with radical spiritism, but his theology came closer than other ministers in the Bay. For more on Cotton's theology and its view of grace, see Pettit, *Heart Prepared*, 130–139; and James Fulton Maclear, "'The Heart of New England Rent': The Mystical Element in Early Puritan History," *Mississippi Valley Historical Review* 42, no. 4 (1956): 637–638.

16. Hall, *Antinomian Controversy*, 156–157, 169, 161, 337–338. Battis writes, Hutchinson "pursued the mild illuminism of John Cotton to its highly subjectivist conclusions." Battis implies a judgment here and elsewhere against Hutchinson; I would emphasize simply the extent to which she took Cotton's teachings further than Cotton himself. Emery Battis, *Saints and Sectaries: Anne Hutchinson and the Antinomian Controversy in the Massachusetts Bay Colony* (Chapel Hill: University of North Carolina Press, 1962), 56. Bozeman, acknowledging their theological difference, offers three "points of connection" between Hutchinson and Cotton: "a portrayal of the saints' direct dependence upon Christ both for ethical purification and assurance, an emphasis upon the Holy Spirit as the agent of assurance, and an unusually strong formulation of the Protestant principle of private judgment." Theodore Dwight Bozeman, *The Precisianist Strain: Disciplinary Religion and Antinomian Backlash in Puritanism to 1638* (Chapel Hill: University of North Carolina Press, 2004), 223.

17. Hall, *Antinomian Controversy*, 73–74. Hall, *Antinomian Controversy*, 69. Stoever offers the best account of this logic and the ordered process that made it possible to reason backward from the final link to the first. See Stoever, *Faire and Easie*.

18. This critique of Puritanism as tied to works seemed to arise naturally, even *inevitably*, from various constituent members of the Puritan movement. As Como writes, "The word 'inevitable' is appropriate in this case if only because mainstream puritanism gave birth to antinomianism not once, nor even twice—but multiple times, under distinct and apparently unrelated local circumstances, in entirely different parts of England. This suggests that whatever else we might say about mainstream puritanism, it most certainly lent itself to what might be termed an 'anti-legal' critique, in which the antinomian elements of the New Testament could be privileged over and against the moralizing elements." Como, *Blown by the Spirit*, 131.

19. Darrett Rutman, *Winthrop's Boston: A Portrait of a Puritan Town, 1630–1649* (University of North Carolina Press, 1965; reprint ed., New York: Norton, 1972), 115; Elizabeth Maddock Dillon, *The Gender of Freedom: Fictions of Liberalism and*

the *Literary Public Sphere* (Redwood City, CA: Stanford University Press, 2004), 55; Amy Schrager Lang, *Prophetic Woman: Anne Hutchinson and the Problem of Dissent in the Literature of New England* (Berkeley: University of California Press, 1987), 19; Knight, *Orthodoxies*, 99. In *The Precisianist Strain*, Bozeman offers perhaps the most compelling case for explaining antinomianism as a reaction to Puritanism's overregulated and disciplined behavior. These works all contribute significantly to our understanding of Puritanism and I am deeply indebted to each, but here I wish to challenge their view of sanctification and the interpretation of the Antinomian Controversy that often flows from it.

20. Delbanco, *Puritan Ordeal*, 122, 136–137. In 1873, John Adams Vinton noted that most scholars defend Hutchinson for "endeavoring to recall the religious community from an undue regard to the *external* manifestations of piety, and to fix their attention more closely on an *internal*, spiritual experience of the power of divine truth." John Adams Vinton, *The Antinomian Controversy of 1637* (Boston: 1873), 7 (emphasis added). Twenty years later, Lang notes, the historian Charles Francis Adams viewed Anne Hutchinson "as the 'great prototype' of those harmless, if 'misty,' Transcendentalists for whom New England would later become famous." Lang, *Prophetic Woman*, 15. One can see that basic argument and its concomitant division (internal experience vs. external deed) repeated through the decades. According to Battis, for example, there were only two paths to assurance: "intuitional means" (what he also calls "the presence of a 'light within'") or "practical observance of the moral law." Battis, *Saints and Sectaries*, 23. These sorts of battle lines are often accepted regardless of which side a certain scholar seems to promote. Battis, for example, is mostly critical of Hutchinson, while Miller rebukes her for mucking up the elders' "mathematically calculable test" of salvation. Perry Miller, *The New England Mind: The Seventeenth Century* (Cambridge, MA: Belknap, 1982), 389.

21. Thomas Shepard, *The Parable of the Ten Virgins* (Orlando: Soli Deo Gloria, 1990), 95, 101, 133, 254.

22. Ibid., 35, 55. Bulkeley quoted in Stoever, *Faire and Easie*, 74. Stoever summarizes: "*That* a person obeyed the commandments meant little; *how* and *why* he obeyed them were the vital points." Stoever, *Faire and Easie*, 74. As Coolidge writes, "Deeds are only as good as the condition of faith from which they follow." John Coolidge, *The Pauline Renaissance in England: Puritanism and the Bible* (Oxford: Clarendon, 1970), 131. Delbanco is right, therefore, when he claims that for the antinomians, "the meaning of any act ... derives only from the spirit in which it is performed," but wrong when he excludes other Puritans from such a view. Delbanco, *Puritan Ordeal*, 129. Shepard preached that the "greatest work" of the Lord was "not only to change the acts, but to change the heart; not only to put new actions, but a new nature into men." Shepard, *Parable*, 277. Thus, in Shepard's church, "applicants did not present their acts of obedience." Charles Lloyd Cohen, *God's Caress: The Psychology of Puritan*

Religious Experience (Oxford: Oxford University Press, 1986), 213. Baird Tipson shows that in New England, the confessions refer almost exclusively to *internal emotions*. Baird Tipson, "The 'Judgment of Charity' in the Early New England Churches," *Church History* 44, no. 4 (1975): 464–465.

23. Hall, *Antinomian Controversy*, 73, 106–107, 184, 161–162, 286, 322. Bozeman notes that Anne Hutchinson "repudiat[ed] in particular (with Traske and Wheelwright) the 'love [of the] brethren' that Cotton himself in England had affirmed and that long had been a standard sign and a key tenet and the cement of the godly subculture." Bozeman, *Precisianist Strain*, 297–298. He does not, however, excavate what this love of the brethren means or entails.

24. *Winthrop Papers*, I.190. Thomas Shepard, "The Autobiography," *God's Plot: Puritan Spirituality in Thomas Shepard's Cambridge*, ed. Michael McGiffert (Amherst: University of Massachusetts Press, 1994), 73.

25. According to Webster, "Sociability came to be a way of measuring godliness in biographies." Tom Webster, *Godly Clergy in Early Stuart England: The Caroline Puritan Movement, c. 1620–1643* (Cambridge: Cambridge University Press, 1997), 130. In his explication, it appears that such a sign of grace often worked by reference to 1 John 3:14 (see especially pages 130–133).

26. Shepard, "Autobiography," 44. Shepard, *Parable*, 494.

27. Clap, *Memoirs*, 5, 7.

28. Ibid., 7. For an analysis of this love in relation to racial boundaries, see chapters 5 and 6.

29. Ibid.

30. Ibid., 9.

31. Ibid., 9, emphasis added.

32. Ibid., 9–10. Caldwell notes that Clap's prior assurances culminate with a love of saints, but adds that it "clearly does not serve; the account breaks off." Her larger point—that "in conversion narratives experience was felt to be more than could be rhetorically contained in a perfunctory arrangement of steps"— seems valid. But in Clap's messy cobbling together of evidence, he never discounts his love of saints. See Patricia Caldwell, *The Puritan Conversion Narrative: The Beginnings of American Expression* (Cambridge: Cambridge University Press, 1983), 165–166. Shea summarizes Clap's combination of assurances this way: "His principal assurance of grace derived from the quasi-mystical experience in which he shed tears and cried out, 'He is come'; but the analytic device Clap relies on to discover more objective evidence is the widespread notion, derived from 1 John 3:14, that only the elect can truly love their brethren." Daniel Shea Jr., *Spiritual Autobiography in Early America* (Princeton, NJ: Princeton University Press, 1968), 124. The combination seems accurate, but Clap does not prioritize as Shea suggests: he might have found most comfort in rapture *once*, but the "principle assurance of grace" on a daily basis was grounded in 1 John 3:14.

33. Hibbins quoted in Larzer Ziff, "The Social Bond of Church Covenant," *American Quarterly* 10, no. 4 (1958): 462.

34. Thomas Shepard, *Thomas Shepard's Confessions*, ed. George Selement and Bruce C. Woolley, vol. 58, *Publications of the Colonial Society of Massachusetts* (Boston: Colonial Society of Massachusetts, 1981), 70.

35. Ibid., 77, 94, 126–127. Some might object that in several of these cases, testimonies turn from a love of brethren to a moment of rapture. In each case, however, these moments only cap earlier experiences of comfort, validating them as genuine. In Shepard's congregation, the love of brethren was never set aside in favor of a single, religious experience; instead, it preceded religious experience and returned later to offer comfort when ecstasies subsided. Cohen has observed this point as well, noting that "love for the godly also indicated the presence of grace, both preparatory and saving, in the individual soul." Cohen, *God's Caress*, 221. My study is indebted to Cohen's and builds on it: concurring on a fundamental tenet of Puritan doctrine, I focus less on "the psychology of Puritan religious experience" (Cohen's concern) and more on the controversies, rhetorical devices, narratives, and intercultural relations of seventeenth-century Puritanism bound up both in this principle and in the other doctrines that evolved from or affected Puritan concepts of sympathy. For example, the love of brethren does not appear in Cohen's account of the Antinomian Controversy. See Cohen, *God's Caress*, 262–270.

36. Shepard, "Autobiography," 43, 47.

37. Ibid., 54.

38. Ibid., 54–55. Shepard, *Parable*, 20–21.

39. Shepard, *Confessions*, 36, 54, 65, 86, 94, 74. For other examples of this emotional double-negative (proving oneself godly by being hated by the ungodly), see 107 and 194.

40. Ibid., 87, 127. Caldwell notes that "America itself, by being perceived in the proper way, or by kindling the proper feelings, or, above all, by deflecting the wrong feelings, offered to clarify one's spiritual condition; and one's reaction to the whole experience … could be turned into one huge 'evidence' or 'effect' of grace." Caldwell, *Puritan Conversion Narrative*, 130. Caldwell mainly focuses on the emigrants' experience after they had crossed the sea and suggests that for many, the move to New England produced "a kind of grim, gray disappointment." Caldwell, *Puritan Conversion Narrative*, 31. In their narratives, however, confessors often relate the mere *desire* to emigrate as a valid sign of conversion. Wanting to live among godly people was itself evidence of grace—long before saints set sail and regardless of what they discovered upon landing.

41. I say "relatively" ordinary throughout because the whole point of the experience was a testimony of the Holy Spirit, which necessarily set it apart from any old feeling. The experience was linked to common emotions and arose from them, but it also had the dimension of offering some assurance of salvation.

In many cases, that experience of assurance was itself what took an ordinary feeling and made it into a testimony of the Spirit. Yet this was still a far cry from ecstatic union, rapturous religious experiences, or the more semimystical demands of the antinomians. It was, instead, a relatively ordinary feeling and affection.

42. Hall, *Antinomian Controversy*, 106, 184. In addition, Cotton claimed that 1 John had been written to those who "did know their good estate, by the knowledge of the Father; before they knew their good estat by their brotherly love." Hall, *Antinomian Controversy*, 184. To back up his reading of 1 John 3:14, Cotton quoted at length from Calvin's commentary on the verse. Hall, *Antinomian Controversy*, 106. Scholars have sometimes argued that Cotton was more Calvinist than his opponents, and at least in his interpretation of 1 John 3:14, they are right. For Calvin's views on sanctification and justification, see Beeke, *Assurance of Faith*, 72–78. But Calvin's overall view was somewhat more nuanced. In a sense, both parties had Calvin on their side. Calvin defines faith as personal assurance (which seems to support Cotton), but he also distinguishes between "*the definition of faith* and *the reality of the believer's experience*." Thus, "*The sense* or *feeling* of assurance increases and decreases in proportion to the rise and decline of faith's exercises, but *the seed of faith* can never change or fluctuate." As a result, "*Assurance may be possessed without being known*." Beeke, *Assurance of Faith*, 54, 61–62 (emphasis in original).

43. Mark 9:24 (King James Version). Of this man, Winthrop writes, "The weake beleever was poore in spirit, yet saw his own Faith weak though it were." Hall, *Antinomian Controversy*, 232.

44. As Delbanco explains, "New Englanders ... were less afflicted by complacence than by anxiety." Delbanco, *Puritan Ordeal*, 142. I agree, though I disagree that such apprehension arose out of preparationist demands. Winship also claims that "partisans on both sides of this controversy had higher priorities than civic tranquility." For him, however, the highest priority was truth for truth's sake: Shepard "repeatedly warned against tolerating his opponents' errors for the sake of peace." Winship, *Making Heretics*, 119. In fact, however, Shepard was often concerned primarily for the peace of troubled souls that he saw being shattered by antinomian demands. Stoever is good on this point. He observes that the elders' position "addressed a keen pastoral problem," embracing the large number of Puritans who were "dependent for knowledge of their estate on the 'inferior light' of conscience concluding from the effects of grace in themselves." Stoever, *Faire and Easie*, 137. McGiffert emphasizes Shepard's concern for weak Christians in general: see McGiffert, "Thomas Shepard," 21–26.

45. According to Foster, the conflict can be reduced to a "barely concealed fear of inspired violence." Stephen Foster, "New England and the Challenge of Heresy, 1630 to 1660: The Puritan Crisis in Transatlantic Perspective," *William and Mary Quarterly* 38, no. 4 (1981): 646. Gura claims that the real

threat (in the elders' perspective) was the Hutchinsonians' radical social and political egalitarianism. Gura, *Glimpse*, 78–80, 174. Others locate the political threat in the supposedly looser morality of the antinomian way. See Battis, *Saints and Sectaries*, 263; Everett Emerson, *Puritanism in America, 1620–1750* (Boston: Twayne, 1977), 75; Gura, *Glimpse*, 53, 58. Moral laxity *did* worry elders, but it seems that scholars have, at times, made too much of this fear. The relative absence of morally loose persons itself suggests that the charge was rather hollow. The radicals were, as Winship puts it, "performatively orthodox." Winship, *Making Heretics*, 59. Foster solves this problem by asserting that the fear was more imagined than real: New England elders imported their understanding of antinomianism from England's radicals and foisted it upon their opponents. Foster, "Challenge of Heresy," 647. Como also argues that the claims of Hutchinson and her sympathizers "were immediately plotted onto a known map of recognized heretical opinion, identifying their purveyors as hidden antinomians." Como, *Blown by the Spirit*, 442. For a selection of political readings, see Ronald Cohen, "Church and State in Seventeenth-Century Massachusetts: Another Look at the Antinomian Controversy," *Journal of Church and State* 12, no. 3 (1970): 475–493; James Cooper Jr., "Anne Hutchinson and the 'Lay Rebellion' against the Clergy," *New England Quarterly* 61, no. 3 (1988): 381–397. Kai Erikson, *The Wayward Puritans: A Study in the Sociology of Deviance* (New York: Wiley, 1966); Lyle Koehler, *A Search for Power: The "Weaker Sex" in Seventeenth-Century New England* (Urbana: University of Illinois Press, 1980); Darren Staloff, *The Making of an American Thinking Class: Intellectuals and Intelligentsia in Puritan Massachusetts* (New York: Oxford University Press, 1998), chapters 3–4; Ann Fairfax Withington and Jack Schwartz, "The Political Trial of Anne Hutchinson," *New England Quarterly* 51, no. 2 (1978): 226–240.

46. Hall also emphasizes this aspect as central to the Antinomian Controversy, particularly Shepard's stake in it. See David Hall, *A Reforming People: Puritanism and the Transformation of Public Life in New England* (New York: Knopf, 2011), 169–171. In this concern for weak Christians, the elders joined in the general focus of Puritan casuistry. As Keith Thomas relates, "Puritan casuists sought to drive away despair, and to indicate ways by which the soul could be saved. For William Perkins, the greatest case of conscience 'that ever was' was *How a man may know whether he be the child of God or no?*" Keith Thomas, "Cases of Conscience in Seventeenth-Century England," in *Public Duty and Private Conscience in Seventeenth-Century England: Essays Presented to G.E. Aylmer*, ed. John Morrill, Paul Slack, and Daniel Woolf (Oxford: Clarendon, 1993), 34. As Beeke shows, the increasing emphasis on sanctification as legitimate evidence of justification (in the influential works of Beza and Perkins, for example) came about primarily through a pastoral "concern for weak believers." See Beeke, *Assurance of Faith*, 82–86 and 112–113.

47. The "demands of preparation," Delbanco claims, "reduced at least some New Englanders to the condition of paralyzed dread, and thereby authorized any form of solace"—a solace that found expression in Cotton, who "encouraged … an expectancy [for rescue] by broadening the terms in which it could be recognized as authentic." Delbanco, *Puritan Ordeal*, 143. According to Gura, the "offer of a 'naked Christ' … greatly simplified the requirements for and demands of sainthood." The belief "in justification by God's free grace alone" enabled people "to obtain some reprieve from the intolerably high level of anxiety by which ministers like Shepard and Hooker asked people to live." Gura, *Glimpse*, 52–53. Under Shepard's system, Rosenmeier concurs, "the burden of finding the assurance of salvation becomes heavy indeed." Jesper Rosenmeier, "New England's Perfection: The Image of Adam and the Image of Christ in the Antinomian Crisis, 1634 to 1638," *William and Mary Quarterly* 27, no. 3 (1970): 444. Lang likewise asserts, "From this moment forward [the moment of 'the Spirit's invisible witness to election'], the antinomian lives in a world free of the sometimes productive, sometimes disabling anxiety characteristic of the Puritan saint." Lang, *Prophetic Woman*, 7–8.

48. Shepard, *Parable*, 192, 194. Hall, *Antinomian Controversy*, 203.

49. Hall, *Antinomian Controversy*, 75, 66–68 (emphasis added).

50. Ibid., 185. For the relevant pages debating this metaphor, see Hall, *Antinomian Controversy*, 55, 75, 138–139, 155, 185.

51. John Calvin, *Commentaries on the Catholic Epistles*, trans. John Owen (Edinburgh: Calvin Translation Society, 1855), 218.

52. By the 1630s, moreover, this metaphor and its debate had one more significant connotation: it could have been code for an antinomian underground. John Eaton, an antinomian leader, interpreted Revelations 12:1 in the following manner: "*I saw a Woman Clothed with the Sun* [That is, the Church Clothed with the Righteousness of Christ, to her Justification] *and the Moon,* [that is, Sanctification] *under her Feet.*" This quotation actually comes from Giles Firmin recording a memory of the antinomian Henry Firmin, who endorsed the same interpretation as Eaton. In other words, the sun and its lesser lights directly engaged antinomian controversies of the day, and possibly signaled one's membership in the antinomian community. See Como, *Blown by the Spirit*, 326–327.

53. Shepard, *Parable*, 221. Hall, *Antinomian Controversy*, 64, 63 (emphasis added). Thus, when Shepard speaks of being "filled with the Spirit of Christ," he qualifies his statement according to different measures: "I speak not now of extraordinary fullness, which prophets and apostles had, nor of that fullness which is in glory, as if we must have that here; but of that which the saints attain to in this life, every one according to his need and measure of capableness of the same." Shepard, *Parable*, 555.

54. Knight argues, for example, that desire was key to the theological system taught by Sibbes and continued by Cotton. Knight, *Orthodoxies*, 131, see also 112–113.

According to Lovejoy, the "intense desire for closing with the Spirit was the very heart of enthusiasm"—and thus of the Hutchinsonian way. David Lovejoy, *Religious Enthusiasm in the New World: Heresy to Revolution* (Cambridge, MA: Harvard University Press, 1985), 71.

55. Hall, *Antinomian Controversy*, 74. Matthew 5:6 reads, "Blessed are they which do hunger and thirst after righteousness: for they shall be filled" (King James Version). In John 7:37, Jesus proclaims, "If any man thirst, let him come unto me, and drink" (King James Version).

56. Shepard, *Parable*, 65, 468–470, 220.

57. Shepard, *Confessions*, 41, 43, 69, 74, 170.

58. Hall, *Antinomian Controversy*, 96. Cotton repeats later, "That which shall satisfie [a saint], is not to drink refreshing out of his thirst, but from the Spirit of life which [Christ] shall give him." Hall, *Antinomian Controversy*, 122.

59. Hall, *Antinomian Controversy*, 93, 96, 121.

60. Ibid., 68. Shepard, *Parable*, 203, 225. Hall, *Antinomian Controversy*, 64.

61. Shepard preached, "He that performs any duty ultimately to ease his conscience, he is married yet unto the law." Shepard, *Parable*, 39.

62. Edward Johnson, *Johnson's Wonder-Working Providence, 1628–1651*, ed. J. Franklin Jameson (New York: Scribner's, 1910), 132, 134, 136. Shepard, *Confessions*, 74–75. Knight has claimed that in the Sibbesian theological system (Cotton's system) a "Christian had only to express delight," but that "only" could imply an enormous demand. Rapture was not easy for all. Knight, *Orthodoxies*, 128.

63. Hall, *Antinomian Controversy*, 130, 85–86. That also seemed to be Wheelwright's answer to the elders' concern for weak Christians. To the objection that his doctrine would "be a meanes to discourage those that are weake Christians, and do them a great deale of hurt," Wheelwright responded, "Let the Gospell be never so cleerely held forth, it never hurteth the children of God, no, it doth them a great deale of good." Hall, *Antinomian Controversy*, 166. In effect, Wheelwright seemed to be claiming what Cotton argued: that by ridding people of false comfort, he was opening them to transforming grace.

64. Hall, *Antinomian Controversy*, 141. Shepard, *Confessions*, 55–56. Hall, *Antinomian Controversy*, 113. For more on Cotton's theology and, in particular, his view of comfort, see Coolidge, *Pauline Renaissance*, 129–138.

65. Hall, *Antinomian Controversy*, 113, 89, 128, 107.

66. Several scholars have argued that when the General Court banished Hutchinson, it also rid the colony of spiritual ecstasy. In Hutchinson's trial, as Delbanco puts it, we can "glimpse the moment at which the idea of a suprarational spirit was beginning to be beaten down in New England." Delbanco, *Puritan Ordeal*, 137. "In place of a warm pietism," Everett Emerson writes, "preachers increasingly emphasized rigid morality." Emerson, *Puritanism in America*, 79. In *Letters from New England*, Emerson describes even more forcefully this quashing of religious fervor: " 'Heart-religion,' identified now with the Hutchinsonians,

became a thing of the past in New England until the time of the Great Awakening." Everett Emerson, ed., *Letters from New England: The Massachusetts Bay Colony, 1629–1638* (Amherst: University of Massachusetts Press, 1976), 212. Such views again map onto the common reading of this controversy as a contest between feeling and discipline—with the latter winning out. Winship, on the contrary, rejects the argument offered by Miller, Delbanco, and Knight that the Antinomian Controversy resulted in the triumph of Shepard's and Hooker's "moralistic and 'legal' style of preaching" over Cotton's "more charismatic and mystical variety." Cotton's preaching, both before and after the controversy, he argues, was "mystical, mild, and doctrinally restrained." Winship, *Making Heretics*, 238. I agree, and many lay Puritans could continue to accept such a style of faith after the Antinomian Controversy closed.

67. Shepard, *Parable*, 476–477, 181–182. Shepard, *Confessions*, 41.

68. Winship, *Making Heretics*, 85.

69. Knight, for instance, claims that Shepard "policed ecstatic expression in church gatherings" and that he "restricted expression of his own high emotion to the private pages of his journal." For Shepard, unlike for Cotton, the confessions were undertaken with "a motive of surveillance" not necessarily "edification"; they served a "regulatory rather than evangelical" function. Knight, *Orthodoxies*, 78, 177.

70. See Shepard, *Confessions*, 163–164.

71. Shepard, *Parable*, 450, 568, 381. McGiffert, "Thomas Shepard," 27. McGiffert offers a strong account of both perspectives on conversion narratives—that they served either as surveillance or as evangelical invitations. See McGiffert, "The People Speak: Confessions of Lay Men and Women," in *God's Plot*, 135–148.

72. Cohen, *God's Caress*, 208.

73. *Winthrop Papers*, III.328, III.344. In shaping his spiritual autobiography to didactic ends, Winthrop joined a wider Puritan tradition. Such narratives existed precisely to teach lessons gleaned from experience. See Shea, *Spiritual Autobiography*, 95, 112–113. There is no evidence that Winthrop delivered his relation publicly, but Winship, who also believes that Winthrop was seeking "to reach a theological common ground with his opponents," speculates that he "may have circulated this document to demonstrate his saintly status by any standard being used in Massachusetts." Winship, *Making Heretics*, 103–104. I argue that Winthrop's narrative is less about assuring himself or others and more about critiquing and commenting on the standards of assurance in place.

74. *Winthrop Papers*, III.339–340.

75. Ibid., 340.

76. Ibid., 340–341.

77. Ibid., 341–342.

78. Ibid., 343.

79. Ibid.

80. Ibid.

81. Ibid. Cohen claims that Winthrop's narrative "builds to a climax, union with Christ, and then winds down." Cohen, *God's Caress*, 260. Yet the way in which it winds down matters as much as the moment of climax. Winthrop's denouement suggests the temporality and danger of even the strongest religious experience.

82. Winthrop, *Journal*, 239.

CHAPTER 3

1. *The Winthrop Papers*, vols. 1–7 (Boston: Massachusetts Historical Society, 1929–), II.174–176.

2. Richard Mather and William Tompson, *An Heart-Melting Exhortation* (London, 1654), 3–4, 9–10.

3. Ibid., 10 (emphasis added).

4. Norton, *The Answer to the Whole set of Questions of the Celebrated Mr. William Apollonius* (1648), trans. Douglas Horton (Cambridge, MA: Belknap, 1958), 4.

5. *Winthrop Papers*, III.520.

6. David D. Hall, ed., *The Antinomian Controversy, 1636–1638: A Documentary History*, second ed. (Durham, NC: Duke University Press, 1990), 25, 29, 29, 33. Everett Emerson, ed., *Letters from New England: The Massachusetts Bay Colony, 1629–1638* (Amherst: University of Massachusetts Press, 1976), 216–217. A similar dynamic can be seen among the varying degrees of puritans in England: ties of affection bind moderate and hotter puritans together despite disagreements about particular ecclesiastical details. For more on this dynamic, see Peter Lake, *Moderate Puritans and the Elizabethan Church* (New York: Cambridge University Press, 1982).

7. John Winthrop, *Winthrop's Journal, 1630–1649*, ed. James Kendall Hosmer (New York: Scribners, 1908),196–197.

8. Ibid., 198–199. The theological dispute at this point concerned descriptions of the indwelling of the Holy Spirit. Wheelwright, Hutchinson, and others of their persuasion argued that the "person" of the Holy Spirit dwelt within each believer in a "real union." Winthrop, on the other hand, considered such language unscriptural and worried about its implications. He agreed that *some* kind of union existed, but he did not want to define it too closely, and so he argued with Wheelwright that for the peace of the church, the terms "person" and "real union" should be "forborn." Winthrop, *Journal*, 199.

9. Winthrop, *Journal*, 201. In *Ways of Writing*, Hall shows that Puritans sometimes relied on "scribal publication"—handwritten manuscripts—because of "a strong preference for a mode of communication that was less disruptive of social peace. The goal of preserving that peace was among the most explicit priorities of the colonists." David D. Hall, *Ways of Writing: The Practice and Politics*

of Text-Making in Seventeenth-Century New England (Philadelphia: University of Pennsylvania Press, 2008), 50.

10. Winthrop, *Journal*, 201. For more on the Puritans' vigorous opposition to "human invention," see Theodore Dwight Bozeman, *To Live Ancient Lives: The Primitivist Dimension in Puritanism* (Chapel Hill: University of North Carolina Press, 1988), 51–80, 136–139.

11. Winthrop, *Journal*, 202.

12. Ibid., 203, 204, 217, 205, 209.

13. Winship writes, "Perhaps it took conference and reflection before hostile observers realized that they had the materials with which they could finally construct Wheelwright as far enough out on a limb that he could be lopped off." Winship identifies the turning point at Wheelwright's *trial*, rather than his sermon, marking it as the transition from "a polarized theological dispute" to "a polarized political dispute." Michael Winship, *Making Heretics: Militant Protestantism and Free Grace in Massachusetts, 1636–1641* (Princeton, NJ: Princeton University Press, 2002), 114, 126. Foster agrees: "The whole idea of an adverse 'party' became particularly useful because it allowed the zaniest or most impromptu outburst of any single 'member' to be collectively attributed and because it was liable to conjure up the very monster it presupposed." Stephen Foster, "New England and the Challenge of Heresy, 1630 to 1660: The Puritan Crisis in Transatlantic Perspective," *William and Mary Quarterly* 38, no. 4 (1981): 651. For both Foster and Winship, the impetus for division lay with the elders. I admire these studies, but I disagree. As I intend to show, the impetus for division came from the same martyr persona that Puritans had nurtured in England and that antinomians continued in New England.

14. Hall, *Antinomian Controversy*, 153, 154, 157.

15. Ibid., 158–159. For more on the theology of the controversy, see chapter 2.

16. Hall, *Antinomian Controversy*, 159, 161. See also David Hall, *A Reforming People: Puritanism and the Transformation of Public Life in New England* (New York: Knopf, 2011), 121–122.

17. Ibid., 159, 163. For the mentality of persecution and martyrdom in early New England, including how it surfaces in the Antinomian Controversy, see Adrian Chastain Weimer, *Martyrs' Mirror: Persecution and Holiness in Early New England* (New York: Oxford University Press, 2011).

18. Theodore Dwight Bozeman, *The Precisianist Strain: Disciplinary Religion and Antinomian Backlash in Puritanism to 1638* (Chapel Hill: University of North Carolina Press, 2004), 7. Bozeman reveals how a minority status traces back to the early days of English Puritanism. Even in the 1570s and 1580s, he writes, "the godly chose and indeed accented and savored a minority status within their church and town." The clergy even called themselves "a 'very smal' presence, 'a smal, poore, … flocke,'" language which Wheelwright's sermon echoes. Beyond a minority status, Bozeman also describes a "sense of embattlement"

among the early dissenters—a stance that Wheelwright also embraced. Bozeman, *Precisianist Strain*, 53, 53, 55, 87. In New England, however, that attitude had to be checked and reversed. As Gura argues, "The revolutionary dynamic within Puritanism unravelled by an internal logic of its own, whether extended against English bishops or Massachusetts theocrats." Philip Gura, *A Glimpse of Sion's Glory: Puritan Radicalism in New England, 1620–1660* (Middletown, CT: Wesleyan University Press, 1984), 29. The history of such an argument dates back at least to 1921. See James Truslow Adams, "An English Opposition Becomes a New England Oligarchy," in *The Founding of Massachusetts: Historians and the Sources*, ed. Edmund Morgan (Indianapolis: Bobbs-Merrill, 1964), 72. For more on the problems of transitioning from minority dissent to majority rule, see T. H. Breen, *The Character of the Good Ruler: A Study of Puritan Political Ideas in New England, 1630–1730* (New Haven, CT: Yale University Press, 1970); Timothy Wood, *Agents of Wrath, Sowers of Discord: Authority and Dissent in Puritan Massachusetts, 1630–1655* (New York: Routledge, 2006), 1–15.

19. Hall, *Antinomian Controversy*, 158, 166, 172, 159, 165.

20. Hall, *Antinomian Controversy*, 168. As Coolidge has noted, Ephesians 4 was a principal text for deducing the nature of the Church in early Puritanism (and, before that, in the Reformers Bucer and Calvin). See John Coolidge, *The Pauline Renaissance in England: Puritanism and the Bible* (Oxford: Clarendon, 1970), 48.

21. Hall, *Antinomian Controversy*, 155, 167, 172.

22. Ibid., 210–211.

23. Ibid., 297. This quote comes from the *Short Story of the Rise, reign, and ruine of the Antinomians, Familists & Libertines*. Winthrop has generally been considered the author, but recently Hall has argued against that notion. Most of it was probably transcribed by a witness named John Higginson hired by magistrates to record the debates and trials, who may then have assembled the package of texts that served as the copy text for the printing of *Short Story*. Hall claims the document should be treated "as an example both of social authorship and of texts that have no author in any meaningful sense." Hall, *Ways of Writing*, 66. In the body of my text, therefore, I cite "the elders," rather than Winthrop, when quoting from this text.

24. Hall, *Antinomian Controversy*, 293, 297.

25. Ibid., 292 (emphasis added), 290. Gordis has argued that "Hutchinson's contemporaries saw her social prominence as a significant aspect of Hutchinson's disruptive power." Lisa Gordis, *Opening Scripture: Bible Reading and Interpretative Authority in Puritan New England* (Chicago: University of Chicago Press, 2002), 168. Certainly her power of disruption gained with her prominence. Yet it seems that her division between one covenant and another did not gain authoritative status until Wheelwright preached it from the pulpit.

26. Winthrop, *Journal*, 209. In his preface to a second edition of *The Antinomian Controversy 1636–1638: A Documentary History*, Hall comments, "Reading

through these documents anew, I am struck by the rhetorical quality of the charge that so-and-so was preaching a 'covenant of works.' Like its twin, the charge of 'familism' cannot always translate into issues of doctrine." Hall, *Antinomian Controversy*, xvi. Winthrop, it seems, would have agreed. These divided sympathies caused disaffections which cut through every level of society and disrupted the Puritans' ideal of harmony. Gordis reads Hutchinson as "reluctant to relinquish a vision of interpretative community in which those who disagreed discussed their concerns and perplexities openly." Gordis, *Opening Scripture*, 181. Gura likewise claims the New England Puritans early in 1637 gave up theological debate and "sought to impose conformity of doctrine upon the population." Gura, *Glimpse*, 250. Yet in Winthrop's eyes, it was Wheelwright and Hutchinson who had shut down the possibility of debate by creating their own family and opposing it to those whom Wheelwright called "Antichristians spirits." Theological disagreements could be worked out only within a broadly conceived unity of the spirit; once that spirit divided, debate could not continue.

27. Hall, *Antinomian Controversy*, 297, 300. Nelson offers a good, brief reading of the word "enemy" in Winthrop's *A Model of Christian Charity*: the sermon requires both a love of enemies (when considered fellow colonists) and a defeat of enemies (when considered opposed to the settlement). See Dana Nelson, *The Word in Black and White: Reading 'Race' in American Literature, 1638–1867* (New York: Oxford University Press, 1992), 4–5. The elders applied that same division to Wheelwright's sermon, critiquing him for using the latter approach *within* the communion of saints.

28. *Winthrop Papers*, III.424, III.425, III.470–475.

29. Hall, *Antinomian Controversy*, 312. Two versions of the trial survive: the elders' edited version in the *Short Story*, and a second account in the appendix of Thomas Hutchinson's *History of the Colony and Province of Massachusetts Bay* (1767). Hutchinson transcribed the account from an "ancient manuscript," which has since been lost. (See Hall's introduction in *Antinomian Controversy*, 311.) This opening comes from Thomas Hutchinson's account.

30. Hall, *Antinomian Controversy*, 313, 266, 267.

31. In this respect, I agree with New who argues, "Whatever her ultimate effect, and however her questioners saw her, Hutchinson's mandate was not in itself to threaten, topple, or replace the outward forms of patriarchy." New's larger point is that Hutchinson's spirituality did not envision *any* kind of political institution: she "sued not for a new law ... but for Christ's inner power." Elisa New, "Feminist Invisibility: The Examples of Anne Bradstreet and Anne Hutchinson," *Common Knowledge* 2, no. 1 (1993): 101.

32. Hall, *Antinomian Controversy*, 262. A great deal of excellent work has studied the gender dynamics of the Antinomian Controversy. For a good selection, see Ben Barker-Benfield, "Anne Hutchinson and the Puritan Attitude toward Women,"

Feminist Studies 1, no. 2 (1972); Lyle Koehler, *A Search for Power: The Weaker "Sex" in Seventeenth-Century New England* (Urbana: University of Illinois Press, 1980); Amy Schrager Lang, *Prophetic Woman: Anne Hutchinson and the Problem of Dissent in the Literature of New England* (Berkeley: University of California Press, 1987); Mary Beth Norton, *Founding Mothers and Fathers: Gendered Power and the Forming of American Society* (New York: Vintage, 1996); Amanda Porterfield, *Female Piety in Puritan New England: The Emergence of Religious Humanism* (New York: Oxford University Press, 1992); and Ross J. Pudaloff, "Sign and Subject: Antinomianism in Massachusetts Bay," *Semiotica* 54, no. 1–2 (1985): 147–163. For further important readings of gender set in a more transatlantic context, see Elizabeth Maddock Dillon, *The Gender of Freedom: Fictions of Liberalism and the Literary Public Sphere* (Redwood, CA: Stanford University Press, 2004), 49–115 (especially 71–83); Jim Egan, *Authorizing Experience: Refigurations of the Body Politic in Seventeenth-Century New England Writing* (Princeton, NJ: Princeton University Press, 1999), 66–81; and Phillip Round, *By Nature and By Custom Cursed: Transatlantic Civil Discourse and New England Cultural Production, 1620–1660* (Lebanon, NH: University Press of New England, 1999), 106–152. Silva, building on Pudaloff and Dillon, summarizes the most recent approach to gender in the Antinomian Controversy: "Hutchinson was not prosecuted because she was a woman, but her prosecution produced the terms through which to understand the status of womanhood in early colonial New England, as well as the deployment of political power in the colony." Christobal Silva, *Miraculous Plagues: An Epidemiology of Early New England Narrative* (New York: Oxford University Press, 2011), 88.

33. Hall, *Antinomian Controversy*, 317, 317 (emphasis added), 320. Winship argues that during Hutchinson's trial, she went from being one of many troublemakers to "the principal agent." Winship, *Making Heretics*, 182.

34. Hall, *Antinomian Controversy*, 327, 327. Ministers were wary to take an oath because oaths were tied to the third commandment (do not take the Lord's name in vain). As Withington and Schwartz write, "Puritans believed that if they swore to anything that was false they were guilty not only of perjury but of blasphemy and would therefore be damning themselves irrevocably." Ann Fairfax Withington and Jack Schwartz, "The Political Trial of Anne Hutchinson," *New England Quarterly* 51, no. 2 (1978): 233. The testimony concerned a meeting held almost a full year before, and even if the ministers told the truth as best they could, they might get something wrong. That made them skittish to swear, though it also weakened their testimony.

35. Hall, *Antinomian Controversy*, 334, 334, 335, 335.

36. Edmund Morgan, "The Case Against Anne Hutchinson," *New England Quarterly* 10, no. 4 (1937): 647.

37. Hall, *Antinomian Controversy*, 337.

38. Ibid., 342, 274, 274.

39. Ibid., 345.
40. Ibid., 346–347. On Israel Stoughton's role in the trial, see Louise Breen, *Transgressing the Bounds: Subversive Enterprises Among the Puritan Elite in Massachusetts, 1630–1692* (New York: Oxford University Press, 2001), chapter 1.
41. Hall, *Antinomian Controversy*, 201. Henry Vane, John Wheelwright, and Anne Hutchinson all faced the accusation that they had broken the colony's peace. See Ibid., 203, 253, 290, 317, and 384.
42. Ibid., 203.
43. *Winthrop Papers*, III.258.
44. There are some very good accounts of how transatlantic relations and the literary public sphere of England affected the print history of the Antinomian Controversy. See especially Dillon, *Gender of Freedom*; Jonathan Beecher Field, "The Antinomian Controversy Did Not Take Place," *Early American Literature* 6, no. 2 (2008), 448–463; Hall, *Ways of Writing*; and Round, *By Nature and By Custom Cursed*.
45. *Winthrop Papers*, II.328, III.398.
46. Round, *By Nature and By Custom Cursed*, 104. Dillon puts the situation well: "Ultimately," she writes, "the *inability* of the Massachusetts authorities to regulate the flow of information back to England concerning the colony required that they, too, add their voices to the chorus of competing accounts in an attempt to accrue public sentiment to their vision." Dillon, *Gender of Freedom*, 78. Thomas Hooker warned of publicity in England and the damage it could do in a letter to Shepard already in 1637; see Hall, *Ways of Writing*, 55–67.
47. Certainly the language of seduction did not go missing from the civil trial: an exasperated Winthrop proclaimed that the meetings at Hutchinson's house were "not to be suffered," in part because they provided an occasion "to seduce many honest persons." Yet even this mention of seduction ends with a concern "that families should be neglected for so many neighbours and dames and so much time spent." Hall, *Antinomian Controversy*, 316. In the church trial, the words "seduce" and "seduction" appear much more frequently.
48. Ibid., 365, 370, 385, 388.
49. Here I build on Lang, who calls Weld's preface "the story of New England's seduction." Lang, *Prophetic Woman*, 54–59.
50. Hall, *Antinomian Controversy*, 202, 204, 203, 204.
51. See chapter 2 for a fuller explanation.
52. Hall, *Antinomian Controversy*, 205. Multiple scholars claim that "it was the content of [Hutchinson's] message that won her adherents." Norton, *Founding Mothers*, 366. For two examples, see Foster, "Challenge of Heresy," 638; Bozeman, *Precisianist Strain*, 326. That may be true of some, but it is not true of how the elders presented the case for a transatlantic audience: in his discussion of this supposedly easy way, Weld shows just how much effort it took to make people accept it.

53. Hall, *Antinomian Controversy*, 205.

54. Ibid., 204–205.

55. Ibid., 205–206.

56. Ibid., 206.

57. Ibid., 206.

58. *Winthrop Papers*, II.289. Hall, *Antinomian Controversy*, 253, 317.

59. Tom Webster, *Godly Clergy in Early Stuart England: The Caroline Puritan Movement, c. 1620–1643* (Cambridge: Cambridge University Press, 1997), 333, 336.

60. Round, *By Nature and By Custom Cursed*, 132.

61. Hall, *Antinomian Controversy*, 213.

62. For the most compelling case that the Antinomian Controversy revealed a rupture of interpretative consensus requiring a new agreement on fundamental doctrine, see Gordis, *Opening Scripture*, 145–186.

63. Emerson, ed., *Letters from New England*, 213.

64. Hall, *Antinomian Controversy*, 217.

65. *Winthrop Papers*, III.343. Hall, *Antinomian Controversy*, 201. For a similar reading see Lang, *Prophetic Woman*, 54.

66. Egan demonstrates well how new responses to the plague in the seventeenth century map onto the way Winthrop handled his own antinomian outbreak. See Egan, *Authorizing Experience*, chapter 4. Here, I add a distinction between punishments and trials. See also Silva, *Miraculous Plagues*, chapter 2.

67. *Winthrop Papers*, III.272, III.353.

68. Anne Bradstreet, *The Works of Anne Bradstreet*, ed. Jeannine Hensley (Cambridge, MA: Belknap, 1967), 292.

69. Hall, *Antinomian Controversy*, 201, 307–308.

70. Gura, *Glimpse*, 253.

CHAPTER 4

1. *The Winthrop Papers*, vols. 1–7 (Boston: Massachusetts Historical Society, 1929–), II.105.

2. John Norton, *The Answer to the Whole set of Questions of the Celebrated Mr. William Apollonius*, trans. Douglas Horton (Cambridge, MA: Belknap, 1958), 10.

3. Richard Mather and William Tompson, *An Heart-Melting Exhortation* (London, 1654), 9–10.

4. Most scholars believe John White wrote *The Humble Request*, as William Hubbard asserted, though no one can know for sure. Those who signed it were John Winthrop, Charles Fines, George Philipps, Richard Saltonstall, Isaac Johnson, Thomas Dudley, and William Coddington.

5. "The Humble Request," in *The Founding of Massachusetts: Historians and the Sources*, ed. Edmund Morgan (Indianapolis: Bobbs-Merrill, 1964), 187–188.

6. Bremer combines *The Humble Request* with Winthrop's *Model of Christian Charity* and John Cotton's *God's Promise to His Plantation* as three founding documents of New England that "represent an effort to balance the desire of Winthrop and his supporters to bring forth further fruits of reformation in New England while denying any separation from the Church of England which might either be suspected by those who remained at home or desired by some of those emigrating." He then notes the linked imagery of the Church of England as a nursing mother. Francis Bremer Jr., *John Winthrop: America's Forgotten Founding Father* (Oxford: Oxford UP, 2003), 175.

7. John Cotton, *Gods Promise to His Plantations* (London, 1634), 18.

8. "Humble Request," 188.

9. Ibid., 188–189. This emphasis on affection in *The Humble Request* fits a broader early modern epistolary culture. Gary Schneider explains that "emotion-laden rhetoric ... regularly mediated political negotiation in early modern England, but was most often associated with the familiar letter." Political communications, in particular, were often mediated by "rhetorical expressions of familiarity, affection, friendship, and love." Gary Schneider, *The Culture of Epistolarity: Vernacular Letters and Letter Writing in Early Modern England, 1500–1700* (Newark: University of Delaware Press, 2005), 101–102.

10. Catharine Maria Sedgwick, *Hope Leslie: Or, Early Times in the Massachusetts*, ed. Mary Kelley (New Brunswick, NJ: Rutgers University Press, 1991), 12.

11. William Bradford, *Of Plymouth Plantation*, ed. Samuel Eliot Morison (New York: Knopf, 2006), 14. Sedgwick, *Hope Leslie*, 13.

12. I borrow the language of "masking" from Burnham, who argues that tears often serve both to mark and to mask transgressive agencies. Michelle Burnham, *Captivity and Sentiment: Cultural Exchange in American Literature, 1682–1861* (Lebanon, NH: University Press of New England, 1997). Here, tears mark the Puritan departure from England even as they cover it up: the separation causes tears, yet the shedding of tears enables the Puritans to deny that they are separating.

13. *Winthrop Papers*, IV.84.

14. Love summarizes the situation: "As Englishmen they bemoaned the divisions in their native land, and as Christians they fasted and prayed for the triumph of God's kingdom in the midst of the turmoil." William DeLoss Love, *The Fast and Thanksgiving Days of New England* (Boston: Houghton Mifflin, 1895), 151. For the mixed feelings of New England Puritans concerning possible war, see Francis Bremer, *Puritan Crisis: New England and the English Civil Wars, 1630–1670* (New York: Garland, 1989), 97–101. For an excellent account of colonial neutrality before and during the wars, see Carla Gardina Pestana, *The English Atlantic in an Age of Revolution, 1640–1661* (Cambridge, MA: Harvard University Press, 2004), chapter 1. As Pestana emphasizes, such a stance emanated primarily from self-preservation, not a lack of concern for England.

15. *Winthrop Papers*, IV.205.

16. Quoted in Harry S. Stout, "The Morphology of Remigration: New England University Men and Their Return to England, 1640–1660," *Journal of American Studies* 10, no. 2 (1976): 156. Stout's article provides a good assessment of this reverse migration, particularly the movement of university-educated men. For the definitive book on remigration, see Susan Hardman Moore, *Pilgrims: New World Settlers and the Call of Home* (New Haven, CT: Yale University Press, 2007). The phrase "stood in the gap," meanwhile, comes from Psalm 106:23, and Puritan ministers frequently used it in reference to leaders of the godly cause. For more on this phrase and others associated it with, see Lonna Malmsheimer, "Daughters of Zion: New England Roots of American Feminism," *New England Quarterly* 50, no. 3 (1977): 493–494.

17. In what follows I focus on two Fast Day sermons delivered by Hooke, in part because of all the Fast Day sermons preached in New England during the English Civil Wars only these two found their way into print in the 1640s. One probable reason for their publication lies in Hooke's connections: Hooke's wife Jane was the cousin of Oliver Cromwell, and both sermons were dedicated to "a worthy Member of the honourable House of Commons"—most likely Cromwell. See Bremer, *Puritan Crisis*, 259; Love, *Fast and Thanksgiving Days*, 155. Yet the content also seemed directed to a transatlantic audience, perhaps because Hooke knew (or hoped) they would be published.

18. William Hooke, *New Englands Teares, for Old Englands Feares* (London, 1640), 2, 4, 5 (emphasis in original here and throughout, unless otherwise stated).

19. Delbanco describes *New Englands Teares* as "a call to some kind of transoceanic solidarity," but he does not analyze *what* kind of solidarity—or how Hooke attempts to achieve it. Andrew Delbanco, *The Puritan Ordeal* (Cambridge, MA: Harvard University Press, 1989), 196. On these matters Hooke is not vague: he calls for sympathy and he attempts to stir it up. Likewise, although Bremer gives attention to a language of sympathy in other parts of *Congregational Communion*, he strangely never mentions it in regards to this sermon, instead calling it "one of the earliest interpretations that the nation's woes were a judgment that called for repentance and religious reform." Francis Bremer Jr., *Congregational Communion: Clerical Friendship in the Anglo-American Puritan Community, 1610–1692* (Boston: Northeastern University Press, 1994), 126–127.

20. Hooke, *New Englands Teares*, 7, 9.

21. For a good description of this situation, see Pestana, *English Atlantic*, chapter 2.

22. Hooke, *New Englands Teares*, 10. William Fenner, *A Treatise of the Affections, or, the Souls Pulse* (London, 1650), 96–102. Fenner's works were published after Hooke's, but they were written earlier (Fenner died in 1640), and they summarize common Puritan rhetorical principles of the day. For the summation of Renaissance rhetorical principles as expressivity and vividness, see Deborah Shuger, *Sacred Rhetoric: The Christian Grand Style in the English Renaissance* (Princeton, NJ: Princeton University Press, 1988), 11.

23. William Perkins, *The Art of Prophesying* (Edinburgh: The Banner of Truth Trust, 1996), 75. Richard Bernard, *Faithfull Shepeard*, revised ed. (London, 1621), 32, 34, 257–258. For the same reason, Perkins advised against memorizing sermons word for word. Such a practice, he explained, "hinders freedom of pronunciation, action and the spirit-given flow of spiritual affections, because our minds are almost obsessed with whether our memory ... is going to fail us." Better to remember a series of points and move through them "without being overly anxious about the precise words we will use." Perkins, *Art of Prophesying*, 70.

24. Bernard, *Faithfull Shepeard*, 37. Perkins, *Art of Prophesying*, 75. For more on the necessity of spiritual affections for rhetorical delivery, see Francis Bremer Jr., *Shaping New Englands: Puritan Clergymen in Seventeenth-Century England and New England* (New York: Twayne, 1994); David D. Hall, *The Faithful Shepherd: A History of the New England Ministry in the Seventeenth Century* (Chapel Hill: University of North Carolina Press, 1972), 52–55. Bremer writes, "Though as time went on it became more common for Reformers to criticize the new theaters and the professional players and playwrights, it is also true that many Puritan preachers of the seventeenth century were known for the drama of their pulpit performances." Bremer, *Shaping New Englands*, 31. Haller puts it more succinctly, "The Puritans in condemning the theatre did not lose the knack of showmanship." William Haller, *The Rise of Puritanism* (Philadelphia: University of Pennsylvania Press, 1938), 250. Gustafson observes a similar principle at work much later in Jonathan Edwards. Citing what Edwards's contemporary biographer wrote about his preaching—that Edwards "made but little Motion of his Head or Hands in the Desk, but spake so as to discover the Motion of his own Heart"—she claims that such a statement reveals "the logic behind Edwards's rejection of Stoddard's more physical style ...: motions of the head or hands detract from, rather than reveal, motions of the heart." Sandra Gustafson, *Eloquence is Power: Oratory and Performance in Early America* (Chapel Hill: University of North Carolina Press, 2000), 65. Such a debate about bodily restraint and emotional delivery dates back to the earliest Puritan manuals on preaching. As Bremer and Rydell note, "Scholars ... have commonly failed to recognize the dramatic nature of the Puritan sermon." See Francis Bremer and Ellen Rydell, "Performance Art? Puritans in the Pulpit," *History Today* 45, no. 9 (1995): 50–54.

25. Hooke, *New Englands Teares*, 11. Hooke's portrayal of war is powerful enough to receive praise from Moses Coit Tyler, a critic who did not laud lightly. See Moses Coit Tyler, *A History of American Literature, 1607–1765*, reprint ed., vol. 1 (New York: Putnam's, 1949), 190.

26. Hooke, *New Englands Teares*, 12.

27. Ibid. Edmund Calamy, *Gods free mercy to England* (London, 1642), 22–23.

28. Hooke, *New Englands Teares*, 16–17, 22, 17. Glenn Hendler, *Public Sentiments: Structures of Feeling in Nineteenth-Century American Literature* (Chapel Hill: University of North Carolina Press, 2001), 5.

29. Hooke, *New Englands Teares*, 9. Harry S. Stout, *The New England Soul: Preaching and Religious Culture in Colonial New England* (Oxford: Oxford University Press, 1986), 51. D'Addario briefly notes a use of sympathy in Puritan transatlantic relations of this time, observing both disparity and similarity. See Christopher D'Addario, *Exile and Journey in Seventeenth-Century Literature* (New York: Cambridge University Press, 2007), 29. Benedict claims that the dual presence of connection and separation is a paradox inherent to sentimental literature. See Barbara Benedict, *Framing Feeling: Sentiment and Style in English Prose Fiction, 1745–1800* (New York: AMS Press, 1994), 11. In a similar vein, Burnham argues that communities based in a principle of sympathy—of like will to like and the easy substitution of self for other—actually mask difference and inequivalence. She writes, "What is sentimental about the imagined communities novels create is the obscured fact that they are not based on likeness," adding: "The tears generated by sympathy function as a veil that masks the incommensurability between these two levels of identification, obscuring difference within the fantasy of sameness and commonality." Burnham, *Captivity and Sentiment*, 47–48. Long before novels (and Puritan captivity narratives, where Burnham begins), Hooke illustrated some of these same ideas in his sermonic call for sympathy.
30. Hooke, *New Englands Teares*, 19, 22.
31. Ibid., 23.
32. Ibid., A2r–A2v.
33. William Hooke, *New-Englands Sence, of Old-England and Irelands Sorrowes* (London, 1645), 4, 19. Bremer shows that the New Haven minister John Davenport, like Hooke and others, preached prayer as a weapon that could be used in place of material aid. Bremer, *Congregational Communion*, 68–69.
34. Hooke, *New-Englands Sence*, 20–1.
35. Ibid., 28–29, 31. For more on this tradition of early modern sympathy and its use of the compass/magnet as a principle example, see chapter 1.
36. Anne Bradstreet, "A Dialogue between Old England and New; Concerning Their Present Troubles, Anno, 1642," in *The Works of Anne Bradstreet*, ed. Jeannine Hensley (Cambridge, MA: Belknap, 1967), pp. 179–188, ll. 5–12.
37. While the first stanza of Bradstreet's "Dialogue" establishes the foundational importance of feeling, few critics have asked how it works. Instead, "A Dialogue" has often been lumped together with Bradstreet's "public" poetry—the political, theological, and *non*emotional verse of Bradstreet's *The Tenth Muse*. Piercy, for example, reads "A Dialogue" as the statement of "a patriotic English woman." Josephine Piercy, *Anne Bradstreet* (New York: Twayne, 1965), 53. Gillespie disagrees, but maintains an exclusive focus on imperial politics. According to her, "Bradstreet take the potential for competition among women … and applies it to the struggle between empire and colony." Katharine Gillespie, "'This Briny Ocean Will O'erflow Your Shore': Anne Bradstreet's 'Second World' Atlanticism

and National Narratives of Literary History," *Symbiosis* 3, no. 2 (1999): 111. Beyond politics, Jeffrey Hammond reads the poem for what Bradstreet would have considered "lessons of sacred history." Jeffrey Hammond, *Sinful Self, Saintly Self: The Puritan Experience of Poetry* (Athens: University of Georgia Press, 1993), 101. These readings are not necessarily wrong. Yet such investigations have stopped short of asking how Bradstreet's language of affection might inflect such issues. For the most part, scholars have studied emotion only in Bradstreet's "private" verse, the domestic lyrics she wrote later. This divide between Bradstreet's public and private poetry first emerged in Kenneth Requa, "Anne Bradstreet's Poetic Voices," *Early American Literature* 9, no. 1 (1974): 3–18. Salska later expanded the binary and applied it to all of Puritan poetics. See Agnieszka Salska, "Puritan Poetry: Its Public and Private Strain," *Early American Literature* 19, no. 2 (1984). In more recent years, critics have tried to break down this dichotomy; for examples, see Sara Eaton, "Anne Bradstreet's 'Personal' Protestant Poetics," *Women's Writing* 4, no. 1 (1997): 60; Paula Kopacz, " 'To Finish What's Begun': Anne Bradstreet's Last Words," *Early American Literature* 23, no. 2 (1988): 177; Kimberly Latta, " 'Such is My Bond': Maternity and Economy in Anne Bradstreet's Writing," in *Inventing Maternity: Politics, Science, and Literature, 1650–1865,* ed. Susan Greenfield and Carol Barash (Lexington: University Press of Kentucky, 1999), n. 16, p. 80; Rosamond Rosenmeier, *Anne Bradstreet Revisited* (Boston: Twayne, 1993), 114. For one of the best accounts of gender in Bradstreet's *The Tenth Muse*, focusing on the representation of it as "public" poetry, see Ivy Schweitzer, *The Work of Self-Representation: Lyric Poetry in Colonial New England* (Chapel Hill: University of North Carolina Press, 1991), chapter 4.

38. *Winthrop Papers*, IV.314. As Hiliker observes, this poem "constitutes a radical break in the traditional representation of the relationship between colony and metropole. The poem portrays 'Old England' as wounded and weak, and 'New England' as her help-meet offering advice on how to improve her state." Robert Hilliker, "Engendering Identity: The Discourse of Familial Education in Anne Bradstreet and Marie de l'Incarnation," *Early American Literature* 42, no. 3 (2007): 450.

39. Bradstreet, "Dialogue," l. 10.

40. I borrow the phrase "affective body" from Matthew Brown, who uses it to describe the feminine position men adopted in devotions in order to become "a helpless vessel for divine action." See Matthew Brown, *The Pilgrim and the Bee: Reading Rituals and Book Culture in Early New England* (Philadelphia: University of Pennsylvania Press, 2007), 17.

41. Ibid., ll. 29–30, 33, 59, 157–158, 160–163.

42. Ibid., ll. 194, 201–212. Pender observes the "physicality of the metaphor" in Old England's final speech, but she reads it as a "rhetorical technique of dissection, anatomy and display to enact a disciplinary punishment of the mother country." Patricia Pender, "Disciplining the Imperial Mother: Anne Bradstreet's *A Dialogue*

Between Old England and New," in *Women Writing, 1550–1750,* ed. Jo Wallwork and Paul Salzman (Victoria: Meridian, 2001), 121. It does not seem, however, that this final speech concerns "disciplinary punishment." As noted earlier, where punishment is required, New England has admitted her share of guilt (l. 159). Pender is right, however, that Bradstreet uses rhetorical techniques of dissection, anatomy and display. These devices enable not punishment, but pity. Martin also notes this emphasis on the effects of war, but reads it as a critique of patriarchy. Wendy Martin, *An American Triptych: Anne Bradstreet, Emily Dickinson, Adrienne Rich* (Chapel Hill: University of North Carolina Press, 1984), 38. In an excellent book, Porterfield writes more broadly about the Puritan use of female suffering as an image of redemption; Bradstreet, for example, "attained recognition through an expertise in female piety that did not relieve suffering so much as give it redemptive meaning." Amanda Porterfield, *Female Piety in Puritan New England: The Emergence of Religious Humanism* (New York: Oxford University Press, 1992), 7.

43. Bradstreet, "Dialogue," ll. 218, 214–215, 219, 299.

44. Rosenmeier adopts this view, arguing, "The daughter's ability to 'simpathize' with her mother's condition and her ability to stay mindful of her mother's state seem to be important. In the end, however, even though she once shared her mother's body and as much as she now pities her woes, she pulls away from empathy and makes clear that what both of them have long prayed for is now happening, however painful that happening may be." Rosenmeier, *Anne Bradstreet Revisited,* 50.

45. Bradstreet, "Dialogue," ll. 216–217.

46. Ibid., ll. 14–17 (emphasis added), 18–19.

47. Ibid., l. 96.

48. As Stevens explains, sympathy implies likeness and tends to circulate within the Christian community, while pity implies "the mercy born of religious devotion" and can extend "to a broad spectrum of relations among humans or between humans and God." Yet the difference also amounts to power: pity "tends to describe relationships marked by an imbalance of power between those feeling and those provoking this emotion"; moreover, Stevens adds, most in the seventeenth century understood pity "as an emotion that emerged from an acknowledgement of obligation." Laura Stevens, *The Poor Indians: British Missionaries, Native Americans, and Colonial Sensibilities* (Philadelphia: University of Pennsylvania Press, 2004), 8–9. Just such dynamics surface in Old England's final speech, including the notion of obligation entailed by her plea that New England "recompense that good I've done to thee." On Bradstreet's role as a dutiful daughter (in this poem and others), see Carrie Galloway Blackstock, "Anne Bradstreet and Performativity: Self-Cultivation, Self-Deployment," *Early American Literature* 32, no. 3 (1997): 222; Pender, "Disciplining the Imperial Mother," 116; Cheryl Walker, "Anne Bradstreet," in *American Writers: A Collection of Literary Biographies,* ed. Leonard Unger (New York: Scribner, 1976), 110.

49. John Winthrop, *Winthrop's Journal, 1630–1649*, ed. James Kendall Hosmer (New York: Scribners, 1908), II.221, II.139, II.294, II.334. Pulsipher describes this "contest of authority" lucidly. See Jenny Hale Pulsipher, *Subjects unto the Same King: Indians, English, and the Contest for Authority in Colonial New England* (Philadelphia: University of Pennsylvania Press, 2005), especially chapters 1 and 2. Some scholars, such as Edmund Morgan, delineate a grow-ing lack of interest in English events during this time. See Edmund Morgan, *The Puritan Dilemma: The Story of John Winthrop* (Boston: Little, Brown and Company, 1958). Bremer opposes such a view, claiming that New England Puritans remained intensely involved in England's affairs. See *Congregational Communion and Puritan Crisis: New England and the English Civil Wars, 1630–1670* (New York: Garland, 1989). Foster, meanwhile, provides something of a middle ground: he traces the development in the 1630s of a "de facto Separatism" and argues that in the 1640s "it became necessary to build paper bridges to the Presbyterians while denying any direct debt to the Separatists." Stephen Foster, *The Long Argument: English Puritanism and the Shaping of New England Culture, 1570–1700* (Chapel Hill: University of North Carolina Press, 1991), 158, 169.

50. These numbers come from Love, *Fast and Thanksgiving Days*, 466–469.

51. Norton, *Answer*, 3.

52. Edward Johnson, *Johnson's Wonder-Working Providence, 1628–1651*, ed. J. Franklin Jameson (New York: Scribners, 1910), 252–253.

53. Ibid., 23. Scholars have long recognized that Johnson's history conveys more feeling than fact. Many early critics, frustrated with Johnson for historical inac-curacies, nonetheless praised him for preserving "the spirit and aroma of New England thought and experience in the seventeenth century." Tyler, *History*, 122. Jameson claimed that *Wonder-Working Providence* "gives us, what neither Bradford nor Winthrop could supply, the history, or at any rate the essential spirit of the Massachusetts colony depicted from the point of view of the rank and file." J. Franklin Jameson, "Introduction," in *Johnson's Wonder-Working Providence, 1628–1651* (New York: Scribners, 1910), 14–15. For later commenta-tors, that "spirit" became the whole point. As Gallagher explains, "Johnson was not just trying to inform, but overtly to affect his reader." Edward Gallagher, "An Overview of Edward Johnson's *Wonder-Working Providence*," *Early American Literature* 5, no. 3 (1971): 37, 47. Gallagher repeatedly uses the word "feeling" to discuss the text; see "The Case for the *Wonder-Working Providence*," *Bulletin of the New York Public Library* 77, no. 1 (1973): 26–27; "Overview," 32; "The *Wonder-Working Providence* as Spiritual Biography," *Early American Literature* 10, no. 1 (1975): 86. In the same vein, Kilman writes, "Johnson's work shows the feelings of specialness that the common citizen held—the feeling that his nation was unique in God's eyes." John Kilman, "A Joiner Looks at Colonial New England: Edward Johnson's Special Providences," *Southern Folklore Quarterly* 45 (1981): 144. The force of *Wonder-Working Providence*—its success or failure as

a defense of New England—lay in its ability to depict, express, and transmit a "feeling" of New England's destiny, an impression of its special significance.

54. Mary Louise Kete, "Sentimental Literature," in *The Oxford Encyclopedia of American Literature*, ed. Jay Parini (Oxford: Oxford University Press, 2004), 546. Some scholars miss this appeal for unity. Rosenmeier, for example, claims that "it is Johnson, the Non-Separatist, who finds his voice and, for better or for worse, makes one of our earliest proclamations of cultural independence." Jesper Rosenmeier, "To Keep in Memory: The Poetry of Edward Johnson," in *Puritan Poets and Poetics: Seventeenth-Century American Poetry in Theory and Practice*, ed. Peter White and Harrison Meserole (University Park: Pennsylvania State University Press, 1985), 159. Likewise, Brumm reads the Puritan departure scene in Johnson as a clean break: it marks "their death as Englishmen, which is the beginning of a new birth as Americans." Ursula Brumm, "Edward Johnson's Wonder-Working Providence and the Puritan Conception of History," *Jahrbuch für Amerikastudien* 14 (1969): 149. Such readings leave little room for Johnson's disavowal of desertion. It is the flipside—the assertion of union—which Johnson bases in the heart.

55. Johnson, *Wonder-Working Providence*, 50–51.

56. Ibid., 51–53. Schweitzer suggests that the two friends were Winthrop and Cotton. She describes the force of this scene as sentimental, arguing that "a male friendship embodies the feminine soul's longing for her spiritual counterpart." Ivy Schweitzer, *Perfecting Friendship: Politics and Affiliation in Early American Literature* (Chapel Hill: University of North Carolina Press, 2006), 97. In that sense, while the figures here are male, the weeping remains feminine. It is also highly sentimentalized. Compare this departure scene, for example, to Jane Tompkins's analysis of sentimentalism in *Uncle Tom's Cabin*: "not words, but the emotions of the heart bespeak a state of grace, and these are known by the sound of a voice, the touch of a hand, but chiefly, in moments of greatest importance, by tears." Tompkins, *Sensational Designs: The Cultural Work of American Fiction, 1790–1860* (New York: Oxford University Press, 1985), 131.

57. Johnson, *Wonder-Working Providence*, 53–54. Marianne Noble, *The Masochistic Pleasures of Sentimental Literature* (Princeton: Princeton University Press, 2000), 129. This idea of negotiating a transatlantic relationship through the language of affection often goes unnoticed. Instead, scholars seem to comment on a theological and political relationship uninflected by feeling. Bercovitch, for example, claims that Johnson made New England "the vanguard of universal history." As a result, "the relationship of the American to the English movement [is] that of harbinger or leader to successors or followers." Sacvan Bercovitch, "The Historiography of Johnson's *Wonder-Working Providence*," *Essex Institute Historical Collections* 104 (1968): 155–156. In the same way, Perry connects the two through a "common cause" described solely in theological and political terms. Dennis Perry, "Autobiographical Role-Playing in Edward

Johnson's *Wonder-Working Providence,*" *Early American Literature* 22, no. 3 (1987): 294. Such readings miss the emotional core of Johnson's history—the argument that affection keeps England and New England one.

58. Johnson, *Wonder-Working Providence,* 137. Bremer notes that John Cotton could also adopt more of a peacemaking role after the Congregationalists gained power: "As the threat of a Presbyterian establishment ... began to fade in the late 1640s, Cotton became more energetic in his irenic efforts." Bremer, "In Defense of Regicide: John Cotton on the Execution of Charles I." *William and Mary Quarterly* 37, no. 1 (1980): 109.

59. Johnson, *Wonder-Working Providence,* 256. Note the resemblance between Johnson's injunction and Tompkins's description of sentimental novels: "For all sentimental novels take place, metaphorically and literally, in the 'closet.' Sentimental heroines rarely get beyond the confines of a private space ... but more important, most of what they do takes place inside the 'closet' of the heart. For what the word *sentimental* really means in this context is that the arena of human action ... has been defined not as the world, but as the human soul." Tompkins, *Sensational Designs,* 151.

60. Johnson, *Wonder-Working Providence,* 51, 151. Van Sant notes this same aspect in sentimental novels: "If readers read for sensation ... the evidence of a writer's talent lies in the reader's body. With the signs of a writer's ability located in the physiology of the reader, accomplishment has to do only secondarily with treatment of formal features or adherence to publicly stated standards." Ann Van Sant, *Eighteenth-Century Sensibility and the Novel: The Senses in Social Context* (Cambridge: Cambridge University Press, 1993), 117.

61. Johnson, *Wonder-Working Providence,* 59, 63. Bercovitch reads Johnson's depiction of the Puritan voyage typologically—a reenactment of "the Israelites' sea passage." Bercovitch, "Historiography," 147. While typology certainly affected Puritan literature, it does not seem to apply as well here. In Exodus, the Israelites faced danger on land (in Pharaoh's army), and the sea opened as an escape. In *Wonder-Working Providence,* the sea proves its own danger. The Lord sustains the emigrants through "Leakes, Stormes, Rockes, Sands, and all other wants a long Sea-voyage procures." Johnson, *Wonder-Working Providence,* 56–57. Such hazards, it seems, represent not a typological point but an emotional strategy.

62. Johnson, *Wonder-Working Providence,* 136. At one point, Johnson even apologizes for relying on particularity: "it was not intended to speake in particulars of any of these peoples departure from thence," he writes. But he seems unable to stop himself, turning next to "the wonderous worke of Christ in preserving two of his most valiant Souldiers, namely Mr. John Norton, and that soule ravishing Minister Mr. Thomas Shepheard." Johnson, *Wonder-Working Providence,* 93–94. For more on particularity and its relation to "sympathetic visibility," see Van Sant, *Eighteenth-Century Sensibility,* 28–31. On the issue of particularity

(and verbal images) in the Renaissance (tracing its classical roots), see Wendy Olmsted, *The Imperfect Friend: Emotion and Rhetoric in Sidney, Milton, and Their Contexts* (Toronto: University of Toronto Press, 2008), chapter 3.

63. Johnson, *Wonder-Working Providence*, 134, 51.

64. The examples of titles are from four texts published in the 1640s: John Norton's *Answer to … Mr. Apollonius*, Thomas Shepard and John Allin's *Defense of the Answer made unto the Nine Questions*, Thomas Hooker's *Survey of the Summe of Church Discipline*, and John Cotton's *Way of the Congregational Churches Cleared*. But as shown previously, Norton's *Answer* begins with a prefatory letter that picks up the scholarly debate because a love of brethren had been established and detected. For more on this love of brethren and its relation to persuasion, see chapter 3.

CHAPTER 5

1. Michael Clark, ed., *The Eliot Tracts: With Letters from John Eliot to Thomas Thorowgood and Richard Baxter* (Westport, CT: Praeger, 2003), 128. The Eliot tracts comprised eleven different publications over three decades that Clark has collected and edited. In this chapter I read them together to highlight a focus on feeling and affection that unites them; I thus cite his edition rather than each particular tract.

2. Perry Miller, *Errand into the Wilderness* (Cambridge, MA: Belknap, 1956), 59. John Preston, *The New Covenant, or the Saints Portion* (London, 1629), 1.

3. As Howard writes of sentimentality, "What is at stake is authenticity: the spontaneity, the sincerity, and the legitimacy of an emotion are understood to be the same." June Howard, "What is Sentimentality?" *American Literary History* 11, no. 1 (1999): 65. In Barker-Benfield's encyclopedic account, he writes, "The culture of sensibility clung to the simpler notions of utter sincerity and the immediate legibility of gesture and expression. Sentimental novels repeatedly sounded the value of 'openness of heart,' 'frankness,' 'candour,' and 'unequivocal sincerity.'" G.J. Barker-Benfield, *The Culture of Sensibility: Sex and Society in Eighteenth-Century Britain* (Chicago: University of Chicago Press, 1992), 221–222. Gesture and expression were seen as better witnesses of sincerity than words (especially in women). See also Janet Todd, *Sensibility: An Introduction* (New York: Methuen, 1986), 86. By the later eighteenth century, that approach had begun to turn on itself in Britain; in America, however, a culture of sentimentalism and its paradoxes of sincerity lasted much longer. For a good introduction to the links between sympathy and discipline—the way, for example, black sufferers in antebellum America had to imagine themselves through white eyes—see Christopher Castiglia, "Abolition's Racial Interiors and the Making of White Civic Depth," *American Literary History* 14, no. 1 (2002): 32–59. I trace a similar dynamic in this chapter. My work here is most indebted here to Laura

Stevens. In her excellent book, Stevens claims that British missionary writings "anticipated many of the ideas and gestures that would constitute the culture of sensibility." I build on her scholarship by showing how Praying Indians went beyond what she calls "spectatorial objectification" while also revealing the crucial link between sympathy and sincerity. Laura Stevens, *The Poor Indians: British Missionaries, Native Americans, and Colonial Sensibilities* (Philadelphia: University of Pennsylvania Press, 2004), 6–7, 13.

4. See Jean O'Brien, *Firsting and Lasting: Writing Indians out of Existence in New England* (Minneapolis: University of Minnesota Press, 2010), 3–4. The literature on the Native cultures of New England is vast, but see also Kathleen Bragdon, *Native People of Southern New England, 1500–1650* (Norman: University of Oklahoma Press, 1996); Kathleen Bragdon, *The Columbia Guide to American Indians of the Northeast* (New York: Columbia University Press, 2001); Lisa Brooks, *The Common Pot: The Recovery of Native Space in the Northeast* (Minneapolis: University of Minnesota Press, 2008); and Matt Cohen, *The Networked Wilderness: Communicating in Early New England* (Minneapolis: University of Minnesota Press, 2010). Other sources are cited throughout this chapter. For the complexities undergirding a long tradition of ascribing oratorical power to Native Americans, see William Clements, *Oratory in Native North America* (Tucson: University of Arizona Press, 2002).

5. Edmund Morgan, ed., *The Founding of Massachusetts: Historians and the Sources* (Indianapolis: Bobbs-Merrill, 1964), 175. Alexander Young, ed., *Chronicles of the First Planters of the Colony of Massachusetts Bay, 1623–1636* (Boston: 1846), 133. Morgan, ed., *Founding of Massachusetts*, 320.

6. This seal is a reference to Acts 16:9, where a Macedonian appears in a vision to Paul and convinces him to take his message to Macedonia with these same words.

7. Young, ed., *Chronicles*, 133–134. I borrow the term "affective model" from Richard Cogley, *John Eliot's Mission to the Indians before King Philip's War* (Cambridge, MA: Harvard University Press, 1999), 18. Most scholars affirm that the Puritans never intended to send out missionaries, relying on "conversion by example, not conversion by evangelism." Charles Segal and David Stineback, *Puritans, Indians, and Manifest Destiny* (New York: Putnam, 1977), 34. As Axtell puts it, "The initial goal was … one of passive seduction, not active reduction." James Axtell, *The Invasion Within: The Contest of Cultures in Colonial North America* (New York: Oxford University Press, 1986), 219. The fact that the Puritans finally *did* begin active missions thus calls for more explanation than their delay. The one place where active missionary work occurred early was at Martha's Vineyard: there, Thomas Mayhew took it upon himself to teach Christianity to Wampanoag Indians. Apart from his endeavor, the Puritans kept their preachers to themselves. For more on Martha's Vineyard, the missionary activities there, and Native American responses, see David J. Silverman, *Faith and*

Boundaries: Colonists, Christianity, and Community among the Wampanoag Indians of Martha's Vineyard, 1600–1871 (New York: Cambridge University Press, 2005).

8. These groups were also "the most isolated from other Indian polities and their trade networks." Neal Salisbury, "'I Loved the Place of My Dwelling': Puritan Missionaries and Native Americans in Seventeenth-Century Southern New England," in *Inequality in Early America*, ed. Carla Gardina Pestana and Sharon V. Salinger (Lebanon, NH: University Press of New England, 1999), 116. See also William Simmons, "Conversion from Indian to Puritan," *New England Quarterly* 52, no. 2 (1979): 116.

9. Scholars differ on how idealistic or political the Puritans were in their efforts to convert the Indians. Early on, Vaughan and Jennings established two inter-pretive poles—Vaughan offering a generous reading of Puritan missions and Jennings summing them up as the "cant of conquest." See Francis Jennings, *The Invasion of America: Indians, Colonists, and the Cant of Conquest* (Chapel Hill: University of North Carolina Press, 1975); Alden Vaughan, *New England Frontier: Puritans and Indians, 1620–1675*, revised ed. (New York: Norton, 1979). As for the start of missionary efforts, many scholars relate it to transatlantic politics (the need for a bolstered image) and a realignment of authority: see especially Ralph Bauer, "John Eliot, The Praying Indian, and the Rhetoric of a New England Errand," *Zeitschrift für Anglistik und Amerikanistik* 44, no. 4 (1996): 331–345, and Kristina Bross, *Dry Bones and Indian Sermons: Praying Indians and Colonial American Identity* (Ithaca, NY: Cornell University Press, 2004), chapter 1; but see also Axtell, *Invasion Within*, 138–139; Jennings, *Invasion of America*, 237–242; Neal Salisbury, "Red Puritans: The 'Praying Indians' of Massachusetts Bay and John Eliot," *William and Mary Quarterly* 31, no. 1 (1974): 30–31. For a good account of the power dynamics between Puritans and Native Americans at this time, see Jenny Hale Pulsipher, *Subjects unto the Same King: Indians, English, and the Contest for Authority in Colonial New England* (Philadelphia: University of Pennsylvania Press, 2005).

10. Cogley, *John Eliot's Mission*, 56.

11. For more on the various motivations to convert, see James Axtell, "Were Indian Conversions Bona Fide?," in *After Columbus: Essays in the Ethnohistory of Colonial North America* (New York: Oxford University Press, 1988); Elise Brenner, "To Pray or To Be Prey: That Is the Question: Strategies for Cultural Autonomy of Massachusetts Praying Town Indians," *Ethnohistory* 27, no. 2 (1980): 135–152; Cogley, *John Eliot's Mission*, 56–58, 75; Robert Grumet, *Historic Contact: Indian People and Colonists in Today's Northeastern United States in the Sixteenth through Eighteenth Centuries* (Norman: University of Oklahoma Press, 1995), 57–58; Keely McCarthy, "Conversion, Identity, and the Indian Missionary," *Early American Literature* 36, no. 3 (2001): 353–369; Salisbury, "Red Puritans," 35–40; Simmons, "Conversion from Indian to Puritan"; Alan Taylor, *American Colonies* (New York: Viking, 2001), 198–199; Craig White, "The Praying Indians'

Speeches as Texts of Massachusett Oral Culture," *Early American Literature* 38, no. 3 (2003): 437–467; Hilary Wyss, *Writing Indians: Literacy, Christianity, and Native Community in Early America* (Amherst: University of Massachusetts Press, 2000).

12. Clark, *Eliot Tracts*, 318.

13. As White asserts, "The Massachusett converted so that their words and ways might survive." White, "Praying Indians' Speeches," 461. That survival entailed a selective transformation, a mix of Christianity and Native culture. On this point, see Brenner, "Pray or Be Prey"; Cogley, *John Eliot's Mission*, 58; David Murray, "Spreading the Word: Missionaries, Conversion and Circulation in the Northeast," in *Spiritual Encounters: Interactions Between Christianity and Native Religions in Colonial America*, ed. Nicholas Griffiths and Fernando Cervantes (Birmingham: University of Birmingham Press, 1999), 43–64; Daniel Richter, *Facing East from Indian Country: A Native History of Early America* (Cambridge, MA: Harvard University Press, 2001), 111–129; Salisbury, "Place of My Dwelling."; Wyss, *Writing Indians*.

14. See Cogley, *John Eliot's Mission*, 50. For Cutshamekin's first response to Eliot, see Michael Clark, "Introduction," in *The Eliot Tracts: With Letters from John Eliot to Thomas Thorowgood and Richard Baxter* (Westport, CT: Praeger, 2003), 10; Clark, *Eliot Tracts*, 84.

15. See Axtell, *Invasion Within*, 273. This number includes the Praying Indians on Martha's Vineyard.

16. Bauer offers a good account of the role of missions in New England (and the concomitant views of Eliot); see Bauer, "John Eliot."

17. For a history of The New England Company, see William Kellaway, *The New England Company, 1649–1776: Missionary Society to the American Indians* (London: Longmans, 1961).

18. For more on the Puritan understanding of "affections," see the introduction.

19. Baxter, *Call*, 39. This view was common to Puritan theology. The influential Richard Sibbes, for example, distinguished "counterfeit from true faith by the religious affections. ... For assurance of salvation it is not enough to know; one must also feel a desire to be saved with all one's heart in the affections." Sidney Rooy, *The Theology of Missions in the Puritan Tradition* (Delft: W. D. Meinema N. V., 1965), 20.

20. Clark, *Eliot Tracts*, 117, 122. Bross turns these questions into a distinct genre. Calling them "performances of faith that make grace visible," she reads them for "traces of Indian resistance" and situates them in the context of the Antinomian Controversy. See Bross, *Dry Bones*, 94–111 (quotes, pp. 98, 94). For another good reading of Indian questions, see Linda Gregerson, "The Commonwealth of the Word: New England, Old England, and the Praying Indians," in *Empires of God: Religious Encounters in the Early Modern Atlantic*, ed. Linda Gregerson and Susan Juster (Philadelphia: University of Pennsylvania Press, 2011), 70–83.

21. Clark, *Eliot Tracts*, 200. The Puritan investment in knowledge as a necessary precondition of grace entailed the promotion of practices and institutions that would increase it. Believing literacy essential for spiritual improvement, Eliot established Indians schools and worked with others to translate the Bible, catechisms, and other religious material. In the "great Indian work which lyeth upon me," he wrote, "my continual care, prayer, desire and endeavour" is "for their schooling and education of youth in learning, which is a principal means for promoting of [the mission work] for future times." Clark, *Eliot Tracts*, 187. Several scholars have commented on the centrality of education to Puritan conversion. See, for example, Axtell, *Invasion Within*, 179, 223–224; Kellaway, *New England Company*, 109–113; Sidney Rooy, *Theology of Missions*, 238–239; Normal Earl Tanis, "Education in John Eliot's Indian Utopias, 1646–1675," *The History of Education Quarterly* 10 (1970): 308–323; Vaughan, *New England Frontier*, 280–285.

22. Clark, *Eliot Tracts*, 109, 93, 116, 254. This form of evidence has received the most attention among scholars because of its impact on Native culture. As Richard Pointer aptly puts it, "In seventeenth-century New England, Puritans endeavored to re-create Indians in their own image." Richard Pointer, "From Imitating Language to a Language of Imitation: Puritan-Indian Discourse in Early New England," in *Puritanism and Its Discontents*, ed. Laura Lunger Knoppers (Newark: University of Delaware Press, 2003), 145. Scholars have viewed the extent of cultural destruction—and the Indian response—in multiple ways. For varying interpretations, see: Axtell, *Invasion Within*; Brenner, "Pray or Be Prey"; Cogley, *John Eliot's Mission*; Jennings, *Invasion of America*; Roy Harvey Pearce, "The 'Ruines of Mankind': The Indian and the Puritan Mind," *Journal of the History of Ideas* 13, no. 2 (1952): 200–217; Vaughan, *New England Frontier*.

23. Clark, *Eliot Tracts*, 61–62. Offered as a proof of grace, this vignette reveals other possibilities for such tears, such as the power of the English army rather than the English God. Wequash led an eastern branch of Niantics with the English against the Pequots and witnessed the massacre at Mystic Fort—the specific incident cited here. Roger Williams spoke skeptically of Wequash's conversion: see Roger Williams, *A Key into the Language of America*, reprint ed. (Bedford: Applewood, 1997), preface. Whatever the reason for his feelings in this scene, what matters is how the English chose to represent them— namely, as the first step of conversion. In her upcoming book titled *Becoming Colonial: Indians, Immigrants, and Early American Aesthetics*, Joanne van der Woude links Puritan mission efforts to the Mystic Massacre, reading both in light of the aesthetic investment in tears and Indian bodies. I am grateful to van der Woude for sharing her manuscript in advance.

24. Clark, *Eliot Tracts*, 60. Thomas Shepard, *The Sincere Convert*, ed. John A. Albro (Ligonier, PA: Soli Deo Gloria, 1991), 8. Richard Baxter, *A Call to the Unconverted* (London, 1658), 9. I thus disagree with Axtell's claim that catechistical instruction formed "the first step in evangelization and Christian nurture." Axtell,

Invasion Within, 435. Before they could learn from the catechism, Praying Indians had to be willing to listen. This point also, incidentally, furthers the Puritan principle of persuasion described in chapter 3: that love precedes logic. Affection comes before and enables the possibility of persuasion.

25. Clark, *Eliot Tracts*, 166, 183, 84.

26. Shepard, *Sincere Convert*, 89, 15. In this formulation I reverse Bross's assessment of the situation: she claims that "even tears, no matter how heartfelt, did not prove to English observers that converts understood Christianity, nor did they demonstrate an experience of full conversion." Bross, *Dry Bones*, 90. Bross is right, but the reverse also held: no amount of knowledge could prove a complete conversion without an accompanying inner feeling—without the affections that made knowledge efficacious.

27. Clark, *Eliot Tracts*, 83. Of this moment, Murray claims, "[Eliot's] awareness that strange language carries mystical power places him (although he would never have admitted it, of course) in the company of priests offering prayers in Latin or sachems drawing authority from archaisms." Laura J. Murray, "Joining Signs with Words: Missionaries, Metaphors, and the Massachusett Language," *New England Quarterly* 74, no. 1 (2001): 74. In one sense that is true—and one more way of alluring Indians to his message. But Eliot's own explanation focuses on his ability to be expressive while speaking, which he can only do in English. Eliot must perform the seriousness and sincerity of his efforts—a performance intended to win the desires and affections of his hosts.

28. Clark, *Eliot Tracts*, 272, 285, 281, 294.

29. Ibid., 228–229. Shepard, *Sincere Convert*, 23. Baxter, *Call*, 125, 284. Almost every Praying Indian testified, as Ponampam did, "I heard that my heart must break and melt for sin, and beleeve in Christ, and that we should try our hearts if it be so." Clark, *Eliot Tracts*, 280. Eliot eventually translated both Shepard's *Sincere Convert* and Baxter's *Call to the Unconverted* into Algonquian.

30. Shepard, *Sincere Convert*, 93, 108. Clark, *Eliot Tracts*, 89.

31. Clark, *Eliot Tracts*, 59, 94. As Murray explains, "Tears were not ornament but guarantee for Indian confessions, especially in the face of missionaries' suspicions about the confessions' sincerity or the accuracy of their translation." Laura Murray, "Joining Signs," 80. Bumas notes that "tears became something of a liquid trope" that English Protestants could use to distinguish their efforts from the Spanish. E. Shaskan Bumas, "The Cannibal Butcher Shop: Protestant Uses of Las Casas' *Brevísima relación* and the Case of the Apostle Eliot," *Early American Literature* 35, no. 2 (2000): 125. Rivett ties the interest in Indian tears to an emerging scientific revolution, whereby "empirical techniques and ethnographic observations" investigated the workings of grace on Native American souls; she claims that the new science led translators and transcribers to record a "racialized spectacle of religious affect" as they searched for signs of grace. Sarah Rivett, "Empirical Desire: Conversion, Ethnography, and the New Science

of the Praying Indian," *Early American Studies* 4, no. 1 (2006): 20. Rivett's larger project links Puritanism to Enlightenment science. See Sarah Rivett, *The Science of the Soul in Colonial New England* (Chapel Hill: University of North Carolina Press, 2011). Brown and Stevens also note the frequent use of tears. See Matthew Brown, *The Pilgrim and the Bee: Reading Rituals and Book Culture in Early New England* (Philadelphia: University of Pennsylvania Press, 2007), 188–192; Stevens, *Poor Indians*, 67–68. Other scholars have also observed the superabundance of tears and offered additional explanations. Axtell claims, "Natives torn from their cultural roots understandably were emotionally fragile when they were confronted by the depressing tenets of Christian sin." Axtell, *Invasion Within*, 232. Salisbury attributes the tears to "hostility arising from the humiliation and deprivation experienced at the hands of the English." Salisbury, "Red Puritans," 50. Cogley notes that Shepard and Eliot were "particularly impressed" by Native weeping, but does not explore why—or what function the representation of such weeping might have served. Cogley, *John Eliot's Mission*, 73.

32. Clark, *Eliot Tracts*, 137–138, 232, 266. For an important account of performance in the context of Puritan missionary work, see Joshua David Bellin, "John Eliot's Playing Indian," *Early American Literature* 42, no. 1 (2007): 1–30. I build on Bellin's insights by focusing on the way performance became inscribed in sentimental literary forms.

33. Shepard, *Sincere Convert*, 26. In this concern, the Puritans faced in an earlier form the same paradox haunting sentimental fiction. As Hendler explains, "Although sentimental fiction asserts that theatricality is dangerous because it can evoke an 'improper,' inauthentic form of sympathy, its representations of even the most authentic sympathy are often indistinguishable from theatricality." Glenn Hendler, *Public Sentiments: Structures of Feeling in Nineteenth-Century American Literature* (Chapel Hill: University of North Carolina Press, 2001), 130.

34. Shepard, *Sincere Convert*, 93. Clark, *Eliot Tracts*, 138, 233. As Tinker writes, "Fearing a reversion to old cultural habits, [Puritans] constantly policed their converts, rooting out suspicious behaviors." George Tinker, *Missionary Conquest: The Gospel and Native American Cultural Genocide* (Minneapolis: Fortress Press, 1993), 20. On the one hand, such tactics reveal a different treatment of the Indians: no elder snuck around Boston peering through windows at potential converts. On the other hand, no elder ever needed to: New England Puritans remained under constant scrutiny from their families and neighbors. The difference here—which is not insignificant—lies not in surveillance, but in which aspects of one's former life English and Indian converts had to reject. In this regard, Pointer is exactly right: "In retrospect, it is clear that what Puritans asked of natives was not what they asked of themselves but instead its precise opposite. Rather than recovering the purity and simplicity of some 'primitive' past, the call to convert to Christianity and English ways for the Ninnimissinuok [the Indians of Southern New England] entailed breaking with the past, being

innovative and adaptive, standing at odds with one's community and its standards." Pointer, "Imitating Language," 160.

35. Clark, *Eliot Tracts*, 88, 127, 129, 133.

36. Shepard, *Sincere Convert*, 65.

37. These contagious tears actually covered up some important dynamics. Most New Englanders knew Cutshamekin to be a problem, accepting Christianity mainly to retain his authority. Eliot would eventually claim that "hee is constant in his profession, though doubtfull in respect of the thoroughnesse of his heart." Clark, *Eliot Tracts*, 228. But in the first throes of conversion, Eliot remains hopeful; more importantly, he wants to make his readers hopeful by narrating the contagion spreading from Cutshamekin to the entire, tear-filled wigwam.

38. Clark, *Eliot Tracts*, 234–235, 96.

39. Ibid., 190–191.

40. Ibid., 84, 189, 266, 242, 223.

41. Cohen has argued that the emotional experiences Native Americans recited proved insufficient evidence of conversion. His reading focuses almost entirely on the doctrinal and emotional *content* of the confessions. Charles Cohen, "Conversion Among Puritans and Amerindians: A Theological and Cultural Perspective," in *Puritanism: Transatlantic Perspectives on a Seventeenth-Century Anglo-American Faith*, ed. Francis Bremer (Boston: Massachusetts Historical Society, 1993), 233–256. Here I want to focus attention on their *performance*. In that regard, my reading comes closer to Rivett's, who claims that "the testimonies *did* provide adequate evidence for the praying church," but failed to evince a "natural taxonomy of grace." Rivett, *Science of the Soul*, n. 40, p. 153. However, my emphasis lies not with empirical science and natural philosophy, but with the role of sympathy in the evaluation of sincerity.

42. Clark, *Eliot Tracts*, 278.

43. Ibid., 280–281. Ponampam actually had two personal confessions; the other ended, "I now desire to repent, and beleeve in Christ, and that Christ will pardon me, and shew mercy to us all." Ibid., 279.

44. Ibid., 281–282.

45. Ibid., 372–373, 376. It should be noted that in the final round of testimonies, to save time and make sure the Praying Indians could be approved on that day, elders opted to have two confessions read instead of spoken; but these testimonies came from Native Americans who had formerly confessed orally: the Puritan elders had already seen their performance of sincerity.

46. Grumet notes that "persuasion and peer pressure rather than force were used to develop support." Grumet, *Historic Contact*, 58.

47. Williams, *Key*, 55, 185. See also Bragdon, *Native People*, 173, 218.

48. As Bragdon writes, "The sachem and his advisors generally held the role of speaker, while the common people acted as witnesses and as a kind of 'chorus.'" Kathleen Bragdon, "'Emphaticall Speech and Great Action': An Analysis

of Speech Events Described in Seventeenth Century Sources," *Man in the Northeast* 33 (1987): 105. Clark, *Eliot Tracts*, 269.

49. Bragdon, "Emphaticall Speech," 105.

50. Here I follow the lead of scholars such as Gustafson, who examines Samson Occom's extension of Algonquian practices into his position as a Christian minister. Sandra Gustafson, *Eloquence is Power: Oratory and Performance in Early America* (Chapel Hill: University of North Carolina Press, 2000).

51. Ives Goddard and Kathleen Bragdon, eds., *Native Writings in Massachusett*, vol. 1 (Philadelphia: American Philosophical Society, 1988), 373. Goddard and Bragdon point out that Massachusett petitions "reflect formalized patterns of speech" and direct readers to four known examples similar to this one. See Goddard and Bragdon, eds., *Native Writings*, 19, 173, 179, 225, and 373.

52. Shepard, *Sincere Convert*, 21–22. Mather's letter can be found reprinted with annotations in Cotton Mather, *Magnalia Christi Americana*, vol. 1 (Hartford: Silas Andrus and Son, 1855), 570. For a good reading of Cotton Mather's notes to this letter, see Constance Post, "Old World Order in the New: John Eliot and 'Praying Indians' in Cotton Mather's *Magnalia Christi Americana*," *New England Quarterly* 66, no. 3 (1993): 416–433.

53. Mather, *Magnalia*, 569. Clark, *Eliot Tracts*, 256. In an excellent book, Branch traces the connections between an insistence on free prayer in Dissenting circles and a rising "cult of spontaneity" that helped develop sentimental philosophy. See Branch, *Rituals of Spontaneity: Sentiment and Secularism from Free Prayer to Wordsworth* (Waco, TX: Baylor University Press, 2006), 35–61.

54. Richter writes, "Though similar in the general outlines, the renditions vary markedly in detail and emphasis, suggesting considerable spontaneity in the speakers' performance." Richter, *Facing East*, 117. A glance through the confessions of Shepard's church reveals this same tendency.

55. When detailing the many prescriptions for gesture and outward display in Puritan services, Brown refers to the event as "a theater of worship." Brown, *Pilgrim and the Bee*, 120. Bross also notes "the inherently theatrical spectacle of public confession," claiming that it "is perhaps nowhere so well documented, certainly nowhere so well publicized as in the spectacle of Praying Indians." Bross, *Dry Bones*, 41. For more on sentimentalism's concern with theatricality, see Hendler, *Public Sentiments*, 33; Julia Stern, *The Plight of Feeling: Sympathy and Dissent in the Early American Novel* (Chicago: University of Chicago Press, 1997), chapter 1; and David Marshall, *The Surprising Effects of Sympathy: Marivaux, Diderot, Rousseau, and Mary Shelley* (Chicago: University of Chicago Press, 1988).

56. Baxter, *Call*, 57. Rooy, *Theology of Missions*, 43. Clark, *Eliot Tracts*, 58.

57. John Eliot, *John Eliot's Indian Dialogues: A Study in Cultural Interaction*, ed. Henry W. Bowden and James P. Ronda (Westport, CT: Greenwood Press, 1980), 61, 95, 97.

58. Ibid., 98, 103.

59. Ibid., 107, 113.

60. Roger Clap, *Memoirs of Capt. Roger Clap* (Boston: 1731), 7.

61. In the seventeenth century, most did not define race primarily through skin color, but rather through matters of culture and environment. At the same time, I follow here the approach of Joanna Brooks, who defines race in this period more by how it was experienced than by how it was theorized. See Joanna Brooks, "Working Definitions: Race, Ethnic Studies, and Early American Literature," *Early American Literature* 41, no. 2 (2006): 313–320.

62. Clark, *Eliot Tracts*, 65.

63. Ibid., 94, 107, 109, 123. See Bross, *Dry Bones* for an extensive reading of these many "Indian sermons."

64. Clark, *Eliot Tracts*, 136. Axtell observes, "In colonial eyes, [the converts] were still Indians and always would be, no matter how 'civilized' or 'Christian' they became." James Axtell, "Some Thoughts on the Ethnohistory of Missions," in *After Columbus: Essays in the Ethnohistory of Colonial North America* (New York: Oxford University Press, 1988), 51. For the most powerful exploration of this point, see Stevens, *The Poor Indians*.

65. Clark, *Eliot Tracts*, 93 (emphasis added), 137. Natural compassion goes missing in most accounts of Eliot's desire for Native missionaries. Axtell, for example, argues that Eliot wanted Indian preachers because they enjoyed "the advantages of linguistic fluency, cultural familiarity, and less need for creature comfort." Axtell, *Invasion Within*, 225. Most scholars agree: see Cogley, *John Eliot's Mission*, 170; Kellaway, *New England Company*, 115; McCarthy, "Conversion," 362; Tanis, "Education," 318. Sehr adds that an increase in Native missionaries "took on millennial implications." Timothy Sehr, "John Eliot, Millennialist and Missionary," *The Historian* 46, no. 2 (1984): 200. Such reasons are not wrong; they are simply incomplete. Eliot emphasized that Indian missionaries had *natural compassion* that would aid their work and possibly issue in spiritual love—the communion of saints.

66. Clark, *Eliot Tracts*, 236, 269, 284, 382.

67. Ibid., 359. As Murray observes about *Indian Dialogues*: "where the distinction is really made is between Christian and pagan, as one of the Christian Indians, Piumbukhou, is at pains to explain to his kinsman." David Murray, *Forked Tongues: Speech, Writing and Representation in North American Indian Texts* (Bloomington: Indiana University Press, 1991), 127.

68. See the introduction for a fuller account of this chorus, especially footnote 20.

69. Clark, *Eliot Tracts*, 107, 217, 260, 360, 110. In a section entitled "Reading as Performance," Brown details many Puritan books which called on readers to be moved or affected, responding with tears to what they read. See Brown, *Pilgrim and the Bee*, 76–87.

70. Clark, *Eliot Tracts*, 64, 145, 364.

71. Thus, the Eliot tracts demonstrate the "powerful conjunction of the performative, vocal and textual dynamics" that Stern locates in revolutionary literature 150 years later and links to Adam Smith. As Stern notes, "Correspondence in the early American novel simultaneously functions as a window onto the outer world of collective affairs and a mirror illuminating the inner states of solitary selves." In its latter function, epistolarity "becomes a dedicated channel for the reflection of fellow feeling." Stern, *Plight of Feeling*, 16–17.

72. Clark, *Eliot Tracts*, 294–295. Dying children itself represents a trope of literary sentimentalism, and in focusing for a moment on childhood deathbed scenes, Eliot precipitated a wider Puritan fascination with such material. In 1672, James Janeway's *A Token for Children* became widely popular, and Cotton Mather put out his own collection of such stories in 1700, titled *A Token for the Children of New England.* Farrell links these works to the nineteenth-century sentimental novel *Uncle Tom's Cabin.* See Molly Farrell, "Dying Instruction: Puritan Pedagogy in *Uncle Tom's Cabin*," *American Literature* 82, no. 2 (2010): 243–269.

CHAPTER 6

1. Stern summarizes Rowlandson's many firsts: "Rowlandson's is the first female voice to speak in published prose in the New World; her narrative creates and inaugurates a native American genre, the captivity tale; and her story could be considered the first early American best-seller, reprinted well into the nineteenth century." Julia Stern, "To Represent Afflicted Time: Mourning as Historiography," *American Literary History* 5, no. 2 (1993): 378. More recently, scholars have emphasized transatlantic and global captivity narratives that preceded and surrounded Rowlandson's. For an excellent review of the turn toward transatlantic captivity narratives (especially those of North Africa), see Gordon Sayre, "Renegades from Barbary: The Transnational Turn in Captivity Studies," *American Literary History* 22, no. 2 (2010): 347–359. Colley also draws attention to the transatlantic and imperial context of captivity narratives, but notes that American captivity narratives are often distinguished by their "marked sentiment," calling them "arguably more feminised, and certainly more domestic and personal, than the generality of their North African and Asian counterparts." Linda Colley, *Captives: Britain, Empire and the World, 1600–1850* (New York: Anchor Books, 2004), 150. In this chapter, I link the domestic and personal aspects of Rowlandson's captivity narrative to Puritan sympathy and the long history of sentimentalism.

2. Lauren Berlant, *The Female Complaint: The Unfinished Business of Sentimentality in American Culture* (Durham, NC: Duke University Press, 2008), 3. Breitwieser also depicts Rowlandson's narrative as disconnected from public time and events. See Mitchell Breitwieser, *American Puritanism and the Defense*

of Mourning: Religion, Grief, and Ethnology in Mary White Rowlandson's Captivity Narrative (Madison: University of Wisconsin Press, 1990), 4–5.

3. What to call this conflict has long been in dispute. "King Philip's War" labels the conflict from the perspective of the English and emphasizes, perhaps too much, the role of the Pokanoket sachem Philip. But Philip's name was Metacom, so the war has also been called "Metacom's War" or "Metacom's Rebellion," along with a host of other names. I have chosen to call it King Philip's War because I will be analyzing a Puritan captivity narrative and so attempting to understand a particular English perspective on the conflict. For more on the "name of war," see Jill Lepore, *The Name of War: King Philip's War and the Origins of American Identity* (New York: Vintage, 1998), ix–xxiii.

4. John Easton, "Excerpt from A Relacion of the Indyan Warre, 1675," in *The Sovereignty and Goodness of God*, ed. Neal Salisbury (Boston: Bedford, 1997), 117.

5. See James Drake, *King Philip's War: Civil War in New England, 1675–1676* (Amherst: University of Massachusetts Press, 1999). Drake emphasizes the tensions caused by the rise of Christian Indians (see especially chapters 3 and 4). Lepore provides an extensive analysis of Sassamon's role; see Lepore, *Name of War*, chapter 1. For a recent, good overview of the war and its wider context, see Jenny Hale Pulsipher, *Subjects unto the Same King: Indians, English, and the Contest for Authority in Colonial New England* (Philadelphia: University of Pennsylvania Press, 2005).

6. On Philip's death, see Benjamin Church, "Entertaining Passages Relating to King Philip's War," in *So Dreadfull a Judgment: Puritan Responses to King Philip's War, 1676–1677*, ed. Richard Slotkin and James Folsom (Middletown, CT: Wesleyan University Press, 1978), 451–452. On the display of his head, see Lepore, *Name of War*, xvi, 173–175.

7. See Kathryn Zabelle Derounian, "The Publication, Promotion, and Distribution of Mary Rowlandson's Indian Captivity Narrative in the Seventeenth Century," *Early American Literature* 23, no. 3 (1988): 239–261.

8. Scholars have a wide range of views on Rowlandson's doctrinal purity. As Stern notes, Rowlandson's account "is read as doctrinally pure, an exemplary jeremiad, or seen to express a kind of protofeminism, a dissenting retort to the Puritan patriarchs." Stern, "To Represent Afflicted Time," 378. For examples of the former, see David Downing, "'Streams of Scripture Comfort': Mary Rowlandson's Typological Use of the Bible," *Early American Literature* 15, no. 3 (1981): 252–259; Gary Ebersole, *Captured by Texts: Puritan to Postmodern Images of Indian Captivity* (Charlottesville: University Press of Virginia, 1995); Charles Hambrick-Stowe, *The Practice of Piety: Puritan Devotional Disciplines in Seventeenth-Century New England* (Chapel Hill: University of North Carolina Press, 1982), 258–264. For examples of readings that see Rowlandson *resisting* dominant Puritan values, see Christopher Castiglia, *Bound and Determined: Captivity, Culture-crossing, and White Womanhood from*

Mary Rowlandson to Patty Hearst (Chicago: University of Chicago Press, 1996); Deborah Dietrich, "Mary Rowlandson's Great Declension," *Women's Studies: An Interdisciplinary Journal* 24, no. 5 (1995): 427–439; Tara Fitzpatrick, "The Figure of Captivity: The Cultural Work of the Puritan Captivity Narrative," *American Literary History* 3, no. 1 (1991): 1–26. Most scholars (including some of these) see Rowlandson as both embracing and resisting orthodoxy. Breitwieser introduced the idea of the narrative's "best intention" continually subverted by an "alternate teleology." Breitwieser, *American Puritanism*, 8. Derounian-Stodola and Levernier review the ways that scholars attribute two voices to her narrative and add their own terminology: "*empirical narration* (the 'colloquial' style) defines the author's role as participant, while *rhetorical narration* (the 'biblical' style) defines her role as interpreter and commentator." Kathryn Zabelle Derounian-Stodola and James Arthur Levernier, *The Indian Captivity Narrative, 1550–1900* (New York: Twayne, 1993), 101. Fitzpatrick calls this "the dual, sometimes dueling textual voices of the captives and their ministerial sponsors." Fitzpatrick, "Figure of Captivity," 2. The ambiguity and the multiple dimensions of Rowlandson's narrative are, in part, what makes the text so fascinating to so many still today.

9. I am not the first to link Rowlandson's narrative to sentimental literature. See also Nancy Armstrong and Leonard Tennenhouse, "The American Origins of the English Novel," *American Literary History* 4, no. 3 (1992): 386–410; and Michelle Burnham, *Captivity and Sentiment: Cultural Exchange in American Literature, 1682–1861* (Lebanon, NH: University Press of New England, 1997). I build on these accounts by resituating Rowlandson's captivity narrative in dialogue with Puritan sympathy.

10. Mary Rowlandson, *The Sovereignty and Goodness of God, Together with the Faithfulness of His Promises Displayed: Being a Narrative of Mrs. Mary Rowlandson,* ed. Neal Salisbury (Boston: Bedford, 1997), 65. The authorship of the preface is ascribed to "Ter Amicum," which presumably is a typo for "Per Amicum," that is "by a friend." Most scholars presume that "friend" to be Increase Mather. For more on the preface and the publishing of Rowlandson's narrative, see Neal Salisbury, "Introduction: Mary Rowlandson and Her Removes," in *The Sovereignty and Goodness of God*, ed. Neal Salisbury (Boston: Bedford, 1997), 44–49.

11. Increase Mather, "A Brief History of the Warr with the Indians in New-England," in *So Dreadfull a Judgment: Puritan Responses to King Philip's War, 1676–1677,* ed. Richard Slotkin and James Folsom (Middletown, CT: Wesleyan University Press, 1978), 104.

12. Lang writes that Rowlandson's "story is meant not to thrill but to instruct. It is a story not of Indian atrocities but of Christian affliction." Amy Schrager Lang, "Introduction," in *Journeys in New Worlds: Early American Women's Narratives,* ed. William Andrews, et. al. (Madison: University of Wisconsin Press, 1990), 21.

See also David Minter, "By Dens of Lions: Notes on Stylization in Early Puritan Captivity Narratives," *American Literature* 45, no. 3 (1973): 335–347. Relatedly, Toulouse reads the narrative as a text engaged in "internal (colonial) and external (royal English) challenges" to cultural control. Teresa Toulouse, *The Captive's Position: Female Narrative, Male Identity, and Royal Authority in Colonial New England* (Philadelphia: University of Pennsylvania Press, 2007), 16.

13. Increase Mather, *Essay for the Recording of Illustrious Providences* (Boston, 1684), 39 (emphasis added).

14. Rowlandson, *Sovereignty and Goodness*, 65–66 (emphasis added).

15. Green quoted in Derounian, "Publication," 249. Derounian, "Publication," 249.

16. Richard Allestree, *A discourse concerning the beauty of holiness* (London, 1679), 114. Anonymous, *The Confession and Execution of the Five Prisoners that Suffered on the New Gallows at Tyburn* (London, 1678), 4. Several scholars have noted the emotional power of Rowlandson's story—Derounian-Stodola and Levernier, for example, call it "unusual for its strong emotional impact"; Hall describes it as "rich in pathos"; Slotkin and Folsom claim that the narrative becomes "a uniquely human and touching document"—but few interpret that emotional power as the primary reason for publication. Derounian-Stodola and Levernier, *Indian Captivity Narrative*, 110; David D. Hall, *Worlds of Wonder, Days of Judgment: Popular Religious Belief in Early New England* (Cambridge, MA: Harvard University Press, 1989), 122; Richard Slotkin and James Folsom, "Mary Rowlandson: Captive Witness," in *So Dreadfull a Judgment: Puritan Responses to King Philip's War, 1676–1677*, ed. Richard Slotkin and James Folsom (Middletown, CT: Wesleyan University Press, 1978), 304.

17. On modern calendars, this would be February 20, 1676.

18. Rowlandson, *Sovereignty and Goodness*, 68–69.

19. This need for pathos also helps explain Rowlandson's focus on the body throughout. For more on this focus, see Mary Carruth, "Between Abjection and Redemption: Mary Rowlandson's Subversive Corporeality," in *Feminist Interventions in Early American Studies*, ed. Mary Carruth (Tuscaloosa: University of Alabama Press, 2006), 60–79. For a study of Rowlandson's hunger—and thus a shift from materiality to sensation—see Jordan Alexander Stein, "Mary Rowlandson's Hunger and the Historiography of Sexuality," *American Literature* 81, no. 3 (2009): 469–495.

20. Rowlandson, *Sovereignty and Goodness*, 69–70. As Slotkin writes, "Family ties, *above all*, are violently disrupted." He goes on to describe "the breakup of families" as "the center of the trial by captivity." Richard Slotkin, *Regeneration through Violence: The Mythology of the American Frontier, 1600–1860* (Middletown, CT: Wesleyan University Press, 1993), 106, 108 (emphasis added).

21. Rowlandson, *Sovereignty and Goodness*, 71, 75, 78. Familial separation also became a defining feature of captivity narratives going forward. See Burnham, *Captivity*

and Sentiment, 50–51. According to Derounian-Stodola and Levernier, female captivity narratives "stress that captivity's main metonymy was the dramatic and decisive fracturing of the original family unit." They add, "As early as Mary Rowlandson's narrative, we find the moment of attack defined by maternal/filial reactions." Derounian-Stodola and Levernier, *Indian Captivity Narrative*, 112, 146. This feature of captivity narratives reveals a link to sentimental literature. As Dillon observes, "The celebration of the mother-child bond and the threatened violation of this bond are thus the central topics of sentimental literature." In fact, she argues, "doing violence to the mother-child bond is the catalyst for the plot of the sentimental novel. The closed domestic space of privacy is thus violently shattered in the sentimental novel, yet only this violence enables the public 'display' that will generate the very meaning and value of privacy. Ironically, then, familial bonds within sentimentalism are made to be broken in order to recharge them with affective value and recirculate them as social currency." Elizabeth Maddock Dillon, *The Gender of Freedom: Fictions of Liberalism and the Literary Public Sphere* (Stanford: Stanford University Press, 2004), 198, 207. Such a description applies strikingly well to Rowlandson's captivity narrative.

22. "Articles of Agreement," *New England Historical and Genealogical Register* 13 (1859): 295. Edmund Morgan, ed., *The Founding of Massachusetts: Historians and the Sources* (Indianapolis: Bobbs-Merrill, 1964), 460, 465.

23. Morgan, ed., *Founding of Massachusetts*, 465. William Gouge, *Domesticall Duties* (London, 1622), 18. Gouge added that the family was "a schoole wherein the first principles and grounds of government and subjection are learned: whereby men are fitted to greater matters in Church or commonwealth."

24. Eleazar Mather, *A Serious Exhortation to the Present and Succeeding Generation in New-England* (Cambridge, 1671), 20. Morgan notes that the "duty to enforce good behavior in the family was the germ of all political and ecclesiastical authority." Edmund Morgan, *The Puritan Family* (New York: Harper & Row, 1966), 7. Norton has observed that the Puritans "saw family and state as analogous institutions, linked symbiotically through their similar historical origins, aims, and functions." Mary Beth Norton, *Founding Mothers and Fathers: Gendered Power and the Forming of American Society* (New York: Vintage, 1997), 4. This worldview has been called Filmerian after Sir Roger Filmer, who set forth a theory of patriarchal power. On the Filmerian system, see Norton, *Founding Mothers*, 3–24.

25. Increase Mather, "An Earnest Exhortation to the Inhabitants of New-England," *So Dreadfull a Judgment: Puritan Responses to King Philip's War, 1676–1677*, ed. Richard Slotkin and James Folsom (Hanover, NH: University Press of New England, 1999), 181. Tompson, "New Englands Crisis," *So Dreadfull a Judgment*, 218. Discipline, order, and subordination are the aspects most stressed in Morgan's account of the Puritan family. Toulouse also identifies such qualities as the defining feature in Rowlandson's narrative: see Toulouse, *Captive's Position*, 39.

26. William Hubbard, *The Happiness of a People* (Boston, 1676), 19. Mather, *Serious Exhortation*, 16, 30. For more on Puritan views of natural affections in the family, see the introduction.

27. William Perkins, *The Work of William Perkins*, ed. Ian Breward (Appleford: Sutton Courtenay Press, 1970), 225. The idea of Christians united as a family springs from Paul's letters to the early church. Hellerman has argued that the "most significant social characteristic of early Christianity" was its "metaphor of the church as a surrogate kinship group." Joseph Hellerman, *The Ancient Church as Family* (Minneapolis: Fortress, 2001), 21.

28. Mather, *Serious Exhortation*, preface. Mather, "Brief History," 136.

29. Rowlandson, *Sovereignty and Goodness*, 75, 84.

30. Ibid., 104, 108, 111 (all emphases in the original unless otherwise stated).

31. See Jane Tompkins, *Sensational Designs: The Cultural Work of American Fiction, 1790–1860* (New York: Oxford University Press, 1985), 164–165; Gillian Brown, *Domestic Individualism: Imagining Self in Nineteenth-Century America* (Berkeley: University of California Press, 1990), 25; and Marianne Noble, *The Masochistic Pleasures of Sentimental Literature* (Princeton: Princeton University Press, 2000), 66.

32. Mather, "Brief History," 110–111. As Potter notes, "From the beginning, it is Rowlandson's knowable role as a mother to which she clings while she struggles concurrently to create and negate her identity as captive slave." Tiffany Potter, "Writing Indigenous Femininity: Mary Rowlandson's Narrative of Captivity," *Eighteenth-Century Studies* 36, no. 2 (2003): 158.

33. Rowlandson, *Sovereignty and Goodness*, 77–78, 88, 91, 86. The importance of homesickness in this text intersects with the work of many different scholars. Lepore notes that houses were a central metaphor of King Philip's War, and that Rowlandson maintained her English identity in captivity by stressing her revulsion of all things Indian and her homesickness for all things English. Lepore, *Name of War*, 91–92, 130. Logan, likewise, claims that "the work of Rowlandson's narrative is to reestablish a social, ideological, and discursive 'home' for her." Lisa Logan, "Mary Rowlandson's Captivity and the 'Place' of the Woman Subject," *Early American Literature* 28, no. 3 (1993): 258. Such readings temper Breitwieser's and Ebersole's accounts in different ways. Breitwieser claims that the "destruction of the ordinary" in Rowlandson's text serves as "the clearing away of the spurious clarities of the daily in order to make way for sound significance." Breitwieser, *American Puritanism*, 81. Yet as Breitwieser himself acknowledges (though in a different way), precisely the opposite also occurs: the ordinary *becomes* the significant. As Armstrong and Tennenhouse observe, "The voice of someone captured by Indians speaks with authority because it speaks out in isolation and testifies to the individual's single-minded desire to return home." Armstrong and Tennenhouse, "American Origins," 394. Most importantly, this longed-for home is an *idealized* one. Anderson

comments that for Rowlandson, "home as it emerged was less experienced than imagined." Benedict Anderson, "Exodus," *Critical Inquiry* 20, no. 2 (1994): 319. What Rowlandson desires, what she remembers with such nostalgia, was an image of peace—a home composed in her memory of *only* security and bliss.

34. Anne Bradstreet, *The Works of Anne Bradstreet*, ed. Jeannine Hensley (Cambridge, MA: Belknap, 1967), 292–293. For more on how Anne Bradstreet's poetry circulates proto-sentimental imagery and themes beyond this one poem, see Abram Van Engen, "Advertising the Domestic: Anne Bradstreet's Sentimental Poetics," *Legacy* 28, no. 1 (2011): 47–68.

35. Increase Mather, *The Day of Trouble is Near* (Cambridge, 1674), 10–11. Mather, "Brief History," 109. Mather, "Earnest Exhortation," 176, 182. In *The Day of Trouble is Near*, he makes this link explicit: "I do believe, that one reason why the Lord threatneth to send upon us that Calamity of War at this day, is because of wars and fightings which he hath seen, and been provoked with in the midst of us." Mather, *Day of Trouble*, 23.

36. Hubbard called for a greater degree of religious tolerance in the face of Increase Mather's urgent exhortations for reform. He also attributed the calamities of the war not primarily to the judgments of God but to poor military skills and leadership. For more on the Hubbard-Mather rivalry, see Anne Kusener Nelson, "King Philip's War and the Hubbard-Mather Rivalry," *William and Mary Quarterly* 27, no. 4 (1970); and Richard Dunn, "Seventeenth-Century English Historians of America," in *Seventeenth-Century America: Essays in Colonial History*, ed. James Morton Smith (New York: Norton, 1972), 195–225.

37. Hubbard, *Happiness*, 16, 19. Hubbard claimed, "Thus in the body politick, where it is animated with one entire spirit of love and unity, and setled upon lasting and sure foundations of quietness and peace, all the several members, must and will conspire together to deny, or forbear the exercise of their own proper inclinations, to preserve the union of the whole, that there be no Schisme in the body." Hubbard, *Happiness*, 16.

38. Thomas Walley, *Balm in Gilead to Heal Sions Wounds* (Cambridge, 1669), 9. Hubbard, *Happiness*, 16. Tompson, "New Englands Crisis," 217 (emphasis added). Hubbard also preached that the loss of love bred error: calling on his community to revive their Christian charity, he claimed that such love may "be the most likely means to heal us and revive things amongst us, to their primitive state of purity and perfection, for when did iniquity abound, but when the love of many began to wax cold." Hubbard, *Happiness*, 60. So also Eleazar Mather called on his listeners to "*maintain a Spirit of love towards God, and towards one another,*" claiming that if the Lord left, it would be because the people had lost their love. Mather, *Serious Exhortation*, 25.

39. Danforth wrote, "The Lord heaps mercies, favours, blessings upon us, and loads us daily with his benefits, but all his love and bounty cannot heat and warm our hearts and affections. Well, the furnace is able to heat and melt the coldest

Iron: but how oft hath the Lord cast us into the hot furnace of Affliction and Tribulation, and we have been scorched and burnt, yet not melted, but hardened thereby, *Isa.63.17*." Samuel Danforth, *A Brief Recognition of New-Englands Errand into the Wilderness* (Cambridge, 1671), 12–13.

40. Perry Miller, "Errand into the Wilderness," in *Errand into the Wilderness* (Cambridge, MA: Belknap, 1984), 1–15. Despite the similarities, Winthrop's sermon was almost certainly unknown to Danforth since it was never published or mentioned. For more on the history of Winthrop's sermon and Miller's use of it, see Abram Van Engen, "Origins and Last Farewells: Bible Wars, Textual Form, and the Making of American History," *The New England Quarterly* 86, no. 4 (2013): 543–592.

41. Rowlandson, *Sovereignty and Goodness*, 105. *1599 Geneva Bible* (White Hall, WV: Tolle Lege Press, 2006), 906.

42. Rowlandson, *Sovereignty and Goodness*, 73, 77, 80, 84.

43. John Winthrop, "A Model of Christian Charity," in *The Winthrop Papers*, vols. 1–7 (Boston: Massachusetts Historical Society, 1929–), II.283, II.289. Rowlandson's captivity narrative has often been seen as an American site for the emergence of modern individualism. According to Armstrong and Tennenhouse, the story presents the tale of a heroine "detached—and thereby individuated" from her culture, who returns and seeks reincorporation. Armstrong and Tennenhouse, "American Origins," 399. Bauer claims that Rowlandson differs from John Winthrop and William Bradford precisely because her narrative "does not present the Atlantic removal as the experience of a community 'closely knit together'; rather, it is the experience of the lonely modern individual in the wilderness of the world all by herself." Ralph Bauer, "Creole Identities in Colonial Space: The Narratives of Mary White Rowlandson and Francisco Nuñez de Pineda y Bascuñán," *American Literature* 69, no. 4 (1997): 684. Breitwieser notes that Rowlandson inhabits a distinct, "afflicted time" that was "dissevered from public time"; she was out of sync with her community. Breitwieser, *American Puritanism*, 5. Burnham associates the "complexity and inconsistency" of Rowlandson's character with the rise of the novel. Burnham, *Captivity and Sentiment*, 38. Deronian-Stodola and Levernier see individuality occurring in the split between soul and psyche. Derounian-Stodola and Levernier, *Indian Captivity Narrative*, 104. Fitzpatrick, meanwhile, locates in Rowlandson an "American rhetoric of self-creation"; through Rowlandson and other captivity narratives, she traces "the breakdown of the Puritan communal ideal." Fitzpatrick, "Figure of Captivity," 3, 8. MacNeil offers a similar reading, claiming Rowlandson as a heroine in the wilderness who "realizes that society and culture, both in the category of outward things, are of secondary importance to the experience of the individual." Denise MacNeil, "Mary Rowlandson and the Foundational Mythology of the American Frontier Hero," *Women's Studies: An Interdisciplinary Journal* 34, no. 8 (2005): 641. Finally, Traister argues that *The Sovereignty and Goodness of God* "gestures suggestively

toward a modern—indeed, secular—understanding of the human encounter with pain and trauma." Bryce Traister, "Mary Rowlandson and the Invention of the Secular," *Early American Literature* 42, no. 2 (2007): 325. My point is that even as such a development occurs, Rowlandson actively resists it and treats it as a special form of suffering.

44. Tompson exhibited the same hope in his description of King Philip's War, suggesting that its destruction might usher in the good of renewed affections. He writes, "This monster war hath hatched a beauteous dove / In dogged hearts, of most unfeigned love, / Fraternal love the livery of a saint / Being come in fashion though by sad constraint, / Which if it thrive and prosper with us long / Will make New England forty thousand strong." Tompson, "New Englands Crisis," 225.

45. Rowlandson, *Sovereignty and Goodness*, 73–75. Of the description of the dying Sarah, Derounian-Stodola and Levernier comment: "Rowlandson presents here a verbal pieta of tremendous emotional force, a combination of biblical echoes, precise observation, and lucid expression." Derounian-Stodola and Levernier, *Indian Captivity Narrative*, 107.

46. Rowlandson, *Sovereignty and Goodness*, 76, 81, 84.

47. Ibid., 88.

48. Rowlandson, *Sovereignty and Goodness*, 70, 71, 73. Lougheed likewise notes that Rowlandson is less interested in the deeds done during the tale as in the emotional response to those actions—not the scalping so much as the triumphing that accompanies the scalping. Pamela Lougheed, "'Then Began He to Rant and Threaten': Indian Malice and Individual Liberty in Mary Rolandson's Captivity Narrative," *American Literature* 74, no. 2 (2002): 295.

49. Sewell focuses on a different foundational line, but one that contains the same force. The first words in Rowlandson's narrative spoken by the Indians are "Come go along with us." Of this line, Sewell writes, "In a sense, the whole history of the American captivity is a response to that imperative, an attempt to deflect its force, deny its authority, correct it as ungrammatical in a syntax of Indian-white conversation in which the imperative mood is supposed to operate in only one direction." David Sewell, "'So Unstable and Like Mad Men They Were': Language and Interpretation in American Captivity Narratives," in *A Mixed Race: Ethnicity in Early America*, ed. Frank Shuffelton (New York: Oxford University Press, 1993), 40.

50. Rowlandson, *Sovereignty and Goodness*, 81, 94. For more on Roger Clap and this love of the brethren, see chapter 2.

51. Clap, *Memoirs*, 7. Rowlandson, *Sovereignty and Goodness*, 108, 111. Lepore notes this focus on an English emotional response in other texts of King Philip's War where the civilized respond to cruelty with "compassion, astonishment, and tears": proper emotional reactions preserve proper Englishness. Lepore, *Name of War*, 11–15. Bauer situates the "intense focus on racial distinctions" within a larger

colonial concern to show that true creoles did not "go native"—that they were as Spanish or English as those born in Europe. Rowlandson especially, he notes, "deemphasizes Christianity as a unifying force, emphasizing instead racial difference in exposing the 'true' nature of the 'Praying Indians' who seem to undermine the imaginary 'hedges' and 'walls' built around (white) New England by Puritan frontier ideology." Bauer, "Creole Identities," 678–680. Lepore identifies a similar context, demonstrating that New England Puritans repeatedly defined themselves as *not Indian* and *not Spanish*. Lepore, *Name of War*, xiv, 1–9. These racial distinctions, I want to stress, relied on emotional experiences and displays.

52. Rowlandson, *Sovereignty and Goodness*, 78.

53. Rowlandson, *Sovereignty and Goodness*, 111, 71. Mather, "Brief History," 128. Rowlandson, *Sovereignty and Goodness*, 109, 112, 111. Breitwieser's account of *The Sovereignty and Goodness of God* focuses on Rowlandson's grief for Sarah. In general, where he reads for Rowlandson's mourning, I read for the mourning she wants *others* (her readers) to do. But I agree with Breitwieser that the intensity of Rowlandson's grief breaks through her best intentions—including the intention to create a model society of mutual affections—and I support his insight that the strong desire for reintegration is precisely what prevents it. See Breitwieser, *American Puritanism*, 187. As Stein says of Rowlandson's failed reintegration, "The truth of her story is simply that you had to be there." Stein, "Mary Rowlandson's Hunger," 483. Rowlandson's failed reintegration has been addressed by many scholars. See, for example, Armstrong and Tennenhouse, "American Origins," 402; Breitwieser, *American Puritanism*, 121–127; Castiglia, *Bound and Determined*, 50–51; Kathryn Zabelle Derounian, "Puritan Orthodoxy and the 'Survivor Syndrome' in Mary Rowlandson's Indian Captivity Narrative," *Early American Literature* 22, no. 1 (1987): 82–93; and Toulouse, *Captive's Position*, 53–55.

54. Lepore, *Name of War*, 148.

55. Rowlandson, *Sovereignty and Goodness*, 68–70, 79, 85. This movement in Rowlandson's text has received a great deal of critical attention. Breitwieser puts it perhaps best, noting that "Rowlandson is one of the very few American Puritans to have recorded the fact that she discovered another being [a human Indian figure], or rather had it discovered to her." He claims that this emergence resulted from "the incapacitation of typology by grief." Breitwieser, *American Puritanism*, 132.

56. Rowlandson, *Sovereignty and Goodness*, 82.

57. Ibid.

58. Ibid. (emphasis added)

59. Ibid., 88. Rowlandson speaks with Indians throughout the text, but it is never explained whether she learned their language or whether they knew hers.

60. Ibid., 97.

61. Rowlandson thus categorizes similar acts of sympathy differently. As Potter observes, "Upon her release, she describes a situation nearly identical to that

she experienced while in captivity, right down to her 'poor, and distressed, and beggarly condition,' but the responses are characterized as acts of specifically Christian charity and thus are valued differently. With such an obvious parallel structure and parallel language in this closing segment, one must wonder whether Rowlandson might herself have been aware of the similar humanity of her treatment in both contexts, but regardless, as a proper Puritan woman, she characterizes the difference as one of God's removing her from 'that horrible pit, and [setting her] in the midst of tender-hearted and compassionate Christians.'" Potter, "Writing," 164. Rowlandson needed to denigrate the Indians precisely because they acted, occasionally, too much like Winthrop's ideal.

62. Ibid., 91.

63. Ibid., 97.

CONCLUSION

1. Paul Boyer and Stephen Nissenbaum, eds., *Salem-Village Witchcraft: A Documentary Record of Local Conflict in Colonial New England* (Boston: Northeastern University Press, 1972), 23–24.

2. Ibid., 21–22.

3. As Hoffer notes, in 1563 England required that "real harm accompany the act of using magic" in order for it to be a felony. While James I passed a stiffer law in 1604, it still required actual harm committed before someone could be put to death. New England's laws from 1648, on the other hand, made merely being a witch into a capital offense (though in practice, authorities still looked for actual harm). In the loss of Massachuset Bay's charter in 1684, they reverted, momentarily at least, to the statute from 1604. But the precise law of the land concerning witchcraft was ambiguous and still under dispute. See Peter Hoffer, *The Devil's Disciples: Makers of the Salem Witchcraft Trials* (Baltimore: Johns Hopkins University Press, 1996), 72–79.

4. Boyer and Nissenbaum, *Salem-Village Witchcraft: A Documentary Record of Local Conflict in Colonial New England*, 24.

5. Deodat Lawson, *Christs Fidelity the Only Shield Against Satans Malignity* (Boston, 1693), 75, 68, 58. The preface has no page numbers or printer's marks.

6. K. David Goss, *The Salem Witch Trials: A Reference Guide* (Westport, CT: Greenwood Press, 2008), 95–96.

7. Paul Boyer and Stephen Nissenbaum, eds., *Salem Witchcraft Papers: Verbatim Transcripts of the Legal Documents of the Salem Witchcraft Outbreak of 1692,* Compiled and Transcribed in 1938 by the Works Progress Administration, vol. 2 (New York: Da Capo Press, 1977), 551–554.

8. Lawson, *Christs Fidelity* (London, 1704), 118.

9. James Cooper Jr. and Kenneth Minkema, eds, *The Sermon Notebook of Samuel Parris, 1689–1694* (Boston: The Colonial Society of Massachusetts, 1993), 197–198.

10. Cooper and Minkema, *Sermon Notebook*, 199–203. In introducing this notebook, Cooper and Minkema note that Parris's "sermons reveal his preoccupation with the spiritual war between Christ and Satan, with distinguishing saints from reprobates, and with an impending demonic invasion." Moreover, they observe his frequent reliance on military, war-like metaphors and a persecution mindset. "By the beginning of 1692," they write, "Parris had succeeded in stereotyping any who opposed him as reprobate enemies of Christ and any who supported him as the chosen friends of Christ, members of the invisible church." *Sermon Notebook*, 13, 19–20. In these ways, Parris sounds a good deal like John Wheelwright in the Antinomian Controversy almost sixty years earlier.

11. Nathaniel Hawthorne, *The Scarlet Letter* (New York: Modern Library, 2000), 45.

12. Robert Calef, *More Wonders of the Invisible World* (London, 1700), 103–104.

13. Boyer and Nissenbaum, *Salem-Village Witchcraft: A Documentary Record*, 87.

14. Calef, *More Wonders*, 98.

15. David D. Hall, *Worlds of Wonder, Days of Judgment: Popular Religious Belief in Early New England* (Cambridge, MA: Harvard University Press, 1989), 191.

16. Boyer and Nissenbaum, *Salem-Village Witchcraft: A Documentary Record*, 28.

17. Calef, *More Wonders*, 107–108.

18. See William DeLoss Love, *The Fast and Thanksgiving Days of New England* (Boston: Houghton Mifflin, 1895), 256–262. Hall notes of such rituals more generally following the Salem witch trials, "What gave [this shared Puritan culture of rituals] force was the intensity with which these people valued the coherence of the body social. All these currents converged on the meaning of the martyr, murder, and witch-hunting. But as neighbors fell to quarreling, as outsiders like the Baptists settled down, as towns became distended, the symbolism of community came to lose some of its significance. With it waned the power of the rites that restored fellow feeling." Hall, *Worlds of Wonder*, 196.

19. Although Cotton Mather most famously used this formulation at Burroughs's execution, it was actually present from the beginning of the trials. In Lawson's early sermon, preached on the same day as Rebecca Nurse's examination, he unfolds the scriptural text from Zechariah that forms the basis of Mather's statement, frequently repeating the idea of the devil disguised as an Angel of Light in order to make sense of people like Rebecca Nurse.

20. For more on the sudden and massive turning of opinions against the Salem witch trial convictions, see Mary Beth Norton, *In the Devil's Snare: The Salem Witchcraft Crisis of 1692* (New York: Vintage, 2003), chapter 8. These quotations are borrowed from her book, p. 312.

21. *A Manifesto or Declaration, Set forth by the Undertakes of the New Church* (Boston, 1699), 2. For more on the founding of Brattle Street Church and the controversy it caused, see Mark Peterson, *The Price of Redemption: The Spiritual Economy of Puritan New England* (Redwood City, CA: Stanford University Press, 1997), 169–172. Pettit argues that ministers such as Stoddard enabled a "return to the sanctity

of the inner life, immune from the probings of others" and claims that in the late-seventeenth century, "indifference to the inner life became more and more pronounced"—a statement he supports as well with the example of Brattle Street Church. See Norman Pettit, *The Heart Prepared: Grace and Conversion in Puritan Spiritual Life*, second edition (Middletown, CT: Wesleyan University Press, 1989), 205–206. For a good account of Stoddard's innovations, see E. Brooks Holifield, *The Covenant Sealed: The Development of Puritan Sacramental Theology in Old and New England, 1570–1720*, reprint ed. (Eugene: Wipf and Stock, 2002), 206–220.

22. William Hill Brown, *The Power of Sympathy*, ed. Carla Mulford (New York: Penguin Classics, 1996), 61, 102.

23. Ibid., 61.

24. Ibid., 67–68.

25. Ibid., 68, 72–73. *The Winthrop Papers*, vols. 1–7 (Boston: Massachusetts Historical Society, 1929–), I.184, I.188.

26. Even distinguishing between "domestic" and "abroad," however, misleads one into assuming a clearer enunciation of boundaries than actually existed. Brattle Street Church, for example, attempted to embrace many of the latest fashionable ideas emerging out of Europe and purposefully hired a minister who had been ordained in England. The founding of the church was a domestic event that arose from transatlantic influences.

27. For a good, brief summary of the Cambridge Platonists, see Sarah Hutton, "The Cambridge Platonists," in *The Stanford Encyclopedia of Philosophy (Fall 2008 Edition)*, ed. Edward N. Zalta <http://plato.stanford.edu/archives/fall2008/entries/cambridge-platonists/>. For a longer account linking Cambridge Platonists to Latitudinarians, see Isabel Rivers, *Reason, Grace, and Sentiment: A Study of the Language of Religion and Ethics in England, 1660–1780* (Cambridge: Cambridge University Press, 1991–2000). For a study comparing Cambridge Platonists to Puritanism, see Norman Fiering, *Moral Philosophy at Seventeenth-Century Harvard: A Discipline in Transition* (Chapel Hill: University of North Carolina Press, 1981).

28. Ralph Cudworth, *A sermon preached before the Honourable House of Commons at Westminster, March 31, 1647* (London, 1647), 4–5. For Cudworth's comments on human goodness as divine rays, see pp. 68–69.

29. Cudworth, *Sermon*, 55.

30. Cudworth, *Sermon*, 34–35, 50. Translation of the Greek in Cudworth comes from a 1770 reprint of the sermon. See Cudworth, *A Discourse Concerning the Evidence* (New York: Gaine, 1770), 22.

31. Cudworth, *Sermon*, 51, 53.

32. Cudworth, *Sermon*, 64–65.

33. As Rivers recounts, "In the 1660s the number of the latitude-men was relatively small and their influence restricted, though increasing; by the 1690s the latitudinarians ... were the dominant, though not the majority, party in the Church of England." Isabel Rivers, *Reason, Grace, and Sentiment: A Study of the Language*

of Religion and Ethics in England, 1660–1780, vol. 1 (Cambridge: Cambridge University Press, 1991), 26.

34. This brief summary relies mainly on Rivers, *Reason, Grace, and Sentiment*, and Irene Simon, *Three Restoration Divines: Barrow, South, Tillotson: Selected Sermons*, vol. 1, ed. Irene Simon (Paris: Société d'édition "Les Belles Lettres," 1967): 1–300. Rivers summarizes that "for the latitude-men the religious life is essentially moral, its pursuit brings pleasure and happiness in this world, and it is achieved by active human effort in co-operation with divine grace." Rivers, *Reason, Grace, and Sentiment*, 73. For the tenet that religion offers temporal benefits here and now—that holiness produces happiness—see also pp. 58–59. On the anti-Calvinism of the Latitudinarians, Simon comments that these preachers "bade John Calvin good night." Simon, *Three Restoration Divines*, 131.

35. Rivers, *Reason, Grace, and Sentiment*, 77.

36. John Tillotson, "The Fruits of the Spirit, the Same with Moral Virtues," in *Three Restoration Divines: Barrow, South, Tillotson: Selected Sermons*, ed. Irene Simon, vol. II.ii (Paris: Société d'édition "Les Belles Lettres," 1976), 576. On Tillotson's extensive influence (in both England and New England), see Norman Fiering, "The First American Enlightenment: Tillotson, Leverett, and Philosophical Anglicanism," *New England Quarterly* 54, no. 3 (1981): 307–344. Fiering argues that the American Enlightenment is in fact more indebted to John Tillotson than to John Locke. Tillotson's sermons, as Fiering explains, "were probably the most widely read works of religious literature in America between 1690 and 1750." Fiering, "American Enlightenment," 309. The possibility of continuity between Puritanism and Latitudinarianism can be glimpsed in the fact that for all of Tillotson's difference from Calvinism, he was beloved even by the Mathers. Increase Mather called him the "great and good Archbishop Tillotson" and supposedly claimed that if all archbishops had been like him, "New England had never been." Fiering, "American Enlightenment," 309. Differences there were, to be sure, but many continuities as well.

37. Tillotson, "Fruits of the Spirit," 571–572.

38. Ibid., 574.

39. Ibid., 580.

40. The conclusion intends neither a declensionist story, nor a narrative of progress; instead, I mean to track what seemed to continue and what seemed to change in the movement of sympathy from the seventeenth to the eighteenth century. For a good account of the emphasis on practice over sign in later sympathy—along with the attempt to build a universal rather than a particular community—see Leigh Schmidt, "Cosmopolitan Piety: Sympathy, Comparative Religions, and Nineteenth-Century Liberalism," in *Practicing Protestants: Histories of Christian Life in America, 1630–1965* (Baltimore: Johns Hopkins University Press, 2006), 199–221.

Index